Street-Level Democracy

Political Settings
at the Margins of Global Power

Street-Level Democracy

Political Settings at the Margins of Global Power

Jonathan Barker

with

Anne-Marie Cwikowski

Christie Gombay

Katherine Isbester

Kole Shettima

Aparna Sundar

Between the Lines
Toronto,
Ontario

Kumarian Press
West Hartford,
Connecticut

Street-Level Democracy
©Jonathan Barker, 1999

Published in Canada by
Between the Lines
720 Bathurst Street, Suite #404
Toronto, Ontario
M5S 2R4

Published in the U.S. by
Kumarian Press, Inc.
14 Oakwood Avenue
West Hartford, CT 06119-2127
for exclusive distribution in the
U.S., U.K., and Europe

THE CANADA COUNCIL | LE CONSEIL DES ARTS
FOR THE ARTS | DU CANADA
SINCE 1957 | DEPUIS 1957

Between the Lines gratefully acknowledges assistance for its publishing activities from the Canada Council for the Arts, the Ontario Arts Council, and the Government of Canada through the Book Publishing Industry Development Program.

Cana⬤

Canadian Cataloguing in Publication Data
Barker, Jonathan, 1938-
  Street-level democracy: political settings at the margins of global power
Includes bibliographical references and index.
ISBN 1-896357-29-6
1. Political participation.   2. Political participation—Case studies.
3. Political participation—Developing countries.
4. Political participation—Developing countries—Case studies.
I. Cwikowski, Anne-Marie.   II. Title.
JF99.B37 1999   323'.042   C99-932052-1

Library of Congress Cataloging-in-Publication Data
Barker, Jonathan, 1938-
  Street-level democracy: political settings at the margins of global power /
  Jonathan Barker ; with case studies by Anne-Marie Cwikowski ... [et al.].
      p. cm.
  Includes bibliographical references and index.
  ISBN 1-56549-106-8 (pbk. : alk. paper)
  1. Political participation—Developing countries—Case studies.
  2. Social movements—Developing countries—Case studies.
  I. Cwikowski, Anne-Marie. II. Title.
JF60 .B38 1999
306.2'09172'4—dc21   99-045383

Cover and text design by Margie Adam, ARTWORK
Printed in Canada by Hignell Book Printing

Between the Lines
(416) 535-9914
btlbooks@web.net
www.btlbooks.com

Kumarian Press
(860) 233-5895
kpbooks@aol.com
www.kpbooks.com

Contents

Acknowledgements
vii

1. Introduction: Integral Lives in a Fragmenting World
Jonathan Barker
1

PART I
**Public Action in Local Contexts:
The Concept and Theory of Political Settings**

2. Power Shift: Global Change and Local Action
Jonathan Barker
8

3. Political Settings: An Approach to the Study of Popular Action
Jonathan Barker
27

PART II
Political Settings in Local Communities

4. Empowerment from Above? Development Projects and Public Space in
Northern Nigeria
Kole Shettima
58

5. Sea Changes: Organizing around the Fishery
in a South Indian Community
Aparna Sundar
79

6. Participation and Insecurity: Small Towns in England
and the United States
Jonathan Barker
115

PART III
Political Settings and Special Constituencies

7. Eating and Meeting in Owino:
Market Vendors, City Government, and the World Bank in Kampala, Uganda
Christie Gombay
150

8. Claiming Space for Women:
Nicaragua during and after Revolution, 1977-94
Katherine Isbester
183

9. The Mosque as a Political Space in Pakistan
Anne-Marie Cwikowski
213

PART IV
Lessons and Conclusions

10. Local Action and Global Power: Shifting the Balance
Jonathan Barker
238

Appendix
Mapping Local Politics: Methods, Measures, and Morals
Jonathan Barker
252

Selected Bibliography
272

Index
274

Acknowledgements

Jonathan Barker's chapters in this book pull together ideas germinated in his graduate-student days at Berkeley and worked on, from time to time, in subsequent years. The intellectual atmosphere in the Department of Political Science at the University of Toronto supported thought far from the mainstream of political science, and a congenial early retirement in 1996 gave him the opportunity to work on his ideas in a sustained way.

Jonathan's first intellectual debt is to his father, Roger G. Barker, who shared his thoughts about "behaviour settings" with a graduate-student son skeptical about positivistic social science. From his father he gained a view of the power of the social environment and also the burden of struggling with the idea of an eco-behavioural science. Jonathan cannot be certain that Roger would agree with the reworked idea of "activity setting," but he is certain that his father would have enjoyed seeing the diverse research that has made use of his thinking.

Jonathan owes special thanks to Dickson Eyoh, Paul Idahosa, Alkis Kontos, David MacDonald, Phil Schoggen, Carmen Sheffelite, Bob Shenton, Gavin Smith, Nick Thompson, Allan Wicker, Linzi Manicom, and Patty Stamp for comments on drafts of chapters. He did what he could with their sage advice and happily accepted their encouragement. His "debate" with Colin Leys in *Southern Africa Report* and subsequent discussions with Colin and John S. Saul convinced him that he had something to say and that he needed to try to say it better.

He received a similar benefit from the opportunity to give talks at Carleton University, Queen's University, the University of Toronto, and the Canadian Association of African Studies. The Centre for Urban and Community Studies at the University of Toronto, under the directorship of Richard Stren, gave the co-authors a pleasant place to meet and discuss drafts.

Jonathan's part in the field research and some of the work of Kole Shettima, Aparna Sundar, and Christie Gombay were made possible by a grant from the Social Science and Humanities Research Council of Canada. Kole's research in Nigeria was supported by a grant from the Rockefeller

Foundation. Aparna thanks the Thirumalai Ashram community, S. Joseph and Roselyn in Chinna Muttam, and S. Arul Mary "Teacher" in Enayam Puthenthurai for hospitality; and Y. Mary Therese and G. Sunny Jose for help with interviews, observation of meetings, and translation. Katherine Isbester is grateful to the International Development Research Centre for the Young Canadian Researcher Award that supported her work in Nicaragua and to her mother, Mrs. A.F. Isbester, for standing behind her daughter's choices.

We all owe special thanks to the people, the community leaders, and the officials in and near Machina, Dagona, Kanyakumari, Oskaloosa, Leyburn, Owino, Managua, and Lahore, who accepted researchers bearing questions, gave generously of their time and knowledge, and often made us their friends. The willing help of research assistants in all of these places contributed indispensably to the research.

Nancy Sears Barker read the text from a reader's standpoint, and her comments induced us to remove several opportunities for confusion. The writers and readers alike are the beneficiaries of Robert Clarke's editing skill; we thank him for making our meaning easier to grasp. But it is our meaning, and we take full responsibility for the text, mistakes included.

Jonathan Barker
Anne-Marie Cwikowski
Christie Gombay
Katherine Isbester
Kole Shettima
Aparna Sundar

Chapter 1

Introduction: Integral Lives in a Fragmenting World

Jonathan Barker

In the last few years reports about change in the countries of Africa, Asia, and Latin America have yielded little to cheer about and much to bring anger and despair. For a time, a few impressive statistics about increasing life spans, decreasing infant mortality, and increasing food production brought some comfort in the face of growing absolute numbers of hungry and vulnerable people in the world; but more recently the good news trends have levelled off or turned downward, inequalities have widened, threats to health have spread, and the incidence of disaster and war has increased. In Africa continuing stagnation and the spread of AIDS, in Asia the economic crisis, and in Latin America growing inequality and economic uncertainty are sobering reminders that the shine is off the brave new post-Cold War experiment in global economic liberalization. The earnest remedies advocated and enforced by leading development institutions demonstrate only meagre success, and their consequences are widely criticized for the human suffering that follows them.

In this seeming grip of gloom, though, I have noticed an odd paradox: when I travel to Africa, Asia, and Latin America and visit villages and neighbourhoods that everyone would classify as poor, I feel my spirits rise. The evidence of difficulty and injustice is palpable, but something makes the experience positive. Why should this be? Why does the situation inspire more hope when I see it up close than when I observe it via research reports and news stories?

Is it that the media have a systematic preference for negative news and send their reporters to zones of war and famine? Bias there is, and some good news may routinely be excluded from the printed record, but direct observation does not contradict the impression, garnered from the media, that recent trends are negative. The key difference between reading about it and being there is something more subtle: the sense that people are taking concrete action to turn things around. Many people simply cope and survive as best they can, but some are active in seeking wider change. And what begins as coping may contribute to larger change. Ordinary men and women may look a bit beyond their most immediate problems to change some aspect of the local situation that seems wrong to them. Local leaders may act upon a wider vision of how the locality fits into the larger picture, and regional and national activists may organize and analyze on a wider scale still, and look for promising sites and forms of action.

The existence of such people may be enough to raise one's spirits and restore a sense of human resilience, but their actions in the longer run may be futile, given the enormity of the forces and trends arrayed against them. Financial firestorms driven by gales of investment moving in and out of fragile economies leave wrecked livelihoods behind. Environmental pressures build with the force of tectonic shifts as ocean fish stocks disappear, water tables fall, land frontiers close, and global weather patterns change. Such pressures can undermine local production, and there is no guarantee that the political response will be cogent and effective. Fear, ambition, and ideology may swing power to figures who appeal to narrow and exclusive identities and detonate conflicts that make whole regions uninhabitable. Given the translocal and transnational nature of many economic and social forces, where does local action come from, what drives it, how does it work, and what hope does it have of engaging real issues in any but an ephemeral way? Why do people in some places respond especially productively to challenges while people in other places do not?

These questions lie at the root of the present book. Its backdrop is global change in the configuration of political power. The questions are too big and have too many ramifications to allow for answers in all their facets, but when I began to pose them several years ago I saw an unusual opportunity to at least begin to find answers. Several students I was working with at the University of Toronto were doing studies of various aspects of local action in a wide range of localities in Africa, Asia, and Latin America. If I could get them to look systematically at local political action as part of their research, perhaps we could bring our observations together and try to shed light on broader questions: in particular, the sources of local political action and its potentiality for counteracting the threats to quality of life and livelihood, some of them induced by the neo-liberal economic project the world is experiencing. The students were willing, and the Social Science and Humanities Council of Canada agreed to fund the research.

Since our research strength was on the local side, we decided to focus on the analysis of local action and to shape it to connect with analyses of global forces of change relevant to our particular local studies. We could also give attention to local change that is quite autonomous from global forces, and we could estimate the range of the scope for autonomous action. Our interest was more than academic, because we all had personal ties, in some cases family roots, in the places we would write about. We wanted our work to be connected to progressive action, but we also knew that the context of action contained complex relationships and contested meanings as local cultures and ways of making a living were changing from within and buffeted by global and national gusts of change from without. At the same time, we were skeptical of the claims of those organizations that, in seeking support for their development projects, make action look simple. They trumpet the gravity of the needs to which they minister and advertise the success stories to which their work contributes: the children fed, the wells dug, the clinics built. But seldom do we get a sense of what local action was required, how it came about, what obstacles it had to overcome, or how well-established the capacity for change has become. We hoped that our research could also throw light on this underlying question by starting with concepts that capture the small-scale potentials for action and provide insights into how those actions can be set in motion.

We therefore saw a need for research that met academic standards of care, rigour, and open-mindedness. However, no academic theory of Third World change or local-central relations or globalization offered convincing answers to our questions, although several—relating to civil society, social movements, gender relations, institution-building, and class dynamics, among others—were clearly sensitive to the issues that motivated us. We decided that our starting point, then, would be a good description of events of local action with due attention to context. We needed the concepts and theories that would make that description possible and that would also advance the construction of a fuller political theory of local action.

I had developed and begun to apply an idea about how to describe and how to begin to theorize popular action that I believed was ready to try out on a larger scale.[1] As chapter 2 demonstrates, the political settings approach, as we came to call it, adds a firm descriptive grounding to more familiar approaches built around conceptions of social movements, local institutions, civic associations, and arts of resistance. It also takes into account the changing spatial configuration of politics that follows from the effects on nation-states of proliferating organizations and associations within them and shifting global forces around them. Chapter 3 addresses two further tasks: to articulate the practical details of the political settings method and to contribute to a theory of local political action.

The work also presented me with the difficult task of describing yet another "approach" to social research and theory to people who may have little taste for talk about concepts or who may have already been subjected to a surfeit of such talk. Two arguments for presenting the approach convinced me to write about it. One is that it yields excellent studies that can be read by any interested reader. There is very little special jargon to master. Readers who so desire can jump right to the content-rich case studies and the concluding comparison (chapters 4 through 10) and ignore the conceptual chapters (chapters 2, 3, and the appendix). The other argument is that committed researchers are looking for ways to describe more fully and more revealingly the complex social realities they come to know, but the concepts and theories they bring to the task are geared to fitting observations into fully articulated interpretations. The political settings approach is designed to capture enough richness to ground thinking about several different interpretations or even to imagine a new one.

Readers thinking through their own action-oriented or academic research projects will, I believe, find the approach and the related research techniques useful. For that reason I have included an appendix on methods, measures, and morals. It describes ways of identifying political settings and getting information about them and includes samples of the research forms we used, showing the kind of information we found it useful to pursue. The problem of "morals" is included because, like all researchers, we faced practical ethical issues related to our research methods. From the perspective of political settings, we had to recognize that we became part of the political landscape as we convened meetings to talk about meetings and became observers in other settings.

Our approach to the study of local action had to fit the conditions of our research and the strengths of the research team. First and foremost it had to find common themes in six studies covering nine very different places, asking dissimilar questions and fitting into distinct interpretive strategies, each one drawing upon detailed knowledge of the culture and society of the place. The solution was to focus upon the most fundamental units of collective public action and to address basic issues of grassroots public life: how popular action arises, what forms it takes, and what it can accomplish. Those units we called *political settings*. Two qualities in political settings make them attractive for field research: they are public, and readily observable. They are public in the sense that people speak and listen in the presence of one another and the activity does not belong to domestic private life. Both field researchers and local people find political settings easy to observe and describe because they have a determinate location in space and time with clear-cut temporal and geographical boundaries, and they usually have common names. As a first approximation one can think of them as public meetings and government offices. We will have much to say about them in the following chapters.

The common element in the component studies was the collection of information on political settings in the research locality and reflection on basic issues of street-level political action. Otherwise each study focused on its own set of issues and collected information on those offices and meetings that were most pertinent to its research theme.

Of the studies, three included more-or-less comprehensive surveys of the political settings in villages or small towns. Chapter 4 grows out of Kole Shettima's undertaking to compare three development projects in northern Nigeria for their success in promoting popular participation. He includes a survey of meetings and offices, concentrating on those connected to the three projects. He knew the cultural context well, for his research was in the region where he had grown up and gone to school. Chapter 5 is part of Aparna Sundar's comprehensive look at the political response to changes in the fishery in the coastal villages of Kanyakumari district in Tamil Nadu state, India. She includes an inquiry into the role of meetings and other collective public actions in villages where the small-scale fishery was under threat. She knew the region well, having done support work with the union of fishers for a year before starting her graduate studies. She had also grown up speaking Tamil.

Chapter 6 is my re-analysis of research done in the 1960s of public meetings in a U.S. and an English small town. This was research in which I had participated in small ways as a young man when it was carried out in the 1950s and 1960s by my father, Roger Barker, then professor of social psychology at the University of Kansas. My reinterpretation is informed by my own personal experience of the towns in question and by familiarity with the context and character of the original research. This chapter has substantive and methodological objectives. Substantively, it aims to show that the overall level of public participation in a U.S. small-town setting is much higher than it is in a similar English town. It also shows that the U.S. rate of participation comes at a price. It makes the position of leaders less secure and pushes more people to take on a greater burden of responsibility before their peers.

Three more studies had a more specialized thematic or geographic focus. Chapter 7 comes from Christie Gombay's work on the political economy of access to food in urban Africa. He examined public action to manage everyday problems and forces of change in a large urban market in Uganda. He knew Kampala well. He had lived there in his youth and had previously done other kinds of research in Kampala and in Owino Market. In chapter 8 Katherine Isbester applies social movement theory to the case of the women's movement in Nicaragua. She enriches that theory with a focus on meetings and deepens our understanding of how the movement spread and adapted to political changes. Before her two stints of field research in Nicaragua she had done support work there. In chapter 9 Anne-Marie Cwikowski's research about the democratic potential of political Islam has its focus on mosques as political spaces in Pakistan. She draws on years of travel in the region as well as her language studies, area studies, and research on Islam.

To this unusually able and well-qualified group of researchers I contributed my own experience of local research in Senegal and Tanzania and my ideas about political settings as an approach to research. I joined directly in the research on political settings in Nigeria, Uganda, and India.

After returning from our field work, when most of us were writing, we met to discuss common themes and to read and discuss one another's work. The chapters that follow are the result of the interaction between the individual research agendas of the writers and their response to the information they gathered on political settings, plus the discussions we had about how to interpret that information. My efforts to describe our method; to compare the component studies; to draw out the common themes; and to elaborate practical, conceptual, and theoretical implications owe a great deal to our discussions together.

The local studies are joined together by more than their attention to political settings: all the localities were, and are, subject to the force of strong external trends. The common backdrop to our work is global change in the configuration of political power—change that challenges normal and accepted notions of the shape of politics and the functions of states. The new shape of global power also places daunting obstacles in the way of efficacious local action.

Note

1. Jonathan Barker, "Political Space and the Quality of Participation in Rural Africa: A Case from Senegal," *Canadian Journal of African Studies* 21,1 (1987): 1-16.

PART I

Public Action in Local Contexts

The Concept and Theory of Political Settings

Chapter 2

Power Shift: Global Change and Local Action

Jonathan Barker

The pattern of global change is fraught with ambiguity. Thinking in terms of decades and centuries, we may find it difficult to confirm the often-asserted weakening of the nation-state in favour of global economic and cultural institutions. The world is only 40 or 50 years away from the decolonization of large parts of Asia, Africa, the Caribbean, and Oceania, and the end of the Soviet empire is more recent still. The dream of many nationalists at mid-century was for an era of strong, mainly secular, nation-states. That dream is not dead, but the trends are now quite diverse.

The industrialized states do remain strong and secular, but they have begun to enter into transnational trade and political agreements that limit autonomous control of their economies. The weaker states that emerged from colonial control, notably those in Africa, still struggle to consolidate their governing institutions for tasks of stability and progress. Along with many older and stronger states in Latin America and elsewhere, they also face neo-liberal international constraints imposed through economic adjustment programs and international trade agreements. Those programs strengthen the pressure on governments to formalize favourable terms for transnational investment and trade. At the same time, transnational actors want to deal with states able to make and enforce economic agreements and policies; in many cases that means strengthening parts of the state apparatus.

Many states are being challenged by cultural movements, some of them operating across national borders in more than one country and some of them having national ambitions of their own. Some states adopt well-defined cultural policies and seek to exert strong social control within their territory in the name of a cultural vision. In so doing they often stimulate movements of opposition or secession.

While governments adjust to changing global forces, local movements and agencies emerge to express issues that governments ignore or to fill gaps in government services. Some of these local entities have translocal and transnational connections and support. Like the governments, the local organizations are learning how to manage in a changing global power structure. As the ideological divide of the Cold War recedes, the neo-liberal tenets of market efficiency and possessive individualism have a strong grip on the high ground of international financial institutions, but critical perspectives are gaining strength. No comprehensive alternative to neo-liberalism has coalesced, but local organizations that feel threatened by economic globalization can find allies in liberation theology, environmentalism, feminist theory, and other critiques of mainstream development thinking. Changing power structures have provoked much debate about the value and future of nation-states and the ramifications of globalization.[1] The long-held assumption that politics can be represented as a single and unified political space no longer seems to hold.

The Athens Effect

One reason that the proliferation of local political actions and the multiplication of transnational political linkages challenge political analysis is that our idea of politics is influenced by what I call the Athens Effect. The thinkers of classical Athens saw politics as a simple unity because that small city-state encompassed the lives of its residents and citizens and controlled, insofar as any social unit could, the conditions of their well-being. Moreover, in democratic Athens a limited number of open political settings in which all or many citizens could participate took in the full range and drama of the city's public political life. Of these the most crucial was the Assembly, in which citizens (a designation that excluded women, slaves, and foreigners) gathered to make laws and other decisions for the people of Athens. During the period of radical democracy the Assembly met near the Agora in an open-air walled space that would hold about 6,000 people. The size of the space seems to have been calculated to make it easy to determine that the required quorum of 6,000 citizens was present. Aristotle, an exceptionally observant non-Athenian resident, explains that the Assembly was the deliberative element of the political constitution, concerned with "the common affairs" and "sovereign (1) on issues of war and peace, and the making and breaking of alliances; (2) in the enacting of laws; (3) in cases where the penalty of death, exile, and confiscation is involved; and (4) in the appointment of magistrates and the calling of them to account on the expiration of their office."[2] Athenians could therefore see the public discussion, controversy, and decision-making on most major public matters played out in one locale, one political setting.

In his ideal polis Aristotle has a striking architectural vision of how this space, "associated with the buildings devoted to public worship," should be situated: "This site should be on an eminence, conspicuous enough for men to look up to and see goodness enthroned and strong enough to command the adjacent quarters of the city. Below this site provision should be made for a public square, of the sort which is called in Thessaly by the name of Free Square. This should be free of all merchandise: and no mechanic, or farmer, or other such person, should be allowed to enter, except on the summons of the magistrates."[3]

Usually near the centre of each Greek city-state was a second kind of public space, the *agora*, the marketplace where merchants bought and sold goods of all kinds. Like marketplaces in many less industrial regions today (such as Owino Market in Kampala, Uganda, described in chapter 7), it was the meeting place for people of many classes and cultures, a place for exchanging news, gossip, and opinion. In his plan for an ideal polis Aristotle stressed its exclusively commercial utility: "The market square for buying and selling should be separate from the public square, and at a distance from it: it should be at a site which provides a good depot, alike for commodities imported by sea and those which come from the state's own territory."[4] Distinct from both public spaces were the households of the city and the farmsteads of the surrounding country, which collectively formed the private space of Athens.

Public and political settings in the Greek city-states were compact and visible. Aristotle could write concretely about the disposition and functioning of the market square and political square.[5] With a little more abstraction he could describe differences and changes in the rules of admission to the Assembly, which determined whether all citizens, only the wealthy, or a small group of self-proclaimed oligarchs could take part in the debates, decisions, and judgments. Recent analysis of all the documents and archaeological evidence about the Assembly and the closely allied public political settings of the Council and the Courts concludes that in the period of radical democracy (462-404 B.C.E.) the "level of political activity exhibited by the citizens of Athens is unparalleled in world history, in terms of numbers, frequency and level of participation."[6] Each citizen devoted 10 to 20 hours a year to political participation, and rules of rotation and selection by lot ensured that almost every citizen took part.

Not surprisingly, then, Greek political thought in language and substance was preoccupied with the special qualities and problems of action in the political sphere. It addressed the issues of the competence of leaders and institutions in relation to the purposes of the community and the consequences of political actions and arrangements for the quality of community life. With deep concern for the vitality of the public sphere, Hannah Arendt has shown how important for the Athenian thinkers was the public display of the ability to exercise power. For them verve and pertinence in speaking and persuading, leading, and demonstrating have an excellence surpassed only by philosophy itself. Furthermore, she concludes:

> The reality of the public realm relies on the simultaneous presence of innumerable perspectives and aspects in which the common world presents itself and for which no common measurement or denominator can ever be devised. For though the common world is the common meeting ground of all, those who are present have different locations in it. . . . Being seen and being heard by others derive their significance from the fact that everybody sees and hears from a different position. This is the meaning of public life, compared to which even the richest and most satisfying family life can offer only the prolongation or multi-plication of one's own position with its attending aspects and perspectives. . . . Only where things can be seen by many in a variety of aspects without changing their identity, so those who are gathered around them know that they are seeing sameness in utter diversity, can worldly reality truly and reliably appear.[7]

The work of Aristotle, Arendt, and Mogens Herman Hansen addresses the important features of political space, which, among other things, contains a plurality of people reflecting their different perspectives. The more its occupants reflect the variety of people in the surrounding community, the more fully political it is. Its activities include performing in public: speaking, persuading, taking positions, and contributing to discussions and decisions before other people. The decisions and actions that occur in political settings intend effects on activity elsewhere in the society. Their wider implications make the performances of people in political settings the more prepossessing. Political settings are subject to rules of admission and acceptable behaviour that limit who can participate and what participants can discuss and do; and although political and economic actions are different and distinct, the rela-tion between them is close and strong. That relation needs scrutiny, but it is not the whole story. There is much debate about the nature of the relations between political and economic action and motivation. In my view the idea put forward by Arendt that political settings work better when purged of claims driven by economic need is forlorn and mistaken. Our case studies find that some of the most effective and democratic political action is driven in large part by responses to economic need.

Inspiring and influential as it is, the case of Athens can be misleading. In Athens political space had a unity and contiguity that do not pertain to the large and complex nation-states of our era. The idea of politics originating in the Greece of the fourth century B.C.E. held that politics could be the attribute only of a diverse and relatively self-sufficient community with a specialization of economic functions and a set of inhabitants with the leisure to devote to public matters. Women, slaves, and foreigners were essential to the economy, but they were deemed unfit for the responsibilities of citizenship. The polis combined smallness with completeness in a way that no longer can be found, and it embodied an exclusionary vision of democracy that is no longer convincing.

Already in Athens the idea of a single unified political space was a theoretical convenience that did not entirely fit the reality. Aristotle made it clear that political actions and important influences on political outcomes were not confined to the citadels and marketplaces of the Greek city-states. There were the guard-houses in which young men gathered, sports grounds, gymnasia for the education of those youths whose families could afford it, and smaller public squares. Indeed, Aristotle wanted to structure political space so as to consolidate it and protect it from the influence of non-citizens and to reinforce the influence of older men and holders of public office. "To be under the eyes of the magistrates will serve, above anything else, to create a true feeling of modesty and the fear of shame that should animate free men."[8] Already Aristotle was concerned about preserving the unity and purity of political space.

The size and political focus of the Greek city-states made it possible for the political thought of the period to combine a strong conception of the unity of politics with careful attention to the context of political actions and institutions. Today a singular political arena is distant from social reality, yet the pattern of public life in Athens, with a few tens of thousands of inhabitants and several thousand citizens, has imprinted itself on the language we use to describe politics. Political science takes the state, the political system, the government as its objects of inquiry. Often it contrasts them with the economy, the market, and the private sector. It thereby expresses a theoretical aspiration to uncover or to create for each nation-state a single political sphere. Yet empirical studies of legislatures, pressure groups, administrative apparatuses, and political parties reveal a complex hodgepodge of semi-isolated institutional spaces with limited interactions far different from the metaphor of a singular and contiguous political space.

Theories of the state, the political system, and the ruling class try to reduce the gap by postulating an underlying unifying process. These efforts have the value of selecting information relevant to important issues of the overall exercise of power in a nation-state, but they select for power at the expense of context. They tell us about the most central institutions of government: how stable, hierarchical, integrated, and encompassing they are (or should be). But they tell us little of the immediate context of central politics or of how it connects with the political practices and contexts of citizens of various conditions and situations.[9] National governments remain the biggest engines of political action, and their claim to unify political space, at least metaphorically, may merit reinforcement. Yet for them to be effective in the changing universe of power and action they need to respond to the political dynamics of local contests and the connections between local and global forces that can and do often bypass national control.

The fragmentation of political space and the impact of global power on national institutions do not form the whole story. There has been a marked increase in the number, range, and energy of non-state, non-family, and non-business voluntary associations—a trend noted in Asia, Africa, and Latin America. On a general level this trend is a social response to the expansion of market logic into social relationships that have more than economic meaning to people. This is the "double movement" that Karl Polanyi refers to in his writing on the logic of expanding market economies.[10] Societies react against the reduction of land and labour and money to the status of commodities. This is also the political reaction that Karl Marx's theory of capitalist development predicts, though not according to the letter of his analysis.[11] For Marx the political revolution would occur in a single concentrated cataclysm, possibly in a world war, once the proletariat gained the necessary organization and autonomy; instead we frequently see a dispersed series of piecemeal actions and only rarely observe the revolutionary overthrow of governing institutions. In the political realm, lines of thought other than those of Marx and Polanyi, but not necessarily in contradiction to them, have resonance today.

Three Hopeful Localisms and the Scale Mismatch

Three perspectives dominate efforts to understand the reaction to globalization.

The Ebbing Tide: New Social Movement Analysis. A few years ago, as class politics seemed to subside, many activists interested in progressive change invested hope and work in new social movements formed around interests and identities not captured by class relations. Some of these movements were related to citizen interests, such as civil rights and environmental health. Others were connected to liberation from oppressions of gender and race and culture not reducible to class or nation. Major theoretical efforts stressed resource mobilization and identity formation, and these concepts have entered the repertoire of contemporary political analysis just as social movements have remained part of the political scene. At the same time hope for a transformative politics based on new social movements has ebbed as they have reached the limits of their constituencies, met counterpressures, and lost the energy and excitement of their beginning phases.[12]

Two different strains of social movement theory address the question of political action. The resource mobilization approach highlights the material and organizational resources that movement actors need to assemble in order to undertake actions and establish the political opportunity structure that aids or inhibits their efforts. The core idea is that the high transaction costs of organizing and a "free rider" problem continually undermine collective action and that successful movements are those that can overcome these obstacles. "Free riders" are people who hold back from joining in collective action in hopes of harvesting the benefit of the actions without incurring the costs of activism. There is evidence that many people engage in social movements for social reasons and for the good feelings it brings. But even if the attractions of participation overwhelm narrow cost-benefit calculations, the costs of organizing support, distributing information, holding demonstrations, and evading repression are heavy when populations are dispersed, communications are poor, controls are great, and resources are few. Therefore, it is argued, successful movements are those that can mobilize resources.[13]

Resource mobilization theory makes evident some real limitations of popular action against the forces of globalization. The fractured political and social contexts in which people attempt to organize against the effects of neo-liberalism do, indeed, prove difficult for organizers, and the costs of organizing are a factor in the success or failure of local actions to get off the ground. Transportation is scarce and expensive. Leadership with the necessary knowledge is hard to find. Minimal office equipment, telephones and telephone connections, a literate constituency, and mass communications equipment are all likely to be in short supply. Official intimidation, harassment, and arrest are powerful hindrances to action and coordination. Therefore the cost of effective organization is high relative to the supply of resources, especially when transnational organization is attempted. In addition the experience of vulnerability that motivates many new social movements occurs among disconnected social units. In the case of patriarchy, for example, even where practices that exploit, attack, and humiliate women are widespread and frequent, the injury is experienced in the isolation of separate households. It takes effort and organization for those injured to construct an idea of their shared experience as women. Something similar is true for the experience of youth, for peasant farmers, for workers in small-scale production units, and for unemployed people.

A second approach to social movements stresses the force of culture over the material dimension of action. It focuses on the capacity of people to create new identities.[14] For example, out of dialogue, learning, and organization comes a sense among women of being women. But there are also cultural obstacles to wide organizing. Women may also have identities as members of a cultural group, a religion, or a class. Indeed, many new social movements reinforce and create identities that divide people and get in the way of responding to the pressures of globalization. There may be room for collaboration, but often the politics of identity offers small grounds for compromise. Cultural differences also reflect or create divisions of knowledge, divisions often heightened in the case of transnational movements. Different groups will know different things about the forces troubling them and have different ideas about the resources and actions on which they can draw. Mobilizing resources and forming identities can and do set social movements going, but they also carry with them conditions that limit the scope and effect of movements, especially in the context of globalization. As movements escape the mediation of the political process of nation-states, at least one leading social movement theorist believes they are more likely to be destructive than (like those of the 1960s) creative: their "power will at first be ferocious, uncontrolled and widely diffused, but later ephemeral."[15]

The Weight of the Past: Civil Society Studies. Recent invocations of civil society, drawing on the thought of Alexis de Tocqueville, argue that vibrant and numerous non-state voluntary associations and social customs of interpersonal trust are necessary preconditions of healthy representative democracy. A central claim is that people's relations to government are mediated by associational relationships that do not belong to family, business, or governmental spheres. Social clubs, voluntary associations, and service organizations are the stuff of civil society, the ground of citizen politics. Critically understood, civil society stands in an ambiguous relationship to representative democracy, because associations can use their freedom to act in ways that undermine democratic institutions as well as in ways that support democracy.[16]

Those who celebrate civil society believe it provides a social ground that reunites political space. It quietly draws attention away both from the disempowerment of the national institutions that globalization has wrought and from the fragmentation of identities and interests that economic and cultural forces have brought. Even if we ignore the fragmentation of political space and the contradictory ways in which it can be used, the best research shows that the unifying social ground of civil society is slow-growing and not easily achieved through purposive action, although it is a wonderful gift when you have it, and where it exists efforts should be made to prevent its erosion. The careful research reported by Robert Putnam, for example, discovers that the conditions for a healthy civil society are long in the making and, in Italy at least, have origins lost in the mists of time a millennium ago.[17] Institution-builders who are more time-bound in their vision believe that shorter-term strategies for creating civil institutions may exist, but the fragility of many recent democratizations gives pause to this thought.

One current in this search for a social basis for democratic politics follows the neo-liberal banner and looks everywhere except the state for positive change. Other currents surge from analysts trying to understand how marginalized people can gain more control over the conditions of their lives, how to make local action more effective and productive. A few observers optimistically note the appearance of many transnational groups devoted to action on issues of civil rights, the situation of women, and ecological destruction. Some write of the creation of a transnational civil society that can match the forces of globalization.[18] Although such organizations do leave room for hope (and they play a part in our case studies), they in no way constitute the equivalent to the civil society that latter-day Tocquevillians believe frames a democratic and popular political space in the best-established capitalist democracies. Where in patrimonial, caste-ridden, violence-torn societies within weak and (at best) semi-democratic states is the trust that cements the relationships of an inclusive and democracy-supporting civil society? In the marginal zones of the global social economy of interest here, civil society theory reveals one more obstacle to local action. Long-standing traditions of social trust and association-formation are in short supply.

Domination Pluralized: Theories of Class, Gender, Culture, and Age. Class analysis is far from dead, and most of the good research on political action still makes use of it.[19] The trend it identifies is quite contrary to the theory that gave Marx and Engels the idea that revolutionary, liberating political change was a real possibility. Those who use class theory to understand globalization see a strengthening and unifying of global capital. The dominant classes are following the Marxist script pretty well. But Marx's revolutionary hope came from the perception that exploitation would not only impoverish the subordinate classes, but also unify and organize them.

Recent class analysis, following Antonio Gramsci or Max Weber or Barrington Moore, focuses on how cross-class influences such as cultural attachments and ties of kinship and organization work against action on the part of classes pure and simple.[20] The concept of class itself, when addressed to the subordinate classes, now seems to take in more fragmented and less inclusive categories than it once promised. It unifies groups at the high end of the economic hierarchy through corporate networking, government assistance, and the conviviality (for the transnational managers of capital) of world cities. At the lower margins it includes groups whose production is dispersed among distant regions and countries, divided between men and women, tied to small-scale producers, and most often fragmented.

Some excellent class analysis focuses on those places in which larger industrial units have been established.[21] It discovers extensive proletarianization, often with special features such as the employment of women in electronics and micro-chip factories or special laws and customs that restrict the reach of labour legislation in maquiladora or export zones. The class patterns resulting from export-promoting policies and economic adjustment are usually patchy and complex. Industrial zones may be isolated from the broader society and kept under military surveillance. In the larger cities the informal sector expands. Its small units and labour contracts, in which wages are mixed with benefits in kind such as food and housing, do not generate class conflict or class consciousness of the classical kind. Some export promotion favours smallholder production that uses family labour, while in other cases larger production units do hire labour but the labourers themselves may have some land.

Class analysis—asking about the different ways in which workers are linked to means of production—is a useful and crucial step in a social analysis of globalization. But it yields no automatic insight into how people will organize to protect or promote their livelihoods. Scattered agglomerations of exploited industrial workers, masses of informal-sector workers and self-employed, many kinds of rural tenancy and credit claims, and widespread gender-based exploitation within family production units make forming a common front of the exploited a difficult task. Adding to the difficulty is the division of subordinate classes by old and new identity movements and generational differences. Class analysis helps us mightily to understand local contexts, but it offers strong evidence of great obstacles to class-defined united action by subordinate classes.

Scale Mismatch and Discovery of Local Contexts

What do these theories, taken together, suggest about the social response to the neo-liberal agenda of globalization? Although they recognize the existence of a good deal of coping activity, they tend to find serious weaknesses in the expected reactions. They warrant scant hope that local action can construct a more positive path of change. Local pressures are likely to motivate local political action, but that action will face a set of obstacles, forces, and problems that militate against effective organization and action. Class interests of low-income earners are fractured, costs of organizing across small-scale and dispersed production sites are high, and identity movements may discourage effective interest-based coalitions. The trust necessary for collaborative coalitions of action is likely to be absent, and it cannot readily be built in the midst of action itself. Moreover, whether motivated by class solidarity, economic interests, or sense of identity, local activism often begins on a defensive note: groups that spring up to oppose government cutbacks or to stop the licensing of a resource company that will pollute fishing grounds have a hard time making the transition to positive pursuits.

Many of the obstacles to effective local action can be summarized as a problem of scale mismatch. Transnational firms own or contract with production facilities in several countries. One centre bargains with or contends with many sets of workers. The efforts of any one set of workers to organize and make claims against their employer have little effect, and the employer can play different sets of workers against one another. The obstacles to organizing all workers in all production units in all countries are difficult to overcome, blunting the edge of worker action everywhere. Similarly, local branches of social movements can struggle against deforestation in one place or the failure of local courts to protect women's inheritance, but the larger forces of deforestation and disregard of women's rights persist. Lively associational action in a village or neighbourhood is unlikely in itself to reach to the places in governments and businesses where economic and social decisions are made. Scale mismatch always favours the bargaining power of centralized administrations, corporations, and communications systems. Transnational businesses and international financial institutions, in particular, consistently benefit from the mobility of capital and management that are central to the rules of globalization.

Together these theories give us some purchase on the problem of local action. They point to a grave scale mismatch and important obstacles to effective local action. But they do not succeed in specifying the true options of local action. For example, Putnam surmises a strong connection between networks of social interaction and the quality of political encounters, especially those between representatives and citizens, but his impressive data on the history of associational membership include little concrete information about the nature of the associational activity that would account for its great influence on politics. Putnam's data suggest that how people do politics, including the politics of non-governmental associations, is crucial for their ability to respond well to economic and social challenges, and he offers stimulating reasoning about two possible political cultures that perpetuate themselves and resist change. But the evidence is strictly circumstantial. His accounts do not allow us to see the norms of reciprocity or distrust in operation, nor do we observe how those norms are created or destroyed, reinforced or weakened. Hence the anticlimactic response to the question of how to move from "uncivic" to "civic" ways. Somehow we need gradually to supply the missing associational institutions. How to do so in practice remains cloaked in a fog of uncertainty.[22]

Do we not, in addition, need to look inside the institutions for information on how political encounters work and how norms operate in the everyday political and social activities that seem so fundamental to the difference between "civic" and "uncivic" societies? There is a void in the empirical and theoretical understanding of all three kinds of theory. Where do identities and motives for collective action come from? Whence derive the early stages of trust? How do people living side by side but fragmented in their class and social ties relate in a public and political way to one another? Until we know more about the micro-level of collective and public action, it is hard to say whether or not the pessimism that follows from the three theories of political action is justified.

The problematic nature of political activity has generated growing interest in local politics and a lengthening list of innovative research projects and inventive interpretations that highlight the complexity of local contexts of action and meaning. There are several projects from which there is much to learn, writings that are especially stimulating in their own right and that suggest a way to solidify and enhance the study of local political action. One of those is the work of James Scott, who brings into focus the hidden politics of highly repressive societies. He shows that there are secret arenas and hidden scripts in which a critical view of political and social power is elaborated by those who experience domination. The pre-existence of an alternative vision of politics explains how seemingly new ideas can appear so unexpectedly and spread so rapidly in revolutionary situations. One is led to ask, however, what about the arenas and the discourse of public discussion in less repressive societies? Is there not a continuum of degrees of hiddenness of political dialogue? Cannot the same sensitivity elucidate a wider range of political settings?[23]

Norman Long and Magdelena Villareal draw attention to the critical interactions between state officials and representatives of culturally distinctive localities. These "interfaces" are the scene of vitally important communications and miscommunications. Again one might ask whether or not degrees of cultural differences exist in all situations in which officials or agents of central powers come face-to-face with ordinary citizens in their localities. Clearly there are extremes of bifurcation that require special analysis, but many political encounters share many of the characteristics of "interfaces."[24]

Akhil Gupta shows the richness of front-line government offices and the intricacy of encounters between officials and citizens. He rightly resists placing all social relations with the state under the single category of civil society. He looks at how local newspapers create and express a public culture and a way of imagining the state, one influenced by transnational forces. These are important observations, yet it seems useful to look systematically at all the encounters between citizens and the state and all the encounters and publications in which citizens concertedly discuss the state.[25]

Sara Evans and Harry Boyte emphasize how popular political action creates free spaces that are venues for open political encounter without much exercise of control by higher authority. These are a crucial feature of radical democracy. While accepting the importance of spaces of free political encounter, it also seems worth attending to the kinds of controls exercised over political encounters that are less than open. Are there not degrees and directions of free political activity? How does unfree or controlled political space work? Does it not make sense to broaden the search of political space to all its kinds?[26]

These revealing views of special and significant spaces of political interaction demonstrate the need for a general conception of political settings that can take account of the dispersal of power and responsibility and also reflect the wide variety of political encounters in society, without losing sight of the roles that central governmental institutions do play in practice. Each of the analyses can fit within the general political settings approach that I am proposing; each represents a focused view of an especially interesting kind of political space. A general approach to political settings promises to be well-suited to a study of issues of central-local relations, politics of non-governmental associations, interactions of officials and citizens, the gradation from hidden to open political discourse, and the full scope of political participation. It can contribute a valuable new layer of evidence and analysis to theories of social movements, civil society, class relations, gender dynamics, and identity politics.

The power mismatch is not the last word in the analysis of local political space. Instead stands an invitation to think beyond the Athens effect. The view from street-level, as our case studies demonstrate, suggests that moderately open polities contain many settings of public political action and several sites of power—local, national, and international—on which to act. Certainly the settings and the sites differ in how central they are and how powerful they are, but given the complexities of the global power shifts the relationships among political settings are no simple matter to describe, to grasp, or to plan. Our theories and visions of political space are in need of imaginative and empirically informed reconstruction. The idea of political settings can play a part in that task.

Another Approach: Political Settings

This book inquires into how people create and use local political settings, or collective public actions located in space and time close to where they live and work. Although the action is local and often geographically distant from centres of political authority, local political settings are often linked to higher and more wide-reaching systems of power at national and international levels. Our inquiry is conceptual and empirical, theoretical and practical. It presents a method and a perspective together with accounts of particular cases. It also reaches beyond the cases to address issues raised by profound changes now occurring in the way in which public life is delimited, structured, and used. The changes call into question commonly accepted assumptions about how politics works and how it ought to work. They therefore raise important theoretical questions about how to understand contemporary political action and practical questions about how to respond to changes that appear to be singularly destructive.

Our method has three dimensions: identification, description, and interpretation. The first dimension—and often an early step in research—is to identify the smallest and most basic units of collective public action in localities undergoing significant change and to make them a focus of field research. These units, or "political settings," then, are all the gatherings of people in specific places at specific times to discuss questions, make decisions, and undertake other actions about matters of common concern for the locality. Local people usually have names for political settings in their midst; often the same setting recurs at more or less regular intervals. Examples are the weekly meeting of the town council in Kanyakumari village in Tamil Nadu state in India, the open hours of the office of the Market Vendors Association in Owino Market in Kampala, and the AMPRONAC conference of mothers, demanding news of their disappeared children, held in Managua in July 1978. Our definition of political settings is founded on a theoretical premise: public discussion, in which people give voice to their knowledge and opinions about matters of general concern in the presence of other people, is central to human political life. This definition does not assume that political settings offer unbiased or unproblematic arenas of full and open communication, as the second dimension of the research method demonstrates.

That second dimension is description: research examines in detail how specific political settings are formed and changed and how discussion and action in them are regulated. The descriptions draw upon two different kinds of theoretical presuppositions. Sometimes they employ principles of selection derived from theories of political action. For example, inspired by the theories of new social movements, two of our case studies describe how settings mobilize resources and form social identities (Pakistan, Nicaragua).

Others emphasize the aspects of settings that relate to institution-building (Nigeria) and to defence of economic interests (Uganda, India). Another focuses on the opportunity they offer for experience of leadership and responsibility (Kansas, Yorkshire). Several descriptive themes are common to most of the case studies: the frequency, scale, and location of political settings; the relationship between gender and participation; the link between political settings and the apparatus of government; the relations between political settings and the economic and cultural pressures associated with globalization; the sources of influence and leadership in political settings; and the relationship between political settings and the defence of livelihood.

Some of the research uses participatory techniques that attempt to orient the content of the research to issues identified by the people in the research localities themselves. Typically people wanted to gain stronger influence over basic issues of livelihood: better regulation of the market by vendors in Kampala, improved protection of the fishery for local fishers in southern India, more sources of water and of income-generating activities in Nigeria. A final and crucial common theme, one related to all the others, is the generation of a sphere of public action. For example, the research into mosques in Pakistan looks closely at how the Friday sermons define issues of government and citizens; the study of fishworkers in India notices the public role of women, the sources of leadership and initiative, and the methods of bringing pressure on the government; the research in Nicaragua focuses on how women create a political identity in the settings of the women's movement; and the research in Nigeria attends to how political settings define and address issues of local economic action and local development.

The third dimension of the research method is to interpret the features of the political settings identified and described by the research. Each case study has its own mode of interpretation, but they all share one important principle: good interpretation is grounded in good factual accounts of political settings. The interpretations relate to issues selected by the researchers, but also to the issues that the people in the localities and countries in question select by their actions and words: the politicization of Islam in Pakistan, the struggles waged by the Sandinistas in Nicaragua against internal and external enemies, the expansion and impending redevelopment of the organized markets in urban Uganda, the environmental pressures on agriculture in northern Nigeria, the balance between central control and local initiative in England and the United States, and the threat posed to the fishery off southern India by changes in technology and by the licensing of foreign fishing vessels.

Interpretation can make use of such familiar categories as social movements, civil society, institution-building, social class, gender, and public space. Within these divergent perspectives the focus on political settings opens to examination a crucial and neglected area of analysis: the interface between (a) socially formed individual persons with their interests and desires and interpretations of the world, and (b) historically rooted social structures and forces that give shape to political settings. The focus on political settings recognizes at a basic and local level the dictum of Marx that people make their own history but not under conditions of their own choosing. Anyone who has called a meeting in an effort to change something has experienced the challenges and the ironies of action in which yesterday's creativity binds today's free construction, which in turn constrains tomorrow's attempts at social innovation.

We seek to demonstrate that political settings are a useful tool for understanding the continuing contest to construct freedom in a time of extensive and rapid changes in patterns of political power. Theories of democratic practice and free communication give us standards for evaluating the degree of democracy in political settings, and studies of the controlling power of class, gender, and cultural inequalities alert us to the powerful forces that often throttle freedom. Our cases show that people in places that might be supposed to lack the historical experience and the skills to create effective and democratic political settings can be adept and prolific in generating them. In these cases at least, the history of local democratic practices includes varying mixes of experience with electoral politics, ancient traditions of consultation, local popular struggles, and the influence of broader associations, such as churches, unions, and schools. Local popular action is not only surprisingly dense and dexterous, but also not entirely local. There is grist here for the analytical mills that would grind away at questions of the resiliency of local democratic practices and why some local actions are relatively democratic while others fall under the autocratic power of a few.

Political action, especially popular demonstrations, can be contagious.[27] What limits the spread of popular action and how it is contained and controlled are valid questions to raise. The regulation of political action does not always take the form of an autocratic minority dictating terms of action to the people. Regulation is accomplished by accepted or seemingly accepted customs about which political settings exist and recur and how the settings in general operate: who sets agendas, who speaks, how decisions are reached. The customs and practices that silently regulate political settings might be said to contain the "common sense" and the kind of "hegemony" that Gramsci thought could become ingrained in class-divided societies, limiting the expression of working-class interests. Looking at collective action in terms of political settings may help to show how hegemonic discourses hold their dominance and how they begin to change.

There are only two sources of evidence about what people think and want: their speech (spoken and written) and their actions. Speech and action take place in social settings that are far from neutral. Every social setting is loaded with formal and informal forces that control and limit the speech and action of every person present; but the very forces that limit speech and action also enable speech and action. For example, people joined together in a church service are under strong pressure to do and say those things that we call praying and worshipping. At the same time the freedom to pray and worship, to be effective, requires the existence of church-type settings. The social freedom of people, broadly speaking, depends upon the range of kinds of activity settings available to them and upon their ability and scope to form new activity settings to meet new desires and objectives. Political freedom, therefore, is much more than the absence of oppression and much more than an internal capacity of individuals to act. It is all that and something more: a quality of the social landscape that offers a range of activities to choose among and, most importantly, offers an opportunity to discuss and to act upon the activity settings that exist, as well as the latitude to found new ones. By definition the settings that offer such opportunities are political settings.

Democracy, then, requires that all citizens be able to take part in the existing political settings and to form new political settings. In addressing matters of broad concern political settings seek to evaluate, regulate, create, and cancel other activity settings. But most regulation of speech and action in political and in other settings occurs through a non-political and often implicit exercise of customary or administrative social power. Where the scope of customary and administrative power is large and the scope of overt political regulation is small, local popular politics is conservative and tends to legitimate existing relations of social power. The story changes when and where customary and administrative regulation is called into question and once-accepted patterns of action are drawn into political discussion; we then speak of the politicization of social life. Under those conditions democratic politics might be a major force for change.

In our research we found that local democratic action was widely present and extremely energetic in unexpected places. This is good news for democrats, but it is only half the story. In some cases street-level democracy produced little change; it legitimated and adjusted an existing system of social power. Even when voices raised in local political settings were calling aspects of that order into question, local democratic action in the form of meetings and demonstrations did not necessarily translate into political power to enforce changes. Moreover, in all the cases recounted in this book there was a chance that local action would simply be overwhelmed by large-scale changes in markets, technology, and communication; or that agendas of intolerance, exclusion, and elimination would drive democratic practices underground. Yet the actions we observed were often robust and strongly supported. Despite their vulnerability, they clearly constituted essential steps to democratic power and raised for us a question about how wider networks of information, communication, and coordinated action can reinforce local democratic activities.

Notes

1. See, for example, my exchange with Colin Leys: Colin Leys, "The World, Society and the Individual," *Southern Africa Report* 11,3 (April 1996), pp.17-21; Jonathan Barker, "Debating Globalization: Critique of Colin Leys," *Southern Africa Report* 12,4 (September 1997), pp.20-22; "Colin Leys Replies," *Southern Africa Report* 12,4 (September 1997), pp.22-23.

2. Aristotle, *The Politics of Aristotle*, trans. Ernest Barker (Oxford: Clarenden Press, 1952), p.189.

3. Ibid., pp.109-10.

4. Ibid., p.310.

5. Ibid., pp.189-93.

6. Mogens Herman Hansen, *The Athenian Democracy in the Age of Demosthenes: Structure, Principles and Ideology*, trans. J.A. Crook (Oxford: Basil Blackwell, 1991), p.313.

7. Hannah Arendt, *The Human Condition* (Garden City, N.Y.: Doubleday/Anchor, 1959), pp.52-53.

8. Aristotle, *Politics*, p.310.

9. David Easton, *A Framework for Political Analysis* (Englewood Cliffs, N.J.: Prentice-Hall, 1965).

10. Karl Polanyi, *The Great Transformation: The Political and Economic Origins of Our Times*, with an introduction by Robert M. MacIver (Boston: Beacon Press, 1957).

11. Hal Draper, *Karl Marx's Theory of Revolution*, vol. II, *The Politics of Social Classes* (New York: Monthly Review Press, 1978).

12. Alain Touraine, "Beyond Social Movements," in *Social Movements: Critiques, Concepts, Case-Studies*, ed. Stanford M. Lyman (Houndmills, Basingstoke, Eng.: Macmillan, 1995), pp.371-93.

13. Sidney Tarrow, *Power in Movement: Social Movements, Collective Action and Politics* (Cambridge: Cambridge University Press, 1994), pp.13-23. See also Margit Mayer, "Social Movement Research in the United States: A European Perspective," in *Social Movements*, ed. Lyman, pp.168-95.

14. Alberto Melucci, *Nomads of the Present: Social Movements and Individual Needs in Contemporary Society*, ed. John Keane and Paul Mier (Philadelphia: Temple University Press, 1989). See also Alberto Melucci, *Challenging Codes: Collective*

Action in the Information Age (Cambridge: Cambridge University Press, 1996), pp.145-62.

15. Tarrow, *Power in Movement*, p.198. For a more positive view see Warren Magnusson, *The Search for Political Space: Globalization, Social Movements and the Urban Political Experience* (Toronto: University of Toronto Press, 1996).

16. Lawrence Whitehead, "Bowling in the Bronx: The Uncivil Interstices between Civil and Political Society," in *Civil Society: Democratic Perspectives*, ed. Robert Fine and Shirin Rai (London: Frank Cass, 1997), pp.94-114.

17. Robert Putnam, *Making Democracy Work: Civic Traditions in Modern Italy* (Princeton, N.J.: Princeton University Press, 1993).

18. An early exponent was Guy Gran, *Development by People: Citizen Construction of a Just World* (New York: Praeger, 1983). Soon after "globalization" entered the lexicon came David C. Korten, *Getting to the 21st Century: Voluntary Action and the Global Agenda* (West Hartford, Conn.: Kumarian Press, 1990). For a balanced overview, see Jamie Swift, *Civil Society in Question* (Toronto: Between the Lines, 1999).

19. A pertinent example is Atul Kohli, *The State and Poverty in India: The Politics of Reform* (Cambridge: Cambridge University Press, 1987), pp.237-41.

20. Antonio Gramsci, *Selections from the Prison Notebooks*, ed. and trans. Quintin Hoare and Geoffrey Howell Smith (London: Lawrence and Wishart, 1971); Max Weber, *Economy and Society: An Outline of Interpretive Sociology*, ed. Guenther Roth and Claus Wittich (Berkeley: University of California Press, 1978); and Barrington Moore, *Social Origins of Dictatorship and Democracy: Lord and Peasant in the Making of the Modern World* (Boston: Beacon Press, 1966).

21. See Inga Brandell, ed., *Workers in Third-World Industrialization* (Houndmills, Basingstoke, Eng.: Macmillan, 1991).

22. Putnam, *Making Democracy Work*.

23. James C. Scott, *Domination and the Arts of Resistance: Hidden Transcripts* (New Haven, Conn.: Yale University Press, 1990).

24. Norman Long and Magdelena Villareal, "Exploring Development Interfaces: From the Transfer of Knowledge to the Transformation of Meaning," in *Beyond the Impasse: New Directions in Development Theory*, ed. Frans J. Schuurman (London: Zed Books, 1993).

25. Akhil Gupta, "Blurred Boundaries: The Discourse of Corruption, the Culture of Politics, and the Imagined State," *American Ethnologist* 22,2 (1995), pp.375-402.

26. Sara M. Evans and Harry C. Boyte, *Free Spaces: The Sources of Democratic Change in America*, 2nd ed. (Chicago: The University of Chicago Press, 1992).

27. Elmer Eric Schattschneider, *The Semisovereign People: A Realist's View of Democracy in America* (New York: Holt, Rinehart and Winston, 1965), makes the point; and Elias Canetti, *Crowds and Power* (London: Gollancz, 1962), provides striking images.

Chapter 3

Political Settings:
An Approach to the Study of Popular Action
Jonathan Barker

"**O**pening political space." The metaphor is a telling one. What images does it evoke? Perhaps it's a huge crowd of three or four thousand demonstrators who risk truncheons, water cannons, and bullets as they take over a public square to shout against the ruling junta. Or 25 women who leave their homes against the entreaties and shouts and commands of their husbands and fathers to gather in a church meeting room to talk about their need for child care and jobs and respect. Or a newspaper that for the first time prints a series of articles on opposition to government repression in an outlying province. As a metaphor political space draws a parallel between a newfound freedom to address new issues and a physical place-time in which speech and action can be freely chosen. Certainly the experience of a freedom to think new political thoughts and to express them in speech and writing is a real and important one. The metaphor reminds us, however, that political participation requires a space in which people can meet; it requires a time when people can be present together and hear one another. It is worth thinking further about political space in this physical and concrete way.

Constricted political spaces are closed and guarded. Often their location is a secret known only to a few. They may even be inside a military base or in a fortified, underground bunker. Streets and public squares are widely open to public access. They are public property under state control and often the first arena of claims for open and democratic political participation. Usually the venue of individual journeys, small errands, and limited interpersonal encounters, they can be wrested from state control and transformed into the site of focused demonstrations and giant meetings to hear speeches and roar demands. Demonstrators can claim them as popular political space. The state sometimes resists the claim and reverses the action, closing the venues of demonstrations or restricting access to them. Curfews bar entry to streets and parks. Gatherings of three or more persons, even on the sidewalk, are outlawed. Tanks occupy the square. Informers report on conversations in cafés and bars. Besieged authorities attempt to reoccupy the free spaces by mounting their own massive rallies and demonstrations.

Only rarely are mass demonstrations the main source of social energy keeping political space open for large numbers of citizens; and tanks are seldom the primary front-line force containing and closing popular political space, although their threat may be a continuing presence. More frequently local organizations and small meetings are the means for opening and retaining popular political space. Some of them amplify their discourse by producing publications. Through discussion they create and refine ideas, and their decisions make claims on actual and potential participants. They send messages to institutions with authority and distribute resources to support other activities.

If political space is concrete and physical, what are the social forces that create and destroy that space, open and close it? How do the forces work? How do people think about political settings and go about creating and changing them? What are the human and social consequences of different forms, sizes, and dynamics of political space? An orthodox response to these questions starts with a set of people, a group, and inquires into what they are doing and why they are doing it. Note that there is some ambiguity here, for the idea of group implies some way of collecting individuals together conceptually as sets of people either similar in some way or organized in some way. Research often asks individuals about their political action and relates action to personal characteristics and experiences. What kind of people vote a certain way? What kind of political action is frequent among university students? What differences explain the various forms of political action taken by rich and poor, men and women, old and young? Make no mistake, we need this form of analysis and this approach to understanding action. But to pursue the orthodox approach does not preclude also taking another perspective.

The political settings perspective—a more unorthodox approach—starts with collective political actions and asks about their properties and frequencies. It also asks how people are drawn to a setting or discouraged from entering it. By definition settings are collective actions, and each political setting has its unique location in space and in time, its own spatial-temporal address. In common language we call them meetings, demonstrations, rallies, picket lines. More general terms are venues, occasions, situations. The general terms suggest that it is quite possible to look at much or all human activity in terms of the occasions, situations, or venues through which the activity is structured.

In this book we call the general units of collective activity "activity settings," but our focus is on political activity settings. The most numerous types are meetings and offices, but there are many less frequent but very important kinds: demonstrations, rallies, picket lines, polling places, discussion groups, sit-ins, and many others. To do research on political settings is to scan the world of human activity for meetings and offices and other political settings and to consider their characteristics and properties and relationships. People are not at all neglected or denied in this approach, but it is their activity as parts of and participants in political activity settings that is the first order of observation.

The approach holds that activity settings are foci of social energy; they contain and organize social forces that impel action just as surely as individual needs, desires, and strategies do. The interplay between individual motives and situational forces is a fundamental theme in the politics of political settings. You may have had occasion personally to experience the powerful pull of a large political demonstration, or felt the revulsion mixed with fear inspired by a rally of a movement you believed to be dangerous. We have all been driven against some part of our will to attend a gathering we wanted to avoid. And many of us have brought social pressures to bear on other people to go to a meeting that we believed merited attendance. Such experiences constitute introspective evidence for the existence of social forces attracting or repelling participation in political space.

Within political settings social forces are also evident. Who has not hesitated at a doorway, gathering the inner strength to cope with the demands of the social situation they were about to enter? We have all seen how customs of precedence, social hierarchies, and forms of address as well as skills at personal manipulation, agenda-management, symbol-mongering, and reasoned argument have shaped decisions made in meetings. Both outside and within political settings, forces are at work that give shape to political action, define its form, and filter its content. What are these forces and how can we best grasp them?

Often the people who take action to close or open political space have a clear idea of what they are doing, not that things always work out according to plan. The autocratic postcoup junta decrees that political opposition is treason, and it sends police to close down the meetings of labour unions, oppositional political parties, and human rights associations. Postrevolutionary governments often legitimize the popular political settings that brought them to power—the meetings, discussion groups, demonstrations, and publications that pushed for change. Typically the passion to create political space subsides and the government fear of continued popular action returns. The new rulers may move to bring popular action under control, and some activist political settings fade away or lose their dynamism. How to build long-term popular action on the surge of popular revolutionary action is one of the great questions for a successful popular democratic movement.

Each locality has a larger or smaller repertoire of types of political action. Political settings are usually orderly, even routine, in their basic form. Even spontaneous demonstrations often follow a kind of script as they open space for political action. Participants know that they will march to the public square, hear some speeches, and shout their demands that the rulers step down and make room for elections. And they know they risk being attacked by police or army units. The women who call a meeting to set goals and map strategies know what an effective meeting looks like, how to manage it, and how to give it a structure. Most people have some understanding about how political settings work, and some people are experts in organizing and managing them. They often have good practical knowledge of the forces operating in political settings. Researchers can learn a great deal from the local activists about how individual drives and strategies interact with situational forces.

Activity Settings

The contextual or situational unit out of which the idea of political space is built, an *activity setting,* consists of a person or a set of people at a place and time engaged in a program of activity along with the objects and environmental features to which the activity is coordinated. All action by all people takes place in one or another activity setting.[1]

Although activity settings are units of collective activity, they are units in which individual and collective intention and creativity abound. A key question in social science method is where to anchor activity. For many purposes it is appropriate to attach activity to the individuals who do the acting. These people are easy to discern, they have consciousness as well as action, and they correspond to the subjective experience of researchers. We can search within the dynamics of the person for the source of actions, and we can look at individual minds and lives to determine the consequences of actions. However, going beyond individualistic analysis to consider the larger contexts makes the meaning of actions clearer and the logic of their occurrence easier to grasp. The actions of a midfielder in soccer/football make little sense without seeing them in relation to the game in which they take place: the rules, the score, the location of the ball, the position, movement, and skills of the other players, and the time left to play. An election is made up of a finite number of individual acts of voting, but, as election monitors know, the meaning of each voting act is determined by how the polling station works and how the ballot is structured and handled. Polling stations are political settings that in principle are designed to let individual choices flow through without hindrance or influence. Other political settings are usually designed to shape the quality of collective action and even its content. Meetings, for example, are often structured to include certain people and exclude others, to encourage the raising of some issues and discourage mention of others. In general, all actions are embedded in larger social contexts; for some purposes of research and analysis we need to anchor actions to larger extra-individual units rather than to individual persons. Activity settings are such units, and they have qualities that make them particularly appropriate for the study of political action and participation.

In defining and characterizing activity settings I first take the standpoint of an empirically oriented naturalistic social science, one that assumes researchers who are trying to make careful, communicable, and reproducible observations of a social reality that exists independently of their observations. Later I will consider two important facts that take us to an interpretationist view of political settings: first, activity settings also exist in the emotional and intellectual consciousness of participants; and, second, for their ability to make observations at all, the self-defined "scientific" observers are dependent upon the people whose activities they observe. Activity settings are useful to an understanding of social life that stresses the social construction of meanings and activities.[2]

A social science researcher sees the keys to the identification of activity units as (1) congruence among activity, material objects, and environment and (2) boundedness in time and space of the activity itself. In other words, (1) the program of activity and its material surroundings are shaped to each other and (2) they have a beginning and an end, both temporal and geographical. Activity settings differ from groups in two ways. Unlike groups, activity settings include the material surroundings and the objects related to the activities: persons, place, and things plus the activities that put them all in motion. Also, unlike groups, activity settings are in existence only when and where they occur. They may repeat regularly—daily, weekly, monthly, yearly—but when they are not happening, they exist only in the intentions and expectations of possible participants and those who know about their existence. Some activity settings occur once only and do not repeat at all.

The boundaries of many activity settings are easy to see. The special meeting of the Northeast Arid Zone Development Project in Machina, Nigeria, was held in the space in front of the Emir's Palace from 8 to 10 p.m. on February 18, 1993; it discussed forming a community bank in the town. In the village of Kovalam in Kanyakumari district in Tamil Nadu state, India, the base committee met in the main street of a neighbourhood from 3 to 5 p.m. on February 4, 1995, to discuss the problems of alcohol abuse and the shortage of social services. Often walls and doors, and regular days and hours, set bounds to a recognizable and coherent program of activity.[3] Usually there is an obvious qualitative change in activity at the boundary. The boundary criterion, for the most part, designates activity settings that correspond to places, venues, occasions, meetings, happenings, occurrences, and events that people spontaneously identify as they organize their own activities for the day, the week, or the year or as they look back to identify what they have done or what has happened in the social world they think about.

That a formal definition and common sense correspond is a clue to one of the important attributes of activity settings: to a significant extent activity settings coincide with the cognitive maps of people who see them and participate in them. Researchers define them as units of observable collective activity, but they (or some version of them) are also units in life worlds, life spaces, and cognitive maps of many people.[4]

Activity settings are comprehensive units of observable human activity. If one could observe all individuals all of the time (the god's eye perspective), one would observe all the human activity there is. Similarly, to observe all activity settings would be to observe all activity. All activity occurs at identifiable locations in time and space and is shaped to its material environment. Still, observable activity omits some important things about people. To observe that people leaving a movie theatre appear to be lost in thought or that the demand of the manager of a bicycle assembly plant for greater speed on the job appears to place workers under stress says only a little about what the people concerned are thinking or feeling, and those thoughts and feelings can have profound significance. To take a history-changing example, we know that the weekly meetings of the Oyster Club took place in the 1780s in Edinburgh and that James Hutton there presented his revolutionary ideas about the evolution of land forms and geological formations. But that brute fact says nothing about the force of his ideas or about the effects of the discussion on the inner thoughts of David Hume and Adam Smith, intellectuals who were to make their own signal contributions in the Scottish renaissance.[5]

Unlike the eye-of-god, human observers cannot look directly into the hearts and minds of the people whose activity they observe, although they can often deduce likely responses from the context and sometimes get first-hand reports about what the people concerned were thinking and feeling. Knowing the context of interaction opens the way to empathic questioning and interpretation, as it does in the case of John McPhee's writing about Hutton. The researcher who has seen, heard, and smelled the speeded-up bicycle assembly line will have a better grasp of the reasons for the subsequent strike than someone without that concrete knowledge. Nonetheless the gap between the contextual knowledge of any observer and the experienced reality of the participants is a fundamental datum of activity settings, one on which their intrinsically political character is grounded.[6] That the persons (their character, intentions, impulses, sensibilities, and experiences) are not totally subsumed by the activity settings in which they take part is a fundamental advantage of using activity settings as units descriptive of social action. It opens the way to a better understanding of the constant potential for change. Because people bring to the settings in which they participate ideas, information, and emotions belonging to their own life worlds, they can and do sometimes remake the activity setting, or push its activity in new and surprising directions, which in turn alters the experience of more people, opening the possibility of cascading changes.

Time-space units are familiar in social analysis and everyday language. On a large scale, historians discover distinct epochs, eras, and episodes that divide the flow of historical time into units with some homogeneity and logical integrity. Modern Europe, classical Greece, frontier America, and Mogul India are social-historical entities recognized by historians, whose interpretive strategies may differ in important ways. Social geographers find large geo-social units in which human settlement and transportation patterns have received an impress that marks them off from neighbouring regions: the Andean highlands, the great plains of North America, the Maghreb, the Ganges basin. On a much smaller scale, journalists —trained to flag the "where" and the "when" of the news —report on "the meeting of the Security Council on February 12," "last Wednesday's press conference by the Prime Minister in Ottawa," or "the robbery Sunday night at Pip's Milk and Banana Shop." And ordinary people record in their calendars commitments like "Woody Allen film at the Century Cinema" and "dinner 7 p.m. with Alex at Ben's Smoked Meat Restaurant." In all these cases there is a perception of an activity unit bounded or unified by the nature of the activity itself.[7]

To see the world of human action in terms of activity settings is to see units of different kinds: trafficways (people and vehicles in roads and streets moving about, talking, and looking around); retail shops (customers entering shops, looking around, choosing objects, exchanging words with a proprietor or employee, giving of money, getting of object, exiting shop); meetings (people sitting in a room facing a table with several people behind it, chair presents agenda, participants discuss items and make motions, chair calls for vote). Many activity settings repeat themselves at regular intervals and become well-known features of the social landscape; they may even be marked on maps and catalogued in the pages of the telephone book. All are specific entities with a unique address in time and space; most have a name familiar to their participants.

Activity settings are especially useful intermediate units for relating to the experience of individual persons on one side and social organizations and structures on the other. Persons are essential parts of activity settings: no people, no setting. But few settings are dependent upon any particular person for their existence. From the standpoint of the setting, people are among its components. Activity settings can be seen as fields of social forces that attract some people to them and repel others and that steer or regulate the activity of their participants within rather narrow limits. Individuals experience the different fields of social forces as they move in the course of their day from one activity setting to another. R.D. Laing notes that each setting "requires a more or less radical transformation of the persons who comprise it. Consider the metamorphoses that one man must go through in one day as he moves from one form of sociality to another—family man, speck of crowd dust, functionary in the organization, friend. These are not simply different roles; each is a whole past and present and future, offering different options and constraints, different degrees of change or inertia, different kinds of closeness and distance, different sets of rights and obligations, different pledges and promises."[8]

Activity settings have a multifaceted, dense, and profound relationship to individuals.[9] They form the immediate environment of individuals; all the external stimuli that reach the receptors of people originate in or traverse activity settings, and many stimuli are sorted and structured by the situation more or less independently of the will or action of the person who receives them. This means that settings limit and create opportunities for action and experience for individuals. More particularly, settings structure patterns of personal causation in the environment; they have a causal structure that comes into play when a person takes action as a means to an end. They are the contexts of choice and of the realization of individual and group projects: they can contain their own micro-politics.

The Micro-Politics of Settings

From the standpoint of political science, activity settings have a surprising feature: when allowance is made for the difference of scale, the definition of activity setting and the definition of state are strikingly similar. Both states and activity settings have territory, population, and some process by which their pattern of activity is regulated and their boundaries are maintained. Activity settings, unlike states, cannot claim sovereignty or a monopoly of the legitimate use of physical force, but they can have "coercive" powers.[10] At the core of each setting is a program, a body of knowledge and instruction in some ways analogous to the constitution of a state, something that gives direction about what activities should be undertaken and how to carry them out. Usually the program is found in the minds of leaders; sometimes a written constitution or rule book gives it formal expression. Preserving and transmitting knowledge of the program are crucial for maintaining the setting.

Moreover, as in a state, a setting includes "a hierarchy of positions with respect to influence upon the setting and responsibility for its functioning."[11] Different positions in the setting have different degrees of power over the setting. To stress their micro-political function, I call them "power zones."[12] Zone 1 is onlooker to the activity of the setting; zone 2 is invited visitor; zone 3 is paying audience, voting member, or buying customer; zone 4 is functionary who administers the program of the setting; zone 5 is joint leader responsible for seeing that the program of the setting is carried out; zone 6 is sole leader responsible for activity in the setting. Together zones 4, 5, and 6 are the operating or performing zones of the setting, and the people who occupy them are the operators or performers with power and responsibility for the activity of the setting. Again, the parallel with political categories is striking: zone 1 is like non-resident visitor; zone 2 like resident foreigner; zone 3 like citizen or subject; zone 4 like government administrator; zone 5 like member of collective leadership or oligarchy; and zone 6 like president, prime minister, or monarch.

The political analogy goes deeper. Employing the language of systems analysis, ecological psychologists have stated that activity settings "generate forces that impose the programmed temporal-spatial pattern upon their component parts, impel the necessary people and material into them, and repel and expel disrupting people and material from them." Undergirding the activity setting "is a control system that maintains [it] intact when the properties of its components and the characteristics of its large context vary widely."[13] The process includes *sensing* information related to the functioning of the setting; *evaluating* whether and how well the program is being achieved; and *switching* as required between actions that implement the program and actions that maintain the setting. The theory emphasizes maintenance actions and the choice between deviance-countering actions that correct inappropriate behaviour and vetoing actions in which poorly functioning components, including persons, are ejected from the setting.

The structure of power in a setting and the processes of sensing, evaluating, and deciding about switching between implementation and maintenance translate readily into political language. Defining politics as discussion, conflict, decision, and action over issues of power and other matters of general concern, one can readily identify the micro-politics of an activity setting. It involves discussion, conflict, decision, and action over issues of power and matters of general concern *within the setting.* In some cases, however, the homeostatic mechanisms are dispersed and there is no micro-political dialogue: individual inhabitants monitor the adequacy of the performance of themselves or of one part of the activity of a setting. In other cases a single person senses, evaluates, decides, and acts with "discussion" that is purely within a single mind. In such cases the politics of the setting is more potential than actual. It is easy to see that discussion about how to implement a program and how to maintain a setting can always erupt and then spill over into discussion about more fundamental recasting of the program and reorganizing of the setting. Micro-politics can move beyond home-ostatic mechanisms to engage processes of change and transformation.[14]

The inherent potential tension between the goals of individual participants and the program requirements of the setting also points to the deeper level of micro-politics: of creating and changing the programs of activity settings. It seems indisputable that discussion will sometimes move from questions of the adequacy with which the program of a setting is functioning to questions about the adequacy of the program itself, including the possibility of fundamentally changing or extinguishing it. One more factor makes the emergence of an active micro-politics even more likely: change in the surrounding conditions that influence the resources, including people, on which the setting draws. Just how to give theoretical expression to issues of change and adaptation in activity settings is an important issue.[15] Here we suggest adopting a political approach.

To look at settings from a political standpoint is to ask where the program comes from, how it is changed, how it fits with the goals and ideas of the various participants in the setting, and, most distinctively, how change in the program of a setting is placed on the agenda of activity in that setting or in another one. The political approach stresses the self-reflecting aspect of activity, the part of an activity setting that considers the setting itself.[16] Think of a small free-standing social club that elects one officer whose job it is to chair the part of each monthly meeting in which the members decide about the time, place, and activity of the next meeting. With respect to the club, the most consequential political action was the founding of the club itself. David Easton's influential definition of politics as "the authoritative allocation of values for a society" (the activity setting in this case) is gravely insufficient. A better understanding emphasizes the use of social power "to initiate, to invent, to bring about."[17] One thing that it can bring about is new social activity, new activity settings.[18]

But initiating and inventing activity are usually not as thorough-going as founding a new setting; more often people initiate activity within the broad program of an existing setting. The normal micro-politics of the social club is the discussion and decision about the next meeting and the periodic election of a chairperson. One could ask about how the discussion was structured, which members spoke, whether decisions were reached through voting or consensus or other methods, and how the public meeting related to behind-the-scenes conversations and negotiations. One could also ask about deeper "constitutional" issues. How was the club founded? How did the understanding about the program of activity arise? How can it be changed? A meeting may come in which members themselves raise deeper issues. A member might move that the club take a public position on a community issue, that it buy a permanent locale, or that it disband. An observer could ask why such issues arise and inquire into how they are discussed and resolved, or left unresolved.

A political focus adds a fundamentally new dimension to the study of activity settings.[19] It asks about the origin of settings, change in their programs, and their dissolution. Does the program of a setting originate or change as the result of an overt decision, or is there a kind of silent adjustment or evolution? Is the program a familiar replication from a well-known cultural repertoire, or is it an original creation in whole or in part? Is it the work of the participants in the activity setting or is it imposed from outside by a larger authority system? If imposed, how remote is the imposing power? How much, if any, of the program is subject to self-reflective discussion and decision by members of the setting about whether to change, maintain, or dissolve it? Are its internal social relations egalitarian or hierarchical? How is its power structure generated and maintained? Are discussion, decision-making, and conflict in the setting open, restricted, or absent? Is communication in the setting symbolic and expressive or is it descriptive and practical? What are the mechanisms of program enforcement? Such questions take the analysis back to the concerns for hidden politics, cultural gaps in communication, experience of associational relations, and degrees of autonomy that writers on the varieties of local politics have recently stressed. They relate to a fundamental and general issue about the way in which activity settings work. How is the activity of activity settings regulated? What are the possible kinds of regulation?

Politics in the form of discussion, deliberation, conflict, and decision is one way of concerting activity. It can also instigate new activities, but with respect to regulating or maintaining activity we need to note that in many activity settings micro-politics is reduced to communicating and enforcing a set of principles of social regulation that almost everyone accepts either actively or passively. Activity settings in which the program of activity has any of the five following patterns, for example, are regulated without much discussion, deliberation, or conflict once the regulatory principles are established: the program (1) smoothly follows a well-known traditional pattern, (2) comes under the detailed direction of other hierarchically superior settings, (3) spontaneously conforms to the desires of individuals, (4) obeys the instructions of a single manager, or (5) conforms directly to market rules and price signals. To list these patterns of regulation is to suggest the existence and acceptance of languages or scripts that settle provisionally many of the issues that might be raised and disputed about the purpose and functioning of the setting. The patterns are drawn from social theory of several kinds. The principles of regulation they assume are, respectively, regulation by tradition, by hierarchical management, by anarchical mutual adjustment, by authoritative individual direction, and by market forces. How well and how generally these and other possible modes of regulation apply to the internal ordering of activity settings are matters for research and analysis that have so far been given very little attention. Research on workplace settings that are supposed to be regulated by a combination of market logic and hierarchical control suggests that a kind of micro-political regime is necessary to support the seemingly non-political regulation of the workplace.[20] The topic of the relation between micro-political and non-political forms of regulation of activity settings merits more study. An important question to investigate asks whose interest the non-political regulation serves.

A fundamental quality of activity settings—those with a well-developed micro-politics and those without it—is their potential for micro-politicization, a process that may spill over into full politicization if issues of government are invoked. Workers who yesterday obeyed the orders of management without question may today become surly and resistant and tomorrow organize and make demands for change in working conditions. A religious service is a tradition-regulated gathering, but one that can occasionally become an important space for voicing demands for social and political justice. Market forces lose their power to regulate activities within settings once larger issues of organization, technology, and strategy are raised; managers—and perhaps even employees—are forced to discuss and decide. Hyperinflation and depressions also undermine market regulation. Even the free-form play in a city park can turn into gang conflict or an attack on police, or, under certain conditions, it can even be reshaped into a political rally.

Choice and change also occur on a larger scale. People enliven and reduce or cancel settings by choosing to frequent them or no longer to frequent them. The array of available settings represents an important feature of quality of life for people. The close relationship between the structure of situations and the opportunity for experience and for consequential action means that people commonly identify well-being with the availability to them of a desirable array of activity settings.

Classifying Political Settings

The availability of activity settings can be studied empirically. For a given settlement area or organization all the activity settings can be listed in a matrix. On the left side in a column is a list of all activity settings. Across the top are noted relevant features of the settings, such as number of participants, attributes of participants, hours of occurrence per year, kind of activity, and so on. Some basic analysis can be read from such a matrix. For example, the number of participants on average multiplied by the hours of occurrence per year yields the total annual person-hours of occupancy time for that activity setting. Since the number of hours in a year is finite and the

number of people in a locality often varies little in one year, the total occupancy time for all activity settings in a locality is also finite. How people distribute their time among activities is an important datum and an interesting
analytical challenge.[21] We can ask, for example, how much time what kinds
of people spend in political activity. What kinds of political activity? With
what changes in recent years?

A pivotal theoretical and practical question is how to classify activity settings. What differences are worth noting? How can the matrix be organized to reflect the structure and dynamics (and for our purposes, the politics) of the settlement, neighbourhood, or organization in question? What
are the criteria for identifying political activity settings? The issue becomes
clearest if we think of a relatively autonomous community, and use three
principles of classification: similarity of program of activity (program types);
linkages via chains of authority (systems); and predominance of certain patterns of action (types of action pattern). The first makes it possible to distinguish business meetings from retail shops and police stations from sports
matches, and to classify all instances of each of these program types together. One researcher estimates that in the United States there may be 400 different *program types*.[22] Several types of meetings have special importance for
our focus on politics and participation, but demonstrations and polling stations are among other politically relevant program types.

The second basis of classification singles out a special kind of inter-
dependence among settings: the exercise of authority over the program of
one setting by actions in another controlling setting. The public business
hours of the credit union and the staff meeting of the same organization are
very different activities, but they are both subject to the authority of the
credit union management committee meeting. *Authority systems* group settings into something akin to institutional clusters (all settings under the control of the Market Vendors Association Central Executive Committee meetings in Owino Market, Kampala, Uganda) and then group the clusters
according to type of authority system, one of which is government. The government authority system and other authority systems, such as political parties, whose activities are oriented to government are of particular interest to
research on political space.

The third basis for classifying settings is the predominance of a
pattern of activity with a certain orientation. Community studies have rated
settings for the presence of 11 action patterns (including business, education,
nutrition, recreation, and physical health). Business, for example, is exchanging goods, services, and privileges for payment; education is formal teaching
of students by teachers. For our purposes the "government action pattern" is
of particular interest.

Research using activity settings can also classify people in various ways: age, gender, social class, ethnic identity, educational achievement, health, place of residence, years in the community or organization, for instance. These categories reflect familiar strategies of analysis, but they can be put to an unfamiliar test. On the matrix of all activity settings it will be obvious which categories of people enter (and which do not enter) which classes of settings. How different is the setting selection of men and women, blacks and whites, young adults and older adults? In what settings are each of these categories concentrated? From which is each largely excluded? Data on differential participation by categories of individuals can be used to explore ideas about social forces and bases of individual choice. If class is defined as social position within a person's primary income-earning settings, then a theory of class determination of other activities translates into a hypothesis about some lines of force or logic that connect a position in income-earning settings to selection of and access to other settings. A theory of the fundamental importance of gender translates into ideas about how many kinds of settings treat men and women differently and/or how gender identity influences the ways in which people choose settings and find a place in them.

Government Authority Systems

We need a vocabulary for distinguishing the boundaries of political space and for analyzing its structure and dynamics. The account of activity settings provides an excellent starting place because of its emphasis on action, authority, and concrete space-time units. Given that all the human activity in a locality or a country, or the whole Earth for that matter, occurs in activity settings, to determine the boundaries of political space we need a way to identify the collection of activity settings that belong to that particular space. One way of categorizing activity settings attends to the nature of the activity itself. It looks for activity settings that specialize in political action, which is action oriented to evaluating, influencing, and implementing the workings of government and more generally to defining and acting upon matters of general concern for a set of people. Another categorization attends to the system of authority that controls the activity; it looks for activity settings subject to the controlling intervention of executive settings of government agencies. It identifies governmental space, defined as all the activity settings that fall under the control of government agencies. There are important zones of overlap between political and governmental space. The polling stations and vote-counting venues that constitute an election, for example, are usually administered by a government agency (making them a part of governmental space), and they also contain activity oriented to choosing office-holders, an important matter of general concern for the people of a governmental jurisdiction (making them a part of political space).

Political theory stresses the special quality of government authority systems. The tradition of political thought stemming from ancient Greece relates politics to that form of human association that is most self-sufficient and occupied with the general well-being of the society as whole. According to the standard Weberian definition, government alone claims a monopoly over the legitimate use of violence. Current definitions and assumptions continue in a similar vein: government allocates values, sets goals, and initiates activities for the whole society; it has, or claims, the power to make and enforce laws regulating activity throughout a society. The political space perspective also recognizes that government claims to make and enforce laws, such as those in the criminal code, that apply to all settings and that define certain actions, such as physical assault, as being illegal wherever they occur. It also recognizes that government authority systems claim and usually exercise more comprehensive control than other kinds of authority systems.[23] However, the political space perspective regards the question of the scope, intensity, and unity of governmental control as an empirical matter. We expect to find considerable variation in the kind, degree, unity, and uniformity of government intervention in and control over social space from country to country and locality to locality. Understanding the actual scope, unity, and intensity of political space will aid thinking about the scope, unity, and intensity that political space ought to have.

In formal terms, the authority systems of government agencies in a country or locality consist of those settings controlled by executive settings of local, provincial (state), or national governments. A listing of the government agency authority systems in a locality and a mapping of the activity settings over which they exercise control through intentional interventions give a clear idea of the scope and content of local governmental space. For example, in two small towns, one in Kansas and one in Yorkshire, in the 1950s-70s the government authority systems included these kinds of settings (listed in alphabetical order): agricultural advisers' offices, civil engineers' offices, court sessions of county and district courts, election polling places, fire stations, government business and records offices (for town, county, and national agencies), health department offices, jails, judges' chambers, machinery repair shops, meetings of town and county councils, physicians' offices (in Yorkshire), police stations, post offices, school administration offices, sewage disposal plants, sheriffs' offices (in Kansas), soil conservation service offices, tax assessment offices, and welfare offices.[24] The lists of local offices of government in towns in northern Nigeria and southern India (chapters 4, 5) bear considerable resemblance to this one.

The focus on government authority systems reveals the boundaries of governmental space: are medical services, education, and banking services included or excluded? It also illuminates the internal structure and dynamics of governmental space. One quality of governmental space, for instance, concerns the scope or range of activities that come under direct government management. A second is the intensity and direction of general government surveillance over all settings, either protecting or limiting political rights. In what measure is political communication and action free from government control? In what measure are they protected from abrogation by private enforcers of social power or morality? It makes an important difference to the quality of political participation if general police surveillance includes listening for and reporting on the expression of political opinions in public meetings and public meeting places such as bars, restaurants, cafés, and social clubs. It also matters if police allow landlords or "strongmen" or religious hierarchies to close meetings and harass organizers.

A third interesting feature of internal structure is the degree of concentration of governmental control in one or a few agencies (such as a department of internal affairs or a regional development office) or its dispersal among a plurality of agencies. Most local governmental space may be under the direct control of a single government department, or different parts may belong to different agencies or be dispersed to boards that enjoy some autonomy from the main government agencies. Moreover, some activity settings formally under government direction may escape direct government control because they operate as parastatal enterprises or crown corporations required to generate their own revenue or to answer to their own constituencies. A more pluralistic system of agencies of governmental authority will probably be more open to local influence—though that influence may be the work of a local elite rather than a democratic body.

A fourth quality of governmental space in a locality relates to the issue of autonomy. Are the controlling settings found within or close to the locality, or are they centred in distant towns and cities?[25] The controlling setting is the one that selects officers, sets agendas, makes rules, establishes budgets, defines membership, and otherwise controls the program of the setting. If the controlling setting is located in the local political jurisdiction, local autonomy is high; autonomy diminishes as the level (and often the distance away) of the controlling setting increases to county, state or provincial, national, or transnational centres.[26] The finer features of local-central governmental relations come into play. Local settings may have day-to-day administrative autonomy but nevertheless receive most of their revenue from central government; they therefore have to gain general governmental approval from time to time. Still another kind of control by government may be exercised through licensing requirements, insurance programs, and bargained agreements between government agencies and other organizations. Again, nearby centres of governmental authority are probably more subject to local pressures than are distant ones.

Research on activity settings in government authority systems can find differences in the range of activities controlled by government, the scope and intensity of government surveillance, the number of government agencies, and the degree of local autonomy they exercise. In this way it can identify and analyze different kinds and patterns of authoritative control in localities. Research in public administration, although it makes little explicit use of activity settings, does shed light on how government authority systems are organized and how they exercise control over societies. The political space approach adds a useful way of seeing how government agencies fit into the full scope of public activity in a locality.

Political Action

Political actions are not confined to settings in the government agency authority systems. Public meetings about government and its activities, demonstrations for or against government policies, and workshops to inform people of their rights under the law are just a few examples of political action occurring in activity settings that are not part of government authority systems. To identify the activity settings in which political activity is concentrated, we need a way of defining political activity. The definition offered earlier—action oriented to evaluating, influencing, and implementing the workings of government and more generally to defining and acting upon matters of general concern—needs to be further considered. Note first that what marks action as political is its orientation, its object or purpose, not its form. Demonstrations, meetings, training sessions, elections, and opinion polls may or may not constitute political action. It all depends upon the orientation of the activity. To bring into focus the changing shape of politics, I propose a definition that goes beyond government and local opinion. The core of the definition remains action oriented to government authority systems and to the regulations and policies that they decide and implement or that people want them to decide and to implement.

To this I would add action that is oriented not to government but instead to the work of non-governmental authority systems in areas that people consider to be of general public importance. Examples are education and health systems controlled by churches or voluntary associations. Finally, in recognition of the self-defining quality of politics (a key matter of common interest is the determination of the content of the common interest) and of the role of people outside any given political locality in determining the scope of its politics, I would add a third clause to the definition: action oriented to matters that intellectual convention or significant opinion considers to be of general and public importance. Such a conventional or imposed definition should, of course, be specified and justified. For example, researchers may wish to consider protection of an important production-related ecosystem as a public issue of general importance even though neither local government nor local people yet recognize it as such. Any analyst who presents as political certain actions that are not oriented to government or to matters locally considered of common concern is obliged to make the case for their being political. In making the case the analyst is performing a political action and should be understood to be so doing. Indeed, portraying and accepting the local opinion about what matters are of common local concern are also political actions. We observers and analysts cannot escape our political role and the responsibilities entailed in that role.

Here then is a formal definition: *political action* is present within an activity setting to the extent that the concrete occurrences within the setting (a) implement or resist the making, interpretation, and execution of laws and regulations by government agencies; or (b) discuss, implement, or resist action by other authority systems on matters local people consider to be of general concern for a locality; or (c) discuss, implement, or resist action on matters significant outsiders consider to be of great public importance.

Political action can involve any of the following: engaging in civic affairs (discussing, informing, demonstrating, voting, deciding, meeting); supplying objects and resources for governmental programs and other public programs; learning and teaching about government and legal programs and other public programs; and evaluating government and other public programs and their leaders.[27]

Political Space

Without claiming quantitative precision I will refer to the group of settings in which action is overwhelmingly (say 80 percent) political as political settings or *political space*. In addition to the settings in which political action is heavily concentrated is a group of settings with more than the background level of government surveillance and political activity. Meetings of recreational associations, service clubs, religious groups, and friendship groups may regularly discuss political issues although that does not constitute their main activity. It will sometimes be useful to refer to this wider arena of politically relevant settings.[28]

There is an area of overlap between governmental settings (activity settings controlled by government agency authority systems) and political settings (activity settings with a high concentration of political action). Government offices, polling stations, courts, police stations, many offices of government service agencies, meetings of legislatures and legislative committees, government-appointed advisory boards, and much else belong to both. However, the differences are significant and each way of demarcating a politically relevant zone has its own uses. Government agencies have direct authority over certain activity settings in which much of the activity is not programmed or controlled by government. Within the government agency authority systems fall trafficways, hallways of public buildings, parks, and playgrounds. By all measures these are large settings that contain much activity, but little of that activity is oriented to government in any way. Only the actions of government employees such as police officers and park maintenance personnel count as government activity. Since the great preponderance of the activity in such settings is not government-related or of general public concern, they are not part of political space. However, a politically oriented rally or demonstration held in a park or in the street and not controlled by government would count as an activity setting in its own right and as a part of political space, not governmental space.

Street-level offices where government employees dispense services to clients are all within governmental space, but their inclusion in political space depends upon whether the client activity fits the definition of political activity. People mailing letters and chatting with friends at the government-operated post office are not engaged in political activity, unless they are, for example, mailing letters to their members of the legislature. Farmers at an agriculture department workshop on good farming practices are not engaging in political activity unless they are (say) learning about government price-support programs; nor are students in the public high school, unless they happen to be studying the rights and duties of citizens. The postal workers, agricultural agents, and teachers are carrying out government regulations in all these cases. The clients are normally not engaging in government-oriented activity. The test is the orientation of concrete activities to evaluating, influencing, making, interpreting, and enforcing government programs or other public programs that fit the definition of political.[29] If a preponderant part of the program of activities (say 80 percent) in the setting consists of such occurrences, then the activity setting belongs to political space.[30] In practice much of political space consists of meetings of various kinds.

Just as non-political parts of the government agency authority systems are excluded from political space, so too are political activities that are not part of government agency authority systems included in political space. In many countries political parties are voluntary associations, but their activity is almost exclusively dedicated to evaluating and influencing government and other public institutions and actions. Interest groups like the farmers' organization, the chamber of commerce, and the women's improvement association have recreational and educational activities, but a significant part of their activity is devoted to evaluating and influencing government. The newspaper office in Yorkshire or the rounds of the town crier in Nigeria, the daily coffee break of several lawyers, professionals, and business people at the Bluebird Cafe in Kansas, or the elders gathering beneath the Talking Tree in Uganda have their own activities, but they all also communicate about political programs. There is, then, a regular zone of politically oriented activity that does not belong to governmental space. Examples of activity settings in the United States and England that belong to business and voluntary association authority systems but in which almost all activity relates directly to government include abstract company offices, attorneys' offices, headquarters and meetings of political party branches, civics classes in the school, and newspaper reporter city hall beats. In stable times and places a society has a consistent zone of direct government authority and another relatively consistent zone of public-oriented and government-oriented activity. In addition to the stable zones we can expect to find a variable zone made up of activity settings that are activated during elections and crises.[31]

Of particular relevance for our focus on political participation is devising a way to identify the space of political participation. Not all political settings have a participatory side. Empirical studies by political scientists define political participation as actions by private citizens intended to influence government decisions.[32] They specifically exclude activities of paid government officials and specialized appointed or elected representatives. This standard definition can also usefully distinguish a subcategory of political settings, namely, those in which the program consists predominately (again, say 80 percent) of political activity undertaken by private citizens. The space of political participation, then, includes activity settings related to political parties, political interest groups, and electoral campaigns. It also includes activity settings such as town meetings, peer juries, elections, and referenda in which private citizens have governmental powers. In these cases administrative and even executive settings in the government authority system are also part of the space of political participation. The definition excludes executive and administrative offices of government run by professionals in which private citizens play a minor role. It also excludes the activities of representative institutions. However, public meetings in which an administrative officer or an elected representative communicates with private citizens do belong to the space of political participation. And if the activity of private citizens is controlled and directed by government officials rather than by private citizens, it does not qualify as participatory activity.

Another kind of activity setting potentially important for participation includes all the government offices in which officials interact directly with citizens. These are the *street-level offices* that dispense social services, enforce laws, and collect taxes. They form the space of direct government service delivery. Much of it is not part of political space, but the quality of citizen-official contacts in education, agricultural extension, health, tax, and police offices expresses and forms the culture of political action more generally.

One other category of activity settings is important for participation. As writers on civil society since John Stuart Mill and Alexis de Tocqueville have observed, the more influential forms of non-governmental associational politics are significant arenas of participation. Our definition of political activity recognizes that the breadth and impact of decisions and actions in non-governmental organizations can rival those of government decisions. Activities that belong to government authority systems in one society may belong to business, religious, or voluntary organizations in another. Thus some associational settings will enclose activity oriented to the government proper or to broad public issues and will therefore belong to political space proper. But the role of associations goes deeper.

The opportunity to be an active participant and to hold positions of responsibility even in authority systems with narrow and specialized agendas may generate a participatory culture and train people in the skills and habits of participation. The role of non-governmental bodies in nourishing a climate of participation may be crucial. Government authority systems, once established, may have inherent weaknesses as creators of participatory political space. Institutionally, as public guardians, they may resist vulnerability to popular whims; and, individually, office-holders have an interest in protection from the pressures of participants. Our research offers evidence that government authority systems are not the best places to experience participation.

There is good reason, then, to bring the smaller-scale and less inclusive versions of politics into the picture. Following the same logic that identifies the general political space of a country or a locality, non-governmental authority systems have their own partial, associational, political space, settings in which the action is oriented to matters of concern for the association. In their own domains non-governmental authority systems can govern themselves in an autocratic or a democratic manner, but some of them will include settings in which members participate actively in the politics of the association. Associational politics, in turn, builds on the micro-politics of activity settings. This wider context of everyday politics merits further discussion.

Settings, Associations, and the Politics of Everyday Life

The political settings approach brings into sharp focus the associational politics of sets of activity settings. Annual general meetings and executive committee meetings are often key spaces for associational politics. Researchers can raise questions about the basis of power within the authority system and about the degree and kind of autonomy exercised by subordinate settings. And there are other interesting questions. How isolated from other authority systems is the internal politics of a particular authority system? Are a few models of the associational politics of authority systems widely spread in a society, or is there an endless variety of forms of associational politics? How closely do the models of associational politics correspond to the models current in politics proper? How do the associational politics of similar authority systems vary from society to society? In a given society or community, are associational politics gathered in a few authority systems or are they widely dispersed among many small authority systems? How do the major authority systems divide up the total associational political activity of the community? How do social influences and resource controls outside authority systems shape decisions and actions? How important are confidential encounters and communications in determining the agendas and decisions of associational political space? What kinds of social divisions—function, class, cultural group, or gender —do authority systems reflect?

The answers to these questions will reveal a great deal about the character of civic activity and its relation to the shape of politics. In addition a kind of informal politics of smaller meetings, whispered conversations, telephone calls, e-mail messages, and other communications coordinates the harmony or presages the conflict in the formal meeting. Such networks are a more flexible kind of associational political activity that constitute a fundamental and well-known aspect of political life.

Outside associational politics and across the boundaries of authority systems, other kinds of communication, exchange, and influence link settings together and shape their activities. The office of the local bank or local moneylender, for example, may provide crucial support for many business settings without exercising direct authority over them. A school classroom, the church meeting room, or a local restaurant may supply a venue for the meetings of certain voluntary associations. Such relationships may influence associational politics, but they do not constitute associational politics. Along with non-political regulation of activity (by tradition, market forces, external command, or spontaneous co-operation), these influences are important features of the environment of politics.

Global Power and Local Action

The empirical conception of political space offers a useful perspective and several valuable tools for considering the impact upon local politics of "globalization"—the project and the tendency to deepen trade and communications around the world under a regime of regulations that favours the unrestricted movement of capital, the spreading influence of global corporations and financial institutions, and the reduction of governmental management of national economies. The critics of globalization document its tendency to undermine the capacity of many local economies to meet local needs, increase economic inequality, produce a large group of people unable to meet their basic needs, attenuate the services government provides, damage local environments, and lower the morale and sense of competence of large numbers of people. The proponents of globalization point to potential (and sometimes actual) gains in income and export earnings from production and sale of new products, improved viability of government finance, reduction in wasteful and ineffective government spending on services, the rise in economic output, and the reduction of budget and trade deficits. The critics have a good point in arguing that the case for globalization simply ignores its effect on the social and institutional context that gives value and meaning to production and consumption. But the proponents of globalization can argue effectively that the critics romanticize cultures that sometimes stifle creativity and uphold elitism and that they attribute all kinds of social malfunction to globalization without specifying the mechanisms through which it works its destructive effects. Neither proponents nor critics venture to say much about what kinds of local institutions channel globalization in beneficial or destructive ways.

The political settings approach gives a clear focus on major arenas of social action, easily including major settings of economic production and exchange. The direct connections of economic, cultural, and political spaces to authority systems that come under transnational control can be readily described, and the major thrust of the controls can be ascertained. Researchers can ask how much the establishment and maintenance of a given activity (business, office, meeting, service) owe to initial and continuing transnational support. The indirect influences of globalization, which are more difficult to gauge, include the positive cultural emphasis on markets and boosting personal income, and the negative view of collective activity and social services. Another major aspect is the ramifying influence of price signals that are driven by the globalized market. On the cultural side, research can ask local people to evaluate the cultural expression of key social and political settings: are they seen to be local or external in origin and inspiration? And researchers can, of course, also make their own reasoned judgments on the matter. With respect to prices, there is no escape from a political-economic analysis that asks about the scope of the market, competition and concentration in it, and the existence of restrictions and subsidies, among other things. At the same time research can ask whether and how discussions and actions in local political space take up the issues that follow in the wake of changing prices, production, and sources of goods.

For people involved in local politics, political settings have an objective existence. People readily answer questions about them and recount stories about what happened and who did what to whom with what effect at particular gatherings or events. Although several other kinds of political settings are important features of local political space, meetings are the most common and significant arenas of political deliberation, and offices are the most common settings of government action. The wrenching changes experienced by many places in the world today stimulate reactions at every level. Economic analysis highlights the decisions made by individual consumers and producers, employees and employers, investors and company managers. Political analysis highlights the decisions of individual voters and the actions of groups and individuals holding and seeking major power. The political settings approach centres on the places and moments of collective deliberation and action within localities and asks about their effects on how people in the locality live.

It also guides questions about change. Each political setting (as well as each authority system that controls political settings) has its own history. By inquiring into the origins and changes in the more important political settings and authority systems one can gain a detailed picture of the people, actions, and circumstances that have brought about political change in a locality. It is also possible to assess the power that each setting exercises, the control to which each is subjected, and the constraints that limit it. All this can be put together with other kinds of social survey, wider historical and social inquiry, and broader analysis of the kinds of social change, often connected with globalization, that the locality is undergoing.

A New Angle of Perception on Politics and Change

The perspective of activity settings yields a new way of looking at familiar political processes. It is usual to think of power as the ability of one person to control the activity of other people. From the perspective of activity settings, power works differently: it influences the context of action. Both the intentional power of powerful people and the structural power of systems are mediated by activity settings: power creates or destroys activity settings, or it alters or controls the way they function. For example, the interest in the process of agenda-setting is based on a belief that setting the agenda of a meeting or a series of meetings can structure or constrain the range of possible decisions. We can go further and imagine a continuum from the most direct action to the most contextual action: registering one's vote, moving a motion, setting an agenda, calling a meeting, founding an organization, establishing a bill of rights, writing a constitution, founding a society. To form the context of action is not to determine the content of action, but it is to limit and direct the possibilities of action. Some actions are ruled out and some are made possible; of those that are possible some are made easy and some are rendered difficult. Power over context, power over the existence and structure of settings, is not the power to command individual action directly, but it is power nonetheless: hence the pulling and hauling, for example, over the establishment of "competitive" elections in several formerly one-party-dominant regimes such as in Mexico and Kenya. Really loosening government control over elections does not mean an opposition candidate will win, but it makes such an outcome possible if the power of voters to register an opposition vote is truly enabled. The word competitive has to be qualified because the real controls on effective voting may change very little.

Political actions sometimes exert forces directly on persons and their activity, taking the material and institutional context as given. For example, the authorities may arrest and incarcerate a political dissident, or a member of the legislature may agree to vote for the government's health care bill if the government agrees to build a prison in his or her district. But many governmental decisions are best seen as attempts to structure the context of action—in some cases political action and in others social action of another kind. For example, a decision to centralize school boards may, intentionally or not, have the effect of reducing the exercise of responsibility by local citizens and shifting control from elected amateurs with local roots to appointed professionals from the capital city.

Activity settings are an excellent way to gain a conceptual grip over the context of action. The social space represented by activity settings is not empty space; it exists and is created through action. Each activity setting is a process of activity that exerts forces on the people within the setting. Activity settings are the structured context of forces most immediately surrounding persons and their activity. The larger social forces postulated by large theories of social change—forces of social class or of cultural identity, for example—must operate on people in the sense of influencing their activity via activity settings. Often the theorists of new historical social forces identify the forces with a new kind of activity setting. Thus the class forces of slavery are identified with slave raids, slaving ships, slave markets, big houses of planters, and fields of slave hands directed by overseers. The cultural force of nationalism finds expression in open and clandestine committee meetings, political education sessions for youth, political rallies, and perhaps in popular militia training camps and military attacks on symbols of alien power. Large-scale historical forces also alter old activity settings. The forces of popular democracy transform coffee houses into clubs for the discussion of political ideas and the planning of political actions.[33] The forces of the concentration of economic power under capitalism change locally run businesses into centrally programmed franchises or centrally owned branches of a large retail or integrated business. A current of ethnic exclusiveness will be reflected in the rules by which associations select participants in their meetings, the way in which restaurant owners welcome and turn away patrons, and how real estate agents behave towards potential house buyers. By such local changes in activity settings large-scale social change makes itself felt in the lives of people.

In examining change, even large-scale historical change, the perspective of activity settings is local and action-oriented. It focuses on the activity and sees actors, in the first instance, as contributors to activity. The forces in the setting generate and program activity. Activity settings are created and disbanded, but as programmed human activity they are entities with staying power. They are among the obdurate realities of the world that people must cope with whether they want to or not.

To alter political space involves contravening habits of language, customs about who speaks and who listens, and beliefs about social hierarchy. It also usually means changing the people and the kinds of people who exercise power over political space. The practices change, and may change rapidly. To the extent that some people are attached to the power balance, the activities, and the symbols of a political setting, its change will awaken strong feelings and may result in turmoil. In the earthquakes of great revolutions, questioning of power in many limited settings finally gains scope to produce overt, and at times dramatic, change when central institutions crack. People move to recast the programs of activity in a wide range of settings: workplaces, schools, places of religious observance, households, and voluntary organizations. Once underway, the process of rapid change is like a contagion and not readily subject to central direction. At a later stage a gradual reaction may set in and some of the earlier changes may be reversed.

Cataclysmic change is important, but most of the time politics changes shape more slowly, by a process more akin to the erosion and accretion of sediments than to the violent transformations of earthquakes. Yet small changes may proceed fairly rapidly, and their accumulation can add up to a significant alteration in how politics works—and in how people experience that politics.

Notes

1. The concept of activity setting comes from ecological psychology. The research and theoretical work by ecological psychologists on what they call "behaviour settings" demonstrate the possibility of wider social science application and development of ecological analysis. To make the concept more accessible and more acceptable to critics of positivistic social science, I use the term "activity setting." Our approach takes important lessons from ecological psychology, but has its own view of the political nature of units of collective activity.

2. Alexander Rosenberg, in *Philosophy of Social Science* (Boulder, Col.: Westview Press,

1988), contrasts the naturalistic perspective, which holds that human action can be studied in the same manner as other material phenomena, with the interpretivist perspective, which bases its understanding on the meanings and intentions that human actors bring to their action. I believe that a focus on activity settings can enrich both perspectives.

3. Where boundaries are less obvious, ecological psychology has developed measures of the continuity/discontinuity of activity to help identify activity-setting units of a standardized minimum degree of integrity.

4. See Joseph P. Forgas, "Episode Cognition: Internal Representations of Interaction Routines," *Advances in Experimental Social Psychology* 15 (1982).

5. John McPhee, in *Basin and Range* (New York: Farrar, Straus, Giroux, 1980), has a nice account of the Oyster Club meetings.

6. Here I take issue with Balzac's claim that he could understand a poor woman's life by following her on the street.

7. The importance and feasibility of identifying time-space units of activity are recognized in several fields of social science, most notably in the Lund school of time geography. Murray Melbin, a sociologist, has even coined a term, "spant," for SPace ANd Time units. See Murray Melbin, "The Colonization of Time," in *Human Activity and Time Geography*, vol. 2, *Timing Space and Spacing Time*, ed. Tommy Carlstein, Don Parkes, and Nigel Thrift (London: Edward Arnold, 1978), pp.100-13. A key question is how to discriminate the boundaries of appropriate space-time activity units. Melbin's proposal is simply to make a convenient four-dimensional grid, such as 10 metres by 10 metres by one story by six hours, and sample activity cell by cell. However, if we take our cue from larger social units and from everyday language and common perception, we will not be satisfied with arbitrary slices through the continuum of time-space activity. Instead we will look for natural boundaries of some kind. The idea of "realized space" put forward by Don Parkes and Nigel Thrift is a step in this direction, but it proposes no standard means of specifying the boundaries of space-time units. See Don Parkes and Nigel Thrift, "Putting Time in Its Place," in *Making Sense of Time*, vol.1, *Timing Space and Spacing Time*, ed. Tommy Carlstein, Don Parkes, and Nigel Thrift (London: Edward Arnold, 1978), pp.119-29. The discovery of a way to discriminate naturally bounded space-time units of activity has been a signal achievement of ecological psychology.

8. R.D. Laing, *The Politics of Experience and The Bird of Paradise* (Harmondsworth, Middlesex, Eng.: Penguin, 1967), p.28.

9. See G. Kaminski, "Cognitive Bases of Situation Processing and Behavior Setting Participation," in *Issues in Contemporary German Social Psychology*, ed. Gun R. Semin and Barbara Krahé (Beverly Hills, Cal.: Sage, 1987).

10. In his writings and conversations about behaviour settings, Roger Barker frequently referred to their capacity to "coerce" their inhabitants.

11. Roger G. Barker and Phil Schoggen, *Qualities of Community Life* (San Francisco: Jossey-Bass Publishers, 1973), p.10.

12. Ecological psychology uses the term "penetration zones."

13. Barker and Schoggen, *Qualities of Community Life*, p.11.

14. A foreshadowing of this deeper kind of politics occurs in ecological psychology's theory of behaviour settings. That theory seems to posit a potential tension between two kinds of directed forces that guide activity in an activity setting. One force is the drive to carry out the program of the setting. In most settings it is the explicit job of the leaders and functionaries in power zones 4, 5, and 6 to make sure the program is implemented and to take measures needed to that end. The second force is the effort of individual inhabitants of the setting to attain their own goals. Their goals may be quite varied, including specific forms of income, prestige, sociability, power, and

security. There is no guarantee that the goals of individual participants will mesh with the program of the setting; yet if inhabitants do not achieve their goals in the setting, they will leave it or refrain from entering it the next time around (unless some external power makes exiting impossible). Thus a potential theme in the sensing, evaluating, and deciding about the implementation of the program of a setting concerns discrepancies between program requirements and inhabitant goals and what to do about them. See Roger G. Barker, *Ecological Psychology: Concepts and Methods for Studying the Environment of Human Behavior* (Stanford, Cal.: Stanford University Press, 1968), pp.137-85; and Allan W. Wicker, *An Introduction to Ecological Psychology* (New York: Cambridge University Press, 1983), pp.70-82.

15. Ecological psychology originally stressed that its theory of activity settings was a theory about the properties of settings. Each of the component parts, whether they be persons, internal combustion engines, vegetable gardens, or computers, operates according to its own laws. It is only in respect to their quality as media or components for the setting that people are encompassed by the theory of behaviour settings. The psychology of individuals is an altogether different field of phenomena that requires its own concepts and has its own scientific laws. Wicker has proposed to apply social-psychological theories of organizations to activity settings. He includes theories about their social construction. Urs Fuhrer, too, has sought to link the study of subjective life space and objective social environment. See Urs Fuhrer, "Bridging the Ecological-Psychological Gap: Behavior Settings as Interfaces," *Environment and Behavior* 22,4 (July 1990), pp.518-37.

16. Ecological psychology does recognize the two-sided relationship between people and settings in its own aspiration to help humans-as-makers of settings to make ones that accord as well as possible to the goals and needs of humans-as-components. For example, ecological psychology has a theory that activity settings that are consistently underpopulated or understaffed (below the population needed for fully adequate functioning of the program) will make more demands on their participants for more various and more responsible behaviour. Furthermore, participants will be more tolerant of social differences among fellow participants who can do the needed tasks. An example is the way that in World War II labour-short factories welcomed women into work that had previously stood behind a males-only gender bar. On a smaller scale the nine people beginning a game of pick-up basketball will welcome anyone who can barely hold onto the ball to fill out the roster of ten required by the game. The people who are sought after to fulfil the program of an understaffed setting gain the experience of being needed, useful, and wanted. The psychological result for participants will probably be greater self-esteem, more social versatility, greater willingness and ability to take responsibility, and less readiness to discriminate. (The specifics of these important linkages are examined here in chapter 6.) Knowledge of such relationships could have obvious relevance to a group of members or leaders discussing how to improve the setting and its program, and it could also lead to larger questions about why the balance between the supply of participants and the demand for their participation in productive settings appears to be so different in different places and in different epochs.

17. Sheldon Wolin, *The Presence of the Past: Essays on the State and the Constitution* (Baltimore: The Johns Hopkins University Press, 1989), p.154.

18. The change entails an important shift of analytical standpoint. Ecological psychology stresses (as against the current emphasis on cognition in psychology) how people are the components or media or bearers of patterns of activity imposed by settings. Ecological psychology is aware that settings can validly be seen from two standpoints. From the standpoint of the setting, people are the components and media needed for perpetuation of the program of the setting. But equally validly, from the standpoint of members of a community, settings are the means to achieve personal and collective

goals of many kinds. They define opportunities for experience and can be selected or rejected on the basis of preferences. Barker and Schoggen, in *Qualities of Community Life*, one of the major works of ecological psychology, state their important analytical observations in two languages: ecological (where the habitat generates behaviour) and psychological (where individuals engage in activity).

The political standpoint combines the two perspectives to form a distinctive third perspective. When people examine activity settings in which they engage, they are sometimes aware that the settings coerce and involve their members, including themselves. People can decide to change the program of activity. On these occasions, participants are like researchers in understanding the power of the setting to use its members as media, but unlike researchers they use their knowledge to try to reshape those forces to make the experiences and products of the setting more to their liking. At the same time, researchers are like members of settings: in fact they are members. Whether they are trying to be invisible witnesses, participant-observers, or participatory facilitators, it is now evident that their relation to the setting is shaped by their conception of research and science and by how the setting and its other members define and treat them. The micro-limitations of doing an objective and naturalistic social science stand revealed. Social scientists, like the people they purport to study, are part of the world they are investigating. Moreover, the activity of social science is part of the activity that social science tries to elucidate.

19. The theory of activity settings proposed by ecological psychology has stressed the control systems' homeostatic qualities, which keep settings relatively stable and unchanging in a changing environment. In part the emphasis on a quasi-stationary equilibrium reflects a deliberate intention to study activity in a "normal" context, not one troubled by unusual turmoil or marked by the dramas of a founding. (We will see in chapter 6 that considerable change does occur over a decade in stable small towns in Kansas and Yorkshire, although both communities were far from turmoil.) In part the emphasis reflects an appreciation of the advantage of an equilibrium model for understanding both stability and change. Ecological psychology directed its attention to demonstrating the existence of strong forces regulating behaviour, forces that emanated not from individual psyches but from the social environment. With their primary case now firmly established, researchers in ecological psychology have called for attention to what they call "the life cycle" of activity settings, including their birth and death. See Allan W. Wicker, "Behavior Settings Reconsidered: Temporal Stages, Resources, Internal Dynamics, Context," in *Handbook of Environmental Psychology*, ed. Daniel Stokols and Irwin Altman (New York: John Wiley and Sons, 1987), pp.613-53.

20. The idea of production regime is developed with insight by Michael Burawoy in *The Politics of Production: Factory Regimes under Capitalism and Socialism* (London: New Left Books/Verso, 1985).

21. The relationship between individual persons and activity settings is an area rich in possibilities for a variety of theoretical projects. Karl A. Fox, an economist, in *The Eco-Behavioral Approach to Surveys and Social Accounts for Rural Communities: Exploratory Analyses and Interpretations of Roger G. Barker's Microdata from the Behavior Setting Survey of Midwest Kansas in 1963-64* (Ames, Ia.: Iowa State University, North Central Center for Rural Development, 1990), emphasizes the potential for use of allocation models in the study of activity settings. Instead of allocating scarce purchasing power, people allocate the finite quantity of time they have at their disposal. Confronted with an array of activity resources, people choose among them where to allocate their 5,856 waking hours per year. The observed array of activity settings over a year can be taken as the result of a large number of individual allocation decisions. The allocation for a hypothetical closed community could be represented on a single large matrix with a row for each resident and a column for each activity setting. The hours each resident commits to each setting over a

year might be entered in the appropriate cell of the matrix. Analysis might seek to verify assumptions about what qualities residents were maximizing in their time-allocation decisions. Or it might ask about the kinds of barriers that faced certain kinds of residents wanting to enter certain kinds of settings. The sum of each column would equal the person-hours of occupancy or occupancy-time of that setting. If all domestic and public settings and all sleeping and waking time were included, each row would sum to the 8,760 hours (8,784 hours in leap years) that each person "spends" each year.

22. Karl A. Fox, "Behavior Settings and Social System Accounting," a chapter in Phil Schoggen, *Behavior Settings: A Revision and Extension of Roger G. Barker's Ecological Psychology* (Stanford, Cal.: Stanford University Press, 1989), p.295.

23. As Schoggen notes in *Behavior Settings*, pp.115-17, the perspective also recognizes the existence of government regulations that apply to selected classes of activity settings, such as regulations about food handling for settings that serve food to the public. However, since governmental laws and regulations of these kinds rarely instigate or determine the program of activity in a setting they are excluded from consideration for identifying the settings that belong to the government authority system.

24. Barker and Schoggen, *Qualities of Community Life*, pp.113-14.

25. Information about any and all authority systems (not only government) can be used to measure the degree of local autonomy or central control over activity settings in a locality.

26. Barker and Schoggen, *Qualities of Community Life*, pp.215-29.

27. Barker and Schoggen, *Qualities of Community Life*, pp.108-09, define 11 "action patterns" (aesthetics, business, education, government, nutrition, personal appearance, physical health, professional involvement, recreation, religion, and social contact) that may be found in any activity setting. They write: "The action pattern Government is present within a behavior setting to the extent that the concrete occurrences within the setting implement or resist the making, interpretation, and execution of laws and regulations by government agencies. This action pattern may involve: engaging in civic affairs; supplying material and behavior objects for governmental programs; learning and teaching about government and legal procedures; appraising governmental programs and officials."

Community studies in ecological psychology have rated activity settings for the presence of each of the 11 action patterns, including the government action pattern. All those settings in which the government action pattern accounts for 80 percent or more of the activity program of the setting make up the "primary governmental habitat" of the community.

28. Barker and Schoggen, *Qualities of Community Life*, pp.10-11, call this wider political zone "the territorial range of government." It includes almost all of the settings of the government agency authority systems because government surveillance is at more than background level in them.

29. Barker, *Ecological Psychology*, pp.58-59.

30. Although not part of political space, street-level government offices are points of contact between state and citizens that can form citizen attitudes towards government and politics.

31. Barker and Schoggen, *Qualities of Community Life*, pp.108-17.

32. Sidney Verba and Norman H. Nie, *Political Participation in America* (Ann Arbor, Mich.: Inter-University Consortium for Political and Social Research, 1976).

33. Ray Oldenberg, *The Great Good Place: Cafes, Coffee Shops, Community Centers, Beauty Parlors, General Stores, Bars, Hangouts and How They Get You through the Day* (New York: Paragon House, 1989).

PART II

Political Settings in Local Communities

Chapter 4

Empowerment from Above? Development Projects and Public Space in Northern Nigeria

Kole Shettima

Conventional assessments of rural development projects and programs evaluate the delivery of social and economic services and tend to focus on problems of efficiency and effectiveness. But here I want to go beyond the conventional approach by using an analysis informed by the concept of empowerment in rural development and linking that concept to the issue of public space. This empowerment approach is one used by a few scholars and activists who place the social and political strengthening of marginalized people at the centre of their preoccupations. For example, after analyzing experiences of bottom-up development Dharam Ghai concludes that the projects are schools of democracy with an impact on other political and social issues in communities, or Robert Putnam, building on his recent work on the importance of civic traditions in Italy, is concerned with how public policy could revitalize civic engagement in the United States.[1] A basic issue here, then, is the role of rural development projects in expanding, constraining, and creating local, public spaces for the exercise of popular power.

There are conflicting views about the forces that shape public space. Scholars interested in social movements and civil society, for instance, make claims for the primacy of class and political-economic status—an emphasis critiqued by writers taking cultural and gender perspectives. I regard the issue as an empirical one. For me the pertinent questions are: Who has access to the public sphere? How is access shaped both by economic status and by gender, age, ethnicity, and other forms of social differentiation? How do the local languages of politics, the nature of associational activity, the quality of public discourse, and the structure of public spaces come into play?[2]

I am interested in the role of development agencies, especially international bodies, in creating public spaces under repressive politics, and here I focus on case studies of three of them: the Better Life Program for Rural

Women (BLP), the Directorate of Food, Road, and Rural Infrastructure (DFRRI), and the Northeast Arid Zone Development Program (NEAZDP). The questions that arise include: What kind of impact does the intervention of both national and global agencies have on the nature of local politics, and vice versa? The development literature tends to note the negative roles of international development agencies, but most of the analyses select large structures and programs without looking at micro-relations and projects. They also tend to focus mainly on delivery services. It is important to ask whether a project that fails in one dimension has a successful outcome in other dimensions, even though that result might be unintended. Apart from these questions, this chapter will, I hope, demonstrate one way of addressing some of the methodological issues raised by the political space approach.

Dagona and Machina

Dagona and Machina are both small trading and administrative towns in Yobe state of northern Nigeria, but they are notably different in history, politics, and religion. Dagona has experienced a relatively recent history of centralization of political structure and consolidation of Islamic belief, and politically the town is pluralistic. Machina has a longer history of centralization of religion and a political authority that remains autocratic.

The core population of Dagona consists of Bade-speaking people who probably migrated to their current settlement in the 18th century. It was only in the 19th century that a process of centralization began among the Bades due to incessant attacks from their neighbours, and Islam became fully established among them only in the 1940s.[3] The town does not have the features of an autocracy, such as a palace and a ruling family. Until the early 1990s, the highest political authority was the Lawan (village head), a position that was not automatically inherited. Also, until recently women played a prominent role in the politics and spirituality of Dagona. There were two women titleholders, Curaku (junior community leader) and Magi (senior community leader). Each of them was elected by the community women and then affirmed by the Lawan.

The people of Dagona are farmers. Farming is done both in *fadama* (flood plain) and *tudu* (upland) zones. *Fadama* farming is mostly irrigated, while *tudu* farming is mostly rain-fed. As a result of irrigation, Dagona is a relatively prosperous community. Land is a major source of contention, partly due to migrant farmers and absentee urban-based elite farmers. In 1993 the town had about 700 households in 500 compounds and a total population of about 5,500. In addition to the Bade majority, ethnic groups included Manga, Hausa, and Sakkwatawa.[4]

According to the court historians of Machina, that settlement was founded in C.E. 980. Most of the territory of the old kingdom of Machina now lies in Niger Republic. Machina town, where the king resided, was a walled community (the old eroded wall is still prominent). Political and economic resources were and are concentrated in the hands of a ruling dynasty, Aliyu, and the political order has had all the characteristics of a ruling aristocracy. In 1993 the ruler of Machina, the Mai Machina, had been on the throne for almost 50 years, and his family had expanded to control many aspects of Machina society. In 1992 the Nigerian government made Machina an emirate and named the Mai Machina Emir: an emirate is the most powerful traditional administrative unit in any state of the federation, and an emir is the highest political authority in an emirate. Islam has been the state religion in Machina for a very long time, but this does not mean that "traditional" religious practices are rare. Women titleholders in Machina do not play a significant role, because the position has been undermined over time.

Machina, like Dagona, is organized politically as a village and is the seat of district administration. Unlike Dagona, it is also the seat of local government and the headquarters of an emirate. In 1991 the town had about 1,600 households in 1,000 compounds and a total population of about 8,000. About 77 percent of the population were of the Manga ethnic group. Other ethnic groups included Fulani and Hausa.

Farming is the major occupation of the people of Machina, with the agriculture all rain-fed. Without *fadama* (irrigated) land, the productivity was lower and the incidence of material poverty higher in Machina than in Dagona.

Three Development Institutions

The Better Life Program for Rural Women started in 1987 as a means of enhancing the status of women and alleviating poverty. It was the pet program of Nigeria's First Lady, Maryam Babangida. At state and local levels the same pattern was repeated: the first lady at each respective level was to head the program. Thus the program was hierarchical. The projects implemented included public education campaigns, knitting and sewing, and trade fairs. Funding for the program was mainly from the federal government and its various agencies. It received supplementary funds from international and bilateral agencies.

The Directorate for Food, Road, and Rural Infrastructure was also implemented by the federal government of Nigeria. It specialized in the provision of rural infrastructure such as roads and wells. At the national level the program was headed by a retired military officer who reported directly to the Office of the President. At the state and local levels the highest political authorities were also heads of the program.

The Northeast Arid Zone Development Program was initiated by the European Community and the Nigerian and Yobe state governments. Its management has had considerable autonomy from both governments, and its funding proved more secure than that of the two government-funded development institutions. The projects implemented by the program have included propagating ox-teams, establishing revolving funds for medicines, and constructing wells.

Community Spaces in Dagona and Machina

Before starting to make a survey of all the community settings, I asked the research assistants in Dagona and Machina where and how people in those communities meet to discuss among themselves issues that affect the community and involve encounters with government officials and receipt of services from governments and projects. My idea of spaces of empowerment is more specific than Robert Putnam's account of social capital. Putnam investigates all forms of social interaction, from bowling to bridge clubs. While group bowling could be an occasion for important community politics, its main purpose and usual focus are recreation; my concern is limited to intentionally public events with a public agenda offering the opportunity for empowering participation.[5]

After walking through the communities and holding discussions with community members I found that the identification of community spaces clearly excluded other important spaces such as private business premises and private productive project settings funded by development projects. Similarly, I have not included settings, such as social gatherings in shaded places, that are not devoted primarily to public affairs. The worship services included in the survey were not those that occurred every day, but only the major events: Friday mosques and Sunday church services. I have not included neighbourhood mosques.

The community settings that met the criterion of containing participatory or empowering activities fell under the authority of three kinds of organizations: *government institutions* (federal, state, local, and associated agencies), *development institutions* (Better Life, DFRRI, and NEAZDP), and *community organizations* (ethnic associations, professional associations, political parties, and religious bodies). Our interest here is in all public meetings, committees, and offices created or strongly influenced by all these various types of organizations.

After we defined the relevant kinds of settings and identified the key organizations, our next task was to map out the various community spaces in the two towns (see Tables 4.1, 4.2, 4.3, and 4.4, pp. 75-78). In Dagona we identified a number of local government offices and services: district head, cement well, bore hole, primary school, health clinic, and village head. The associations and meetings related to these offices and services that were created or expanded by the local government included the Chapnori (meeting of ward heads) and the meetings of village and district heads. A parent-teacher association and a health committee existed in Dagona, but the activity of the former had been influenced by NEAZDP and the latter created by NEAZDP. There was no meeting or committee on the cement well project. The state government provided two services: a Community Viewing Centre (a place where people can watch television and hold meetings), and Yobe State Agricultural Development Program (YOSADP). There was no committee or meeting on the viewing centre project created by the state government, but YOSADP had formed a Kungiyar Fadama (Fadama Association), which brought together farmers engaged in flood agriculture. NEAZDP had, however, established a committee to manage the viewing centre. On very few occasions, federal government agencies like the National Population Commission, the Directorate of Social Mobilization, and the National Electoral Commission held public campaigns in Dagona, but they did not have offices in the community.

As for development institutions in Dagona, NEAZDP had several projects and services: grinding machine, dehusking machine, NEAZDP office, primary health care/drug revolving fund, community bank, conservation, and bookstore. NEAZDP had also partly funded renovation of a bore hole and the community viewing centre. For all these services and offices NEAZDP had either initiated or influenced committees and/or meetings, including the Dagona Village Development Association, Health Committee, Women's Committee, Parent-Teacher Association, Conservation Committee, and the Viewing Centre Committee. Similarly, meetings and training sessions had been held for village development plans, village development promoters, and traditional birth attendants. The development institutions under direct government control had not appreciably expanded the space of empowerment. The Better Life Program had a grinding machine, but with no meeting or committee. DFRRI had funded three feeder roads to and from Dagona but sponsored no meetings or committees. These programs also did not have offices in the community. The lack of meetings (see Table 4.1) and offices connected to these two organizations indicated their top-down approach in comparison to NEAZDP.

The community organizations in Dagona included two ward offices of political parties: National Republican Party (NRC) and Social Democratic Party (SDP). These parties held meetings in the community. There was also the Dagona market, but with no related committee or meeting. There were two Friday mosques: Masallacin Jumma'a (Friday Mosque) and Masallacin Izala (Izala Mosque).[6] Only the Masallacin Izala had a committee to oversee its activities, whereas the Masallacin Jumma'a was the responsibility of the Imam and the village head. Furthermore, a professional association, Kungiyar Masunta (Fishers' Association), met to discuss issues relevant to the profession (see Table 4.4). The number of community organizations in Dagona, though seemingly small, was significant when compared to Machina, and reflected Dagona's pluralistic nature.

Machina had more community settings than Dagona largely because it was (and is) the seat of local government, which had established a large number of offices and services in the town (Table 4.3), including offices and services of the departments of works, treasury, natural resources, administration, primary health care, and health and medical. Other public settings included slaughterhouse, dispensary, two primary schools, market stalls, Islamiya (Islamic school), office of the district head, office of village heads, guest house, legislative council, Local Government Education Authority (LEA), Expanded Program on Immunization (EPI) office, and nursery. Very few meetings or committees were formed to oversee these offices or services initiated or influenced by the local government.

In Machina the Yobe state government had established a number of offices and services: Government Junior Secondary School, Yard Superintendent Office, Water Board, Area Court, YOSADP, Yobe State Agricultural Mechanization Agency, and Community Viewing Centre. These offices and services had no regular meetings or committees connected to them. For its part, the federal government had established a number of offices or services: the Nigerian Police, Immigration Department, the State Security Service, Customs and Excise, the National Electoral Commission, the National Population Commission, the Directorate of Social Mobilization, and the National Directorate of Employment. No associations or regular public meetings were linked to any of these settings, although several of them held internal meetings and, of course, community members received various services from them. In addition, occasional meetings occurred in the public campaigns organized by the National Electoral Commission, the National Population Commission, the Directorate of Social Mobilization, and the National Directorate of Employment (see Table 4.2). As in Dagona the governmental institutions did not have a participatory structure, which means they had a limited impact in expanding community spaces.

The three development institutions had also established their presence in Machina. Better Life had funded a grinding machine and held a community meeting, while DFRRI and the office of the Rural Development Coordinator had partially funded a few other projects. NEAZDP, though, had initiated many activities and contributed to many settings of empowerment. It had established an office, a nursery, a community library, and a community bank. It built a maternity home and dehusking machine house. NEAZDP's

Women's Committee was the only entirely new committee to manage any activity in the community, but NEAZDP had also influenced the activities of the Village Development Association. Several meetings and training sessions were held under the auspices of the NEAZDP, including the meeting on the village development plan, community bank board meetings, regular meetings of village development promoters, and training meetings on Pukko (improved mud stove). Although NEAZDP had sponsored and stimulated a significant number of meetings in Machina, there would have been even more except for the hierarchical nature of politics in the community: the dominance of the public sphere by a ruling family.

Community organizations in Machina included the Parent-Teacher Association, Hausari Social Club, Kautalhore, Butchers Association, Nigeria Union of Teachers, and National Union of Local Government Employees (see Table 4.4). These associations all held meetings. Two religious places identified as public settings were the Church of Christ in Nigeria (COCIN) and the Friday mosque. There were no committees managing or overseeing these services and no meetings held about them, although a mosque committee had been set up to oversee the building of a new mosque. The two political parties, NRC and SDP, had ward and local government offices and held meetings in the community. Even in terms of community organizations, because of the vertical nature of politics in Machina, the public space there was not as extensive as in Dagona.

The surveys of public settings in the two towns reveal three interesting lines of comparison with respect to space for empowerment and participation: Machina vs. Dagona; government agencies vs. development institutions vs. community organizations; and NEAZDP vs. DFRRI vs. BLP. Based on this research we found, first, that community organizations were more likely than government agencies to establish spaces of empowerment and that local levels of government were more likely to do so than higher levels of government. Second, we found that the more pluralistic and less autocratic cultural and political context of Dagona had led to a greater expansion of public settings of participation and empowerment there. We found as well that NEAZDP's greater autonomy from government made it much the most effective in expanding settings of participation and empowerment of the three development institutions in both Dagona and Machina. Still, a closer look at the discourses employed in political settings showed that even in government-dominated settings in an autocratic political environment, people could find scope for meaningful expression of their views and interests.

A comparison of the public spaces created and expanded by the three levels of government, the three development institutions, and the several community organizations revealed an appreciable impact on community public life: there were several settings of useful contact and communication between government and people and within the communities. Machina, though, had more public settings than did Dagona, because Machina was a centre of local government, district government, village government, and an emirate; it was also a development area headquarters and an entry point on the border with Niger Republic. Dagona, a slightly larger town, was only a district and village government centre and development area headquarters. Most significantly, Machina, as a local government headquarters, benefited from the universal policy of the federal government of Nigeria to establish most of the offices and services that had been enumerated under local, state, and federal governments in all local government headquarters. Although Machina had experienced a greater presence of government than Dagona had even before the creation of Machina local government in 1991, certainly the change in Machina's status to a local government headquarters had enlarged the presence of the various levels of government. Some of the services and settings were new, while some pre-existing settings had been transformed. For example, Machina had immigration, state security services, and custom offices by virtue of its position as the major rural town on the border with Niger Republic, but with the creation of the local government these offices were expanded and the services provided increased. Still, these local govern-ment institutions were not participatory.

Furthermore, associational life in Machina had been influenced by the creation of the local government. There were branches of the Nigeria Union of Teachers and the National Union of Local Government Employees even before 1991, but their activities became more pronounced in the fol-lowing years. With the creation of the local government, more local govern-ment personnel and teachers were employed, boosting the membership of the organizations. The role of the town as a local government headquarters also made it easier for the unions to take up the grievances of their members with the employers. In contrast, Dagona was only a district, village, and development area headquarters, and it had only become a district headquar-ters in 1993. Thus, most of the services provided in Dagona derived from its status as a development area headquarters created in 1990 by NEAZDP, a par-ticipatory organization.

While the number of public settings in Machina was greater than in Dagona, this finding did not in any way indicate the quality of the public spaces in the two communities. After all, several of the community settings in Machina were government creations. The government offices and services in Machina had little contact with the local people in terms of public meet-ings, nor did they enrich associational life in the community by forming committees around the services they provided (Tables 4.2 and 4.3). Thus most of them were service delivery sites with very little involvement of the communities. As Tables 4.2 and 4.3 show, despite the existence of several government institutions in the two communities, only 50 meetings took place involving those institutions and the local people. Out of that figure of 50 meetings, 37 were in Machina and 13 in Dagona. However, while the significant difference in those communities reflected the high number of government institutions in Machina, it also indicated the lack of public involvement in their activities. As well, the number of meetings with the public was distorted by the high number of public meetings—25—conducted by the Expanded Program on Immunization (EPI). If we take away those meetings the total figure of the two communities drops to 25; and if we subtract the figure of EPI (25) from the Machina figure, the total drops to 12 meetings. Hence, the difference between the number of public meetings in Dagona and Machina favours the former.

Although it is accurate to say, based on these findings, that governments have not significantly created or expanded community spaces, lower levels of government are more likely to involve their people than are upper levels of government: the meetings score is federal government 9, state government 5 (Table 4.2), and local government 36 (Table 4.3). What is disturbing is that even at the lower levels of government, the two most important agencies that make the most significant policies, Administration Department and Legislative Council, did not have contact with the local communities. The Administration Department was perhaps the most important agency at the local level because that was where the chairperson, deputy chairperson, secretary of the local government, director of personnel, and the supervisory councillors were based. The Legislative Council was where all the councillors were based; they were primarily responsible for law-making at the local level.

The three development institutions had created or influenced more community meetings than had the different levels of government. The development institutions created or expanded 58 community spaces as against 50 for the government institutions. Dagona, with fewer delivery points than Machina, had more associations and committees formed around the services provided in the community by development institutions. Therefore, although Machina had more public spaces than Dagona, these were mainly delivery points and did not expand or create associational life in the community. In Dagona, with fewer public spaces, associational life was much more enriched because associations and committees have been formed around those spaces.

A comparison of community spaces influenced or created by development institutions on the one hand and community organizations on the other shows that the development institutions played a significant role in promoting associational life. While community organizations influenced or created 14 more meetings (Tables 4.1, 4.4), that number primarily reflected the political status of Machina as a local government headquarters. The meetings of the SDP and the NRC were numerous because two party levels existed in Machina: local government and ward. A caution: whereas in the field research, political parties were classified as community organizations, it was the federal government that decreed the existence of these organizations. Similarly, the presence of the Nigeria Union of Teachers and the Nigeria Union of Local Government Employees became more noticeable after the creation of the new local government in Machina in 1991. Without the political parties and the two unions, the number of community-inspired meetings would drop to 18 (10 in Dagona and 8 in Machina); and the difference between the development institutions and the community organizations would be 40 in favour of the former.

Of the 72 meetings of the community organizations in the two communities, Dagona had 25 while Machina had 47. Thus the number of settings was in Machina's favour. But if we subtract the influence of the political parties and the professional associations, Dagona had more community-based meetings than Machina: Dagona had ten meetings while Machina had eight.

The three development institutions, then, showed a significant impact on the number of public meetings in the two communities. The government institutions resulted in 50 meetings, the development institutions 58, and the community organizations 72. A further analysis of the disproportionate influence of some settings, for example, EPI, showed that the development institutions had more impact than at first glance.

Community Discourse

Accounts of social capital in the United States seldom pay much attention to its content. While I agree that social capital might have an intrinsic value, for the purpose of this work I am interested in the quality of meetings and how they reflect institutional and contextual biases. I want to suggest that there is a need to take a step further in the analysis of public spaces not only to count the numbers, but also to look at the nature of the meetings. The nature of meetings will reveal their context and institutional arrangement.

In November 1992 the Village Development Association in Machina called a meeting to discuss a Village Development Plan (VDP), connected to the work of NEAZDP, for the year 1993. The town crier went around informing people in the evening preceding the meeting and again on the morning of the meeting. The meeting was scheduled to take place in the Community Viewing Centre by the Emir's Palace. About 85 people gathered for the occasion. After everyone was seated, the Emir was ushered in surrounded by his advisers and praise singers. The seating arrangement was formal, with about 15 officials and dignitaries of the meeting on one side and the rest of the community—about 70 people—on the other.

Who has access to the meetings? The officials of the meeting were the Development Area Promoter (DAP), Bashir Bukar Albishir, and two NEAZDP officials from the headquarters: the financial controller, who was also the mentor of the Development Area, and the "Manpower" specialist. Other dignitaries present, in addition to the Emir of Machina, were representatives of the Machina local government, the Imam of Machina and his contingent, and NEAZDP field technicians based in Machina. This was the first time the local government had been included in the process of formulating a Village Development Plan, and because the most important agencies for policy-making at the local government levels—the Administration Department and the Legislative Council—had no public forums to discuss their work with local people, the local government participation at this meeting was an important departure. Among the "ordinary citizens" I noticed only one member of the National Republican Convention (NRC), Alhaji Usman. In contrast all the elders and notable members of the ruling SDP were in attendance. No women attended as members or officials, although several girls came as onlookers. Although the Hausa community is one of the major ethnic groups in the community, the only noticeable members of that community present were Ciroma Makale, who was Sarkin Pawa (head of butchers) and Sule S. Pawa, the local government supervisory councillor for works and who a few months later became the Sarkin Hausawa (head of the Hausa community, with rank equivalent to village head). They were both members of the SDP. Most of the elders and officials of the meeting wore *dara*, a type of red cap, and some wore green cloth. These were the symbols of the SDP.

There were seven items on the agenda: opening prayer, welcome address by the DAP, address by the Emir, response by the financial controller, review of the 1992 Village Development Plan and the 1993 Village Development Plan, vote of thanks by the DAP, and closing prayer.

The Imam was invited to open the meeting with prayers. He read Surahs Fatiha (Opening), al Falaq (The Daybreak), and Luqman (Wise). As part of his welcome address, the DAP introduced the guests from the headquarters, the representatives of the local government, and other NEAZDP staff based in Machina. He explained that the purpose of the meeting was to discuss the needs of the community for 1993 and review the activities of NEAZDP in 1992. He ended with an invitation to the Emir to address the gathering. The Emir's comments were brief. He thanked the officials of NEAZDP from the headquarters for their continued support and the people for turning up for the meeting. He went on to emphasize the need for unity in the community. The financial controller, whose speech was translated from English to Hausa by the Manpower specialist, thanked the Emir and the community for their warm reception and support of NEAZDP projects.

He asked the Manpower specialist to lead the discussions on the 1992 and 1993 VDPs.

Two items on the agenda took a long time to resolve: the inability of NEAZDP to complete the implementation of a maternity project in 1992 and the provision of water to Machina in 1993. A maternity home had been planned for Machina in 1992 but only the building had been completed and the necessary equipment and personnel had not been provided. For the people of Machina, the inability to implement the whole project was not acceptable because of the high maternal and infant mortality rates in the community. Moreover, they had confidence and trust in NEAZDP that they would not be disappointed. Many community members raised those concerns. The NEAZDP response was that there was a change in policy at the headquarters to limit the number of maternity projects and study their operations before implementing them on a larger scale. The community members were not impressed with the explanation; they argued that the people who needed the project least were those benefiting: most of the maternity projects were located near the headquarters of the Program but these were also the areas best served by roads and therefore with easier access to hospitals.

Not just the Program but also the local government came under heavy criticism. Because the local government in Machina had no mechanism of policy input through public meetings, the local people saw its participation in this meeting as a strategic opportunity to make their concerns known. The probing was done strategically, during a discussion on a request put forward for a water project. Many speakers made the point over and over that the only basis of judging the performance of any government in Machina was its ability to provide water to the community. People in the community knew that the speeches were not directed at NEAZDP but at the local government. The veiled criticism arose from the widely held belief that the major concern of the local government should be to provide adequate water to the community. The creation of the local government had awakened the hope that the problem of water in the community would be resolved. In the perception of the people of Machina, no serious effort had been previously made to provide the community with water because Machina was not a local government headquarters and the leaders of the local government were not based in the community. In response to the probing the local government officers explained that there was a joint plan with NEAZDP to provide adequate water to the community and meetings would be held to resolve the issue.

The next item was a vote of thanks by the DAP, who thanked all those who attended the meeting and emphasized that NEAZDP was an organization for everyone in the community. The meeting ended with the Imam reading Surah Fatiha (Opening) and Salatul Fati, a prayer reading that radicals interpreted as conservative. The source of this prayer, according to its supporters, is a dream of one of the famous Islamic scholars. They believe that saying this prayer equals reading the whole Quran. Many of the people who say this *addu'a* (supplication) are Sufists and belong to the Qadriyya and Tijaniyya brotherhoods, which had strong support in Machina among the Emir and his followers. Opponents of these brotherhoods—and in Yobe state most of them belong to the Izala movement—believe that no human being can receive any revelation from God because Prophet Muhammad (PBUH) is the seal of all prophets. Moreover, they argue that Salatul Fati contains very few verses and therefore cannot be compared with the Quran. In response, one of the prominent scholars of the Qadriyya brotherhood, Sheikh Dahiru Bauchi, made the interesting argument that the Quran is like a drum of water while Salatul Fati is like a bottle of scent. While the drum of water is more important because it serves various purposes, its cost is not less than that of a bottle of scent. In the context of northern Nigeria's religious politics, therefore, those who read this prayer are said to be conservatives while those who don't are perceived to be radicals.

This meeting, despite its exclusion of some sections of the community (women, Hausa, Izala movement, and NRC members), held a special significance. NEAZDP had for the first time introduced the concept of a Village Development Plan in the community. There had been no history of government and development agencies sitting together with communities to plan a budget for the community. Development plans were supposed to be technical and a monopoly of experts. The participation of local people in the process was important. Moreover, even for NEAZDP this step was important because none of the previous European Community Programs in Nigeria had experimented with the idea of VDPs. In addition, the local government was also involved in the process. Local governments, the closest tier of government to the community, had no similar strategy, and in that meeting their accountability to the local people was questioned. The meeting was also not a mere talk show. Whatever final decision was made about projects for the community reflected the inputs of the local people. Furthermore, the questions asked by the local people on the maternity project showed that this was not merely a meeting for consultation by NEAZDP.

Other aspects of the public meeting reflected community and cultural politics in Machina. There were overt and hidden messages in the prayers and speeches. The first and second Surahs read by the Imam, Fatiha (Opening), and al Falaq (The Daybreak), are also the first (1), and the second to last (Surah 113) of the Quran respectively. All of them were revealed in Mecca. The first Surah Fatiha (Opening) is read on most occasions and is used to start prayers. Surah al Falaq (the Daybreak) urges humanity to seek refuge in God from the evil deeds and envy of other human beings, and its significance seems to be to convey the message that people should not fear to speak their minds, but at the same time should not engage in doing evil to others. This prayer set the moral ground for the discussion at the meeting. The next Surah read by the Imam, Luqman (Surah 31) (Wise), is also a Meccan Surah. Its message is that the righteous receive guidance while those who seek vanity perish. Some of the Ayat (verses) carry strong messages to leaders. Luqman is said to have been a ruler of very humble background who ruled his people justly. He refused power and worldly things. He is said to have given instructive parables similar to Aesop's Fables in Greek history. The Surah also warns against arrogance and immoderation: "swell not thy cheek . . . nor walk in insolence . . . and lower thy voice." The Imam by reading this Surah was sending a message of humility to the meeting.

In the closing prayers, as we've seen, to read Salatul Fati means one is conservative in the context of northern Nigerian religious politics. The Emir's speech was interpreted by those who did not agree with him as an attempt to show his neutrality. The audience saw the emphasis on unity as a call to support the Emir.

In his vote of thanks the DAP made the point that the Program belonged to the community. He took care to stress the neutrality of the Program and that it should not be perceived as being partisan. Those who knew the hidden scripts and were aware of royal politics would interpret his speech differently. It was important for him to make those pronouncements, not only to protect his job but also, for personal reasons, to keep the Program outside the control of the SDP, which dominated the local government and was supported by the Emir. The chair of the local government was a son of the Emir. Therefore, one would have expected the DAP not to care if the Program was used for political purposes. While I think the DAP had a sincerity of purpose, however, the event carried the intrigues of royal politics. The DAP, too, was a son of the Emir—his eldest (and he was later appointed the district head of Machina). He and the chair of the local government had different mothers. The local government chair had a full sister who was also the education secretary of the local government, but on the DAP's side there was no other sibling of high qualification and status. With the Emir at an advanced age, the crucial issue of who would become the next Emir of Machina loomed large. Even as the eldest son, the DAP was in no way guaranteed that he would succeed his father, especially because his half-brother, the former chair of the local government, had established a political constituency at the local and state levels where the SDP had been in control. It was therefore in the personal interest of the DAP to make sure that NEAZDP was not used as a political machine.

The politics of co-wives also plays a part. In Manga culture in any polygynous relationship the core family tends to be more defined by *tuam* (breast-feeding) than by *bu* (blood): those who drink milk from the same breast (maternal brothers and sisters) are closer than those who have the same blood (paternal brothers and sisters).[7] Thus mothers are always conscious of making sure that their children prosper, especially in a family like that of the Emir, where the struggle for power is pervasive. In the same vein each mother makes sure that her children prosper because there is no guarantee that she and her children can inherit much in such a large family.

The DAP's emphasis on the political neutrality of NEAZDP was a veiled commentary about a rough experience with one of the SDP elders who attended the meeting. That politician had reported to the Emir that the DAP was undermining their campaigns in the rural areas. This was because the DAP used to explain in all villages that NEAZDP was not aligned to any political party and belonged to the communities, whereas the politician was quietly spreading the word that NEAZDP belonged to the SDP. By reporting the DAP to the Emir, the politician hoped that the official would be rebuked and politicians could claim that all the projects funded by NEAZDP in the various villages were the work of the SDP. These contextual matters influence the success of rural development institutions, however benign they seem. The incidents illustrate how public discourse and more secretive communication can influence each other.

In contrast to the situation in Machina, in Dagona several committees were responsible for managing different projects. Instead of all resources going through only one channel, as in Machina, there were several channels in Dagona. This was a reflection of the pluralistic nature of politics in the community as opposed to the hierarchical nature of politics in Machina. The pluralistic nature of politics in Dagona went along with a somewhat more inclusive pattern of participation in the public spaces. There were more meetings of several groups, each with a strong sense of involvement in the community. Most important aspects of their lives were managed by participatory committees, including water, health, and education. Although in Dagona SDP members predominated in the public spaces and as beneficiaries of projects, people in the town, including members of the NRC, did not interpret that as a reflection of political bias.

This is not to say that everyone was an equal citizen of Dagona. Just as some people were excluded in the Greek polis, in Dagona women and migrants, especially the Sakkwatawa, were disproportionately disenfranchised. The formal exclusion of women was the rule in all the public spaces in Dagona and Machina, while the exclusion of migrants was more pronounced in Dagona. The Sakkwatawas had benefited from several of NEAZDP's productive projects, but in projects that involved community participation (social projects) they were not active. Perhaps they tried to retain their migrant status and identity by not participating in community activities. It is also very possible that the people of Dagona pointedly treated them as migrants and second-class citizens. Women in both communities and in both development programs participated less than men; and in both communities the participation of women in politics was minimal. Women were not members of any committees other than women's committees. Indeed, women had separate responsibilities from men. Most of the men's responsibilities were assumed to be community-wide, while women's responsibilities were more narrowly assumed to be particular to women. Thus the women's committees of Machina and Dagona were responsible for NEAZDP projects on maternity and dehusking and grinding, which were part of the female sphere, but women were not involved, for example, in the committees of water and conservation, two activities in which they had important responsibilities in the communities but which were part of the male sphere.

Conclusion

As the case studies of three development institutions—the Better Life Program for Rural Women, the Directorate of Food, Road, and Rural Infrastructure, and the Northeast Arid Zone Development Program—show, development projects have the very important role of creating, expanding, and constraining community spaces in which development officials, government officers, and local people meet to discuss issues of importance to the community: claims are foregrounded and negotiated. These projects are also forums for asserting and proclaiming community citizenship. However, discourse in the public sphere reflects not only the socio-economic status of the participants, but also cultural values, historical-political antecedents, and gender relations, and it does so either openly or through hidden scripts—as the case study of a community meeting illustrates. The content of meetings—an aspect neglected in some of the writing on social capital—is also revealing. It shows how a public meeting can begin to enlarge discussion of local issues in a place long kept under firm autocratic control. Critical voices can express themselves artfully using traditional forms and symbols. It takes an observer who knows the culture well to detect how the new assertiveness expands the sphere of participation.

The Northeast Arid Zone Development Program, the development institution that has been most successful in this respect, is the one most insulated from governmental politics by its overseas funding and its independent management. The other two development institutions operated much like other government agencies. Unlike government agencies and government development institutions, which are essentially top-down and oriented to service delivery, the relatively autonomous development institutions created public spaces of empowerment at the village level where community organizations also operate; but the new spaces had begun to address issues of basic material well-being. In the case of NEAZDP, global forces interacted with the local context to construct sufficient autonomy from governmental constraints to create new energies and initiatives. But the nature of the public sphere mirrored social differences including gender, class, and ethnicity that placed barriers to participation in the way of women, marginalized cultural groups, and politically and economically subordinate strata. The barriers were more pronounced in the socially more hierarchical and the politically more autocratic town.

Notes

1. See Dharam Ghai, *Participatory Development: Some Perspectives from Grassroots Experiences* (Geneva: UNRISD, 1988); and Robert Putnam, J-C. Casanova, and Seizaburo Sato, *Revitalizing Trilateral Democracies: A Report to the Trilateral Commission* (Washington: Trilateral Commission, 1995).

2. I use the concepts of public space and community settings to refer to the public sphere, restricting the usage of the terms to activities that are purposely public. I therefore do not include spaces such as cafés. I am aware of feminists' concerns that focusing on the public entails a gender bias against women and emphasizes "high" politics, ignoring the subtle politics that are sometimes expressed in the household. Although decisions made in the public sphere are sometimes determined by backdoor politics in palaces and private rooms, one cannot ignore the significance of public life. Its discriminatory and inadequate nature should be continuously analyzed and critiqued. Andrew Kiondo's account of local development in Tanzania resonates with some of the concerns of this research. See Andrew Kiondo, "The New Local Politics of Development in Tanzania," in *The New Local Level Politics in East Africa: Studies on Uganda, Tanzania, and Kenya*, ed. Kanyinga Karuti, Andrew S.Z. Kiondo, and Per Tidemand (Uppsala: Nordiska Afrikainstitutet, 1994), pp.50-88.

3. Zanna Abubakar Ahmed, "A History of Bade Emirate in the 19th Century: A Study of the Establishment and Consolidation of the Gid Dynasty 1820-1880 AD," M.A. thesis, Department of History, University of Ibadan, 1988.

4. Sakkwatawa is a dialect of Hausa. It is spoken by people from Sakkwato or Sokoto. Even other indigenous Hausa find it difficult to understand the dialect.

5. Robert Putnam, "Bowling Alone: America's Declining Social Capital," *Journal of Democracy*, 6,1 (January 1995), pp.65-78.

6. Izala is shorthand for Jamatul Izalatul Bidiat wa Ikhamatus Sunnah, Movement for the Eradication of Superstition and Upholding of the Sayings of Prophet Muhammad (PBUH).

7. Does this remind you of the contextual nature of the saying "blood is thicker than water" to describe close relationships? Marxists have already made the point that cash is thicker than blood to illustrate the importance of class relations.

Table 4.1

Development Institution Presence
August 1992—August 1993

Number of Public Meetings
Sponsored by Development Institutions

Development Institution	Dagona	Machina	Both Towns
NEAZDP	43	14	57
DFRRI	0	0	0
Better Life	0	1	1
Total	43	15	58

Source: Activity Setting Records and Group Discussions, 1993.

Table 4.2

Federal & State Government Presence

August 1992—August 1993

	Machina		Dagona	
Government	Present	No. of meetings	Present	No. of meetings
Federal				
Police	Yes	—	—	—
Immigration	Yes	—	—	—
SSS	Yes	—	—	—
Custom	Yes	—	—	—
NEC	Yes	1	—	1
NPC	Yes	1	—	1
DSM	Yes	2	—	1
NDE	Yes	1	—	1
State				
Yard Superintendant	Yes	—	—	—
Water Board	Yes	—	—	—
Rural Electricity	Yes	—	—	—
YOSADP	Yes	—	yes	5
YOSAMA	Yes	—	—	—
Area Court	Yes	—	—	—
Viewing Centre	Yes	—	yes	—
Secondary School	Yes	—	—	—
Emirate	Yes	—	—	—
Total	17	5	2	9

Note: SSS=State Security Service; NEC=National Electoral Commission; NPC=National Population Commission; DSM=Directorate for Social Mobilization; NDE=National Directorate of Employment; YOSADP=Yobe State Agricultural Development Program; YOSAMA=Yobe State Agricultural Mechanization Authority.

Source: Activity Setting Records and Group Discussions, 1993.

Table 4.3

Local Government Presence

August 1992—August 1993

	Machina		Dagona	
	Present	No. of meetings	Present	No. of meetings
Works	Yes	—	Yes	—
Administration	Yes	—	—	—
Treasury	Yes	—	—	—
LEA	Yes	—	—	—
Dispensary	Yes	—	—	—
Health Clinic	Yes	—	Yes	—
Veterinary	Yes	—	Yes	—
Primary Schools	Yes	1	Yes	—
Market Stalls	Yes	—	—	—
Guest House	Yes	—	—	—
Legislative Council	Yes	—	—	—
EPI	Yes	25	—	—
Village Head	Yes	2	Yes	3
District Head	Yes	4	Yes	1
Natural Resources	Yes	—	—	—
Nursery	Yes	—	—	—
Slaughterhouse	Yes	—	—	—
PHC	Yes	—	—	—
Islamiya	Yes	—	—	—
Total	19	32	6	4

Note: LEA=Local Education Authority; EPI=Expanded Program on Immunization;
    PHC=Primary Health Care.

Source: Activity Setting Records and Group Discussions, 1993.

Table 4.4

Number of Public Meetings
Sponsored by Community Organizations

August 1992—August 1993

Dagona	Meetings
Kungiyar Masunta	8
Izala Friday Mosque	2
NRC Ward Level	7
SDP Ward Level	8
Friday Mosque	—
Market	—
Subtotal	25
Machina	**Meetings**
Parent-Teacher Association	2
Church	—
Friday Mosque	—
Hausari Social Club	4
Kautalhore	NA
Butchers Association	2
Nigeria Union of Teachers	2
National Union of Local Government Employees	NA
NRC (W/LG)	18
SDP (W/LG)	19
Subtotal	47
Total	72

Note: W=Ward; W/LG=Ward and Local Government

Source: Activity Setting Records and Group Discussions, 1993.

Chapter 5

Sea Changes: Organizing around the Fishery in a South Indian Community

Aparna Sundar

In 1996-97 the small-scale and medium-scale fishworkers of India won a remarkable victory in their three-year-long campaign against the Indian government's deep-sea fishing policy. Under a 1991 policy, licences were issued to industrial fishing vessels owned as joint ventures between Indian and foreign business to fish entirely for export in India's deep seas. As a result of the fishworkers' campaign, the government agreed to issue no new licences, cancel existing licences, and reorient its fisheries policy in favour of traditional fishers. The victory of the Indian fishworkers is particularly significant in the current period of economic liberalization and opening up to foreign capital. If it endures, it will have proved a timely step towards conserving the fishery in the context of worldwide depletion and resource collapse.

At the same time as this campaign was underway, another conflict in the fishery was being played out in the fishing district of Kanyakumari in the southern state of Tamil Nadu. This struggle was between artisanal fishers working on small unmechanized craft (sometimes fitted with outboard motors) and the owners of mechanized trawlers. Blaming the trawlers for damage to their gear, undermining their livelihoods, and depletion of the resources, artisanal fishers have been engaged in opposing the trawlers for decades, fitfully after the introduction of the boats in the 1950s and in a more sustained manner since the 1980s. The government responded with regulations that proved inadequate to ensure resolution of the conflict.

Both struggles[1] are part of a "fishworkers' movement" that has gained strength and prominence over the last two decades, and the contrast between them permits some interesting reflections. Firstly, there is the paradox that, in a period when globalization is seen as the single biggest threat to local livelihoods, a major move towards the entry of global capital was successfully fought off, while a long-standing conflict between small- and medium-scale indigenous fishers continued to elude resolution. What, if anything, does this tell us about the scope for organizing in the context of globalization? I argue here that the threat of "globalization" may itself create new opportunities for national organizing and that the "localization" of an issue does not necessarily serve to make it more tractable. The threat posed by any policy must be measured through the strength of local interests vested in it, the ideological and material resources that opposition can draw on, and the alliances that can be formed.

Secondly, there is Amrita Basu's decade-old prognosis about the fishworkers' and other such movements: "Given their inability to gain state power or to arrest capitalist development, grassroots movements appear to be losing credibility." These movements had "marginalised themselves by underestimating the centrality and complexity of the state."[2] The success of the struggle against deep-sea fishing suggests that this is clearly not the case. Indeed, far from underestimating "the state," the movement exploited to its advantage the state's complexity and the contradictions between its different elements.

Finally, notions of what constitutes "success" for a movement need broadening, for while the struggle against trawling may not have won resolution, it nevertheless reflected, and added to, the fishworkers' power to politicize new issues and settings and to draw them into the struggle.

The "Political Setting" Approach

By locating politics physically, the use of political settings allows us to examine the "micro-foundations" of such abstractions as "the state" in a quite literal sense. Looking closely at settings in which state officials and their clients interact, such as in government offices, or in public demonstrations of protest, provides a sense of the relationships through which images of the state are forged. It positions us methodologically to "disaggregate" the state—both in terms of levels, and in terms of its institutions and policies, to examine the mutual interaction of "state" and "society," and perhaps even to decentre the location of sovereignty.[3]

In addition to allowing us to "disaggregate" the state, this approach enables us to disaggregate a social movement in a way that few of the many accounts of the fishworkers movement do.[4] By doing so, it shows us how struggles around an issue in the fishery are also struggles about power in the village, practices of gender, and the role of the church.[5]

Finally, a focus on political settings enables reflection on forms of politicization and the links between the formal settings of liberal democracy and other forms of participation. By reminding us that "the politics appropriate to a particular occasion always has to be invented,"[6] it brings us alive to the creative and performative functions of politics, and to practice (as distinct from institutions and discourses), aspects of politics neglected until lately by the teleological and prescriptive bent of writing on the "third world."[7]

To focus on practice, and on the local and specific, is not by any means to make the "assertion of authenticity," of "being there" as a superior means to understanding. The political settings method does not treat "the local" as "an unproblematic and coherent spatial unit,"[8] or deny the ways in which the "trans-local" structures the local. Rather, it allows us some empirical means to grasp at these multiple mediations.

The Modernization of the Fishery

India ranks as the seventh marine fishing nation in the world based on total production. The importance of the fishery for India's economy lies in its high employment of some eight million people and in its contribution to export earnings. In 1993 the seafood industry contributed 3.5 percent (U.S.$810 million) to the country's export earnings. The main markets for Indian seafood exports are Japan, United States, Western Europe, and Southeast Asia.[9]

The move to invite joint ventures between Indian and foreign capital in deep-sea fishing is part of the trajectory of development of a sector that has always been shaped by the interaction, in different degrees, of local, regional, national, and international forces—local resource endowments and technological adaptations, national and provincial development policy, and international markets, technology, and "aid."[10]

State intervention in modernizing the fishery began in the colonial period,[11] but the real fillip to planned modernization came with independent India's first five-year plan. Fisheries policy has from the outset had the productivist, technocratic bias that underlay, for instance, the Green Revolution in agriculture. The goals of planned development have been to increase production for export and domestic food supply, generate employment, and improve the living conditions of the fishing communities.[12] These goals are not without their contradictions. Increased export may come at the cost of increased domestic consumption. Increased production does not require investment in the fishing communities and can instead go to interests that compete directly with them. Finally, capitalization of the sector, under the assumption that there is a limitless resource base that will sustain production both for domestic subsistence and export, can rapidly undermine itself by contributing to the erosion of that base.

State policy is only one of the actors in the fishery, and even here the various levels of the state come into play, because jurisdiction over the inshore fishery lies mainly with the states (provinces), and provincial policies, even in the colonial period, varied greatly.[13] In the state of Kerala, for instance, where the differentiation in the fishery and production for export can be seen most clearly, trawlers were first introduced by an Indo-Norwegian Project for Fisheries Community Development in the 1950s. The first step to export frozen prawn to the United States was taken by a private merchant in 1953, and the success of this venture led to increased demand for frozen prawn from Kerala and the entry of other entrepreneurs. Having lost access to fishing rights in Mexican waters in 1962, Japan also soon became a market for prawn exports. The state government began to provide subsidies for the acquisition of mechanized craft in order to take advantage of this export drive.[14]

The process of acquisition of mechanized trawlers and purse seiners was accompanied by the motorization of traditional craft. Here too government subsidies played a part, as did small NGOs and co-operative societies that encouraged the process, and fishermen themselves, who eagerly grasped at motorization as a means of going greater distances, reducing labour, and remaining competitive with mechanized craft. Motorization and the adoption of more sophisticated gear require higher initial investments and bring recurring high costs for fuel and engine maintenance. This increases the need for larger catches to allow owners to break even.[15]

The growing presence of capital-intensive, highly "efficient" technology has resulted in socio-economic differentiation within communities, moved management away from the community, and changed food regimes and consumption patterns, as well as labour processes.[16] Most damagingly, perhaps, the nature of property rights in this fishery, which allows relatively easy access to newcomers, the use of inappropriate technology, the high demand from external markets, the financial subsidies provided by the state to encourage investment in the sector, and the growing population pressure on the coastal commons, have led since the 1970s to a fall in overall fish and prawn harvests and a crisis of ecological overfishing.[17]

Prompted by a balance of payments deficit, and by a clause in the 1982 Law of the Sea that requires a country to open its Exclusive Economic Zone (EEZ) for exploitation by other states if that country is unable to exploit that zone fully itself, the government of India introduced a new deep-sea fishing policy in 1991.[18] This proposed the licensing of foreign vessels under joint ventures between Indian and foreign companies to fish entirely for export in India's EEZ. The incentive package included easy financing and the supply of diesel fuel at international rates (lower than the Indian rates that outboard motor operators, for instance, pay). Units could export their entire catch, processing and trans-shipping it directly at sea; they were not required to dock at any Indian port and could use a foreign port as the base of operation. The government would receive 12 percent of the foreign-exchange earnings of the enterprises.

Of the 41 joint ventures licensed by March 1994, 19 of the foreign partners were companies from South Korea, Taiwan, and other East Asian states, 3 from China, 11 from Russia and the erstwhile Soviet Union, and 7 from Western Europe, the United States, and Japan.[19] The Indian firms were registered mostly in New Delhi or in the east-coast state of Andhra Pradesh, where indigenous deep-sea operations are based.

India's previous attempts at deep-sea fishing had not been success-ful.[20] Critics point out that the Indian deep sea, unlike temperate seas, does not offer adequate spatial and seasonal concentrations of commercially valuable fish that would make a fishery based entirely on their exploitation viable. It remains attractive to foreign vessels, however, because depletion of significant fisheries elsewhere has left many large fleets idle.[21] Given the Indian government's minimal monitoring capacity, there is always the opportunity to stray inshore.

The policy was guaranteed to lead to speedy depletion of the fish resource. Monitoring of catch would be impossible in the absence of an oblig-ation to land it on Indian shores. Since a number of the species straddle the deep sea and inshore area, and since deep-sea vessels would be forced to fish inshore to ensure an adequate catch, this would put enormous pressure on the already overexploited inshore fishery. The policy also had no visible ben-efits in terms of employment generation in harvesting, processing, or mar-keting, since all these operations could be performed offshore. Given that a significant proportion of the catch would be types of fish that were already being harvested inshore, export of the entire amount would reduce the amount available for domestic consumption and for sale by local vendors, many of them women. Deep-sea vessels the world over routinely overfish and then dump overboard large quantities of the bycatch to ensure that their quotas are filled with commercially valuable fish. Many of the species dis-carded as bycatch have traditionally contributed to the protein intake of low-income families.

The Fishing Economy of Kanyakumari District

Kanyakumari district has the largest fishing population in the state of Tamil Nadu. Close to 200,000 people live in 42 villages along the 68-kilometre coastline of the district.[22] Even within this small area, differences in ecology, resource endowment, and level of skill have resulted in a number of highly varied and specialized fisheries.

Tamil Nadu launched its mechanization program in 1955, when subsidies were provided for the acquisition of 30- and 32-foot wooden trawl and gill-net boats. Subsequent five-year plans saw investments in harbours and freezing and processing facilities.[23] The first boats in that period were acquired in the west-coast village of Colachel, whose natural harbour permitted their operation.[24] They were bought largely by *karamadi* (shore seine) owners and other richer fishermen. Many of them borrowed heavily from local merchants to finance their investment, and in a number of cases they were forced to sell their boats to the merchants when they were unable to repay the loans. Lacking an adequate processing and marketing infrastructure in Colachel, and faced with the opposition of the local *kattumaram* fishermen, the trawler owners gradually began to fish in the neighbouring state of Kerala, where the government was investing heavily in infrastructure. Gradually *kattumaram* fishers also began to migrate seasonally to Kerala to work on trawlers there. Very few trawlers were acquired elsewhere in the district until the construction of the harbour at Chinna Muttam on the east coast at the end of the 1980s. With this, the number of trawlers in Chinna Muttam and the adjoining village of Kanyakumari grew from three in 1987 to close to a hundred in 1995. Newer trawlers can be as large as 51 feet long and have up to 120-horsepower engines.

The motorization of traditional craft did not become a government scheme until the Seventh Five-Year Plan in 1985.[25] A Boat Building Centre set up by the diocesan social service society developed new designs of stitch and glue plywood boats (*vallams*) with outboard motors (OBMs) of up to 20 horsepower, which became increasingly popular alternatives to the *kattumarams,* made of the light wood that was fast becoming scarce and dear.[26] The local fishermen's marketing co-operatives provided subsidies for acquisition of these craft or of OBMs for use on *kattumarams*. Notwithstanding these innovations, the traditional *kattumaram*, a keelless beach landing craft formed by tying together three to five pieces of light, rough-hewn wood, remained preponderant. The craft, virtually unsinkable and highly efficient for crossing surf, could be operated with oars, sails, or OBMs, and support a wide variety of gear, from nets of all sorts to long lines. In the 1990s Kanyakumari remained the district with the highest number of unmechanized traditional craft in the state,[27] due to the suitability of the *kattumaram* to local coast and weather conditions and the high cost of the alternatives.

Catch figures for the entire district showed only a small shift in landings between the artisanal (including motorized) and mechanized sectors, with the artisanal sector landing 99.9 percent in 1978-79 and 85 percent in 1993-94. At Colachel natural harbour, where trawlers dominate, the ratio was dramatically inversed, with the artisanal sector landing 98 percent in 1985-86 and only 6 percent in 1993-94. While landings did fluctuate dramatically from year to year, district catch figures showed a secular decline from a peak of 96,130 tonnes in 1984-85 to 29,235 tonnes in 1993-94.[28] This decline was disguised by the incremental rise in the price of the fish over the decades due to the demand from international and new domestic markets.

Dried fish, particularly anchovy, had been exported from Kanyakumari to Burma and Ceylon (Sri Lanka) since at least the beginning of the 19th century. With the prawn export boom in the 1960s, exporters began to send agents to villages in the district. Trawlers, *vallams*, and *kattumarams* all catch prawn, squid, and cuttlefish, as well as other high-value fish. The trawler owners said they concentrated on such exportable species to stay viable; artisanal fishers too made a significant proportion of their income from export.[29]

In the 1990s a small proportion of the men in each village were training for work outside the fishery. Migration to the Persian Gulf countries largely to work on fishing vessels had been a growing trend since the early 1980s. While many villages now had between 50 and 100 men in the Gulf at any one time, this was not enough to reduce the heavy dependence on the fishery for employment. Displaced from net-weaving and with few other avenues for craft employment, girls increasingly stayed in school longer and looked (with limited success) for clerical, teaching, or social work jobs. Processing plants near the fishing harbour at Chinna Muttam employed 50 to 100 young women from the area seasonally; a similar number migrated temporarily to processing plants in other parts of the country, where they lived on the premises of the plant and worked in conditions of poor health and safety and strict labour discipline.[30] A smaller number of older, indigent women worked as fish vendors, buying fish on the beach and selling it in nearby markets.

The situation in Kanyakumari district, then, was of a population highly dependent for its livelihood on a declining fishery and, increasingly, on global markets. Whether the people fished on artisanal craft for export, or migrated to work as labour on trawlers that fished for export in Kerala or in plants that processed shrimp for export, their fortunes increasingly depended on markets for fish and seafood in Japan, the United States, and Western Europe.

The Fishworkers' Movement

The fishworkers' movement had at least two sources: the protests against the trawlers, which began to intensify in a number of the states in the 1970s,[31] and the systematic work by social activists, predominantly from Christian backgrounds and often with the support of church-related social action organizations, in the fishing communities of south Kerala. As the unrest and militancy from other states began to spread to Kerala, these two strands came together nationally to found the National Forum for Kattumaram and Countryboat Fishermen's Rights and Marine Wealth, with the name changed in 1983 to the National Fishermen's Forum (NFF), a representative body of 13 major regional fishermen's unions. The NFF was registered as a trade union in 1985.

The campaign against trawling and other types of indiscriminate mechanized fishing was the spark, and would remain a burning issue, for the movement. Opposition to trawling was framed in terms of social justice (the enrichment of the few at the expense of the many), sustainable development (depletion through overfishing), and food security (local subsistence versus export). The first major campaign of the Forum was to push for a marine bill, which would declare an exclusive fishing zone of 20 kilometres from the shore for non-mechanized craft, regulate the operation of trawlers, and specify a minimum mesh size. A ban on trawling during the monsoon, which is the spawning season, also became a long-standing demand. The central government issued a marine bill in 1980, leaving it to the states to turn the bill into law, and in the next few years a number of the states passed marine fishing regulation acts creating trawler-free zones, preventing night trawling, and, in the state of Maharashtra, declaring a monsoon ban on purse seiners. Almost everywhere that the acts were passed, they were challenged in court by mechanized craft operators, with varying degrees of success. The issue remained unresolved in most states. In Tamil Nadu many districts worked out their own arrangements. In Kerala, despite recommendations from three "expert" committees to regulate access to the fishery in the interests of conserving the resource, a monsoon ban remained highly political—implemented and lifted each year depending on the balance of power between the opposing lobbies and the biases of the government of the day.[32]

The movement took up a wide variety of issues connected to coastal communities and the fish resources: pollution and dumping, beach tourism, nuclear power, intensive aquaculture, and working conditions for migrant women workers in shrimp-processing plants. It made welfare demands: for pensions, education allowances, and buses for the fish-vending women. In Kerala, governments unable to take a firm stand on trawling were eager to make concessions on these demands instead.[33]

The NFF functioned as a federation: common national programs were worked out at annual general meetings, and office-holders travelled incessantly to build links and provide guidance and support; but member unions varied greatly in their ideology, structure, and day-to-day functioning. The national meetings were remarkable affairs, with heated discussions requiring translation into at least a few of the nine languages of the coastal states, as well as Hindi and English.

The movement's leadership was hard to classify in terms of class or ideology. It represented a rare and fortuitous coming together of committed progressive clergy and religious in Kerala (deeply influenced by a theology of liberation),[34] social workers, members and fellow travellers of left parties, journalists, and scholars. That the movement struck roots may be witnessed by the emergence over the years of a layer of skilled activists from within the communities and organizations themselves.

Key women activists worked to develop a gendered approach both to the fishery and to organizing.[35] They understood women's participation in the fishery as including both the paid work of fish-vending and fish-processing and the unpaid work of political organizing, raising of credit, and reproduction of labour and the webs of social life. Negotiations to increase women's presence in the organization became a constant. At the 1989 general meeting of the National Fishermen's Forum, animated discussions preceded the decision to change the name to the gender-neutral National Fishworkers' Forum.[36] At the 1994 meeting, women members staged a walkout to protest what they felt was a lack of action on organizational measures to increase women's participation. Elements of ecofeminism informed attempts to articulate a vision of a nurture fishery—as opposed to the dominant capture fishery—that saw expression in projects such as one aimed at the rejuvenation of the mangrove forests, breeding grounds for a variety of marine life.

Although the NFF was the trade union and political wing of the movement, the movement itself was much broader, and it included marketing co-operatives such as those federated under the South Indian Federation of Fishermen's Societies (SIFFS),[37] and NGOs involved in appropriate technology, fisheries research, and training in community work. From its inception the movement also made alliances with other popular organizations, trade unions, and "people's movements."[38] Peter Waterman's concept of "social movement unionism" is apt in this context.[39]

Consequently, the approaches taken were diverse. The movement became skilled in the repertory of militant oppositional actions described by Madhav Gadgil and Ramachandra Guha: *pradarshan* (collective show of strength), *dharna* (sit-down strike, or demonstration), *gherao* (surrounding of a key authority figure), *rasta roko* (road blockade), *jail bharo andolan* (movement to fill the jails), and *bhook hartal* (hunger fast).[40] It mounted successful legal challenges and put up constructive proposals, such as a draft marine bill in the 1970s, a draft eighth five-year plan for the fisheries in 1990, and an alternative deep-sea fishing policy in 1994. Other methods included public education, as through the 1989 Kanyakumari March around the theme "Protect Water, Protect Life"; ecological restoration of mangroves and artificial reefs; experiments with appropriate technology, such as new designs of beach-landing plywood craft; and economic development through the marketing co-operatives.[41]

These approaches indicated a relationship with the state that was never simply oppositional. Legal challenges, participation in government-appointed committees, drafting of an alternative five-year plan: all of these suggested a willingness to engage with the structures and processes of liberal democracy, even as they attempted to undercut the structural inequity that was at its base.

The campaign against the new deep-sea fishing policy began at the end of 1993 with the NFF and the Small Mechanized Boat Operators together calling for licences for joint ventures to be revoked and a new deep-sea fishing regulation act to be enacted.[42] It took off with a one-day all-India *bandh* (closure) of the fishery on February 4, 1994. The success of that action led to a coalition of different interests in the fishery under the National Fisheries Action Committee against Joint Ventures (NFACJV) to continue the campaign. This was followed by a nationwide "Black Day" in July 1994, a two-day national fisheries strike in November 1994, and a week-long hunger fast by Thomas Kocherry, chair of the NFF and convenor of the NFACJV, supported by relay fasts by fishworkers across the country in May 1995.

The growing national and international support for the fishworkers' cause led the government to appoint a committee (known by the name of its chair as the Murari Committee) to review its policy. After pressure from the NFACJV, the committee was reconstituted to include four representatives of the fishworkers, among them Kocherry. On February 6, 1996, the Murari Committee submitted its recommendations, which included the total cancellation of licences issued to foreign vessels under joint ventures, the provision of training and subsidies to enable small- and medium-scale fishers to harvest the deep sea, and mandatory consultation with the fishing community on all fishery legislation or policy.

With no sign that the government was acting on the committee's report, to force action Kocherry began a hunger fast in Bombay on August 7, 1996. The central trade union federations, the National Centre for Labour (NCL) and the National Alliance of People's Movements (NAPM), carried out support actions across the country. On August 10, fishers and dockworkers began an indefinite blockade of the major harbours. As a consequence of this action, the Ministry of Food Processing Industries agreed to stop issuing new licences and to begin implementing all aspects of the report. Finally, another round of harbour blockades in March 1997 succeeded in getting an agreement to cancel even current licences.

Artisanal fishers and mechanized trawler operators, traditionally enemies, came together under the NFACJV to deal with an enemy larger than both. A major achievement for these workers in the "unorganized" sector was the collaboration gained from the central trade union federations in the organized sector. They also gained strong international support from unions and other organizations. MPs across party and ideological lines raised questions in Parliament that were critical of the government's policy. Both right-wing BJP MPs from Gujarat and Maharashtra and left-wing CPI(M) MPs from West Bengal and Kerala wrote asking for the policy to be reviewed. Some 102 MPs signed a petition to that effect. Various state governments, in particular the government of the western state of Gujarat, expressed their opposition to the central government's policy.

The campaign marked a qualitative advance for the movement. It was able to operate at a national level, uniting hitherto conflicting sectors in the fishery around a single issue and setting the basis for international organizing. It was able to utilize and participate in the formal political process without ceding the autonomy to organize militantly outside it. It was able to draw unprecedented media attention to unconventional issues raised from the outset: management of the resources to ensure their sustainability; the social impacts of technology; questions of exports, markets, practices of consumption, and food security; distributive justice; and community right to the commons.[43] Most importantly, it was able to win recognition of its proposals from the government Review Committee, which recommended a radical reorientation of the country's fishery policy in the interests of community-based producers, domestic consumers, and the sustainability of the resource.

Politics is structured and mediated, though, not only by the routines and conventions of meetings, but also by the combination of geography and architecture that forms the physical characteristics of "place." The political settings approach, then, includes an examination of (i) the physical setting of geography and architecture; (ii) the spaces created by various associations; and (iii) the meetings and collective actions generated by campaigns and other public events and how they intersect with both the physical setting and the associational spaces.

The Physical Setting

That geographical location and architectural arrangements may serve as a metaphor for economic, social, and political relations is rarely better illustrated than in the fishing villages of Kanyakumari. The village I describe, Kanyakumari (or KK), is 20 kilometres from Nagercoil, the district headquarters. It is off to the east of the main highway that runs north-south to end at the Cape of Comorin (Kumari), land's end, a popular tourist spot and Hindu pilgrimage site. The population of close to 10,000 belongs to the two fishing castes of the district—Mukkuvar and Paravar—categorized as "backward" for purposes of affirmative action. Describing the fishing villages of the district, Kalpana Ram writes: "The Mukkuvars are located on the outer fringes of an ancient agrarian civilisation. Beyond them is the sea, on which their livelihood depends, offering them a ready if provisional escape from the low status that caste society affords them. Their geographical location is a metaphor not only for the social and economic marginality of the Mukkuvars but for the possibilities of an independent cultural identity that this marginality provides."[44]

KK stretches barely two kilometres along the coast from northeast to southwest, and one kilometre between the sea to the east and the highway to the west. Small brick and cement houses with tiled roofs line the beach close to the sea; the intervening space is packed with drying *kattumarams*, so that one has to pick out a careful path between them, the drying nets, and the children playing outside the houses. In the afternoons and evenings, men sit in groups close to the beached craft, mending their nets or playing cards. Women also sit in groups closer to their homes, playing games, talking, combing their children's hair. Given the warm climate and the cool sea breeze, people live outdoors as much as in, and the distinction between public and private space is not sharply drawn. This becomes less true as one moves inland, to the west of the village. Families who have entered other occupations—merchants, teachers, white-collar workers of various kinds, and, increasingly, trawler owners—live closer to the highway that runs to the west of the village, in larger, better furnished houses, and have more of an "interior life." The Catholic Church of Our Lady of the Snows marks the centre of the village, the dividing line between the more prosperous and the less so. Along the beach are two other small shrines, where families in the area light candles and the women often go to pray in the evenings.

On land bought from the village, but a little distance from the houses, is the office of the Assistant Director of Fisheries for the east coast of the district. He is in charge of carrying out fisheries surveys, registering craft, and implementing the various schemes of the fisheries department. All active fishers in the village are members of the government co-operative society through which the various schemes are disbursed. Elections to the society were discontinued in the early 1980s, and a government-appointed Special Officer oversees their functioning.[45] Across the highway, within a few minutes' walk from the village, is the police station for the area.

The Collector (the highest administrative authority for the district), the District Superintendent of Police, and the Assistant Director of Fisheries for the district all have their offices in Nagercoil. Tamil Nadu's extensive road system and regular bus service make these offices quite accessible even for fishing villages more distant than KK. Almost every time I paid an extended visit to one of these offices, including the police station, I would encounter fishermen and sometimes women, alone or in groups, coming to inquire about a scheme, make a complaint, or deliver a petition. In KK, children would be sent with the monthly insurance premium to the Assistant Director's office.

The Collector had recently announced that he would hear representations from the fishing villages on the first Monday of every month; on those mornings a crowd of people, often accompanied by their parish priest, could be seen waiting on the grounds of his office, which is on a main road leading into town. Across the road is a bus stop, a tea stall that does a brisk business, and two typing and photocopying shops that are kept equally busy dealing with petitions and other documents people need to present to the authorities. Between the tea stall and the shops is a thatch shed that seems to have become a permanent structure. It accommodates whichever group is carrying out a *dharna* or hunger fast outside the Collectorate on a given day. Protest is thus given its due place, across the road from power.

The Associational Settings

That the state is by no means the only system of authority in the fishing villages is evident from the central presence of the church in KK. Ram writes:

> Since the period of conversion in the sixteenth century, the Church has emerged as a powerful overlord, viewing the coastal belt as its own private territory, in both the economic and the political sense. In the course of four hundred years, the Church has constituted itself as a quasi-State, operating within the boundaries of the official State of the day. It has levied its own taxes, adjudicated disputes between one village and another, or between individuals, and generally mediated the relations of people within its own territory with the outside world. . . . Villagers ironically refer to their parish priests as *kuTTi raja*, "petty prince."[46]

This authority is now more contested as other influences, such as political parties and NGOs, have become stronger. In an effort to counter these, the church itself has initiated much of the associational life in the village.[47] However, this in turn has opened up spaces from which the hegemony of the church is challenged. Besides the pious associations, catechism classes, and youth groups that came out of the Vatican II-inspired movement to laicize the church, the diocesan social service wing—the Kottar Social Service Society (KSSS)—has over the years initiated programs such as the Community Health Development Program, fishermen's marketing co-operatives, and a savings and credit society for widows and other indigent women.

The church has since the 1980s attempted to institute elected parish committees to replace the long-standing system of village government—a nominated committee of men of relative wealth and large family backing. KK village, like many others, has resisted adopting a parish committee structure on the grounds that this would formalize the participation of women and give the diocese too much control over the village's affairs. It does have a village committee, with members elected from each street. In 1995 some 35 men were active in it, all *kattumaram*, *vallam*, or mechanized gill-net fishers. The five or six members who owned trawlers had stopped coming to the meetings. The village committee raises revenues for village activities, settles intravillage disputes, and represents the village to state authorities and other nearby villages.

Inspired by experiments in Latin America, a diocesan priest began his own attempts to set up Basic Christian Communities (BCCs) during his tenure as parish priest in the village of Kodi Munai in the 1970s. From the beginning, the BCCs created the space for the participation of women, and many articulate women activists first found their voice at these meetings. Their active participation has caused many men to stay away, and in general the richer families participate less than the poorer, leading to a description of the BCCs as "meetings for the poor and women."

The fish-marketing co-operatives initiated by the KSSS in the early 1980s are now part of a districtwide federation. Intended to break the exploitative hold of the merchants, to whom the fishermen were bonded by debt to sell their catch at uncompetitive rates, they buy fish from the fishermen and market it, provide credit, and institute compulsory savings.[48] These *sangams* are relatively wealthy organizations in the village, and are often approached to contribute to village causes.

Shantidan, a savings and credit organization for fish-vending and other petty business women, was set up in 1983 by one of the initiators of the men's *sangams*, using funding from a number of international NGOs. The units have registered remarkable savings, and these are pooled at the district office to enable larger loans. Animators paid for by the organization conduct weekly meetings at which savings and loan repayments are collected. In the early 1990s a number of other such thrift and credit organizations for women were established.

Every village has units of all the major political parties—the ADMK, DMK, Congress (I), Janata Dal, MDMK, as well as their youth and women's wings.[49] The fishing villages are well-known as ADMK strongholds. Party units do not meet regularly, but party affiliations are strong and become activated during elections and when villagers want to gain access to the state government in Madras. The numerous film star fan clubs are also bases for political mobilization, as they are across Tamil Nadu, where films and politics are closely associated.[50]

Out of the differentiation of the fishing economy, organizations have emerged to represent the various interests. A Trawler Owners' Association was established in Colachel in 1982; the Chinna Muttam Trawler Owners and Employees Union was formed in 1991 and claims 1,200 members, both owners and workers on the 122 trawlers that operate from the area.

The NFF has also sponsored local organizing. The Tamil Nadu Fishworkers' Union (TFU) was set up in the district in 1989-90, with a formal elected structure growing upwards from units at the village level. Its main organizing strategy in the beginning was the demand to regulate trawling, but it has also campaigned over the years for measures such as buses for fish-vending women and pensions for all fishworkers. Yet the TFU has not put down deep roots in the area; partly because, as often explained, its paid organizers were all women and could not be taken seriously by the fishermen. The TFU is the only one of the fishworker organizations in the district to have women vendors and even women in the community as members along with men.

In 1993 another organization, the Vallam and Kattumaram Fishermen's Union, was formed as an outcome of the escalating tensions generated by the annual monsoon return of the trawlers from Kerala. The initiative this time came from the *vallam* fishermen of the west coast rather than a national organization. Operating through an executive committee but without formal units in the villages, the Vallam Union nevertheless managed to get village committees to contribute funds, and it organized more militantly than the TFU, for instance, through boat captures. More recently the union's leadership and advisers attempted to curb the fishermen's readiness to do battle in favour of more legal means: "peace committees" in the presence of district officials, petitions in court, and lobbying with elected representatives in Madras.

Associational routines include not just meetings and organizational elections, but the rituals of interest representation. Youth groups, parish and village committees, BCCs, the women's thrift and credit organizations, the youth and women's wings of parties, and the TFU have all at various times organized demonstrations and sent petitions demanding improved water supply or bus services, or protesting corruption in the public distribution system. The women's groups in particular have taken up campaigns to stop the sale of illicit alcohol, demand special bus services for fish-vending women, and, in far fewer instances, protest cases of sexual abuse or dowry.

These many associational routines have rarely continued for long without being punctured by some intense and dramatic event. Intervillage or intravillage feuds, or an incident such as the communal conflict of 1982,[51] have brought all such activity to a halt until the problems were settled.

Alternatively, organizational routines are enlisted into larger movements—against the setting up of a private net-making factory in 1977-78 that would displace hundreds of women net-weavers; against the construction of the harbour for mechanized vessels at Chinna Muttam in the 1980s; the frequent campaigns against unregulated trawling; and, most dramatically, the NFF's Kanyakumari March in 1989. Participation in these movements, even when they failed in their immediate aims, has left its sediment in a history of organized resistance, a rich repertoire of political methods, and a population well-rehearsed in public action.[52]

Dialogues and Demonstrations

The Trawler Wars

The first mention of a conflict around the trawlers in the records of the KK police station came in 1977 (1971 in Colachel), although the first boat burnings date to the 1950s.[53] Police records show a steady stream through the years of petitions in court, "peace talks" between the two parties, and, in 1987 and 1989, the burning of trawlers. The "peace talks" refer to talks between the two parties held on neutral grounds such as the Revenue office, the Collectorate, sometimes the Bishop's office, and in the presence usually of a group of officers. Each party put forth its demands, sometimes in a separate meeting with the officers, and then the officers attempted to negotiate an agreement.

The Tamil Nadu Marine Fishing Regulation Act of 1983 laid down a free zone for trawlers (and all mechanized craft) of three nautical miles from shore, thus reserving that zone for artisanal craft. It also empowered district authorities to impose other conditions on times of operation, including seasonal bans if necessary.

Opposition to the trawlers in the Colachel region on the west coast had subsided through the 1980s as more and more men began to work on them and as they began to fish largely in Kerala. It erupted again in 1991 with the declaration of the monsoon ban on trawling in Kerala, and after that erupted summer after summer during the period of May-June to August-September, when the trawlers returned to the district. This struggle also prompted the formation of the Vallam Union.

As the number of trawlers operating from the Chinna Muttam harbour near Kanyakumari village began to increase incrementally by the beginning of the 1990s, opposition to them in the village intensified. Unlike in Colachel, where a majority of the trawler owners were fishers themselves, a good percentage of the new owners in Chinna Muttam and KK were not fishermen, but teachers, merchants, Gulf returnees, and others who had no experience of the fishery. The men they hired to work on their trawlers were *kattumaram* fishermen who continued to alternate working on their own or other people's *kattumarams* and working on the trawlers.

In 1993 the Kanyakumari district administration declared a ban on monsoon trawling but was unable to monitor its implementation, and trawlers were sighted in flagrant violation of the ban. KK village conducted two road blockages calling for the ban to be implemented, and at a subsequent peace meeting village committee members won an agreement, which they decided to uphold as law. They then erected a stone near the entrance to the church with the following inscription in Tamil:

Notice to the General Public of KK Fishing Village

At a meeting at the District Revenue Officer's office, Nagercoil, on 20-8-1993, in the presence of the DRO, the Assistant Superintendent of Police, the Circle Officer, Tahsildar, Assistant Director Fisheries, Kanyakumari, MLA [member of the state legislature], and Police Inspector, representatives of the kattumaram workers of the six villages affiliated with Kanyakumari village and representatives of the trawler owners of Kanyakumari village, having spoken together, have jointly and unanimously agreed on the following decisions:

1. Every year from 15 May (1st of the Tamil month of Vaikasi) till 31 August (15th of the Tamil month of Aavani), there should be no trawling;
2. On all other days of the year, trawlers must go out to fish at 6 a.m. and return to harbour at 6 p.m.
3. Trawl nets should be operated only beyond a 5 km zone from the shore.
4. If a trawler destroys the net of a kattumaram as it crosses its path, complete compensation for all damage should be paid by the owner of the trawler.

Signed:
Parish Priest, Kanyakumari village and the people of the six villages of
1. Kanyakumari
2. Mel Manakudy
3. Keezh Manakudy
4. Kovalam
5. Chinna Muttam
6. Arockiapuram

Villagers then felt that these rules were, quite literally, "written in stone," and the decisions became the basis of all subsequent negotiations. The church was the obvious site for the stone, for it was the central social and political space of the village. As an imposing piece of architecture, with its white spires looming tall against the blue sea as travellers by bus approach the Cape, the church is also much visited by tourists; the stone inscription placed there was thus also a declaration of the village's resolve to the wider public.

In the early months of 1995 villagers began to note more and more transgressions by trawlers that were straying inshore, returning well after 6 p.m., or staying out for a number of days, destroying nets and then refusing to pay adequate compensation. In February-March, talks began to be held between the villagers and trawler owners in the presence of the District Revenue Officer.

On March 6, the day before a new round of talks, trawler owners made a physical attack ("with hands," as the police reports say) on three *kattumaram* fishers. *Kattumaram* fishers in general then refused to attend the talks the next day. When the trawler owners returned, they found that the village crier had been sent around to make an announcement telling people not to go fishing that day. They descended on the parish priest and questioned him about why he had allowed this—going so far as to pull him by his cassock. The *kattumaram* fishers, enraged, gathered in two contingents to attack, and war broke out. Some houses belonging to trawler owners were attacked and damaged. After the police were called in, most people fled to the seashore, though some continued to stay and pelt stones. (Villagers' and police reports on the incident differ.) The police fired and one man was injured. The police continued to maintain a post outside the village—they would never dare to go to the seashore because the threat of being thrown into the sea is an old and oft-repeated one.

That night some 45 huts belonging to *kattumaram* fishers were burnt down. Many of the people living in these homes located in the poorest section of the village worked as coolies rather than owning their own crafts, and many of the houses were made of thatch. A village meeting was called for 4 a.m., and some thousand people gathered. In the days following, no one slept at nights. Groups patrolled the streets, and every house had *chukku* (dried ginger) coffee and betel nuts to offer patrollers. On March 26 another 15 houses belonging to *kattumaram* workers were set on fire.

On April 1, some 35 men bathing in the tanks and ponds outside the village were rounded up for damaging the boat owners' houses. Many of those arrested were schoolboys or youth, and there was no evidence to point to them particularly as the perpetrators of the crime, although some of them may have been involved. The villagers claimed that this was the only way the police could hope to make any arrests—by swooping down on the men outside the village. If they had come into the village with specific search warrants, not only would they never have been able to find the right men, but such an arbitrary roundup would also have been impossible given that they would have been outnumbered and threatened with death at sea.

Instantly, consultations began in the village, with the parish priest as key participant. It was decided, with his agreement, that the women should mount a protest, because it would not have been safe for the men to do so. That very night the women took over the main highway that runs by the village to the Cape. The road was blocked with nets and *kattumarams*.

The committee of representatives from the six contiguous villages was set into action, and the parish priest of the neighbouring village of Kovalam became very involved. The parish priests of KK and Kovalam rushed back and forth between the village and the highway to consult with the women and then with others by phone.[54] The other six villages also went on strike and held up buses. The Vallam Union was called for assistance, but the villagers found that organization's legalism and moderation unacceptable and decided not to heed its advice. In later interviews both sides expressed frustration and dissatisfaction with each other. The Vallam Union called the villagers hot-headed and stupid. Meanwhile, various officials—the District Revenue Officer, the Assistance Director of Fisheries—kept phoning the parish priest, who refused to influence the people. The MLA, a member of the ADMK, also advised them to hold firm, saying that they had no power but people's power and the only way they could achieve anything was if they continued to display their strength. The local MP, a Congress (I) member, also reportedly spoke on behalf of the *kattumaram* fishers.

Nearly a thousand women were present at the peak of the action. Those who did not participate were threatened with being denied access to the communal water taps. The women remained at their post for three days and nights, the young unmarried ones being sent home every night. Children were suckled on the highway, and women took turns going home to look after their families' needs. Prominent women of the village—organizers for various associations, those who had been vocal on this issue in the past—led the slogan shouting and singing.

Finally, on the third day, the Collector arrived at the scene and addressed the women from his car. They asked him why he did not alight. He replied that he was scared of getting enmeshed in their nets. They shouted at him, addressing him familiarly (*nii*) instead of respectfully (*niingaL*), and like a young boy—(*vaa Daa—po Daa*). They asked him what he had done with the suitcase of money (bribe) the trawler owners had paid him. One of the women told me later that they had heard about this from the trawler owners, who were boasting that they had paid the Collector many thousands of rupees. Since they were often related and lived close to each other, there were few secrets between the *kattumaram* fishers and the trawler owners. The Collector told them to hurry up and move. He was hot and tired from standing in the sun for so long (an hour). They were unmoved and scoffed at him for this—they had been sitting on that hot road for three days now. Finally, he agreed with the parish priest to have the 35 men released.

After this, four representatives from the village—two men from the committee and two outspoken women—went to Madras to see the fisheries minister. Their MLA got them the appointment. They told the minister: "Our *kal vettu* [stone inscription] is the law in our village. We can't change it. If you change it, your law will remain in your office, it can't be implemented in our village." They warned him about what a decision against them could mean for the party's political support, because Kanyakumari had always been an ADMK *kooTTai* (fortress). In response, the Commissioner of the Department of Fisheries in Madras came to survey the situation and meet with the contending parties. His decision was to maintain the status quo, which was to uphold the ban on night trawling and monsoon trawling and maintain a trawler-free zone.

Trawler owners filed a request for a stay in the High Court on the grounds that by hiring as many as 10 men on 140 trawlers they were providing employment to over 1,400 men, who would otherwise be unemployed. The *kattumaram* fishers hotly contested this, saying that all those employed on the trawlers also worked on *kattumarams*. The workers supported their stand. The village committee issued a writ prohibiting any of them from working on the trawlers during the monsoon, to prove to the trawlers that they did not need their employment. One of the committee members said: "This is the season when the fish come closer to the shore to spawn. To let coolies [hired labour] work on the trawls at this time would be to let a hundred people murder in the place of one."

Later, on April 16, the trawlers did go out for a day, and the *kattumaram* fishers launched a massive attack on their houses. They also issued a village writ saying that no one should buy the fish the trawlers brought back or they would not be allowed church rites.[55] One of the largest processing and marketing companies, belonging to a man from the village, obeyed the writ because the man had aging parents who might have needed their last rites. The Chinna Muttam Trawler Union stood divided, with those who had been *kattumaram* or mechanized gill-net fishers themselves willing to observe the monsoon ban, and the new entrants to the fishery resisting. The former group could take up other types of fishing during the period and therefore faced less loss of income. One man was forced to sign his agreement with the village when his mother died and was refused burial by the village committee. By July, 33 trawler owners had signed agreements with the village.

The village committee had met nightly throughout this period.

Since they were fishing at night during that season, they would meet from 8 p.m. to midnight and then go out to sea. Some 12 men were present at one of the meetings I attended in July. They kept no minutes, but the leader did outline the agenda for the evening, which included settling a fight between two men in the village. The men were called in and their statements heard, and the more powerful of the two was censured for having picked the fight with someone of lower social standing. Finances were discussed. The president of one of the *sangams* was called in and asked if the *sangam* could contribute to the committee's expenses. He said he would have to consult with his executive. The *sangams* in the village had already lent some Rs.80,000 to the village for their expenses in the conflict. The committee members planned to collect *terippu* (tithe) the coming Saturday: 10 percent of the catch for the day would be collected from all *kattumaram* and *vallam* fishers in the village. This was to go towards regular village expenses such as the monthly church electricity bill. But this time more than one *terippu* a month might be required to pay for the costs of the conflict. Then there was a discussion about the need for someone to go to Madras to check whether the trawler owners had filed a writ in the High Court and what its status was. This would mean a loss of four or five days' income during a good fishing season. One of the men was selected to go, and it was agreed that his family would be paid Rs.100 a day, though it was recognized that this was not really adequate compensation during a time when a fisher could earn as much as Rs.1,000 a day.

The Campaign against Deep-Sea Fishing

Decisions regarding the campaign against the deep-sea fishing policy were taken during 1994-95 at meetings of the National Fisheries Action Committee against Joint Ventures and transmitted to its member organizations. In Kanyakumari, while the Tamil Nadu Fishworkers' Union, which was affiliated to the NFF, had become weak and somewhat ineffective, the diocese supported the campaign and sent a representative to the NFACJV meetings wherever they were held.

In Kanyakumari most major actions were nationally planned. A district action committee was convened by the priest who had attended the NFACJV meetings. This consisted of the diocesan Director of the Basic Christian Communities and other BCC activists; a few other interested priests; a bank officer and activist of the CPI(M)-affiliated Science Forum; and representatives of a few other voluntary organizations. Representatives of the fish merchants and the fishermen's co-operatives were invited but never attended, although they did participate in the strikes.

The BCC provided funds and staff time for mail-outs and the like, but the paid staff of the TFU did much of the legwork. Staff members prepared a street play with youth from the villages and took it to many of the coastal villages, where it was performed in schools or churches. The parish priest of one of the villages wrote and acted in another play, entitled "One Whale or a Thousand Anchovies?" which was performed during the celebration of the feast day of the village patron saint. Another parish priest made a short video film explaining what the deep-sea fishing scheme could mean to artisanal fishers and had it broadcast by cable in a number of the villages. The BCC wrote up the issue in one of its weekly newsletters, which was distributed for discussion in the village BCC meetings. The Bishop sent out a circular in his capacity as the chair of the Labour Commission of the Catholic Bishop's Conference of India (CBCI), calling on local priests and other dioceses to support the campaign. A small number of posters and leaflets were printed due to the limited funds raised locally for the campaign, but in the days before the strike a van toured some of the villages broadcasting the event and calling on people to attend the demonstration in Nagercoil.

The political settings of the campaign generated a variety of political initiatives, including building alliances, providing information, and mounting protest actions.

Building alliances. Two TFU organizers, both women and one of them a nun, went to meet office-holders of the Chinna Muttam Trawler Owners and Employees Union to solicit their involvement in the actions being planned at the district level. They only tried to meet those they knew personally, and so went to the home of the treasurer, a man named V. He was quite supportive of the idea of a two-day strike to be held in November 1994. He said that catches had been very low that year and agreed that the size of fish had become smaller and certain species had disappeared altogether. He said that Taiwanese ships had already been sighted fishing inshore. He said that the TFU organizers should send a letter regarding the information meeting planned for the following week and the upcoming strike to the union office and that they would support it.

Another man present was more adversarial. He said that so far the priests and other activists had been setting the *kattumaram* and trawler operators against each other, and it was unrealistic to expect them to unite now. He was clearly more politically astute than the treasurer and so was less willing to accept that there had been a decline in catch, although he conceded that the increase in the number of fishers had resulted in reducing the catch for each party. He said that other factors, such as a shift in currents, were responsible for the disappearance of some species.

No representatives of the Chinna Muttam Union ever attended any of the meetings or demonstrations. However, parish priests announced the contents of the Bishop's circular at Sunday mass, and the same social links that made difficult any secrets between the two parties in the trawler wars ensured that the trawler operators were well aware of the risks the new policy posed to them. Consequently, they did observe the called strikes.

Providing information. An information meeting was organized by the District Action Committee and held in a meeting room of a lodge (hotel) in Nagercoil. The speakers were two well-known organizers in the field of small-scale fisheries, from outside the district. JJ, an organizer with a small leftist consciousness-raising group, chaired.

Present were some 25 people, five of them from the TFU. The others were from the CPI(M)-affiliated union—CITU, the Science Forum, the Tamil press, clergy, including the directors of the BCC and the KSSS, other voluntary organizations such as the Kanya Pengal Iyakkam (Kanyakumari Women's Organization) and the Praxis Group, and the CPI(M)-affiliated legal adviser to the Vallam Union. Of those present four were women, besides one of the speakers.

The speakers presented the facts of the policy and why it was to be opposed. Those present asked for clarification. The CITU members especially wanted clarification on how the issue was understood politically, that is, whether in terms of political corruption of the ministers concerned or in terms of "globalization of capital." There seemed to be general agreement in favour of the latter. There was some debate on local strategy and what kinds of actions would work, with many urging at least a symbolic demonstration in Nagercoil on the days of the strike, because a strike restricted to the coastal areas was not as likely to get media coverage. No decisions were taken at the meeting, which lasted over two hours. Some of the fishermen present said they had learned a lot from it and that more such meetings should be organized.

Protest actions. A women's *dharna* was held outside the Collectorate. As required by law, police permission had been obtained to conduct the *dharna*. The police were present, some five or six of them, including two women. Also present was the CID (Central Investigation Division—the government intelligence agency) officer. He was well-known to some of the older activists, who were happy enough to tell him what he needed to know.

The *dharna* was supposed to start at 10 a.m. Women began gathering around the tea shop opposite the Collectorate. Some of the activists were already there. Gradually some 80 women gathered, most of them from the eight or nine villages where either the TFU or Kanya Pengal Iyakkam had some following. The majority of the women were fish vendors, older women, often widows, used to having to fight for space—at the fish auctions on the beach where they bought their fish, on the buses where the conductors readily offloaded them if other passengers complained that their fish smelled, in the markets where they hawked their fish. Many seemed to have been released by their age and trade from the norms of modest feminine demeanour; they had strong voices, no-nonsense attitudes, and a biting, irreverent wit.

At 11 a.m. the gathering crossed the road, planning to go into the Collectorate compound (the shed constructed to house protest was occupied by CITU-led unemployed people calling for job creation). But the police stopped them and they had to stand on the fairly wide sidewalk in front of the gate. JJ then addressed them, saying that the sea belonged to the fishing communities, and that foreign vessels would displace them. Then one of the TFU activists said a few words. Following this the animator of the Kanya Pengal Iyakkam started leading the slogans: "hit not, hit not, hit not fish-workers in their stomach," "the district officers are good only for grinding dough [women's work]," and other rude lines about politicians, government officers, and academics (degree holders). The women were animated and acted out things like grinding dough.

At about 11:35 JJ decided the group had done enough and that people should go home. The police and the CID had probably suggested this to him. First everyone was asked to move back across the road to near the tea shop. This upset the women, including the leaders from the TFU and Kanya Pengal Iyakkam, so ten minutes later people were moved back but asked to sit near the gate. After some more sloganeering, JJ again decided it was time to stop. But the women would have none of it and said they could not go home until they had presented a memorandum to the Collector—and, after all, what else had they come for? The TFU secretary hastily drafted a memo and took it to the shop opposite to have it typed. Then a group consisting of two nuns active in the BCC (they had been very vocal in shouting slogans), JJ, two TFU activists, and both the Kanya Pengal animators went to see the Collector. Meanwhile, a woman from one of the village units took up the slogans. A TFU organizer thought of singing the closing song from their street play and having a woman from one of the villages give the closing speech saying that this was the first step and there would be many more if their demands were not conceded. The TFU organizers sang each line with many gestures, and the women repeated them. It was all very moving, and even the police looked interested, if not quite touched.

Meanwhile the group returned and said they had not been able to see the Collector, but would wait and give him the petition. JJ again asked the women to leave, but they were angry and said they still wanted a response from the Collector. An organizer took up the slogans again but, before she could make her speech, the parish priest of KK village, who was there with a group from his village on other work, came up and also started telling the women to leave. Some women got up, but others were not willing to leave without getting a response. They were frank and forthright with the organizers and made clear their displeasure at being asked to move around and leave prematurely.

A number of other protest actions were organized. The two-day national strike called by the NFACJV in November 1994 was observed throughout the district. A men's *dharna* did not get off the ground because organizers had neglected to seek police permission. The final action of that phase of the campaign was a relay fast, with people from different villages fasting for a day, held in solidarity with the fast by Thomas Kocherry in Porbandar. The fast was called off after eight days when Kocherry and other national leaders were invited to Delhi for talks with the concerned minister.

Conclusion

The situation in the Indian fishery requires us to qualify what we mean by "globalization." Indian fishworkers have been producing for the world market for close to three decades now and are dependent for their livelihoods upon its fluctuations. If globalization refers to the intensification of social relations so that the local is shaped by distant events,[56] this process was already well underway before the adoption of the new deep-sea fishing policy. The entry of foreign fleets fishing solely for export, in an area where the monitoring capacities of the Indian state were negligible, posed a significant threat to the state's sovereignty over its resources. It not only marked a new stage in the process of incorporation into a global economy, but also created new opportunities to resist that change.

Production for foreign markets created more leverage for old forms of protest, such as the two-day national fisheries strike in November 1994. In the absence of economically powerful employers for the most part, and in a sector that, unlike food grains, cannot be dubbed "essential," work stoppages in the fishery would have had little political significance in the past. But with the increase of export earnings from the fishery, the state could now be expected to respond to prevent their decline.

The NFACJV leadership made full use of the opportunities created by this move to open up India's seas to foreign vessels and took full advantage of the space provided by nationalist sentiment, the tensions between the different levels and imperatives of the state, and the structures of liberal democracy. It made, for instance, the argument that the access of foreign fleets to India's EEZ could be a potential threat to "national security" and that it was not in the "national interest." This was a skilled move, for liberalizers and protectionists alike seemed to agree on security interests.

The skill of the leadership can also be seen in its bringing together of the artisanal and the mechanized sector. Neither sees itself as having given up the older antagonism permanently, and both recognize that their alliance is fragile. Yet they work together with a basic understanding: "We cannot wait until all the contradictions have been overcome before we begin to organize. We must work with the contradictions and in spite of them."[57]

The deep-sea fishing policy seems to have had few national supporters. The national companies that had entered into joint ventures or were interested in doing so did not constitute an overwhelming lobby. Nor did the policy promise jobs. Its sole contribution was to be in terms of foreign exchange. Nationalist sentiment could be persuaded to oppose a policy with no obvious benefits to any domestic constituency and significant potential harm to a sizeable one, the eight million fishworkers. For instance, the Parliamentary Standing Committee on Commerce, in its Report on Marine Products, declared, "In spite of several hours of examination of dialogue with the Ministry of Food Processing Industries [it was] unable to appreciate the rationale behind the present policy of Joint Ventures in deep sea fishing," and the "fears of the traditional fishing community are well founded." It concluded, "The Committee would certainly want the Government to appreciate the sentiments of our traditional fishermen and modify the policy accordingly."[58]

As important as the lack of a domestic constituency for the policy was the weakness of the international lobby for it. No major new investments had been made, because it was largely a case of redeploying ships lying idle elsewhere, and a significant number of the companies involved were South Korean, Taiwanese, and East European rather than the big U.S. or British multinationals.[59]

With regard to trawling, various scholars, and even fisheries officials I spoke to, have pointed to the contradictions of the state's stand on medium-scale mechanization of the fishery.[60] The commitment of policy-makers to modernization, in the fishery as in all areas of the economy, had led to the provision of all manner of financial and infrastructural support to the mechanized sector. At the same time, legislators dependent on the continued electoral support of their constituencies sought to represent the views of the numerically more significant community of artisanal fishers. The result has been constant equivocation, "peace committees" that seek temporary and local arrangements instead of an enforceable state legislation, "inquiry committees" set up to "examine the matter." Pointing out that "The decision to mediate and not to legislate reflects the contradictions inherent in the state," S.S. Sivakumar et al. argue that any lasting solution is prevented by the politicians' need to keep the issue alive.[61]

The contradiction is not only between policy-maker and politician. It lies within the nature of the policies itself, reflecting the contradictions inherent in the goals set out for fisheries modernization: increased production through "modern" technology at the same time as improvement of the living standards of the fishing community. Thus subsidies have been given not only to assist mechanization but also for the acquisition of OBMs for small craft. The ability of motorized craft to go longer distances increases the area of competition between them and the mechanized trawlers, as well as driving up their costs and thus increasing their need for higher returns.

The ideology of modernization and the view of the artisanal fishers as "backward" is one shared by a cross-section of the general public, including activists and intellectuals in the left-wing associations and the CPI(M) who opposed the deep-sea fishing policy. The mechanization of the fishery is seen as necessary and inevitable. For instance, the villagers of KK argued that the press had been entirely in the trawler owners' favour and that they themselves had been portrayed as ignorant and unruly. Thus the artisanal fishers are unable to draw on support from the wider public. The caste- and community-bound nature of the artisanal fishery has also prevented broad-based links with other sectors of rural "toilers."

Like the NFACJV and the NFF, the people of KK related to the state in complex ways, questioning its legitimacy and sovereignty, yet using its institutions. Village law had sovereignty over that of the state. The group that went to see the fisheries minister in Madras told him: "Our stone inscription is the law here. We can't change it. If you change it, your law will remain in your office, it can't be implemented in our village." Later I was also told: "The three-month trawling ban is not in the Tamil Nadu Marine Fishing Regulation Act, but it is our village regulation and is for the well-being of our village." The village committee was able to issue writs and enforce them through denying the entitlements of membership in the village community: access to the water outlet, church rites. Meanwhile, the state's regulations were routinely flouted by its citizens, the trawler owners. The state's legitimacy based on claims of acting democratically or fairly was contested. In public speeches and private conversations about the conflict, people would ask rhetorically, "Is this a democracy?" (*itu jananaayakam aa?*), "Is this justice?" (*itu niyaayam aa?*). The Collector was openly accused of being corrupt and accepting bribes from the trawler owners.

The productivist bias of state policy was critiqued for its impact on equity and social justice. The trawler owners ascribed the opposition of the villagers to "relations of envy,"[62] but those who had enriched themselves in other ways, through trade or through work in the Gulf, were never the objects of such violent envy. Rather, the basis of the opposition is contained in the rhetorical question, always posed in discussions with the *kattumaram* fishers, "Should ten people be allowed to get rich at the expense of a hundred?" It lies in an understanding of the fishery as a finite resource, the too "efficient" exploitation of which by a few leaves less for the many. When I suggested that the solution might be assistance for all fishers to acquire trawlers, I was told, "And will there be enough fish for that? The government encourages us to 'develop,' to buy trawlers. But can we all do so? Can everyone own a plane or even fly in one?"

The police were reviled and not allowed into the village. Yet both parties made constant visits to the police station to file complaints against each other. They regularly called for peace talks in the presence of district administrative officials and filed writs against each other in the High Court. Well aware of the tensions between the dictates of state policy and the electoral vulnerabilities of elected representatives, villagers sought out their MPs and MLAs for assistance, and threatened them and other ministers with withdrawal of electoral support. Although they acknowledged some truth in Sivakumar et al.'s suggestion that it was in the interests of the politicians to keep the problem alive and to favour mediation over legislation, villagers seemed unwilling to indict the party system, preferring to see in their electoral strength a source of power for themselves. For them the problem lay not so much in the reluctance of the provincial government to legislate more comprehensively, as in the prevarication of the administrative authorities in enforcing legislation.

Clearly, neither struggle "underestimated the centrality and complexity of the state." However, both worked, not outside and against a monolithic state, but within the crevices and openings created by the contradictions between the different levels and imperatives of the state. It was by "seizing on the fissures and ruptures, the contradictions in the policies, programs, institutions, and discourse of 'the state'" that they were able to "create possibilities for political action and activism."[63]

The struggle against the trawlers was not resolved, nor did it succeed in creating consensus within the wider public about the rightness of its demands. Yet the villagers of KK did not experience the fight against trawling as a failure or defeat, but as a source of "empowerment." Objectively, too, it may be seen as having contributed to the building of what Ponna Wignaraja calls "countervailing power," the living, collective consciousness of the people, their vigilance against the abuse of formal power.[64] People can gain a sense of power and efficacy even from struggles that may not succeed in winning major concessions or lasting solutions.[65] Constant engagement succeeds in expanding the space within which "countervailing power" may be built.

Both struggles drew on the existing "popular democratic" spaces created by other organizations—by the progressive local diocese, for instance.[66] While much of the work for the local deep-sea fishing campaign was carried out by the TFU, the union affiliated to the NFF, it was coordinated by a group of priests and publicized through the BCCs. The Bishop's circular calling on the diocese to support the deep-sea fishing campaign was key in getting trawler owners to observe the strike, although they were also aware of the national alliance of other mechanized craft groups and artisanal fishers. In the trawler wars, KK villagers drew heavily for financial support on their fishermen's co-operative *sangams*.

The generative role of these popular democratic spaces becomes clearest when we examine the prominence of women in both struggles. Theorists have argued that women's close involvement in production, consumption, and social life, in communities of primary resource harvesters, such as forest dwellers, fisherfolk, and peasants, makes the growing threat from international markets to livelihood and consumption a strong motivation for them to act.[67] But the confidence and skills they bring to that action depend very much on their prior political participation. Women in KK are explicitly excluded from traditional bodies such as the KK village committee, as well as from fishermen's associations, such as the Vallam Union, and they are rarely present at the official peace talks. Yet their participation in popular democratic settings, many of them church-sponsored, such as the BCCs, and the various thrift and credit organizations, as well as in the spaces created by liberal democracy, such as the women's wings of political parties, has schooled them in public action.

The women staff of the TFU did much of the mobilizing for the deep-sea fishing campaign, and they and other activist women participated in street plays, made speeches, and led slogans. In KK, two of the strongest women leaders, who went to Madras as part of the group of four to meet the ministers, were active in the women's wing of the ADMK party, and had been in the TFU and various pious associations. The women's belief in the importance of their participation was expressed in the much-repeated statement, "The committee men can be bought off, but now that we women have woken up, we will not give in."

The trawling struggle in KK also succeeded in opening up and utilizing new political settings. It was action-packed, fast-paced. Every space became politicized: the beachfront, the lanes between houses, the houses themselves, the church, the highway. No police permission was sought to occupy these spaces. The Collector was forced to come to the women to persuade them to move. The KK parish priest was drawn into the struggle on the side of the large majority of his parishioners, who expected him to exert himself strenuously on their behalf. He could not persuade the women to get off the road—he did not even try, though the officials requested him to. The local fishermen's *sangams* were called upon to contribute financially to the cause.

In contrast to the struggle against trawling, the deep-sea fishing campaign in Kanyakumari district was conducted formally, in sites commonly agreed upon as "political"—meeting halls, the Collectorate. Police permission had to be sought to occupy the Collectorate, and when it was not obtained the demonstration was not held. The Collector remained in his office and the petitioners had to wait to see him. The KK parish priest, who happened to be there, was able to get the demonstrating women to leave when the police decided they had stayed long enough.

For all that the deep-sea fishing campaign was a "campaign" and by definition time-bound, intense, and concerted, in Kanyakumari it nonetheless reflected a state of "normal" or "routine" politics. As Subrata K. Mitra argues, certain forms of political protest, frequently of "uncertain legality," such as the hunger fast or the *dharna* outside the Collectorate, have become routine forms of political representation in India and as such may be seen as part of the mechanisms of liberal democracy.[68] In contrast, the state of politicization during the trawler wars may best be described as "heightened" or "riven"[69]—a state in which the normal limits of action and assurances of safety and predictability have disappeared. The boundaries of political settings break down in a continual, shifting, meeting-action process, and new "ad hoc" settings such as the meetings on the beach or the attacks on the houses are generated. The forms these ad hoc settings take are not always new, but draw upon an established repertoire of actions. The settings of "normal" politics, such as the peace talks, then try to reassert themselves and contain the emotions and conflicts that are breaking down the boundaries. But once opened, the new settings may be hard to shut down irreversibly.

Notes

1. "Struggle" is the term used by the fishing communities in Kanyakumari, and by the movement generally. In any case, it is more apt for the conflict over trawling than the term "campaign."
2. Amrita Basu, "Grassroots Movements and the State: Reflections on Radical Change in India," *Theory and Society* 16 (1987), pp.670, 667.
3. Akhil Gupta, "Blurred Boundaries: The Discourse of Corruption, the Culture of Politics, and the Imagined State," *American Ethnologist* 22 (1995), p.378; Joel Migdal, Atul Kohli, and Vivienne Shue, eds., *State Power and Social Forces* (Cambridge: Cambridge University Press, 1994); and Warren Magnusson, *The Search for Political Space: Globalization, Social Movements and the Urban Political Experience* (Toronto: University of Toronto Press, 1996), p.9.
4. On the fishworkers' movement, see Basu, "Grassroots Movements and the State"; Madhav Gadgil and Ramachandra Guha, "Ecological Conflicts and the Environmental Movement in India," *Development and Change* 25,1 (1994); Gail

Omvedt, *Reinventing Revolution* (New York: M.E. Sharpe, 1994); Harsh Sethi, "Survival and Democracy: Ecological Struggles in India," in *New Social Movements in the South: Empowering the People,* ed. Ponna Wignaraja (London: Zed Books, 1993); Ghanshyam Shah, "Grass-roots Mobilization in Indian Politics," in *India's Democracy: An Analysis of Changing State-Society Relations,* ed. Atul Kohli (Princeton, N.J.: Princeton University Press, 1988); Vandana Shiva, "Fisheries and Conflicts at Sea," in Vandana Shiva, *Ecology and the Politics of Survival: Conflicts over Natural Resources in India* (New Delhi: Sage, 1991). However, the only account examining the dynamics of meetings and negotiations for representation within the movement comes from a key activist of the movement: Nalini Nayak, "The Kerala Fishworkers' Struggle," in *A Space within the Struggle,* ed. Ilina Sen (New Delhi: Kali, 1990). Patricia Kuruvinakunnel, "'Fire on the Seashore': Struggle of Fisherwomen in Kerala," *Manushi* 37 (1987); P.M. Mathew, "Politics of a 'Non-Political' Struggle," *Economic and Political Weekly (EPW)*, Aug. 25, 1984, and Susan Visvanathan, "The Fishing Struggle in Kerala," *Seminar* 423 (1994), also provide good details of specific actions and profiles of participants in the Kerala movement. Recent accounts of how communities manage the fishery as a common property resource, such as Maarten Bavinck, "Fisher Regulations along the Coromandel Coast: A Case of Collective Control of Common Pool Resources," *Marine Policy* 20,6 (1996), and John Kurien, "Income Spreading Mechanisms in Common Property Resource: Karanila System in Kerala's Fishery," *EPW*, July 15, 1995, also detail the local political fields they open up.

5. For studies of other movements that discuss the tensions between the various levels of the movement, or between the movement and villages drawn into it, see Amrita Basu, *Two Faces of Protest: Contrasting Modes of Women's Activism in India* (Berkeley: University of California Press, 1992), on the Shetkari Sangathana in Maharashtra; and Amita Baviskar, *In the Belly of the River: Tribal Conflicts over Development in the Narmada Valley* (New Delhi: Oxford University Press, 1995) on the Save Narmada Movement in Madhya Pradesh.

6. Magnusson, *Search for Political Space*, p.91.

7. James Manor, ed., *Rethinking Third World Politics* (New York: Longman, 1991), pp.2-4.

8. Gupta, "Blurred Boundaries," p.377.

9. Food and Agriculture Organization of the United Nations (FAO), *Yearbook of Fisheries Statistics, 1993*, Rome, 1995; "The Unique Struggle of the Fishworkers," *Labour File* (New Delhi: Centre for Education and Communication) 2,7&8 (July-August 1996), p.13.

10. John Kurien, "Technical Assistance Projects and Socio-economic Change: Norwegian Intervention in Kerala's Fisheries Development," *EPW*, June 22-29, 1985. On the role of international agencies in fisheries development, see Kurien, "Technical Assistance Projects"; Connor Bailey, Dean Cycon, and Michael Morris, "Fisheries Development in the Third World: The Role of International Agencies," *World Development* 14,10-11 (1986); and Knut Pelzer, *Mechanisation of Indigenous Fishing Crafts: The Indo-Belgian Fisheries Project at Muttom—A Statistical Study*, publication no.5 (Nagercoil: KSSS, 1971).

11. In the precolonial period, the state intervened in the fishing economy chiefly as tax collector. For fisheries in the colonial period, see Peter Reeves, "The Colonial State and the Indian Fishing Industry: Attempts to Restructure Artisanal Production, Processing and Distribution, c.1860-1950," paper presented at the Association for Asian Studies Conference, New Orleans, Louisiana, April 11-14, 1991; and Peter Reeves, Andrew Pope, John McGuire, and Bob Pokrant, "Mapping India's Marine Resources: Colonial State Experiments, c.1908-1930," *South Asia* 19,1 (1996).

12. John Kurien, "Ruining the Commons and Responses of the Commoners: Coastal Overfishing and Fishworkers' Actions in Kerala State, India," in *Grassroots Environmental Action: People's Participation in Sustainable Development*, ed. Dharam Ghai and Jessica M. Vivian (London: Routledge, 1992), p.224; Kurien, "Technical Assistance Projects," pp.A-72; N. Subba Rao, *Mechanisation and Marine Fishermen: A Case Study of Vishakapatnam* (New Delhi: Northern Book Centre, 1988).

13. Mechanization of craft in the western states of Gujarat and Maharashtra, for instance, seems to have occurred by and large without the sharp social differentiation and conflict it generated in other states, such as Goa—Robert S. Newman, "Green Revolution—Blue Revolution: The Predicament of India's Traditional Fishermen," *South Asia*, new series 4,1 (1981); Andhra Pradesh—Subba Rao, *Mechanisation and Marine Fishermen*; Kerala—Kurien, "Ruining the Commons and Responses of the Commoners"; and Tamil Nadu—S.S. Sivakumar et al., "From Toori to Thirty-Footer: A Preliminary Study of the Political Economy of Fishing in Tamil Nadu," *Bulletin*, Madras Development Seminar Series, 1979.

14. Kurien, "Technical Assistance Projects," pp.A-74-76.

15. Kurien, "Technical Assistance Projects," pp.A-79-80; Wicky Meynen, "Fisheries Development, Resources Depletion and Political Mobilization in Kerala: The Problem of Alternatives," *Development and Change* 20 (1989); Nalini Nayak, *Continuity and Change in Artisanal Fishing Communities: A Study of Socio-Economic Conditions of Artisanal Fishing Communities on the South West Coast of India following Motorisation of Fishing Crafts* (Trivandrum, Kerala: PCO, 1993); PCO and SIFFS, *Motorisation of Fishing Units: Benefits and Burdens* (Trivandrum, Kerala, 1991); and Pelzer, *Mechanisation of Indigenous Fishing Crafts*.

16. For a careful political economic analysis of these changes, see Jean-Philippe Platteau, "Penetration of Capitalism and Persistence of Small-scale Organizational Forms in Third World Fisheries," *Development and Change* 20 (1989); Kurien, "Technical Assistance Projects"; and John Kurien, "Entry of Big Business into Fishing: Its Impact on Fish Economy," *EPW*, Sept. 9, 1978. For an explanation of why small-scale forms of organizing production persist even in a "modern" fishery, see Jean-Philippe Platteau, "The Dynamics of Fisheries Development in Developing Countries: A General Overview," *Development and Change* 20 (1989).

17. For a more detailed analysis of the "political economy of overfishing," see Kurien, "Ruining the Commons and Responses of the Commoners," pp.225-35; and John Kurien and T.R. Thankappan Achari, *On Ruining the Commons and the Commoner: The Political Economy of Overfishing*, Working Paper no.232 (Trivandrum, Kerala: Centre for Development Studies, 1989).

18. This section on deep-sea fishing policy draws from M. Giudicelli, *Study on Deep Sea Fisheries Development in India* (Rome: FAO, 1992); John Kurien, "Impact of Joint Ventures on Fish Economy," *EPW*, Feb. 11, 1995; Mukul, "Enter, the Big Fish: New Deep Sea Fishing Policy Draws Flak," *Frontline*, Aug. 26, 1994; National Fishworkers Forum (NFF), *Stop Entry of Foreign Fishing Vessels: Continuing Struggle: A Dossier*, 1995; NFF, *All India Fisheries Bandh: A Dossier*, 1994; Ajantha Subramaniam and M.H. Kalavathy, "Between the Devil and the Deep Sea: The Dilemma of Artisanal Fisherpeople," *Frontline*, Nov. 18, 1994; and Bhaskar Srinivasan, "Fishing for Famine," *NOW* (Toronto), Aug. 18-24, 1994.

19. NFF, *Stop Entry of Foreign Fishing Vessels*, pp.107-9.

20. As a result of the prawn-export boom at the end of the 1960s and the entry of big business into fishing, an indigenous deep-sea fleet has been operating off the east-coast port of Vishakapattnam since 1970. After an initial period of high profits, the heavy capitalization led to overfishing and a decline in annual landings per vessel. Of the 180 vessels licensed to fish in that area, by 1991 40 were no longer operational and only 12-14 were making an annual catch that allowed them to break even. See M. Giudicelli, *Study on Deep Sea Fisheries Development in India* (Rome: FAO, 1992); and Kurien, "Impact of Joint Ventures on Fish Economy."

21. It is now generally recognized that world fisheries are at the point of collapse, due mainly to industrial overfishing. See "The Last Frontier," *Down to Earth*, Aug. 15, 1995; "Overfishing: Its Causes and Consequences," Special Issue, *The Ecologist*, March/April, May/June 1995; and "Diminishing Returns: Exploiting the Ocean's Bounty," *National Geographic*, November 1995. *The Ecologist*, in particular, provides good analyses of causes and consequences, as well as country case studies.

22. Assistant Director (AD) Fisheries, *Statistics for Kanyakumari District*, Nagercoil, 1994.

23. Tamil Nadu Department of Fisheries, *Status Report on the Mechanisation Programme for the Development of Marine Fisheries*, Madras, 1986.

24. K.T. Thomson, "Political Economy of Fishing: A Study of an Indigenous Social System in Tamil Nadu," Ph.D. thesis, MIDS, Madras, 1989.

25. Tamil Nadu Department of Fisheries, *Endeavours and Achievements: Fisheries Statistics*, Madras, 1993, p.5.

26. Pierre Gillet, *Small Is Difficult: The Pangs and Success of Small Boat Technology Transfer in South India* (Nagercoil: Centre for Appropriate Technology, 1985); Pelzer, *Mechanisation of Indigenous Fishing Crafts*.

27. Tamil Nadu Department of Fisheries, *Endeavours and Achievements*, Madras, 1993.

28. Catch figures for the entire district are drawn from the Tamil Nadu Department of Fisheries, *Endeavours and Achievements*, Madras, for various years. Those for Colachel harbour are from the Assistant Director (AD) Fisheries, *Statistics for Kanyakumari District*, Nagercoil, 1994. One should be wary of relying too heavily on any of these numbers, since they are neither always consistent nor, as the AD himself pointed out, independent of political considerations.

29. In 1993-94, *sangam* members sold fish worth Rs.45 million through open auction on the beach, largely for domestic marketing, and Rs.30 million through export

companies. Kanyakumari District Fishermen's Sangams Federation (KKDFSF), *Annual Report 1993-94*, Nagercoil, 1994.

30. Gabriele Dietrich, "Women's Struggle for Production of Life: Public Hearings of Women Workers in Informal Sector," *EPW*, July 1, 1995; International Collective in Support of Fishworkers (ICSF), *Proceedings of the Public Hearing on Women's Struggle for Survival in the Fisheries*, Madras, 1995.

31. The largest of the protests against trawlers included a clash between the *kattumaram* fishers and trawler operators in Madras in 1976, the burning of trawlers and the death of some 16 *kattumaram* fishermen there in 1978, and a long chain-hunger strike by the small-scale *rampon* fishermen of Goa in 1977. Details of the beginning phase of the movement are drawn from Jose Kaleekal, "The National Forum," in Indian Social Institute and Delhi Forum, *Struggle to Survive: A Dossier on the Struggle of Fishermen and Fish Workers in India* (New Delhi, 1987); Kurien, "Ruining the Commons and Responses of the Commoners," pp.235-38; Mathew, "Politics of a 'Non-Political' Struggle"; Jose Murickan, *Storm on the Seashore: The Fishermen's Struggle in Kerala* (New Delhi: Indian Social Institute, 1987); and Nayak, "Kerala Fishworkers' Struggle."

32. Kurien, "Ruining the Commons and Responses of the Commoners."

33. Kurien, "Ruining the Commons and Responses of the Commoners"; NFF, *Annual Report*, various years.

34. Mathew, "Politics of a 'Non-Political' Struggle"; Visvanathan, "Fishing Struggle in Kerala."

35. Nalini Nayak, "Women Must Recover Their Spaces," interview, *ICSF Samudra Report* 10 & 11 (December 1994); and Nayak, "Kerala Fishworkers' Struggle."

36. Interestingly, the resistance to the change was based less on opposition to the inclusion of women than on the belief that this would open membership to those from non-fishing communities. Because fishing has traditionally been a caste-based occupation, the term "fisherman" in various vernaculars refers equally to the community as to the occupation. Those who opposed the name change were seeking to limit membership, and access to the fishery, to traditional fishing communities. Unfortunately, it was not just richer entrepreneurial entrants they wanted to exclude, but poorer castes seeking a livelihood in the sector. The name change does not translate perfectly—*machuara* in the Hindi name still conjures up a fisherman—but other unions have more consciously adopted "fishworker": The Kerala Independent Fish Workers (*Malsya Thozhilali*) Federation; the Tamil Nadu Fish Workers (*Meen Thozhilali*) Union.

37. K.G. Kumar, "Organizing Fisherfolk Cooperatives in Kerala," *EPW*, March 19, 1988.

38. The NFF was one of the members of the Alliance of Militant Trade Unions in 1987 and a founder member of the National Alliance of People's Movements formed in 1989; and the National Centre for Labour was set up in 1995 to study and lobby for unorganized labour in the informal sector. Some of its leading activists were also among the founders of the International Collective in Support of Fishworkers in 1986.

39. Peter Waterman, "Social-Movement Unionism: A New Union Model for a New World Order?" *Review* 16,3 (1993), pp.266-67.

40. Gadgil and Guha, "Ecological Conflicts and the Environmental Movement in India," p.121. See also Subrata K. Mitra, *Power, Protest and Participation: Local Elites and the Politics of Development in India* (London: Routledge, 1992), p.9.

41. NFF, *Protect Waters, Protect Life*, 1989; John Kurien, "Collective Action for Common Property Resource Rejuvenation: The Case of People's Artificial Reefs in Kerala State, India," *Human Organisation* 54 (1995); and John Kurien, "Greening the Coastal Sea Ecosystem: Collective Action and Renewable Resource Rejuvenation," *Bulletin*, Madras Development Seminar Series 20,12 (1990); Gillet, *Small Is Difficult*.

42. John Kurien, "Joint Action against Joint Ventures—Resistance to Multinationals in Indian Waters," *The Ecologist*, May/June 1995; "Unique Struggle of the Fishworkers"; NFF, *Stop Entry of Foreign Fishing Vessels*; and NFF, *All India Fisheries Bandh: A Dossier*, 1994.

43. "Unique Struggle of the Fishworkers."

44. Kalpana Ram, *Mukkuvar Women: Gender, Hegemony and Capitalist Transformation in a South Indian Fishing Community* (New Delhi: Kali, 1992), p.xiii.

45. A. Rajagopal, "Tamil Nadu Cooperative Movement in Peril," *EPW*, Oct. 29, 1988.

46. Ram, *Mukkuvar Women*, p.34.

47. On the reformist clergy as Gramscian "intellectuals," who participate in the state's hegemonic projects of "reform, rationalism, development and cultural nationalism," see Kalpana Ram, "Rationalism, Cultural Nationalism and the Reform of Body Politics: Minority Intellectuals of the Tamil Catholic Community," *Contributions to Indian Sociology* 29,1&2 (1995).

48. Pierre Gillet, *Ten Years of Involvement with Fisheries and Fishermen in Kanyakumari District*, publication no. 13 (Nagercoil: KSSS, 1979); Kumar, "Organizing Fisherfolk Cooperatives in Kerala"; James Tombeur, *Led by God's Hand: Reflections on my Faith Experience and Pastoral Ministry* (Trivandrum, Kerala: Nalini Nayak, 1990), pp.52-59.

49. The party acronyms here stand for Dravida Munnetra Kazhagam (DMK), Anna Dravida Munnetra Kazhagam (ADMK), and Maramallarchi Dravida Munnetra Kazhagam (MDMK). For brief, and opposed, analyses of the parties of the Dravidian movement, see V. Geetha and S.V. Rajadurai, "Dravidian Politics: End of an Era," *EPW*, June 29, 1991; and David A. Washbrook, "Caste, Class and Dominance in Modern Tamil Nadu," in *Dominance and State Power in Modern India*, ed. Francine Frankel (Delhi: Oxford University Press, 1989).

50. Sara Dickey, *Cinema and the Urban Poor in South India* (Cambridge: Cambridge University Press, 1993); M.S.S. Pandian, *The Image Trap: M.G. Ramachandran in Film and Politics* (New Delhi: Sage, 1992; and Karthigesu Sivathamby, *The Tamil Film as a Medium of Political Communication* (Madras: New Century Book House, 1981).

51. George Mathew, "Hindu Christian Communalism: An Analysis of the Kanyakumari Riots," *Social Action* 33 (October-December 1983).

52. On the 1977-78 net-making factory, see Gillet, *Ten Years of Involvement with Fisheries and Fishermen*; on the role of popular memory of resistance in fuelling fresh resistance, see Nandini Sundar, *Subalterns and Sovereigns: An Anthropological History of*

Bastar 1854-1996 (New Delhi: Oxford University Press, 1997), particularly p.249.

53. Gillet, *Ten Years of Involvement with Fisheries and Fishermen*; Thomson, "Political Economy of Fishing"; also oral reports.

54. When I praised the role of the priests to an activist from another village, she said that the parish priest of KK had no choice; he would have been physically assaulted and forced to leave the village if he had not done what the people wanted.

55. While the church would not have been able to withhold the rites if pressed, the parish priest would have wanted for his own safety not to make that clear.

56. Giddens, cited in Waterman, "Social-Movement Unionism," p.255.

57. Thomas Kocherry, personal comment.

58. Rajya Sabha, Parliament of India, *Department-Related Parliamentary Standing Committee on Commerce (1995-96)—Twenty-Fourth Report on Marine Products* (New Delhi: Rajya Sabha Secretariat, 1996), p.22.

59. This statement about greater political power for U.S. and European transnational corporations than for Asian ones calls for more discussion and theorizing.

60. Kurien, "Impact of Joint Ventures on Fish Economy," p.A-81; Sivakumar et al., "From Toori to Thirty-Footer."

61. Sivakumar et al., "From Toori to Thirty-Footer," p.591.

62. Amitav Ghosh, *The Relations of Envy in an Egyptian Village*, Working Paper no.149 (Trivandrum, Kerala: Centre for Development Studies, 1982).

63. Gupta, "Blurred Boundaries," p.394.

64. Ponna Wignaraja, ed., *New Social Movements in the South: Empowering the People* (London: Zed Books, 1993), pp.10-12.

65. See also Michael W. Foley, "Organizing, Ideology, and Moral Suasion: Political Discourse and Action in a Mexican Town," *Comparative Studies in Society and History* 32,3 (1990), p.458.

66. That organizations such as the BCCs and co-operatives need not always serve as spaces from which to penetrate the local political system can be seen from Foley's account of organizing in a Mexican town. See Foley, "Organizing, Ideology, and Moral Suasion." Here the "anarchist bent" (p.485) of the organizers, and their notion that these organizations should follow a "distinctive path not corrupted by electoral politics nor coopted by the state" (p.473), had the effect of narrowing their political effectiveness.

67. Amrita Basu, "Grassroots Movements and the State," p.659; Craig S. Benjamin and Terisa E. Turner, "Counterplanning from the Commons: Labour, Capital and the 'New Social Movements,' *LABOUR, Capital and Society* 25,2 (1992); and June Nash, "Global Integration and Subsistence Insecurity," *American Anthropologist* 96,1 (1994).

68. Mitra, *Power, Protest and Participation*, p.9. For a discussion of the relation between institutional participation and more radical forms of protest, see pp.198-205.

69. These terms were suggested to me by Jonathan Barker.

Chapter 6

Participation and Insecurity:
Small Towns in England and the United States

Jonathan Barker

Research carried out in the 1950s and 1960s in small towns in England and the United States by Roger Barker and his associates offers a rare opportunity to delve into the social infrastructure of political life—what we might call the everyday life of civil society. Because the research made full use of the idea of activity settings, and covered the whole of public activity in each of two towns in two different years a decade apart, its quantitative comparisons disclose much about the ambiguities of small-town participation in the two countries at mid-century.[1]

I have to admit that contemplating this kind of information makes a strenuous demand on us latter-day intellectuals, informed as we are by ideas of social construction, qualitative methods, and participatory research. Today we can marvel at the forthright belief in a purely naturalistic social science and the drive to measure a vast range of social qualities, but we can also mine the treasure of painstakingly collected descriptions and enumerations of ordinary and observable aspects of social action that have never before or since been so carefully treated as objects of scientific curiosity. We can learn a great deal about the depth and limits of participatory practice in the two towns and about the paradoxical fruit of broadly participatory institutions.

From this research we learn about a civil society that was familiar personally or symbolically to many of the men and women who contributed to action and thinking about democracy and political change in the postcolonial world. Oskaloosa, Kansas, is but a few hours' drive from the childhood homes of U.S. presidents Harry Truman and Dwight Eisenhower, and the values of small-town U.S.A. were dear to the hearts of social scientists brought up on Jefferson and Tocqueville and steeped in the virtues of frontier self-reliance and prairie populism. For much of the social science that attempted to fathom the emerging world, small towns of the United States and England stood as quintessential embodiments of "normal" civil society.

The civil society in question has a special historical location. The long boom that followed World War Two was taken as normal, and the Cold War was the established regime in the international political economy. It was the era of Dwight Eisenhower and Harold Macmillan; it ended with John Kennedy in office in Washington and Harold Wilson about to lead Labour to victory in the United Kingdom. Around the time of the first survey the U.S. Supreme Court ruled against segregation in public schools, the silicon chip went into production, an oral contraceptive was developed, and the French were defeated in Vietnam. The perturbations and social movements associated with these events were just beginning and hardly made themselves felt in the small towns of middle America and northern England during the time of this research.

Oskaloosa and Leyburn, 1954-63: Differences and Similarities

Both Oskaloosa, Kansas, and Leyburn, Yorkshire, were small rural towns, centres of retail trade and local government, surrounded by lightly populated countryside. They just met the requirements to be classified as "full convenience centres" in the hierarchy of trade centres.[2] Oskaloosa was a county seat and Leyburn the seat of a rural district council and a judicial district. In 1964 the population of Oskaloosa was 830 people; that of Leyburn was 1,310 people. Both were (and are) inland towns situated at similar distances (20 to 45 miles) from larger towns and cities, also of similar sizes.[3]

The towns also differed in several ways. Leyburn had a much longer history: the ruins of Bolton Castle near Leyburn dated from before 1400, while Oskaloosa's historic court house was built in 1867 and had to be replaced after it suffered tornado damage in 1960. Perhaps because it grew up in an era of travel by foot, Leyburn was a more compact town than Oskaloosa, with a population density almost 2.5 times higher; its larger population was concentrated into 260 acres compared to Oskaloosa's 400. Leyburn had rainy and cool summers; Oskaloosa's were dry and hot. Oskaloosa's streets and lots were laid out north-south and east-west in the gridiron pattern common to country roads, city streets, and farm boundaries in the region. Leyburn's narrower streets bent to the contours of the rolling landscape, as did many of the stone walls in the surrounding fields and pastures. In Oskaloosa the boundaries of property were rarely marked by fences or walls; in Leyburn stout walls and fences, with gates—362 of them—for access, stood between neighbouring households, encircled churchyards, and separated public streets from private gardens. While Oskaloosa was surrounded by isolated farms, the population in the area around Leyburn lived in small villages, each with pub, post office, general store, school, and bus stop.[4]

The two towns also had a high degree of cultural similarity, as shown especially by comparing types of activity settings. Indeed, activity settings that belonged to the same setting type were "sufficiently similar that major components (staff, equipment . . .) could be transposed without appreciably disturbing the functioning of either setting."[5] A key question is the amount of training it would take for central performers in setting A to fill a central position in setting B. In activity settings of the same setting type, very little training would be required. On the basis of detailed evaluations of all public settings, the researchers concluded that a person from Oskaloosa would find that one in three of the setting types in Leyburn and one in two of the available settings were so familiar that he or she could participate in them at any level of leadership. The commonality is even greater—about three-quarters of activity setting types and three-quarters of available activity—if settings programs with similar elements distributed in different ways are added. For example, the activity of the postal substation in the stationer's shop in Leyburn would be familiar to a person from Oskaloosa, though in the U.S. town it would belong in a government post office rather than a private business. At the other end of the scale, fully unique setting types accounted for about 7 percent of each town's setting types and 3 percent of its public space.[6] A comparison of culturally more distant communities would result in fewer common setting types and more unique ones. The activity setting types common to Oskaloosa and Leyburn included:

> auction sales, household furniture, and general merchandise
> clothiers and dry goods stores
> excursions and sightseeing tours
> home economics classes
> meetings, business
> parks and playgrounds
> religious worship services

The cultural differences stood out in sports and recreation. Among the activity settings unique to Oskaloosa in both survey years were baseball, basketball, and (U.S.) football games, charivaris, chiropractors' offices, and ice cream socials. Among the activity settings unique to Leyburn were lawn bowling, cricket, and dart games, public bonfires, fish and chips shops, and corsets sales routes.[7] Activity settings that belonged to the government authority system, to political space (as defined here in chapter 3), and to public-service-oriented non-governmental authority systems were similar in many ways, but far from identical; and they differed considerably in size and other ways.

The Nature of Social Space

To write about opening or closing political space implies both a way of telling whether political space exists or not and that there is some way of comparing the size or the openness of political settings in different societies and localities and at different times. Despite the popularity of the term "political space," I know of no writing about how different degrees of openness or different sizes of political space are recognized or estimated. I offer here, therefore, some first steps in an analytical understanding of the nature of political space.

In a basic sense, the human resources available to every collection of people for the construction of social space are very similar. Every set of 100 people has roughly the same number of person-hours of action available for social structuring, assuming similar levels of health. Of course skills, ideas, existing patterns, technologies, and inspirations differ with the result that the social spaces of different collections of people look very different. A first difference is whether and how they make a division between domestic and public social space. Domestic space is occupied with activities that people are engaged in within their own dwelling places. Public space exists outside dwelling places or involves people who do not dwell there. In Oskaloosa and Leyburn, the distinction between private domestic spaces and public social ones was easy to draw. Public spaces may restrict entry, but they draw people from more than one domestic setting. The demarcation of public and domestic spaces may be much sharper in some societies than in others.

The dwellers in any town not only allocate their time between domestic and public spaces, but also divide it between in-town activities and out-of-town activities. The town activities may draw different numbers of people and different amounts of time from out-of-town dwellers. To forestall confusion, the data cited below focus on town-dwellers and exclude out-of-towners. One basic difference among towns will be the proportion of town-dwellers' person-hours that public social space contains. *What proportion of their time do people commit to public, as opposed to domestic, activity settings?* We see immediately that the residents of Oskaloosa spend more of their time in the public spaces of the town than do the residents of Leyburn: 0.76 hours or 46 minutes more per day on average. This is a significant difference.

Table 6.1

Person-Hours in Public Activity Settings, 1963-64

	Oskaloosa	Leyburn
Total person-hours in public settings	1,880,732	2,625,816
Person-hours per day	5,137	7,174
Total person hours via town residents	1,124,134	1,426,115
Above as percent of total	60	54
Mean hours per town inhabitant	1,356	1,089
Mean hours per day per town inhabitant	3.73	2.97
Above as percent of 16-hour waking day	23	19

Source: Roger G. Barker and Phil Schoggen, *Qualities of Community Life* (San Francisco: Jossey-Bass Publishers, 1973), pp.263-65.

For some reason, then, the public activities in Oskaloosa draw town residents more strongly than do the ones in Leyburn. But there are many other possible differences. The same number of people committing the same number of hours to public space might divide their activities very different-ly. The allocation of time among business, politics, religion, education, and other activities may be quite dissimilar. *How do people divide their time commit-ments among different types of public space?* We find, for example, that people in Oskaloosa spend 11 percent of their public time, or about 24 minutes per day, in political space (government-oriented activities); while in Leyburn they spend 6 percent or about 11 minutes per day, on the average.

In classifying activity settings, we can use three ways of designating different features of social space. The first is a fine-grained classification that identifies different activity setting types according to the specific features of the program of activity. In 1963-64 Oskaloosa showed 198 different setting types and Leyburn 213.[8] Several of the tables below list the activity settings types relevant to politics and participation. (For a complete list see the Appendix.) The second designation groups activity settings according to the type of authority system to which they belong. Authority systems are defined by the control that some activity settings exercise over the programs of other settings. Some settings stand alone as freestanding authority sys-tems in their own right, but many are controlled by an executive office or committee meeting. In Oskaloosa and Leyburn five kinds of authority system accounted for all the activity settings: churches, government agencies (other than schools), private enterprises, schools, and voluntary associations.

The third classification groups settings according to the main focus of the activity in the setting: its action pattern. These action patterns are: aesthetics, business, education, government, nutrition, personal appearance, physical health, professional involvement, recreation, religion, and social contact. Unlike the classification by authority system type, these categories are not mutually exclusive. The settings whose activity focuses on "making, implementing, and evaluating government regulations" are the settings that make up political space.[9]

When the people in a locality divide their time among a group of activity settings, they are also structuring their activity into a finite set of activity types, organizing it into certain authority systems, and arranging it according to a number of focuses of activity. Each activity setting also has a set of attributes: frequency of occurrence, duration of each occurrence, average number of inhabitants, number and kinds of positions of responsibility and leadership, degree to which the program of activity is autonomous, and many more. The multidimensionality of settings raises the question of what global measures are appropriate for comparing the different ways in which localities structure their activity.

One measure is person-hours or, from the standpoint of the settings, occupancy-time. How many person-hours are contained in the activity settings under control of government agencies? How many are in those whose programs of activity focus on government regulations? But person-hours tells us little about the range of activity, the possibility of exercising responsibility, or the ready availability of different programs of activity. For example, the same number of person-hours committed to business-oriented activity settings could all go to one setting (say, a Wal-Mart) or it could go to 20 different shops on Main Street. Or two localities that each commit about the same proportion of the total available person-time to politics might structure it very differently; one might have only one major political venue, perhaps a town council, that meets fairly frequently and for long hours, while another might have dozens of different smaller and more specialized committees, each one meeting less frequently.

A composite measure of the availability and richness of activity settings was used extensively in the research on Oskaloosa and Leyburn. I call it a measure of the *amplitude* of a setting or a group of settings, and its units are called *centiurbs* or *cu*. For any activity setting or set of activity settings it takes account of (1) number of settings per year, (2) number of settings per day, and (3) number of settings per hour. It weights these numbers according to the averages for the two towns and then finds the mean of the three numbers. It measures social abundance: *How readily available and varied are the activities*? If the set of activity settings is like the array of a multitude of kinds of dried beans on display in a food market, then the use of person-hours records how many people chose each variety of bean, and the total shows how many chose any kind of beans at all. The amplitude measure is like a measure of the richness of the bean offerings and their availability, according to the number of kinds and their placement in the display.

Besides authority systems, action patterns, person-hours, and amplitude, three structural features of social and political space are of particular political interest. Control over settings can be more or less local in its origin. *How much local autonomy do public settings have?* Activity settings also differ in the number of responsible positions they have, including the number of leadership positions. The point is important for assessing the opportunity for effective participation. *How many positions of responsibility and leadership do the settings have?* In addition, one can ask about the kinds of people who participate in any particular group of settings. What social classes do they represent? How many are men and how many are women? What age categories are present? *What biases are evident in the kind of people taking part in the settings?* Of course, many other questions might be asked and many other measures attempted. The research in Oskaloosa and Leyburn addressed all the questions in italics above, and the information gathered is the basis for the following discussion.

Government Authority Systems

Every activity setting is under the control of an authority system. In some cases the system of control is strictly internal to the setting; the setting then comprises its own stand-alone authority system. In other cases one setting manages several other settings; the controlling setting and all the settings it controls comprise an authority system. For Oskaloosa and Leyburn the researchers assigned all authority systems to one of five groups on the basis of the characteristics of the controlling or executive setting: private enterprise (the controlling setting was operated by one or more private individuals to make a living), church (controlled by central administrative settings of churches), school (a private or public educational agency operates the managing setting—all were public in Leyburn and Oskaloosa), government agency (controlled by executive settings of town, county, state, or federal governments, excluding school-controlled settings), and voluntary association (any other kind of setting exerts control). These are types of authority systems, not singular authority systems. Business settings often stand alone as autonomous authority systems, but each belongs to the class of private-enterprise authority systems. Each voluntary association is likely to comprise a few different activity settings, often including an annual business meeting and more frequent sessions of their specialized activity. The other types of authority system—school, church, and government—are usually made up of a large number of different settings, but the settings are grouped under only a few authority systems. In a very small community there might be only one church authority system and one school authority system. Government agencies may number two or three or more as local, provincial, and national governments each have some concrete presence and may operate through distinct departments. In Oskaloosa and Leyburn each type of authority system embraced two or more authority clusters.

A good measure of the scope of government authority in a locality is the proportion and kind of activity controlled by government agencies. The rest is left to the other four kinds of authority system. With respect to Oskaloosa and Leyburn we measure activity both in terms of *person-hours* committed and in terms of the *amplitude* of the activity.

Of the time they spent outside their homes and in town in 1963-64, the residents of both Oskaloosa and Leyburn spent a little less than half in activity settings controlled by one or another government agency, including schools. All participants (town-dwellers and out-of-towners together) spent just over half their public time in government-controlled settings. That is one measure of the reach of government in the two towns, and it shows that governments are major forces in giving shape to social space in the towns. Government authority systems other than schools accounted for much more of the person-time of Leyburn's inhabitants in 1963-64 (about 31 percent) than they did of Oskaloosa's (about 17 percent). On average Leyburn's dwellers spent 335 hours per year in settings controlled by government authorities other than schools, while Oskaloosa's inhabitants spent 225 hours per year in such activity settings. If we include school-controlled settings, Oskaloosa's residents committed 599 hours per year, more than 11 hours per week, to government-controlled settings. The comparable figure for Leyburn's residents was 495 hours per year or 9.5 per week.

Athough government agencies were in charge of comparable amounts and proportions of the person-hours of the residents of the two towns, the mix of activities they controlled was quite different. Table 6.2 suggests that the school authority system involved many more person-hours in Oskaloosa than in Leyburn, a pattern due in large part to the many community events (basketball and other sports, plays and programs, school-board meetings) sponsored by the Oskaloosa schools.[10] The mix of activities controlled by non-school government agencies in the two towns was also quite different (Table 6.3).

Table 6.2

Government Agency Authority Systems (GAAS), 1963-64

	Including Schools Oskaloosa Leyburn		Omitting Schools Oskaloosa Leyburn	
ALL INHABITANTS				
P-H in GAAS	958,199	1,370,201	308,075	723,517
percent total P-H	51.0	52.1	16.4	27.5
TOWN RESIDENTS				
P-H in GAAS	497,412	647,445	186,896	438,386
percent total P-H	44.2	45.5	16.6	30.8
mean P-H	599.3	495	225.2	335.4

Note: "All inhabitants" includes people in the settings who do not reside in the town. "Total P-H" includes all the person-hours spent in all the non-domestic activity settings in the town. "Total P-H" of town residents includes all the person-hours in non-domestic activity settings in town accounted for by town residents.

Source: Barker and Schoggen, *Qualities of Community Life*, Table 10.3, p.331, Table 10.7, p.337.

Some of the differences stemmed from a different style of organization. Leyburn's mail service was handled through a postal substation in a stationer's shop and by door-to-door delivery, while Oskaloosa had a government post office where people picked up their mail. Leyburn had a police station and Oskaloosa a sheriff's office. Other differences derived from Oskaloosa's position as a county seat with a jail and county court house, even though it was smaller in population. These features were related to the greater decentralization and greater local autonomy that were general features of social space in Oskaloosa as compared to Leyburn. Still, Leyburn's government agency authority systems controlled five types of settings that were entirely absent from Oskaloosa's. The services covered—health, transportation, and communications—were the work of private-enterprise authority systems in Oskaloosa.[11] In controlling the settings where people committed their public time and in the importance of the kinds of activity they controlled, government agencies other than schools played a bigger role in Leyburn than in Oskaloosa. This is the pattern one might expect on the

Table 6.3

Comparison of Setting Types in the Government Agency Authority Systems (GAAS)

Major setting types in Oskaloosa's GAAS; but not in Leyburn's:
 jails
 judges' chambers
 general post offices

Major setting types in Oskaloosa's GAAS; but minor in Leyburn's:
 government business and records offices

Major setting types in both Oskaloosa's and Leyburn's GAAS:
 hallways
 machinery repair shops
 business meetings
 trafficways

Major setting types in Leyburn's GAAS; but minor in Oskaloosa's:
 cemeteries
 parks and playgrounds

Major setting types in Leyburn's GAAS; but not in Oskaloosa's:
 health department offices
 nursing homes
 physicians' offices
 police stations
 sorting post offices
 railway freight offices
 tax assessment and collection offices
 telephone kiosks

Note: "Major" setting types comprise 3 percent or more of the centiurbs of the government agency authority system; "minor" setting types comprise less than 3 percent.

Source: Barker and Schoggen, *Qualities of Community Life*, p.31.

basis of Britain's more positive view of government at the time and the stronger tradition of private enterprise in the United States. What is more surprising is the extensive role of government in the everyday lives of people in both these small towns.

That role appears a little less overwhelming when we use the measure of amplitude of social space, and the comparison between Oskaloosa and Leyburn brings out very different results. In amplitude (availability and richness), Oskaloosa's government agencies controlled about 16 percent of social space in 1963-64 while Leyburn's controlled about 11 percent. By this measure the difference favoured Oskaloosa whether or not the school systems were included. Activity under government authority in Oskaloosa, compared to Leyburn, was divided into more numerous, more various, and more available activity settings.

Table 6.4

Government Agency Authority Systems (Excluding Schools), 1963-64

	Oskaloosa	Leyburn
AMPLITUDE		
no. of AS/year	114	59
no. of AS/day	22.5	16.4
no. of AS/hour	7.1	6.0
amplitude in cu.	17.5	12.4
percent of total cu.	16.3	10.9
RESPONSIBLE POSITIONS		
number	740	416
percent of town total	20	9
VARIETY OF ACTIVITIES		
no. of major types	8	14
no. of types	52	41
percent of total no. types	26	19

Source: Barker and Schoggen, *Qualities of Community Life*, Table 6.2, p.198.

On average during every hour of the year Oskaloosa had seven activity settings under the control of a non-school government agency in operation and Leyburn had six. Leyburn's greater person-hours were placed in fewer settings. Moreover, the number of different government-controlled settings available each day and each year was greater in Oskaloosa, almost twice as great over the course of a year. Occurrences of each setting must have been less frequent and of shorter duration on average in Oskaloosa, but the larger number of activity settings meant more variety.

There are revealing measures of two other aspects of government-controlled settings: local autonomy and participation (in the form of the exercise of responsibility and leadership and the holding of meetings). Oskaloosa scored higher than Leyburn in both. The measure of local autonomy records the percentage of the total amplitude of activity settings controlled by activity settings that fall into each of three categories: those with high local autonomy are controlled locally (within the town and its closely surrounding district); the ones having medium local autonomy are controlled regionally (outside the town and its immediate district, but within Jefferson County for Oskaloosa or Wensleydale for Leyburn); and those exhibiting low local autonomy are controlled from beyond the region (the state and national level in Kansas and the county or national level in North Yorkshire). About 19 percent of the amplitude of government-controlled settings in both Oskaloosa and Leyburn had high local autonomy, but, compared to Leyburn, much more of Oskaloosa's had medium local autonomy (about 53 percent to 28 percent) and much less had low local autonomy (about 28 to 53 percent). However, the difference in local autonomy was less for the government authority system than for any of the others. The greater local autonomy of Oskaloosa's settings was most accentuated in the case of settings controlled by schools, voluntary associations, and churches. And for both towns the government agency authority systems had the least local autonomy of the five kinds of authority systems.[12]

Several measures are relevant to the question of participation. One is the number of responsible positions, including both executive positions (shop manager or meeting chairperson) and operating positions (store clerk or recording secretary). Table 6.5 shows that the government agency authority systems contained 740 responsible positions in Oskaloosa and 416 in Leyburn. The much higher number in Oskaloosa stands out even more when we take into account the smaller population of the town. There were 281 percent more responsible positions in government per person in Oskaloosa than in Leyburn. Yet compared to other authority systems these numbers are low. In Oskaloosa only private enterprise had fewer responsible positions than government, and in Leyburn government had the fewest.[13]

A related measure records the number of position-holdings or unique person-position intersections (PPI) that occurred for all the responsible positions. Thus, if in the course of the year two different individuals held the position of chair of the town council, then two person-position intersections would be generated. In 1963-64 the government agency authority systems of Oskaloosa generated many more person-position intersections in absolute numbers and more than twice as many per inhabitant as did Leyburn's. If all the person-position intersections were spread evenly, more than half the residents of Oskaloosa and more than a quarter of the residents of Leyburn (including children) would have held one responsible position in a government-controlled setting. Yet, in both towns government agency authority systems were relatively small producers of person-position intersections compared to other authority systems.

Table 6.5

Responsible Positions and Person-Position Intersections in Government Agency Authority Systems (Excluding Schools), 1963-64

	Oskaloosa	Leyburn
RESPONSIBLE POSITIONS		
number	740	416
percent of town total	20	9
PERSON–POSITION INTERSECTIONS (PPI)		
via all inhabitants		
total PPI	1,306	824
percent of all PPI	9.2	7.0
via town inhabitants		
total PPI	453	353
percent of town PPI	6.8	8.4
mean PPI per town inhabitant	0.55	0.27

Source: Barker and Schoggen, *Qualities of Community Life*, Table 6.2, p.198, Table 10.4, p.333.

Table 6.6

Business Meetings in the Government Agency Authority Systems in Oskaloosa and Leyburn, 1963-64

OSKALOOSA

Agricultural Extension Agricultural Advisory County Committee Meeting
Agricultural Extension Artificial Breeders Association Board Meeting
Agricultural Extension County Executive Board Meeting
Agricultural Extension Dairy Herd Improvement Association Directors Meeting
Agricultural Extension 4-H County Advisory Committee Meeting
Agricultural Extension 4-H County Council Meeting
Agricultural Extension Home Economics Advisory Committee Meeting
Agricultural Extension Livestock Association County Board Meeting
Agricultural Extension Purebred Beef Association Directors Meeting
Agricultural Extension Township Electors Meeting
Cemetery Board Meeting
City Council and Planning Commission Meeting
City Council Meeting
City Library Board Meeting
City Planning Commission Meeting
County Commissioners Meeting
County Planning Board Meeting
County School Planning Board for School Unification Meeting
County Social Welfare Board Meeting

LEYBURN

District Council Civil Defence Committee Meeting
District Council Regular and Standing Committee Meeting
District Council Public Relations Committee Meeting
District Council Road Safety Committee Meeting
Parish Council Association Branch Meeting
Parish Council Meeting
Parish Council Town Meeting
Playing Fields Committee Meeting

Source: Barker and Schoggen, *Qualities of Community Life*, pp.520-21.

Finally, we can compare the kind and number of business meetings held by government agency authority systems other than schools in the two towns. In 1963-64 there were 19 such meetings in Oskaloosa and 8 in Leyburn. The difference is almost entirely accounted for by the very active Agricultural Extension Service in Oskaloosa, as a list of the relevant meetings (Table 6.6) demonstrates. The lists are of kinds of meetings and reveal nothing about how many times the named groups met, the number of participants, or the length of the meetings. However, they do show that government agencies in Oskaloosa held many more formal business meetings organized by more specialized committees than did government agencies in Leyburn. It is a pattern that repeats itself outside government.

The research on government control of social space reveals significantly different patterns in the two towns. Measured by person-hours committed, Leyburn's government-controlled space was larger than Oskaloosa's, but both were in control of a major part of the hours people committed to non-domestic activities in the towns. Leyburn's governments had a large role in health, transportation, and communications activity, from which Oskaloosa's government agencies were largely absent. Oskaloosa's governments controlled jails and judges chambers, part of its somewhat greater governmental autonomy as compared to Leyburn.

More surprising is the greater richness in number of activities, number of positions of leadership and responsibility, and number of business meetings in Oskaloosa's government-controlled space. In those terms government was a significantly more active and more extensive concern in the U.S. town than it was in the English town.

That is the pattern with respect to government control, a category that corresponds more or less to what political science sometimes calls the output side of political systems. The next section looks at political space, a category that corresponds more or less to what political science sometimes calls the input side of political systems. The differences between the two towns are even greater in political space. It is worth noting that the political space approach we are using shows that a large number of activity settings belong to both categories: political inputs and outputs are sometimes generated together in the same political settings.

Political Space

According to our definition (chapter 3), political space comprises all those activity settings in which 80 percent of the action is oriented to government authority systems and to the regulations and policies that they decide and implement or that people want them to decide and implement. The research in Oskaloosa and Leyburn applied a similar definition: "The action pattern

Table 6.7

Types of Activity Settings of Political Space, 1963-64
(Percent of town's total amplitude)

	Oskaloosa (15.3cu)	Leyburn (8.6cu)
Agriculture		
agricultural advisors' offices	2.8	0
agronomy classes	0.7	0
animal husbandry classes	1.3	0
Civil records and accounts		
abstract company offices	3.3	0
accountants' offices	0	11.0
government business and record offices	21.8	1.4
tax assessment offices	0	5.3
Education		
school administrators' offices	4.4	3.8
Elections		
polling places	1.3	1.7
vote counts	0	0.6
public posting of election returns	0.3	0
Health services		
civil engineering and public health offices	0	3.3
health department offices	0	4.8
physicians' offices	0	4.6
blood collection laboratories	0	0.6
X-ray laboratories	0.3	0.6
Information		
libraries	2.0*	2.0*
civic education booths	0	0.6
Law and order		
police stations	0	7.9
sheriffs' offices	2.8	0
jails	8.2	0
attorneys' offices	11.1	0
solicitors' offices	0	9.3
judges' chambers	3.6	0

continued on page 131

continued from page 130

	Oskaloosa	Leyburn
county court sessions	1.6	0
district court sessions	0.5	0
coroners court sessions	0	1.7
magistrates court sessions	0	0.9
fire alarms and fire-fighting	0.7	0.8
fire stations	2.6	1.0
Meetings		
business meetings	8.5	6.3
discussion meetings	3.1*	0
land condemnation hearings	0.3	0
public inquiries and hearings	0	0.6
cultural meetings	2.0*	1.0*
Post office and communications		
post offices	4.0	0
post offices and stationers	0	5.5
sorting post offices	0	9.6
Sanitation and environment		
sewage disposal plants	0	3.2
refuse disposal services	0	3.8
soil conservation service offices	2.8	0
Transportation and road maintenance		
civil engineering and public health offices (see above)		
civil engineers' offices	2.8	0
machinery repair offices	6.0	5.7
railway freight stations	0	5.8
motor vehicle operators classes	0	0.6
Welfare and other social services		
welfare offices	2.8	0
welfare workers classes	0.3	0
Total*	**101.0**	**101.6**

* These are types of activity settings that appear both in political space and in other zones of activity. The figures represent my estimate of the proportion recorded for the type as a whole that belongs to political space. The totals vary from 100 due to these estimates and to rounding.

Source: Barker and Schoggen, *Qualities of Community Life*, Table 6.20, p.113 and Appendixes A and B, pp.448-540.

Government [primary political action] is present within a behavior setting to the extent that concrete occurrences within the setting implement or resist the making, interpretation, and execution of laws and regulations by governmental agencies. This pattern may involve: engaging in civic affairs; supplying material and behavior objects for governmental programs; learning and teaching about government and legal procedures; appraising governmental policies and officials." As well, "Government is *prominent* within a behavior setting if 80 percent or more of its program involves occurrences of the kinds stated above. . . . Government is *secondary* within a setting if government-connected occurrences are greater in degree than the general police surveillance which applies to all settings, but less than the degree defined for settings where Government is prominent."[14]

There is an overlap with the activity settings under the control of the government agency authority systems, but many political activities usually signalled as important elements of democratic political practice are not controlled by government. They are the work of voluntary associations, churches, and businesses, although, as it turned out in the case of these two towns, the contribution of these agencies to political space was quite small.

Political space in Oskaloosa and Leyburn in 1963-64 included a wide variety of activities, as Table 6.7 shows. The large number of zeros in the table indicates that each town had a different mix of kinds of political activities. They had only three major kinds in common: machinery shops, business meetings, and school administration offices. However, several others can be seen as variants of one another, such as attorneys' offices and solicitors' offices. Comparing this list to the government agency authority systems list shows considerable overlap, as one would expect, between political settings and settings controlled by government agencies. Political space is smaller in amplitude and person-hours in both towns, but much more markedly smaller in Leyburn. In both person-hours and amplitude, political space, in contrast to government-controlled settings, is larger in Oskaloosa than in Leyburn (Table 6.8). People in Oskaloosa are more active than in Leyburn vis-à-vis government both as recipients of active government policies and as participants in the political process. In Leyburn extended political space (settings where action is oriented to government more heavily than the background level, but less than the 80 percent of primary political space) is larger than in Oskaloosa. Leyburn spreads its politics more thinly and more widely.

Oskaloosa (15.3 cu.) has almost twice the political space of Leyburn (8.6 cu.) by the amplitude measure, nearly twice as many different political activities in operation during the average hour (6.8 compared to 3.6) and average day (23.6 compared to 12.8), and decidedly more responsible positions in political settings (327 compared to 248) (Table 6.9). Leyburn's

Table 6.8

Size of Government Space and Political Space, 1963-64

	Oskaloosa		Leyburn	
	GAAS	Pol Space	GAAS	Pol Space
Total person-hours	308,075	218,643	723,517	131,007
P-H via town residents	186,896	122,524	439,386	89,355
Mean P-H per town residents	225.2	147.6	335.5	68.2
Amplitude in cu.	17.5	15.3	12.4	8.6

Source: Barker and Schoggen, *Qualities of Community Life*, pp.110, 198, 288, 331.

Table 6.9

Political Space, 1963-64

	Oskaloosa	Leyburn
EXTENT		
AS/year	69	46
AS/day	23.6	12.8
AS/hour	6.8	3.6
amplitude in cu.	15.3	8.6
percent of total cu.	14.2	7.6
RESPONSIBLE POSITIONS		
number	327	248
percent of town total	3	3
VARIETY OF ACTIVITIES		
no. of major* types	9	14
no. of all types	27	27
percent of town total kinds	14	13
EXTENDED POLITICAL SPACE		
amplitude in cu.	75.5	97.2
percent of town total	70	86

* "Major" setting types account for at least 3 percent of the amplitude of political space.

Source: Barker and Schoggen, *Qualities of Community Life*, Table 6.19, p.110.

political space is spread across a larger number of major setting types. Political activity accounts for a similar small percentage (3 percent) of all the responsible positions in non-household settings, but in amplitude Oskaloosa's political space occupies more than 14 percent of the total public space, while Leyburn's fills less than 8 percent. In both towns political settings are poorer in responsible positions than the average for all kinds of non-household activities.

The pattern of control over political settings was fundamentally similar in the two towns (Table 6.10). Government agencies and private enterprises between them controlled almost 90 percent of political space in both towns, and government agencies alone controlled almost three-quarters in Oskaloosa and over 60 percent in Leyburn. Private enterprise controlled correspondingly more in Leyburn: more than one-quarter compared to about 15 percent in Oskaloosa. Schools came next in both towns. Voluntary associations controlled a surprisingly small portion of political space, less than 1 percent in Oskaloosa and slightly more than 2 percent in Leyburn. The pattern of control shows that a great deal of political activity was the routine work of government agencies and businesses doing work for government. There were also meetings of government officers with citizens, as well as meetings of elected government bodies in which citizen participation was prominent. The relatively low degree of local autonomy of political settings, although markedly higher in Oskaloosa, correlated with the extensive government control over politically oriented activity settings.

Oskaloosa's greater political activity stands out clearly from the data on person-hours spent in political settings (Table 6.11). On average residents of Oskaloosa spent 147.6 hours per year in political activities, while residents of Leyburn spent 68.2 hours. Of all the time town residents spent in non-household social activity in town, residents of Oskaloosa devoted 10.9 percent to political activity. The comparable figure for inhabitants of Leyburn was 6.3 percent.

The same pattern was evident with respect to holding responsible positions (person-position intersections or PPI), in political space (Table 6.12). Town inhabitants of Oskaloosa were almost twice as likely to hold a responsible political position (0.27 position-holdings per person) than were those of Leyburn (0.15 position-holdings per person).

Table 6.10

Control of Political Space, 1963-64

	Oskaloosa	Leyburn
AMPLITUDE OF POLITICAL SPACE IN CU.	15.3	8.6
PERCENT OF POLITICAL SPACE CONTROLLED BY		
churches	0.0	0.6
government agencies	74.7	62.8
private enterprises	14.5	25.8
schools	10.2	8.6
voluntary associations	0.6	2.1
PERCENT OF POLITICAL SPACE WITH		
high local autonomy	20	2
medium local autonomy	49	39
low local autonomy	30	59

Source: Barker and Schoggen, *Qualities of Community Life*, Table 6.23, p.116.

Table 6.11

Person Hours in Political Space, 1963-64

	Oskaloosa	Leyburn
P-H ALL INHABITANTS		
total P-H	218,643	131,007
percent total P-H	11.6	5.0
mean P-H per cu.	14,322	14,299
P-H TOWN INHABITANTS		
total P-H	122,524	89,355
percent total town P-H	10.9	6.3
mean P-H per cu.	8,026	10,435
mean P-H per town inhabitant	147.6	68.2

Source: Barker and Schoggen, *Qualities of Community Life*, Table 9.7, p.288.

Table 6.12

Person-Position Intersections (PPI) in Political Space, 1963-64

	Oskaloosa	Leyburn
RESPONSIBLE POSITIONS		
number	327	248
percent of town total	3	3
PPI VIA ALL INHABITANTS		
total PPI	713	533
percent of gross PPI	5.0	4.5
PPI VIA TOWN INHABITANTS		
total PPI	28	199
percent of town PPI	3.4	4.7
mean PPI per town inhabitant	0.27	0.15

Source: Barker and Schoggen, *Qualities of Community Life*, Table 6.19, p.110, Table 9.8, p.289.

Political space included not only all the meetings listed as belonging to the government agency authority systems for the two towns (Table 6.6), but also a further set of meetings likely to be oriented to government or to government policy (Table 6.13). The first part of their names indicates the authority system they belong to. Again, Oskaloosa stood out as affording much more opportunity for political participation. That town had 29 politically oriented meetings not controlled by government, as compared to 10 such meetings in Leyburn.

Whether taken from the standpoint of the area of government authority or from the standpoint of space of activity oriented to government, people in Oskaloosa were much more extensively involved in political activity than were people in Leyburn. They spent more time at it, had greater local control over it, organized more different venues to engage in it, and created more responsible positions for doing it. The differences are important, but they should not be allowed to obscure a set of underlying similarities. The towns share a great deal: freedom of religious organization and expectation of a plurality of sites of worship; public education; basic civil rights and electoral institutions; a sector of privately owned and operated businesses supplying goods and services to town residents; roads built and

Table 6.13

Meetings in Political Space Not Part of the Government Agency Authority Systems, 1963-64

OSKALOOSA

Business Meetings
>
> Democratic County Club Meeting
> Farm Bureau County Board Meeting
> Farm Bureau County Policy Meeting
> Farm Bureau Northeast District Delegates Meeting
> Mental Health County Association Board Meeting
> Mental Health County Association Organizing Meeting
> Northeast Kansas County Clerks Association Meeting
> Northeast Kansas County Clerks of District Courts Association Meeting
> Northeast Kansas County Engineers Association Meeting
> Northeast Kansas County Officials Meeting
> Northeast Kansas County Probate Judges Association Meeting
> Northeast Kansas County Register of Deeds Association Meeting
> Northeast Kansas County Sheriffs and County Attorneys Meeting
> Northeast Kansas County Treasurers Association Meeting
> Northeast Kansas County Welfare Directors Association Meeting
> Northeast Kansas County Welfare Association Annual Meeting
> Republican County Committee Meeting
> Soil Conservation District Board of Supervisors Meeting
> U.S. Agriculture Stabilization and Conservation County Committee Meeting
> U.S. Agriculture Stabilization and Conservation County Delegates
>   Convention
> U.S. Farmers' Home Administration County Committee Meeting

Cultural Meetings
>
> Republican Women's Club County Meeting

Discussion Meetings
>
> Agricultural Extension Wheat Information Meeting
> Civic Club Meeting
> Civil Defense County Informational Meeting
> Parent-Teacher Association Open Meeting for All Electors with School
>   Unification Committee
> Perry Reservoir Association County Informational Meeting
> Perry Reservoir Association Public Meeting
> U.S. Engineers Meeting with County Commissioners and Citizens of Ozawkie

continued on page 138

Continued from page 137

LEYBURN

Business Meetings

    After-Care Committee Meeting
    Conservative Party Society Committee Meeting
    County Primary School Managers Meeting
    Liberal Party Society Committee Meeting
    Secondary Modern School Board of Governors Meeting
    Tradesmen's Association Meeting
    Young Farmers Club Advisory Committee Meeting

Cultural Meetings

    Agricultural Discussion Joint Meeting with Upper Dale
    Agricultural Discussion Group Meeting
    Conservative Society Open Meeting

Source: Barker and Schoggen, *Qualities of Community Life*, pp.520–21.

maintained by government agencies; a wide range of services and activities provided by voluntary agencies, government agencies, or private enterprise. Because of the similarities, rather than despite them, the notable differences require analysis and explanation. How did the different patterns come about, and how are they maintained? What difference do they make for individual experience and quality of public life?

The Logic of Political Space

The information collected allows only some general comments about the origins of the different patterns of political life in Oskaloosa and Leyburn. General historical and cultural propositions suggest where the cultural images of a proper town might differ between Kansas and Yorkshire. As a U.S. town and one laid out and settled on the 19th-century frontier, Oskaloosa participated in the populist and democratic culture documented by Tocqueville in *Democracy in America*. The society had no feudal order to carry forward cultures of class and station, but did include an idea that a town meant having churches, shops, a public square (perhaps to reinforce the claim to become county seat), schools, and (in the case of Oskaloosa) the will to keep advocates of slavery away. Leyburn, by contrast, grew gradually over the centuries and may never have experienced a wave of populism. Indeed, the remnants of feudal traditions lived on in the form of a landowning gentry. Some eight members of that gentry lived in Leyburn, where they were disproportion-

ately active in the government authority systems but inactive in political settings (Tables 6.14, 6.15, 6.16).

The researchers collected information about the relative participation of class, gender, and racial groups in different activities and social spaces.
The data show a great deal of similarity in class bias with respect to government and politics in the two towns and a much greater difference with
respect to gender. Both towns displayed a strong bias for participation in
political settings by upper-class and middle-class persons and a weaker bias
for participation in activities controlled by government agencies by lower-
class persons. With respect to gender, Leyburn demonstrated a strong bias in
favour of males and against females in political settings, while Oskaloosa displayed no such tendency.

In sum the data on differential political participation do not lend
support to the view that the political cultures had very different class biases.
They do show that members of the upper classes in both towns were disproportionately active in political settings. The much greater gender bias in
Leyburn's political space was a distinctive cultural feature. It was not repeated in the other areas of activity in the town.

Table 6.14

Bias between Political Space and Inhabitant Subgroups, 1963-64

Oskaloosa		Leyburn	
Social class III	87	Females	43
Social class II	89	Gentry	61
ALL INHABITANTS	100	Social class II	96
Females	101	Social class III	96
Males	111	ALL INHABITANTS	100
African-American	176	Males	152
Social class I	184	Social class I	171

Note 1: The measure of bias expresses the average commitment of person-hours of sub
group members as a percentage of the average commitment of person-hours per town
inhabitant. Less than 100 means less than average time commitment and more than 100
means more than average time commitment.

Note 2: Social classes I, II, and III correspond roughly to Warner's upper-middle, lower-mid
dle, and upper-lower classes, and gentry to Warner's upper-upper class. W.L. Warner, M.
Meeker, and K. Eels, *Social Class in America* (Chicago: Science Research Associates, 1949).

Source: Barker and Schoggen, *Qualities of Community Life*, p.381, Table 12.4, p.388.

Table 6.15

Bias between Government Agency Authority Systems and Inhabitant Subgroups, 1963-64

Oskaloosa		Leyburn	
Social class I	86	Social class II	62
Female	97	Female	98
Social class II	98	ALL INHABITANTS	100
ALL INHABITANTS	100	Social class I	101
Male	105	Male	102
Social class III	110	Social class III	124
African-American	153	Gentry	125

Source: Barker and Schoggen, *Qualities of Community Life*, Table 12.17, p.394.

Table 6.16

Number of Town Residents in Inhabitant Subgroups, 1963-64

	Oskaloosa	Leyburn
Total town	830	1,310
Male	415	621
Female	415	689
Social class I	73 (9%)	85 (7%)
Social class II	438 (53%)	543 (41%)
Social class III	293 (35%)	674 (51%)
African-American	26 (3%)	—
Gentry	—	8 (1%)

Source: Barker and Schoggen, *Qualities of Community Life*, Table 11.1, p.368.

We are better equipped to discuss the forces and mechanisms that accompany and maintain the existing patterns. Our view of activity settings and authority systems (chapter 3) argues that a micro-politics of individual activity settings and an associational politics of non-governmental authority systems can be observed and studied through the political settings approach. Much recent research and thought about political participation suggest that micro-politics and associational politics may form the supporting substrata of politics proper.[15] The researchers in Oskaloosa and Leyburn collected systematic information about the exercise of responsibility and leadership across all the activity settings in the two towns. This information shows that the pattern we have found in political settings is a general difference between the two towns. On the whole, activity settings in Oskaloosa were more locally autonomous and they gave (or required) many more positions and acts of leadership and responsibility.

If all the locally controlled settings of 1963-64 in Oskaloosa were to operate at the same time they would require 4,290 responsible people (operatives), while all those in Leyburn would require 1,378 people to carry out essential operations.[16] Furthermore, young people in Oskaloosa received more early training in local leadership and participation than they did in Leyburn. Adolescents were single or joint leaders in 61 settings in Oskaloosa compared to 14 in Leyburn. Furthermore, Oskaloosa's adolescents spent 40.3 hours per year in settings led by adolescents; Leyburn's spent 26.3 hours in such settings.[17] In other words, the churches, businesses, schools, and voluntary associations of Oskaloosa formed a network of cultural support, skill formation, role modelling, and relevant experience for participation in political space proper. Furthermore, the greater local autonomy in Oskaloosa, especially of government and school authority systems, gave a stronger incentive for participation in those areas.

The Quality of Politics

Oskaloosa's more active, more locally controlled, and more participatory politics was underpinned by a broad pattern of greater social activism. Undoubtedly there are differences in attitude and values that can be related to the two different patterns, and we will speculate on some of them shortly. But here we are noticing the existence of different modes of concrete activity. How are those differences reflected in the experience of town residents? How do the different patterns and experiences influence the qualities of political life in the towns?

A good place to begin thinking about these questions is with the meaning of the greater number of positions of responsibility and leadership in Oskaloosa for town residents. Recall that a single position-person intersection

(PPI) occurs when a particular person exercises a position of responsibility as operative or leader in at least one occurrence of a setting. Jim Hamilton preaching at a church worship service, Emily Crowder sorting mail at the post office, Borden Rocklow acting as secretary at a city council meeting, Gladys Morton managing the meat counter at the grocery store, or Briggs Jenkins operating a stall at the school carnival: these are all person-position interactions. Note that preaching one Sunday and preaching on all the other Sundays would both count as one person-position intersection. Since Oskaloosa had more leadership positions than Leyburn, placed more of them in the hands of town-dwellers, and had a lower population than Leyburn, it follows that the number of position-holding tours by each person was larger in Oskaloosa. On average each person served 8 tours in responsible positions in Oskaloosa, 3.2 in Leyburn. These figures reflect a further difference: Oskaloosa replaced its leaders and operatives more frequently than did Leyburn. In 8 tours of duty the average Oskaloosa inhabitant was fulfilling .056 percent of all the position-tours required to operate the public space of the town. In 3.2 tours the average inhabitant of Leyburn was enacting .027 percent of all the position-tours required to operate the public space of the town. Comparing the two figures, we see that as performers Oskaloosa's residents were 2.07 times more valuable to the public activity of their town than were Leyburn's residents. The loss of one of Leyburn's residents would do only half the damage to home-town public activity that the loss of one of Oskaloosa's would inflict.

The same kind of contrast was evident for the leaders of activity settings (Table 6.17). The activity settings of the two towns required leaders in the central power zones. Each setting had a single leader or joint leaders. The same person or different persons might assume a position of leadership at different occurrences of the setting. Any taking of a specific leadership position in a particular setting by one person, whether for one occurrence or for many occurrences, counts as a leader act. Leader acts are a subset of person-position intersections.[18] They were much more numerous in Oskaloosa (2,104) than in Leyburn (1,673). Moreover, more residents of Oskaloosa (339 or 41 percent) than residents of Leyburn (263 or 20 percent) had experience as leaders in 1963-64.

The data also show that leadership was considerably less stable in Oskaloosa than in Leyburn. Whereas 60 percent of the setting leaders in 1963-64 were still in place in 1967, only 39 percent of the corresponding group in Oskaloosa were still in place.

The measures of value to town activity are objective measures of the positions and contexts that people occupied; they say nothing directly about the experience and attitudes of citizens. However, they signal sharp differences in subjective experience. People in Oskaloosa experienced being needed,

Table 6.17

Leadership, 1963-64

	Oskaloosa	Leyburn
Leader acts by all inhabitants	2,104	1,673
Leader acts by town inhabitants	1,482	883
Mean leader acts per town inhabitant	1.8	0.7
No. of town inhabitants who were leaders	339	262
Percent of town inhabitants who were leaders	41	20
Mean leader acts per leader (settings led)	4.4	3.4
No. of town leaders who led same settings in 1963 and 1967	136	157
Percent of town leaders who led same settings in 1963 and 1967	39	60

Source: Barker and Schoggen, *Qualities of Community Life*, Table 8.5, p.270, Tables 8.6 and 8.7, p.272.

important, and responsible more frequently than did people in Leyburn. Leyburn's residents experienced being expendable and redundant more frequently than did Oskaloosa's. Were public space in 1963-64 in Leyburn as leader-intensive as it was in Oskaloosa, 275 Leyburn residents who were not leaders would have been drawn into leadership positions. Not only did the people of Leyburn experience the psychological consequences of being expendable more frequently than did residents of Oskaloosa; they found that the available leadership positions came open less frequently because their leaders stayed in position longer.

There was another difference in the experience of people in the two towns. In Oskaloosa the share of public activity that was under local control was much larger than it was in Leyburn. Therefore the leaders of public activity settings came under more local pressures from below in Oskaloosa and more distant pressures from above in Leyburn. Oskaloosa in 1963-64 had 4,290 locally controlled positions of responsibility; Leyburn had 1,378. Leyburn in 1963-64 had 2,295 positions of power in activity settings whose programs were determined from a distance; Oskaloosa had 500. Local autonomy strengthened people in Oskaloosa: local leaders had more direct power; their power strengthened the ability of local citizens to exercise informal influence directly on responsible leaders; and citizens' formal power to replace leaders and shape the program of settings was more concentrated. Low local autonomy weakened people in Leyburn: local leaders were agents of a distant authority and not entitled to make and implement decisions about the activities they administered; the weakness of local leaders gave less purchase to the informal direct influence of local members; and the formal power of local citizens to replace leaders and change programs was attenuated by distance from county and national elected bodies and by small representation on them.

The greater power of Oskaloosa residents as holders of responsible positions and as members made them more active and interested; the lesser power of Leyburn residents made them more passive and apathetic about public activities. The same contrast fits with the more avid and extensive pursuit of leisure and home activities by the people of Leyburn. The greater pressure on leaders in Oskaloosa's settings and the lesser security of their positions as leaders placed them under greater stress than leaders in Leyburn. According to the researchers, both towns witnessed a "continuing conflict between those who wish[ed] to enhance the value of persons and the power of the people, at the cost of tension, hard work, low standards, and insecurity, and those who wish[ed] to decrease tension and effort, and increase standards and security—to increase efficiency—at the cost of the value of persons and the power of the people."[19]

The outcome of the conflict was different in the two towns: Oskaloosa tended in the direction of lower standards, more insecurity, and higher pressure while Leyburn tended towards higher standards, more security, and less pressure. The pattern of change in the two towns from the mid-1950s to the mid-1960s was also significantly different (Table 6.18).

The lost settings in Oskaloosa included the book exchange services at the school, phased out in a statewide change to rental of textbooks; farm practices classes, phased out when a special program for World War II veterans was ended; and initiation of incoming high school students, which was ended by a decision of the local school board. The researchers saw the loss of physicians' offices and services as temporary because of the active campaign by residents to attract a medical doctor to practice in the town. In subsequent years doctors were induced to open offices in the town, sometimes with the aid of federal programs, but the economic obstacles remained potent. The lost settings in Leyburn included garden allotments, probably a local government decision based on falling demand because of the increased availability of fresh vegetables in the shops; and railway maintenance shops, due to a decline in traffic on the Wensleydale line.

Table 6.18

Change in Activity Setting Types, 1954-55 to 1963-64

	Oskaloosa	Leyburn
Permanently lost		
percent of setting types	12	10
percent of amplitude in cu.	6.2	4.1
Gained and entirely new		
percent of setting types	14	15.5
percent of amplitude	8	4.9
No. new setting types by authority system		
church	1	0
government	4	1
private enterprise	11	2
* school	6	26
voluntary association	5	3

* By decision of a higher education authority a new, modern secondary school was built in Leyburn between 1955 and 1963. The new school settings (which were a high proportion of all the new settings in Leyburn) almost all derived from that change.

Source: Barker and Schoggen, *Qualities of Community Life*, pp.73-79.

The new settings in Oskaloosa related to government (excluding schools) included motor vehicle operators' classes and exams, water supply plant, welfare workers classes, and X-ray laboratories. The only government-related and non-school setting added in Leyburn was motor vehicle operators' classes.

Most of the changes in both towns were traceable to large-scale economic and technical changes: closing of the telephone exchange in Oskaloosa when dial phones and an automatic exchange came in; closing of the gasworks in Leyburn as production of gas from coal ceased to be competitive. Others reflected new interests of citizens: painting classes in Oskaloosa and dog shows in Leyburn, both initiated by voluntary associations. The school system in Leyburn and private enterprise in Oskaloosa were clearly the most innovative authority systems during the research decade, although innovation was much more broadly based in Oskaloosa than in Leyburn.[20]

The change in this period of stability was considerable. The government agency most prominent in change was the school system, especially in Leyburn. The actions of higher reaches of government had definite consequences for activity in both towns. The local agencies most active in change were private enterprises and voluntary associations, especially in Oskaloosa. Local government also played some part, but was not prominent.

With respect to social and political tensions and changes the consequences were double-edged. More people and more leaders in Oskaloosa had the power to make changes in social activity, and the data on change in settings (to found, alter, or cancel them) between 1954-55 and 1963-64 show that they did make more change. But the greater power of leaders made them the logical and available targets for the discontent of town residents. In Leyburn local leaders were less logical targets of discontent because they had less power, and they were also less vulnerable to local pressures because they were more dependent upon external authorities who were geographically distant and often institutionally insulated from local pressures. The tension between non-leaders and leaders, therefore, was greater in Oskaloosa than in Leyburn. The vulnerability of leaders in Oskaloosa to local pressures made them responsive to discontent and often moved them to initiate change, but their "greater insecurity" more often led to their retirement from positions and to the rescinding of changes begun.[21]

The pattern might give pause to those who advocate radical democracy and participatory politics to energize change. That system may be excellent for getting change started, but it may also lead rapidly to countermovements and a failure to achieve the continuity required by stable change. The ability of a local society to change while at the same time giving scope for most residents to defend their preferences and their interests appears from our evidence to come from features that extend much wider and much deeper than the formal systems of government and politics. Leadership and responsibility, innovation and influence operate in a wide range of activities and authority systems. The energy and activism of a locality seem rooted in the deep structures of social interaction. Research on the micro-politics of activity settings and associational politics of authority systems, in connection with the politics proper of the locality, can reveal concrete practices and features of local society that underpin different degrees of responsiveness and innovation.

The best way to open political space and to keep it open, on this reasoning, is to relate it to a new activity in which people have a practical interest. Practices of broad discussion and shared responsibility can more easily be established around the new activity than they can around old activities with well-formed programs. But the practical experience of new ways of discussion around one new activity can set an example and transmit an experience that people will carry into old activities as sources of reform and change. The innovations need not and should not be entirely local. Not only are the pressures that open localities to change global in their impact, but the ideas about new actions tend to connect and spread through networks and organizations. Still—and this point is crucial—the innovation will remain rhetorical and cannot take root until it can be translated into a program of practical activity that fits the motivation and the needs of the people to whom it is addressed.

Notes

1. The distinction between household or domestic activity settings and non-domestic or public activity settings was easy to apply in Oskaloosa and Leyburn. Where people run businesses and offices out of their homes the distinction may be more difficult to make, but often the business activity is set apart in time and has a special room or a special arrangement of furniture and a special set of people and responsible positions to mark it off. I will sometimes refer to the non-domestic activity settings as public settings, taking it in the broadest sense. Many public settings, such as businesses, are privately owned and some may define themselves as "private" clubs in order to escape application of laws governing public places. For the purposes of this chapter the major types of social space are domestic space (private households) and public space (all non-domestic activity settings). Within public space the size and structure of political space, as discussed in chapter 3, are of particular interest.

2. They had more services than a "minimum convenience centre," but fewer specialty retail services than a "partial shopping centre." See Karl A. Fox, *The Eco-Behavioral Approach to Surveys and Social Accounts for Rural Communities: Exploratory Analyses and Interpretations of Roger G. Barker's Microdata from the Behavior Setting Survey of Midwest, Kansas in 1963-64* (Ames, Ia.: Iowa State University, North Central Center for Rural Development, 1990).

3. Roger G. Barker and Phil Schoggen, *Qualities of Community Life* (San Francisco: Jossey-Bass Publishers, 1973), pp.17-20. I write the account in the past tense. Although many physical and social features of the two towns have not changed very much, I do not know what the changes and continuities are. A contemporary survey allowing comparison over 40 years would be a valuable and fascinating research project.

4. Barker and Schoggen, *Qualities of Community Life*, pp.17-20.

5. Ibid., p.31.

6. The quantities compared are measured in centiurbs, a term explained elsewhere in this chapter and in the appendix. Barker and Schoggen, *Qualities of Community Life*, p.69.

7. Barker and Schoggen, *Qualities of Community Life*, p.5.

8. Ibid., p.65.

9. Ibid., p.34.

10. Ibid., p.206.

11. Ibid., p.5.

12. Ibid., pp.213-15.

13. Ibid., pp.211-12.

14. Ibid., p.109.

15. The work of Robert Putnam has been a focus of discussion of variants of this proposition. See Robert Putnam, *Making Democracy Work: Civic Traditions in Modern Italy* (Princeton, N.J.: Princeton University Press, 1993).

16. Barker and Schoggen, *Qualities of Community Life,* p.217.

17. Ibid., pp.375, 380.

18. Ibid., pp.270-71.

19. Ibid., p.403.

20. Ibid., pp.73-79.

21. Most of the argument and much of the language of this and the preceding paragraphs are drawn from Barker and Schoggen, *Qualities of Community Life*, pp.400-3.

PART III

Political Settings and Special Constituencies

Chapter 7

Eating and Meeting in Owino:
Market Vendors, City Government,
and the World Bank in Kampala, Uganda

Christie Gombay

In 1990, 217.4 million people, or 34 percent of the African continent's population, lived in urban areas. Many countries in Africa are urbanizing at fast rates, and current United Nations projections suggest that within 30 years, 57 percent of the population will be living in urban areas. The gross figures mask significant differences in levels of urbanization between the different regions: 22 percent for eastern Africa, 33 percent for western Africa, 38 percent for central Africa, 45 percent for northern Africa, and over 55 percent for southern Africa.[1] For both national and municipal governments this urban growth poses significant challenges, the most significant of which is the growth in urban poverty. While the levels of urban poverty may be higher in other continents, the emerging trends suggest that the same processes that produce poverty elsewhere are occurring in African cities.

During the last decade the World Bank has taken the leading role in shaping an urban agenda. In 1994 in Africa the World Bank had more than 40 projects valued at over U.S.$1.5 billion. The amount of money being invested in urban development is significant in itself, but perhaps more importantly it has propelled the World Bank's interpretation of "improved urban management" to the forefront of how we think about developing cities of the developing world. The Bank's vision will have incalculable implications for how residents of these cities will live and how cities themselves will be able to address urban poverty alleviation. With relatively few exceptions, little critical attention has been paid to what is becoming the dominant agenda for urban development and urban management in Africa today.[2]

This chapter looks at one of the Bank's recent efforts to improve urban management, in particular in Kampala, Uganda. The central argument is that the World Bank's technically proficient approach to "improving urban management" ignores a powerful new reality of life in cities: the vitality of "informal politics" and local community organizing. In much the same way that structural adjustment programs have come to dominate national politics and policy-making, so too has "urban adjustment" monopolized policy at the municipal level.[3] The impact of neo-liberal orthodoxy at the municipal level has significantly reduced the scope of the formal political arena by establishing fiscal restraint, privatization, and cost-effectiveness as the primary considerations for public-sector management at all levels. The result has been to push politics underground, to informalize politics to such an extent that while many decisions may continue to appear to be taken in the public arena, many important ones are being forced into the streets as well as into the offices of municipal bureaucrats and politicians. The informalization of politics at the local level in the urban setting corresponds to the submersion of national struggles as much as to the emergence from below of local struggles driven by individual and group survival strategies.

The imperatives of collective survival, as well as the need to address political considerations that fall outside the narrowing spectrum of official policy, have led to a shift away from formal to informal political systems that are more ad hoc, issue-specific, and situational. This form of politics revolves around survival—but the survival not only of the urban poor, but also of the bureaucracy. It is a politics from below and one that constantly undermines and re-recreates the landscape upon which "upper-level" or macro-politics is based.

One instance of this kind of organizing has occurred among market vendors in Owino Market in Kampala, the country's largest city and its capital. Owino, with about 4,000 vendors and 30,000 employees in 1992, was (and remains today) the country's largest retail and wholesale market. By looking at how the vendors organized themselves, at how they conducted meetings and discussed critical issues related to resources within and outside the market, we can gauge the extent of participation at the grassroots level and derive a more profound understanding of the complex forces at play.

Uganda and Structural Adjustment

After almost 15 years of civil war and chaos, the advent in 1986 of the National Resistance Movement regime led by Yoweri Museveni heralded a new era in Uganda's development. Given the previous experience with political parties both prior to and after the regime of Idi Amin (1971-79), the National Resistance Movement banned political parties and political organizing and created a resistance council (RC) system based upon popular elections from the grassroots up: a territorially based system of local representation in which neighbourhoods elected representatives to a council to speak for them on matters related to their particular communities. These neighbourhood committees (RC 1) in turn elected representatives to sit on parish level councils (RC 2), which then elected representatives to the sub-district level (RC 3)—and so on up to and including the national parliament (RC 5).

After 1987 the government of Uganda embarked upon an adjustment program developed by the World Bank and the International Monetary Fund, which met with considerable success. During the early 1990s the economy grew at over 5 percent per annum, and in 1994-95 the economy grew at a rate of over 10 percent.[4] Uganda became a committed proponent of structural adjustment and did well at meeting fiscal targets—though whether this adherence resulted in significant gains for the poor in Uganda remained in question.[5] Nevertheless, compared to the previous 15 years, the 1990s seemed to promise a return to the days when Uganda was the "pearl of Africa."

Kampala and Urban Adjustment

Urban adjustment, as a component of structural adjustment, began in Uganda even before the advent of the National Resistance Movement government in 1986. Urban management in Uganda kept pace with the shifting thinking on improvements. In 1985 a World Bank sector study, *Uganda: Report on Urban Finance and Management*, focusing on rehabilitation of services, recommended that "better-managed" cities would alleviate pressure on the central government if urban residents took on "a much greater share of the financing" for urban services.[6] During the next year central government transfers to the municipality plummeted, leading to a further reduction in service provision. In 1990 the World Bank shifted its focus and approved the First Urban Project for Uganda, which included rehabilitation of key infrastructure—including the upgrading of three markets, provision of some serviced land, strengthening of urban management, and technical assistance and training.

Kampala had grown considerably. During the decade leading up to 1992, the annual growth rate averaged 4.8 percent per annum. As in many African cities, the provision of services fell far behind the demand. An estimated 75 percent of Kampala's residents lived in crowded, poorly serviced areas lacking basic infrastructure and amenities. Roads were potholed, less than 10 percent of the population had the benefit of refuse collection, and water supply was erratic and unpredictable in many neighbourhoods. Most people survived through a variety of activities; few people had formal employment.

In 1988 the Ministry of Planning estimated that the whole country had only 378,227 formal-sector jobs—or about 5.3 percent of the labour force. Of this, two-thirds were in public-sector employment and one-third in private-sector establishments. Kampala accounted for almost one-quarter of the total, or about 95,000 jobs. But formal-sector employment had its drawbacks. The average monthly gross remuneration of employed persons in January 1988 in the formal sector was USh.3,127. Within this category, government employees were the most underpaid, with an average monthly remuneration of USh.1,175, while their counterparts in parastatal and private sectors received USh.5,786 and 7,312 respectively.[7]

Salaries for those entrusted with "improving urban management" were better but still only constituted a fraction of what was required for a living wage. A town clerk in Uganda made USh.145,300 per year, a department head like the city treasurer made the same, a section chief made 100,330, and a market master made almost 60,000. In June 1992, one U.S. dollar was equivalent to 1,169 Ugandan shillings, which meant a town clerk earned about 10 U.S. dollars a month. A survey conducted in 1989 estimated average monthly household total consumption expenditure for Kampala as almost USh.60,000 per month, roughly 30 times the average monthly wage.[8] While a variety of allowances and benefits went along with some of the positions in the public service, the jobs themselves did not allow for survival beyond more than four or five days a month.

In Kampala public-sector employment was not a livelihood, but a means of access to a livelihood. The job may have had a house or a housing allowance that went along with it, which was critical to surviving in the city, but what was crucial was access to or control over other sources of revenue. Often this access took the form of applying, or not applying, government regulations if the price was right, a practice often referred to as "eating" in apparent reference to its connection with meeting basic needs.

The World Bank and the Uganda First Urban Project

According to the government of Uganda's Basic Household Survey, some 70 percent of Kampala's residents were living below the poverty level, which means that most people in the city were being forced into all sorts of different arrangements to make ends meet. Very few people had the luxury of having formal employment from which they could make a "living wage." The vast majority had to undertake a broad range of activities—especially in the informal sector—to support themselves.[9] These conditions lead to two important and interrelated questions: first, in what ways have these kinds of activities changed how Kampala has developed, and is developing; and, second, what impact has informal economic activity had on the direction of urban management?

Into the 1990s, several World Bank projects had a direct bearing upon how Kampala was being managed; many of them overlapped with and were implemented by different agencies in the city. The most important one from our perspective was the $28.7 million First Urban Project, approved in 1990. The project's objectives were to:

1. improve living conditions and alleviate poverty in Kampala by restoring key infrastructure services;
2. support the development of decentralized local urban management by strengthening the revenue base, financial management, and technical capacities of the Kampala City Council (KCC) and by improving the ability of central government to assist local authorities to increase their revenue base and strengthen financial management;
3. strengthen the country's capacity to manage the process of urban land development; and
4. promote sound cost recovery policies and practices.[10]

The project continued through the decade, with evaluations of its various components planned and anticipated. Two of its components are of special interest here: the first was a program to upgrade markets in Kampala, and the second was a move within the KCC to promote privatization of KCC assets.

Under the auspices of the World Bank First Urban Project in Uganda, a team of consultants was brought in to prepare recommendations for the rehabilitation of Kampala's markets. KCC had promised vendors in Owino Market as early as 1984 that the market would eventually be upgraded, and the arrival of the consultants in 1989, although late, was heralded by the Market Vendors Association (MVA) as a concrete sign that improvements to the market were about to take place. The MVA met with the consultants and made recommendations to them concerning proposed changes to the market. But the project was based on the principle of full cost recovery for any capital expenditure, and many of the MVA's recommendations would have led to significantly escalated costs. The planning for the upgrading of Owino Market was completed in 1990, and the proposed improvements were intended to minimize both cost and disruption to market life by stressing low infrastructural inputs and a phased construction process.

There was one small catch. The market upgrading project involved three markets, two of which were partially situated on private land. One of the conditions of the project was that implementation could not begin until the KCC was full owner of the land on which all three would be built. Negotiations for the purchase of this land turned out to be more complicated than anticipated. Two years later, as the negotiations continued, the KCC put together a Market Development Program. Its objective was to "transform the markets into more habitable places by upgrading and providing better structures and related services. . . . These inadequate services and facilities will be upgraded within the overall planning of the area for the benefit of all vendors and residents of Kampala City."[11] Meanwhile, the Owino upgrading, planned as part of the First Urban Project, was still awaited.

Vendors in and around Owino Market, for their part, could not stand still. They had to take action within the market to maintain the order and security required by their businesses. But the most striking change occurred on the roadways and parking lot adjacent to Owino, where a thriving evening market sprang up; and the politics of survival converged around this "illegal" evening market, for it was there that the survival of vendors, resistance councils, KCC officers, and ministry officials intersected and conflicted. The conflict was not over how much the vendors paid—the rental rates in this "informal," "unregulated" market were the same as those of the official markets run by the KCC—but, rather, over who got the proceeds and how those proceeds were to be divided.

Evening markets—cramped, active, and inexpensive—had long been a daily fact of life in Kampala. Vendors would try to get rid of perishables, and people on their way home from work in the city would stop to make purchases. Owino Market, close to the central taxi park and the bus station, was at the crossroads of the major transportation arteries in the city, an ideal place to stop and shop at the end of the day.

Initially the poor security situation in the area limited the growth of the evening market outside Owino. As it became safer to stay out longer at night, the outside market grew; and as it grew the attractiveness of having a stall in Owino Market itself began to decline, especially for those with stalls in the rear of the market, where rain would often turn passageways into muddy quagmires. In 1990 the MVA and the Market Management Committee (MMC) tried whenever possible to press the KCC and the Ministry of Local Government to deal with the issue of the evening markets, but their efforts met with little success. Indeed, the efforts of the MVA encountered a severe setback when, in September 1990, the minister of local government, Bidandi Ssali, allowed vendors to "temporarily" trade from two of the streets adjacent to the market and in the parking lot after five o'clock every evening. In honour of the minister, the vendors in this evening market named it the Bidandi Ssali Market. The "informal" protection provided to the evening market by the local government minister acted as a dramatic catalyst for its growth. With this step, the fortunes of Owino Market began to go into decline. From October 1990 to April 1991 the arrears in vendor fee payments began to mount and the number of vacant stalls increased. Arrears stood at about USh.14.3 million shillings with 1,383 vacant stalls in May 1991.

Owino Market and Activity Settings

After visitors got used to the sights, the smells, the noise, and the never-ending bustle in the market, another feature often caught their attention: the number of people who seemed to be talking longer than necessary to make a business transaction. Wandering through the market, a visitor couldn't help but be struck by the many clusters of people who seemed to be doing something other than buying or selling. But, as we soon discovered, the meetings in this market were not ad hoc or haphazard, but followed regular patterns and were highly organized. Many of the meetings took place in the open air, in empty stalls, or, in some cases, inside market buildings. Whatever the surroundings, the people in these meetings seemed perfectly capable of blocking out the din around them and focusing intently upon the agenda at hand. Because most of the participants needed to get back to their stalls, the meetings lasted only as long as they had to, and each event was characterized by a certain efficiency and practicality. As we spoke with vendors about the meetings, we learned that they were the work of a large number of organizations that dealt with a wide variety of issues and met a number of different needs.

Vendors in Owino Market faced very real problems in making their market a viable commercial location. The lack of services, the difficulties of unloading goods, the lack of pavement underfoot, the lack of waste disposal, the flooding, and the presence of the evening market all contributed to a sense of tremendous unease in the market. Despite the many obstacles faced, and in part because of them, the vendors in Owino Market had developed a wide variety of organizations to address not only social but also economic and political issues.

Methodology

Anyone doing research in the market had first to meet with the senior market administrator, appointed by the Kampala City Council to head the Market Administration Section, a unit of the KCC within the Finance Department and responsible for collecting market revenues and managing the market's affairs in general. To talk to the vendors, though, we had to deal with the chairman of the Market Vendors Association. The holders of both these positions told us that their particular organization understood how the market worked and pursued the best long-term interests of the vendors and of the market as a whole. But their parallel claims suggested the importance of exploring the extent to which either organization was able to deal with the conflicts that arose among people in the market and between the vendors and local government itself.

The tendency in organizational analysis is to focus primarily upon the organizational structure, rules and regulations, position-holders, and the relationship of the organization to its social environment. While all of these types of analysis can provide certain insights into the nature of an organization, they miss an element of singular importance for organizations that are fluid and evolving—the physicality of the organizations themselves: the location of the organizations, whether they have offices, how often they hold meetings; the agenda of their meetings; who participates and who does not; and so on. In Owino Market, where the vendors would come and go fairly regularly and where organizations could be weak both on the ground and in their abilities to mobilize support and effect change, it seemed important to examine not only the objectives of the organizations, but also their daily realities. We did this through an analytical survey tool that focused specifically upon the political space created by the organizations.

Activity Settings Survey

The information presented here is based upon a political settings survey I conducted in Owino Market in October 1992. The survey was undertaken by a team of four graduates of Makerere University over a period of three weeks, pre-tested on four different groups, and then implemented across a broad spectrum of organizations in Owino Market. These ranged from public-sector activity settings, like the KCC Tax Office, the Ministry of the Interior police post, and the KCC Market Administration office, to various levels of the Market Vendors Association, to private vendor groups. In all, we surveyed and collated data from 20 different settings. We based the selection of organizations for more detailed analysis on our informed impressions of which organizations in the market constituted the most significant sites for political participation and contestation between vendors themselves and between vendors and the public sector. The primary organizations examined were the Market Vendors Association, the Kampala City Council administration, organizations both public and private involved in promoting improved security within the market, social and mutual aid societies, and the Market Management Committee, which was created to serve as a direct channel of communication/control between the KCC and the MVA.

The most striking thing about the meetings in Owino Market was their sheer number. Vendors were involved in all sorts of activities. The market had 30 football teams. It had dance troupes, benevolent societies, training programs for security, training programs for civil defence, basic commercial training—the list went on and on. In addition, various organs of the public sector kept a keen eye on what was going on. The Kampala City

Council collected rents and revenues, the Health Inspectorate monitored health conditions, and the KCC finance department had a tax office in the market, as did the police. The National Resistance Movement was also delivering political education courses for the vendors. What we discovered was that far from being a "free market," the market had its activities very carefully regulated both by the vendors themselves and various public authorities. The meetings fell roughly into two groups, which mirrored the state-civil society relationship. The first group of activity settings, those firmly grounded in civil society, in one way or another reflected concerns of survival of the vendors. The most important organization in that camp was the Market Vendors Association, the largest vendors' organization in the market. I will describe in detail five MVA-related settings, which, taken together, provide a comprehensive picture of a grassroots organization with extensive support and legitimacy. I also describe two other civil society settings: one belonging to a sports club and the other to a security business.

Within the state structure, five different settings reveal the various ways in which organizations in civil society and the state differ from one another. The majority of the state settings deal with the KCC administration and organs of security. The most interesting from the point of view of refracting the tensions between civil society and the state is the setting called the Market Management Committee, which was a structure introduced by a former town clerk of Kampala to bridge the gap between the objectives of the KCC vis-à-vis the market and the vendors' goals themselves. This, and many of the other meetings, show how despite differences on a number of issues, the vendors and the KCC tended to agree on the need for certain services: security and crime prevention, vendor education, refuse collection, water and sanitation, and market upgrading. Indeed, many of the organizations within civil society had developed to replace those of the state that had withered away.

By looking at the meetings I discovered a continuum in how they functioned, ranging from open, accessible, and conciliatory for the settings at the lowest level established by the vendors themselves and becoming more closed, exclusionary, and conflictual the more directly the state controlled them. Within the market, commercial conflicts were dealt with in local vernacular: any interested party was invited to participate and resolutions were designed to accommodate. Between the vendors and local authorities, in the spaces guarded by government organs, relations tended to be more hostile and limited to key players, and only rarely were issues resolved.

Popular Organizations in the Market

Along with the number of meetings a most impressive feature of Owino Market was the level of organization of people in the market itself. Many associations have arisen to address specific issues faced by groups of vendors, and over the years many of these ad hoc organizational structures had coalesced into viable organizations that handled different sorts of problems at different levels. Clearly, the popular organizations in the market were vibrant and able to mobilize a tremendous amount of support both from within the market itself and from outside.

Market Vendors Association (MVA). A vendors' organization was in place in Owino Market even before the construction of the market in 1972. The organization became increasingly active in the 1980s, expanding its role in carrying out essential functions. The expansion of its structure and functions was institutionalized in June 1988, when the Market Vendors Association became a legally recognized body. The MVA's constitution spelled out its objectives:

1. To promote and encourage genuine business practices;
2. To promote the economic advancement and well-being of associate members;
3. To promote and maintain a closer liaison between the market authority (Kampala City Council) and the traders in order to foster better understanding and working relationship between them;
4. To co-ordinate the various activities undertaken by other traders' associations elsewhere in the country and beyond and to collaborate with members thereof in the attainment of the common objectives; and,
5. To set and maintain a set of rules of conduct and ensure the governance of the traders in accordance with the set standards of conduct and behavior for the general good and welfare of all parties involved.[12]

Every Ugandan vendor in the market over the age of 18 was eligible to become a member of the Association, and in theory everyone in the market, excluding porters, was a member. To become a member, a vendor was required to pay a nominal annual subscription fee. Although it was difficult to tell how involved most of the vendors were in the organization, by looking at the structure of the MVA and the nature of its levels and meetings we saw strong indications of its activity and influence.

The constitution of the MVA codified the norms and regulations that governed the market vendors through the first decade in the market.

The constitution, with 31 articles, established the formal rules governing all vendors in the market. Under Article 7, "Observance of Law, Rules, and Regulations," vendors were called upon to be "readily available and willing to participate in communal work for the well being of the market." Article 8, "Qualifications for Female Members," stipulated, among other things, that "Married woman [sic] shall produce a letter of no objection to her trading in the market from her husband and endorsed by the Resistance Council I or other similar appropriate authority of the area of her residence." But the most important sections of the constitution related to the management of the association itself. Articles 12 through 30 focused upon the organization of the MVA and its administrative structure. The constitution stipulated that the association would be governed through a hierarchy of councils and committees beginning at the departmental level, proceeding to the zonal level, and culminating with the central executive. The MVA organized the vendors in the market into 57 departments, which in turn were grouped into four zones. Above the zonal level was the central MVA committee and executive. The executive and committee structures at the departmental, zonal, and central levels were identical and modelled on the resistance councils (RCs) of local government. It was a pyramidal structure with indirect elections from one level to the next.

The boundaries of each of the 57 departments in the market were based on the type of commodity sold (Rice Department, Palm Leaves Department, or Flour Department, for example) or spatial contiguity of stalls in a given area. The size of the departments varied both in terms of number of stalls and space occupied, but each had a similar internal structure and, in theory, a similar program of action. In practice the level of participation varied from department to department, and the type of issues discussed also reflected the most immediate concerns of vendors in each department.

The committee at the departmental level elected an executive to oversee departmental affairs. The executives of all the departments in a zone constituted a zonal committee, and from among themselves they elected an executive to carry out MVA activities at the zonal level. The executives of the four zones constituted the MVA central committee, and they elected an executive from among themselves to govern the entire structure. The executives met regularly to resolve problems within department, zone, and market. Vendors at the departmental level elected a committee of nine every two years to direct and resolve market issues within their departments. All the department executives together made up the zonal committee, and they elected a zonal executive of nine to manage matters within the zone. The central committee was composed of the 28 members of the zonal executives, who in turn elected a central executive of nine to deal with issues that had an impact on the market as a whole. It was the MVA central executive that dealt with the Kampala City Council and outside agencies on issues related to the market as a whole.

The following outline of settings or meetings starts from the bottom, with a departmental-level setting, and moves toward the top of the MVA. Each setting was selected from among the 20 settings documented to provide a specific insight into how the market was regulated and how "civic" the community appeared to be in practice.

Flour Market—Departmental Meeting. The flour department, located in the Inner Market, consisted in 1992 of about 54 vendors. Meetings were held once a month in the stall in the department with the least amount of inventory. Less inventory meant more room for participants to sit down. The flour department was founded in 1985 and had been meeting on a regular basis ever since. In general, meetings lasted around two hours and would have between 10 and 15 participants. The executive committee consisted of a department leader, assistant leader, treasurer, and secretaries of mobilization, health, and women. The department leader was a Muganda who had been in the department for over ten years and was well respected by the vendors in the department. The department leader and assistant were elected by members of the department in elections supervised by representatives of the central MVA. The term of office for all members of the executive was two years. The other five executive members were then chosen by the two elected leaders. The leader and assistant would go from stall to stall to introduce their choices, and if members did not accept the rest of the slate, the whole department would go to the MVA central office for supervised elections of the five department executive members. In this department, the vendors did not contest the leader's appointees. Of the seven leaders in the flour department, two were women, although the leader reported that in general women in the department did not participate vocally in many of the meetings. None of the leaders was paid for the time they put in or work they did as members of the department executive. The executive committee was responsible for collecting MVA dues from members of the department for the central MVA (the annual fee was USh.1,200—about one dollar). The department was allowed to retain 10 percent of the dues it collected from vendors for development work in the department.

Meetings were convened by the secretary of mobilization, who went from stall to stall informing vendors of a meeting in the coming week. The exercise was repeated on the day prior to the meeting. The department leader, Abubukali Katula, told me that the level of participation in meetings in 1992 was low and there was no sanction for not attending. He added that people in his department were primarily interested in their own personal welfare and therefore found meetings "a bother." While business in the department was adequate, the vendors were concerned with the growth of the evening market and were eager for the market reconstruction to begin.

All meetings of the flour department were opened with a prayer, and minutes were kept of all resolutions adopted at each meeting. These resolutions would be forwarded to the central MVA to ensure that they were consistent with the overall objectives of the MVA and to foster accountability from all levels. At executive meetings the issues discussed included financial matters, such as ways of purchasing goods collectively to reduce prices and increase profits and administrative market issues. Hygiene in the department was considered a serious issue, and in 1992 the department passed a resolution forbidding any member of the department to sit on sacks of flour while working. The punishment for such an offence was the denial of work for between two hours and a day, depending upon the number of infractions. They also discussed the role and responsibility of the KCC in matters relating to cleanliness and waste disposal in the market. Department meetings also provided an opportunity for department leaders to convey information received from the central MVA and to inform vendors about progress made on larger market development issues that transcended department concerns.

For one departmental meeting, held on October 3, 1992, for example, the leader and the secretary had informed members the day before about the meeting, and 12 people attended. They were briefed by the leader about the purpose of the meeting: to address the issue of mud in the road just in front of the department. Vendors were sweeping dust from their stalls into the road, and the KCC rubbish collectors did not remove it. The refuse turned into mud during the rainy season. It was resolved that every vendor should dispose of dust in the dustbins provided by the KCC, even the vendors on the other side of the road. The leader asked if there were any other suggestions and there were none. The leader closed the meeting asking those present to tell other members of the resolution.

Case-solving meeting, Kawempe-1 Department. A second activity setting related directly to the departments had to do with the "informal" legal system developed in the market. At all levels of the MVA structure, case-solving subcommittees had been established to deal with civil suits. There was a great deal of conflict in the market, usually to do with commercial relations, either between vendors and customers, or between vendors themselves. Business arrangements had a way of going sour when one of the parties believed they had been shortchanged. During the early years of the market such conflicts were brought to the KCC administration or the central MVA, but as the market grew and the number of disputes increased the vendors needed a new mechanism to deal with the conflicts. The MVA set up a system in 1988, based upon departments, to address such matters. The case-solving meetings were held on an irregular basis as cases arose. During the year prior to our survey the Kawempe-1 department case-solving committee heard about 20 cases. Each meeting lasted about 45 minutes, with the longest taking an hour. From 5 to 35 people participated, including the vendors involved in the controversy and their neighbours. The meetings were open to the general public; other vendors or customers wandering by were allowed to make suggestions and present opinions if they wished to do so. The case-solving meetings in Kawempe-1 department were always held in the open around the leader's stall.

The cases were dealt with by the leader, who was an older woman fluent in Luganda and recognized in the department for her oratorical skills. Cases would be dealt with at the time that they were reported. The leader would handle the case alone if it were a simple matter, but for more complex cases she called her assistant and vendors from stalls near the ones involved in the controversy. Usually, about eight participants gathered around the leader's stall to listen to both parties. The leader then invited suggestions from the participants, including the complainant and the accused, concerning the matter under discussion. The open discussion that followed usually narrowed to an agreed decision. Then the leader passed judgment and asked the individuals involved to comply with the decision. Invariably, vendors would do so although they had a right of appeal to the zonal and central MVA executives if they so wished. If neither party was satisfied with the outcomes from the three levels of the "informal" judicial system, they always had the right to take their case to the formal legal system. Such challenges were both extremely expensive and subject to even greater vagaries, so most vendors preferred to rely on the internal judicial system.

For example, one meeting in Kawempe-1 department in 1992 was called when a woman vendor came to the leader to complain that her partner, another woman, had cheated her. The two women occasionally purchased groundnuts together and shared the profit. When one fell sick for a week the other decided not to give her any of the money realized from the goods purchased that week. The woman who had been sick lodged a complaint, arguing that she was entitled to her normal share. The leader summoned her assistant and four neighbours of the women involved who confirmed the existence of the arrangement between them. After much arguing between the two women, and the expression of different opinions by the participants, it was agreed that the complainant be paid one-fourth of the profits realized since she had her capital invested in the business, although she had not worked for a full week. Both parties accepted the decision, and the meeting was closed after the accused promised to pay her partner at the end of the week. The outcome of this conflict was recorded in the official minutes of the departmental executive and forwarded to the MVA central office.

In general, the case-solving meetings had proved to be tremendously helpful to all concerned. These "commercial courts" were successful at resolving cases because they were open to public scrutiny. For instance, our queries about one case-solving session in the food houses department of Owino Market prompted this response to a question about the role of onlookers: "Onlookers are many because they come to listen for a few minutes and then move on. Others keep coming because the leader's stall is next to the path used by both vendors and customers. Onlookers are very important and on a number of occasions have given valuable suggestions. In fact onlookers are encouraged to participate because some of them might be leaders in other departments with experience of similar cases. Suggestions made by onlookers are as valuable as those of members."[13]

In the absence of efficient and effective legal mechanisms for adjudicating commercial conflicts, the vendors themselves had devised their own system of regulating such conflicts. Given the frequency of such conflicts and the relative dearth of official services within the market, it is perhaps not surprising that such a procedure evolved. It is important to bear in mind that it was not a replacement for, but an adjunct to, the formal legal system.

Inner Market Zone—Executive Committee Meeting. The Inner Market zonal executive committee of the MVA was founded in 1990 at the instigation of the central MVA. It met each month in the senior market administrator's office or in the market administrators' office, both of which were enclosed spaces. The zonal executive committee consisted of a zone leader, an assistant-leader, general secretary, and secretaries for defence, health, information, and women, and a treasurer. In 1992 all but two were men, and the majority of them were from Buganda.

Elections for the zone executive took place every two years and were much more contentious than elections at the departmental level. Whereas in many departments it was difficult to find vendors willing to serve on the executive committees, at the zonal level the competition was more intense. During the elections held in 1992, three members of the previous committee were not re-elected. The zone leaders were chosen from among the 15 top executive members of the departments in the Inner Market Zone. Elections of secondary leaders took place in the zone. The leader mobilized departmental leaders to elect people for different posts. Secondary leaders were chosen from among departmental leaders.

The agendas of their meetings included approving minutes from the last meeting as well as issues under discussion for the day. The date, time, and venue of the next meeting were announced, and prior to the following meeting the information secretary would remind committee members about the upcoming meeting. One or two members might fail to attend, but there

was heavy pressure to attend and those who did not were expected to provide good reasons for doing so.

Each meeting opened with a short prayer asking God to guide the
participants in the discussion so that they might come up with worthwhile
decisions. The prayer could be led by any member, but each major religious
group represented in the zone was given that opportunity. The general secretary then introduced the agenda and asked the participants to give their
views and suggestions concerning particular items. Any participant was free
to add an item to the agenda. When all items had been discussed the chairman went through the agenda reminding participants of what decisions had
been made for each item. The meeting closed with a short prayer. The general secretary was responsible for taking minutes.

The topics of discussion in these meetings covered any number of
items, such as the general cleanliness of the zone and economic problems of
members. In 1992 concern was also expressed about the tendency of vendors
to do business on credit. This was being seriously discouraged because of the
complaints it generated. Another important issue for the Inner Zone executive was what to do about children in the market. According to the Markets
Act of the government of Uganda and the constitution of the MVA, children
were not allowed in markets. Although this act remained formally in effect,
the KCC did little to enforce it. Many women vendors had small children and
there was mounting pressure for a day-care centre to be built in the market.
The executive had prepared a plan and forwarded it to the central MVA, but
no action had yet been taken.

One of the most pressing issues dealt with at the zonal level was
how to contend with the illegal evening market and the problems it had
caused vendors in the Inner Market. However, the powers of the lower-level
groups were limited and whatever opinions participants held were simply
reported to the MVA central executive, which was ultimately responsible for
dealing directly with the city authorities. By 1992 the issue of the evening
market was no longer the central topic of discussion because the vendors
believed that since it was supported in any case by "Big Shots," however
much they might complain nothing would be done. Many vendors adopted
the position that if you can't fight them, join them, and the number of
vacant stalls was on the rise.

To take an example, one 1992 zonal meeting was called by the zonal
leader after he discovered on one of his tours of the zone that vendors in the
Irish Potatoes Department were disposing of their rubbish in the road, apparently encouraged to do so by the Market Management Committee (MMC)
representative for the zone. The information secretary informed members of
the meeting, and the MMC representative was also asked to attend because
the issue to be discussed affected him. The meeting was chaired by the leader,

who opened it with a prayer, informed members why the meeting had been called, and tried to establish whether it was true that the MMC had actually allowed vendors to dispose of rubbish in the road. The MMC representative said that he only allowed the sweeping of dust, not rubbish, into the road, because dust was easily removed by KCC cleaners. It was agreed that the health secretary would go to the department in question with the MMC representative to rectify the misunderstanding. The meeting was closed with a prayer and members dispersed to their respective businesses.

With four zones in Owino Market, the issues raised tended to transcend departmental and even zonal boundaries. Different zones had specific problems, and each would seek solutions to their particular problems within the context of the market itself. But by 1992 all of the zones were suffering from the lack of investment in infrastructure within the market and the growth of the evening market. The zone executive members also sat on the MVA central committee, so the lines of communication between the central directorate and the zone executives were fairly open. The Inner Zone was the one that had been the original planned market. Its members tended to be wealthier than many of their counterparts in the other zones, and they also had the benefit of whatever little infrastructure was still functioning in Owino Market. Although the Inner Zone was considered to be the most sought-after area in the market, the conditions were not noticeably better than other areas. Perhaps because of their relatively superior position within the market, the Inner Zone vendors tended to focus more on larger issues surrounding the role of KCC and the moves to limit the scope of the evening market, than on zone-specific issues. Whereas departmental level meetings were held in Luganda in the open air, as one began to move up the administrative ladder the language switched to English and the meetings were held in enclosed spaces. Both of these measures effectively excluded a large number of vendors from active participation in the deliberations.

MVA Central Office. The MVA Office was one of the two most active offices in the market (the other was the Market Administrators' office). The MVA Office, situated just outside the enclosed Inner Market Zone, came into existence as the result of prolonged pressure from the vendors to secure space from the KCC for its construction. In 1984 the MVA executive applied to the KCC for permission to build an office. After considerable foot-dragging on the part of the KCC, a site was allocated and surveyed. Initially the KCC agreed to pay for the construction but then reneged on its commitment. The MVA went ahead without KCC approval, leading the city authorities to arrest the chairman and the general secretary. They were soon released, and the final outcome was that the KCC allowed the MVA to build an office, but one smaller than originally intended. In the 1990s the space was too small for the way it was being used.

The MVA Office was open 300 days a year, 10 hours a day. Normally there were three to four people present in the office carrying out MVA business, with two of them paid association employees. The two staff members would spend much of the day dealing with disputes brought to them by litigants. For example, in one dispute a woman had been supplied with goods by a man who wanted to "befriend" her. The man demanded payment, but the woman refused to provide any sexual favours. She believed they were in love, because they had previously gone to a hotel near the market and slept together. In this case different witnesses gave their views and a consensus was reached through a majority vote: the woman had to pay some money, but not the whole amount.

In addition to resolving cases, the MVA Office was also the site of executive meetings that dealt with the most important issues concerning all the vendors in the market. These meetings took place on a monthly basis and resolutions passed at this level were the most important in dealing with the daily focus of MVA activities. Most of the discussions revolved around economic problems of vendors, disputes among vendors, and lack of KCC action with regard to taxes, fees, sanitation, health and hygiene, and security in the market. There was also a great deal of discussion about when the First Urban Market Upgrading project would begin.

Market Vendors Association Leaders Conference. Meetings of the Market Vendors Association Leaders Conference were held monthly in a theatre near the market. They served as the policy-making organ for the Market Vendors Association in addition to providing an opportunity for department-level members to communicate directly with the leaders of the MVA. In attendance were all 57 department leaders plus assistants, members of the MVA executive, resistance council representatives, administration officials, and the officer-in-charge of the police detachment in the market. Department leaders were also permitted to invite up to five other members to attend with full authority to participate. Generally attendance amounted to around 150 people.

The Conference was founded in 1988 because the MVA wanted to create a setting in which information and ideas could flow freely between market vendors and MVA leaders. The objective of the meetings was to promote frank discussion between vendors and the administration on all issues of interest to either party. The conference was organized by a committee of 16, which included three advisers and four committee members who sat only on this particular committee group. There was a sitting allowance for attending these meetings so leaders tended to make an effort to be there. Failure to attend could lead to demotion from a particular position.

Again, the meetings, which lasted for about two hours, were conducted primarily in Luganda. Minutes of proceedings were kept, and there was a great deal of participation from the floor. The meetings provided a forum for the executive to discuss progress to date and future strategy with its constituents. A wide range of issues concerning the entire market were discussed—including taxes, the evening market, and the hidden power networks that seemed to play an increasingly important role in the way things were run. Resolutions were passed that authorized the MVA executive to pursue a particular course of action—usually vis-à-vis the Kampala City Council. The largest issue facing the MVA in the late 1980s and early 1990s was the growth on its doorsteps of the evening market.

The chairman would open meetings by asking one of those present to say a prayer. To encourage tolerance in the market between members of different faiths, the prayer was rotated between members of different religions. The chairman would then give his report and the general secretary read the agenda. The agenda items were discussed, including matters arising from the minutes of the last meeting and other business. The meetings closed with a prayer.

At one typical conference in 1992, the chairman congratulated members for the successful completion of the cadre course, a military and political education program organized by the government. He informed members that the course was informative on affairs in Uganda. The chairman wanted to discuss cleanliness in the market. The vendors asked for an explanation about the temporary stalls in the parking yard of the market. There was a brief explanation of the matters raised.

The resolutions passed by the MVA Leaders Conference (like those passed by the MVA central executive) were binding on the members. The fact remained that the Leaders Conferences provided an important and regular channel for communication between the lowest and the highest levels of authority and management in the market. Formal and actual control over many of the meetings at the zonal and departmental level came from the Leaders Conferences. They provided a key sounding board for the main network of power in Owino Market, and, in a concrete way, were a vibrant example of "micro-politics" in action. The resolutions passed became policy positions for the MVA central executive, which became responsible for implementing them. Thus the MVA Executive would adopt the strategies and organize the actions that the Conference endorsed for dealing with issues such as the evening market and the World Bank Market Reconstruction Project. Conversely, the MVA executive's actions depended entirely upon its ability to mobilize support from the membership as a whole. With great challenges to the continued existence of the market, the MVA faced a constant need to demonstrate to vendors at the rank and file level that it was pursuing everyone's collective best interests.

Hot Star Football Club Meeting. A large number of social organizations in the market dealt with social welfare, and others handled cultural activities, but the largest organization focusing on social activities was the market's soccer team. Within the market each department tried to field a soccer team (in 1992 there were 30 such teams, which played against each other), and the best player from these "lower teams" were selected for the market team—the Hot Stars, who played in a larger league.

During the football season, monthly meetings of the Hot Stars Football Club lasted about half an hour, with between 80 and 150 participants. The meetings were held at Nakivubo Settlement School, just beside the market. The team was founded in the early 1980s by the Kyebandula Department and the idea soon caught on and spread to other departments in the market. According to our informant, during its early years the Hot Stars were used by then President Milton Obote's Uganda People's Congress (UPC) to try to attract support in the market. Apparently, views about soccer and who should be on the team were couched in political language along party lines, and the manager of the team was known to be a staunch UPC supporter. In late 1985 the manager was sacked and a new manager with no political affiliation was hired. By 1992 sport and politics in Owino had been separated.

The leader of the setting was the team manager, who also acted as the team chairman. The vice-chairman in 1992 was also the chairman of the Market Vendors Association. These two were assisted by a general secretary and a treasurer and 12 footballers. The composition of those attending the meetings varied considerably from meeting to meeting, but one of the deciding factors seemed to be whether or not individual departments had a representative from their department playing on the team. As fundraising for uniforms and other expenses was an important activity, richer departments held greater possibilities for the management of the football club.

Generally meetings would, once again, open with a prayer, this time delivered by the team manager. A report on management would follow. Department leaders would then report on collection of dues. People would give views on matters raised, and the meeting would close with a prayer. The meetings tended to be practical and direct and dealt with the team and financial issues. Minutes were kept of the proceedings. Women also took part in the discussion and were important backers of the team.

The Hot Stars were clearly seen as an important and central focus of the market vendors, and the team's performance in matches was taken extremely seriously in the market. At a meeting in 1992, for example, the main focus of the discussion had to do with a circular issued by the KCC town clerk banning organizations from collecting dues in the market. The town clerk had abolished the MVA collections, a move that members believed was inappropriate and should not be enforced. The ensuing discussion focused on strategies for approaching the town clerk to get him to rescind this directive. In spite of this directive, the Hot Stars did fundraising through appeals to richer members of the market community. All the leading vendors in the market contributed financially to the football team and acted as an informal board of directors. The MVA, senior market administrator, and the MMC also contributed funds to the Hot Stars.

Umoja Securicor Staff Meeting. Umoja Securicor Company, a private company, provided security services to vendors in the market. It was founded in 1978 out of a need by the market vendors for protection of their goods. Originally goods had been left in the stalls overnight and losses due to theft were often incurred. Vendors decided to select a few individuals among themselves to act as security guards, paying them monthly. Over time the guards found it risky to safeguard people's goods without becoming a registered and officially recognized group. The request for registration was made and the town clerk allowed them to operate with an official letter from him. A change in the form of registration came about when a new town clerk took over. He even advised the guards to get an office. The guards were incorporated in 1986. There was a structural change in 1989 when a wooden storage building they had used burnt down. After that they used an open store.

Umoja Securicor staff meetings took place on an irregular basis and lasted for about an hour. When one of its directors was present, up to 15 people would be in attendance. The meetings were held in the company field office, which consisted of a number of stalls joined together. The first meetings took place in 1986 when the company expanded by hiring five additional guards. At that time the company's general secretary informed the company director that the staff had problems forwarding their views and opinions to the company's executive committee on an individual basis. It was therefore decided to begin holding staff meetings, in which problems and solutions at the lower levels could be discussed and then forwarded to the executive as group decisions.

The meetings were chaired by the general secretary and occasionally the managing director, when he was invited to do so. The language used at the meetings was Luganda, although minutes were kept in English. Staff members were informed of the meetings three days in advance and they were expected to attend as part of their duties. Onlookers were not permitted and were chased away by staff. Occasionally, when sensitive issues were being discussed, the meetings were conducted in English to limit the understanding of people in the nearby area. In general, discussions focused upon the financial problems of employees, particularly increasing salaries for employees and provision of supper for the group employees (casual labourers). They also covered issues such as the functioning of the organization, improvement of security, complaints of clients, and conflicts between Umoja and RCs or police.

One 1992 meeting was called to address the issue of insecurity following an increase in thefts of goods. The general secretary asked his watchmen about the circumstances of the thefts and the type of people who were stealing. Members gave their views of the problem, noting that the market was used as a thoroughfare by many residents of the area, that many entrances had no gates, making it difficult to tell thieves from passersby, and that there was insufficient overhead lighting in the market. The general secretary noted that part of the problem lay in recruiting watchmen without providing them with sufficient training. It was therefore resolved that watchmen be trained after recruitment. The decision was to take effect immediately. The general secretary promised to take the trainees to the Nsambya Police College for better training. The issues of lack of gates and poor lighting were forwarded to the KCC market administrators.

Popular Organizations. The political settings of civil society in Owino Market, far from being ad hoc and transitory, were well established and broadly based. Within the MVA, each of the settings considered here points towards an open and inclusive organization that struggles to respond to the needs of vendors and present carefully articulated positions to outside authorities. The myriad roles that the MVA had assumed by 1992 attest to both its legitimacy among the vendors themselves and its ability to provide an effective forum for the many different peoples vending in Owino Market. The 1992 case-solving meeting in Kawempe-1 Department, for instance, exemplified the elaboration and method of the "informal" judicial system. The meeting of the Inner Market zonal executive committee pointed toward the types of issues that vendors in the market tended to be concerned about on a broader basis. The MVA Leaders Conference showed how policy-making and strategizing among the vendors was conducted in an open and inclusive setting. Going beyond the MVA, the Hot Stars Football Club meeting brought out some of the issues around political manipulation and representation within the market. And finally, the Umoja Securicor setting demonstrated how the vendors had developed a system to buttress the inadequate security arrangements within the market. Even this setting, which had evolved into a quasi-private-sector security firm, showed many of the same features that prevailed among other more public and popular organizations within the market.

What all of these meetings suggest is that the popular organizations created political spaces in Owino Market that were characterized by a high degree of openness and inclusion. They were highly organized and systematized with information flowing rapidly between different groups, and they were productive—both in building up strategies to achieve vendors' objectives as a group, and in resisting encroachment from external forces whenever possible. When we juxtapose these settings with other settings in Owino Market that were tied directly to state apparatus, clear differences are visible.

State Apparatus

Several state organs were active in the market in 1992. The most visible was the Kampala City Council, responsible for administration of the market, enforcement of health and commercial regulations, and revenue collection. In addition, security and crime issues tended to play a preponderant role in events in the market, so the national police force had also established a presence. Included below are discussions of four activity settings that emerged directly from state involvement in Owino Market.

One of the most important issues in the market, in addition to attracting sufficient numbers of customers, was security: what to do with goods at night, what to do in the case of thefts or disagreements, and what to do in the case of physical attack. Much of the institutional infrastructure developed by the vendors was designed to address the adjudication of commercial conflicts, but matters did not stop there. The vendors required protection of their commodities at night, and they needed access to the official legal system. To address these needs a police post had been established in the market. But there was a popular perception among vendors that the police force and, indeed, the entire judicial system were highly corrupt and therefore unlikely to provide vendors with the sort of protection and conflict resolution they needed. As a result the police force (Ministry of the Interior) was bolstered by the private security company, Umoja Securicor. The relationship between the public and the private systems was a constant source of tension between the police and the security company, with the vendors trapped in between.

KCC Market Administrators Meeting. One of the most important settings in the market affecting the vendors was the KCC Market Administrators Meeting, for it was here that KCC directives and circulars were disseminated to the staff who would be responsible for implementing them. These meetings were held twice monthly and generally lasted for two hours. There were between 7 and 13 participants, and although the meetings took place in an enclosed space (the Market Administrators' Office) there were frequent interruptions from individual vendors seeking assistance on various issues. All the participants were employees of the KCC. The market administrators were recruited from all over the country and needed a school leavers certificate to be eligible for the post. In 1992 there were nine market administrators, a senior and an assistant senior market administrator, two cashiers, and six labourers. The market administrators were responsible for the daily administration of the market, including rent and dues collection, implementation of KCC circulars concerning market management, and maintenance of market facilities.

There was no prayer prior to the meetings, but minutes were kept of all proceedings. The senior market administrator (or his assistant, or another temporary chairman) opened the meetings and presented the agenda. The agenda items were discussed, and solutions to problems were found. For example, at a meeting in October 1992 the discussion addressed the performance of the market administrators with respect to revenue collection, cleanliness, and the task of market administration. The senior market administrator and the assistant chief gave advice about improving the level of performance, and the meeting closed.

The market administrators were the front-line officers of the KCC and the Market Administration Section with regard to Owino Market. If someone had to be evicted for failure to pay rent, it was the market administrators who had to do it. Similarly, if one of the vendors had contravened a health regulation, the KCC health inspector would identify the infraction but the market administrator had to impose the sanction. Hence the market administrators were not well liked by the vendors, and indeed by dint of their overzealous enforcement role a few market administrators had come to be widely despised by the vendors. One individual became the focus of heated discussions between the MVA, who sought his removal from the market, and the KCC, who valued his ability to "motivate" the vendors to pay their rent on time.

Vendors might have seen market administrators as necessary evils, but the Market Administration Section did not have an especially high view of the vendors either. Given the low wages within the KCC, and the relative frequency with which those wages went unpaid, attitudes to market vendors were ambivalent. Formally, vendors were constantly denigrated within the KCC, but when it came to personal survival, it was not unusual for Market Administration staff to have stalls of their own that they would in turn sublet to others. For their part, the vendors believed that many of the administrators succumbed to the temptation to pocket rents or daily dues, while KCC members had a keenly felt sense that many of those working in the markets were corrupt. To offset this pattern, the KCC rotated market administrators, not only among positions in a particular market, but also among different markets. In that way, the KCC hoped to keep pilfering to a minimum.

Police Post. The police post was established in Owino Market in 1978 by the inspector-general of police. The officer in charge (OC), responsible for dealing with crime in the market, was assisted by a second in command, a Criminal Investigation Department officer in charge; a Special Branches officer in charge; and a woman in charge. They, in turn, were supported by 25 other uniformed police, five of them women. The police post was open every day the market was open, from six in the morning till eight at night. Generally, the police dealt with cases referred to them by individual vendors or other associations within the market. Cases were brought to the police by any administrative official concerned, and the Criminal Investigation Department (CID) officer at the counter received the case, recorded it, and addressed it to the officer in charge. The officer decided which market department should handle the case and then handed it over to them. The head of department then decided whether to deal with the problem within the setting or to send it to the Central Police Station. CID dealt with major criminal cases, particularly cases of theft. The uniformed officers performed general duties and handled minor cases.

While the types of cases varied considerably, one example involved a case of assault in which a man had entered the home of his lover and attacked her in the presence of her husband, causing bodily harm. The two complainants and the culprit were brought in by the RC 1 defence secretary. When the CID at the counter received the case, he referred it to the officer in charge. The culprit asked to compensate the woman, but she refused to accept compensation. The police sent the case to the Central Police Station and later to court, where the culprit was convicted of assault and sentenced to six months' imprisonment.

While the police were certainly an ever-present force in the market, they were treated with a certain amount of mistrust by the vendors. Like all other civil servants in Uganda, they had low official salaries, and it was widely recognized that they could not survive on that pay alone. Vendors accepted the idea that they must pay for security, but there was a deep-rooted mistrust of the police to the point where anyone with the means would rather pay a private company to guard their goods. Consequently, the police force tended to have an antagonistic relationship with Umoja Securicor and was always happy to entertain complaints against them. For example, early in October 1992 goods worth USh.600,000 were stolen from a vendor. Because it was entrusted with the safekeeping of the goods, Umoja compensated the vendor, but its staff did not call upon the police to help them investigate the case and catch the thieves.

Law Seminar by the Officer-in-Charge (OC). Law seminars were initiated by the officer in charge in 1991 when he found there was no working system of co-operation between police and market administration. The high rate of criminal cases indicated a need for him to talk to vendors to identify areas of insecurity. The seminars, held on a weekly basis in Nakivubo School, lasted for about half an hour. On different occasions the OC invited speakers from outside the market to make presentations at these seminars.

The OC would write to the RC and the MVA office to inform leaders of different departments of the timetable for impending seminars. Vendors who were interested were free to attend, but the emphasis was on getting leaders to attend. The MVA central executive would also single out departmental leaders, who were told to attend. The meetings were opened by the OC, who addressed the participants on their role in leadership in regard to security. After his address he would invite participants to give their suggestions about how security could be strengthened in the market. Participants voiced complaints, particularly about the police, and the OC was obliged to respond. The OC closed the meeting by summing up the proceedings.

These law seminars included an open expression of conflict, particularly on the part of the vendors, with the police force. People took the opportunity to condemn whatever malpractice they believed the police had committed. One major type of issue raised was the mishandling of cases by police, and especially the release of criminals immediately after arrest. People demanded an explanation of that practice.

The meeting I documented was about leaders' powers to handle cases and to what extent they should handle cases, given that most cases were first received in the departments. The meeting was opened by the OC, who explained the purpose of the meeting to the participants. He expressed his concern about some criminal cases that were not forwarded to the police post, mainly because the department leaders were ignorant of the nature of the cases. Participants were invited to give their views and to ask questions, which the OC answered. It was agreed that cases were to be brought straight to the police. When leaders could not determine whether the cases were civil or criminal, the leaders were to consult the OC. The OC thanked the participants for attending.

Women vendors in the market seemed to play an active role in these seminars, voicing complaints and seeking clarification on particular issues. They were concerned about their particular problems in the market, including issues of sexual abuse. For example, one woman sought advice about what to do about a male vendor who had impregnated her niece, who was employed in the man's stall. The man had agreed to give financial assistance to the girl, but the woman wanted him to marry her niece.

Incidentally, as a result of these seminars Kampala's leading English-language daily newspaper, *The New Vision*, published a letter on October 31, 1992, praising the performance of the OC in Owino Market for doing an outstanding job in combating crime in Owino and the surrounding area, and in particular for conducting the seminars.

Market Management Committee Meeting. To deal with the deteriorating relations between itself and the various market vendors associations in the markets around the city, the Kampala City Council, on the advice of the chief market administrator, established one Market Management Committee (MMC) in each market to co-manage the markets. These committees were intended to act as a bridge between the KCC market administration and the vendors. The stated intention was to try to encourage a sense of co-management of the markets. Among other things, the KCC hoped that the MMCs would formulate administrative policy for markets, organize and control groups in the markets, allocate stalls, fight illegal markets, mobilize vendors, and monitor revenue collection. They were composed of representatives from the vendors association, the neighbouring resistance councils, one representative from the market administration, and one independent. Initially each MMC was to be composed of elected representatives of the market vendors plus neighbourhood representatives as well as appointed members from the KCC. The members were to sit for terms of one year and then be re-elected (or not) in annual elections. As an incentive to members of the committee, the KCC approved a sitting allowance to be paid to each individual who attended a meeting. In the case of Owino Market, the original size of the MMC was seven people: three from the vendors, three from RCs, and one from the KCC.

The MVA welcomed the creation of its own MMC in Owino because, it seemed, with such a committee in the market there would be less likelihood of rent increases taking place without consultation. MVA leaders were elected as the vendors' representatives to the MMC to discuss market policy. The first meeting of the MMC took place on July 12, 1990, and an issue that immediately moved to the forefront was that of the evening market, which was continuing to grow far beyond the confines of the sidewalks to which it had been originally allotted. From the MVA's perspective, the growth of the evening market was taking place for two principal reasons: the failure of the KCC to improve conditions such as lighting, flooring, and security in the daytime market; and the KCC's failure to take serious action against the evening market. Initially the MVA leaders brought pressure for movement on both issues as quickly as possible. The KCC was not pleased by this turn of events. During the course of 1991 the issue of the illegal evening market dominated discussions at both MMC and

MVA meetings. Still, despite numerous meetings on various fronts, the evening market continued to grow.

The first and all subsequent meetings of the MMC were held in the office of the assistant chief market administrator in the building of the Kampala City Council itself. The office is enclosed, and no onlookers were permitted. In theory the MMC was supposed to meet twice monthly, but by 1992 the Owino Market MMC was meeting only sporadically. Meetings varied from 45 minutes to three hours depending upon the agenda, with generally between seven and thirteen participants. Each meeting opened with a prayer and minutes were kept of the proceedings—although my repeated requests for minutes did not meet with success. All the members on the MMC were Baganda, all spoke English, and the meetings were conducted primarily in English. The leader of the MMC was the assistant chief market administrator, Central Division, Kampala District.

In many ways the MMC and the MVA had overlapping functions. For example, at a meeting in early 1992 a report on an inspection of the market by MMC officials indicated that fish vendors were working under filthy conditions. Particularly unsanitary was the trench where fish waste was deposited. Department leaders and a few vendors were summoned and addressed by the MMC officials. It was discovered that two vendors' assistants cleaning fish were responsible for the poor sanitary conditions. The meeting resolved that the vendors would go back and clean the department themselves and that in future they would keep close control of those who cleaned the fish. The decision was accepted by both parties and took effect immediately.

The MMC had the authority to deal with all of the public space in the market, including the allocation of stalls to aspiring vendors and the holding of meetings by organizations in the market. All associations in the market were to inform MMC of their meetings, the agenda of the meeting, and of any outsiders invited to attend, and the MMC had the right to proscribe any meeting that it decided did not benefit the people. It would act against a meeting through the senior market administrator, who informed the offending association in writing. For example, one meeting was called by the MVA to address its members without the knowledge of the MMC zone representatives. The secretary reported this to the senior market administrator, who immediately told them to conclude and never again to address people without informing the MMC.

Although the MMC was intended to provide a new participatory vehicle for the management of markets, it was a short-lived experiment. At a meeting of the MMC that I attended in October 1992, I noted three striking aspects that indicated the committee was failing. First, the meeting took place in English; second, it was in an enclosed space—in the senior market administrators' office; and third, it did not have a quorum. The use of English excluded many vendors; and its location in the official offices also implied a certain complicity with the market administration. But, most importantly, the lack of quorum meant that it had already failed to garner widespread support. This example opened up another avenue of research that proved to be extremely useful to understanding political space in and around Owino Market. Representatives of local resistance councils were supposed to be on this committee, but none of them had shown up. Upon inquiry, I discovered that the new representatives had yet to be elected. When I subsequently went to interview neighbouring resistance councils, I discovered that they had no intention of rejoining the Owino Market MMC. Instead, they were focusing their efforts on managing the evening market, largely because they were able to generate more personal income from their involvement there than in Owino.

Conclusion

This overview of the various meetings in Owino Market in 1992 provides a sharply defined picture of how the institutions of the state and the organizations of civil society relate to one another on an everyday basis. Certainly, a wide range of both organs of the state and organizations of the vendors were active in Owino Market. Despite an ongoing need for both sides to work together, the meetings within the vendors' organizations were democratic and participatory, and those of the state institutions tended to be autocratic and unpredictable.

The level of organization and the frequency of meetings among the vendors suggest a high degree of legitimacy and participation. Assuming that of the 4,000-plus vendors in Owino Market, only half were attending the various meetings, each vendor who did attend was spending about 56 hours a year in meetings of the MVA alone. Table 7.1 uses data gathered from the settings survey to indicate the pattern of vendor participation. In this I have assumed that the participation in the lowest levels of the MVA is somewhat sporadic (slightly more than half the vendors might attend), but that as one moves up the chain attendance becomes more regular. What emerges from these calculations is an astonishing amount of time spent by vendors meeting to discuss the various levels of problems faced in the market. Indeed, the vendors in Owino Market were spending over 120,000 hours a year attending meetings of the MVA alone. This strongly suggests that the vendors were finding it both necessary and useful to attend these meetings to ensure that issues involving the regulation of Owino Market did not pass them by.

The large number of meetings in Owino Market and the high level of organization of the vendors are surprising given the political turmoil that dominated Kampala for so many years, and given the dangers of organizing and leadership posed during the years of violent and abusive government

Table 7.1

Vendor Participation in Meetings

	Meetings per year	No. of participants	Duration (hours)	Total person-hours
DEPARTMENT LEVEL				
57 depts (40 vendors per meeting)	12	2,280	2	54,720
case-solving—57 depts	20	1,140	1	22,800
ZONAL LEVEL				
zonal exec. meetings— 4 zones	48	64	2	6,144
case-solving—4 zones	20	40	1	800
general meetings	6	4,000	1	24,000
MVA CENTRAL EXECUTIVE				
executive meetings	12	16	2	384
case-solving meetings	300	6	1	900
MVA leaders conference	24	150	3	10,800
Total MVA meeting time per year in person-hours				120,548

under Idi Amin and Milton Obote's second period in power (1980-85). Clearly, a wide variety of issues needed to be resolved, and the cost of addressing many of them was borne directly by the vendors.

Analysis of the activity settings reveals an important relationship between the costs involved in resolving particular issues and the level at which they were resolved. At the lowest, or individual vendor, level the most common type of problem involved commercial conflict: for example, deals that had gone bad and needed to be resolved. A good illustration is the case-solving meeting that dealt with the disagreement between a woman and a transporter about the prices involved in a particular transaction, which was only one of many similar cases we heard about in the market. In a sense, the resolution of such differences involved time and money for all parties concerned, and generally, if the sums involved were not tremendously high, the cases could be resolved fairly quickly.

The second level of issues has to do with the provision of services such as security and solid waste disposal, which had a wider impact on vendors. All vendors sustained an important part of the costs of these services, but their provision was not equally critical to the well-being of all vendors. In these cases vendors responded to the shortfall in services in two distinct ways.

In the case of the security services, those whose stalls were within the enclosed Inner Zone, where the police post itself was situated, had less to fear than the 4,000 vendors whose stalls were outside the gate and walls. Thus, the clients of Umoja Securicor were, for the most part, richer vendors whose stalls were outside. The account of the growth of Umoja Securicor indicates that the town clerk was implicitly supporting the idea of the privatization of this service because the KCC did not have, or was unwilling to provide, sufficient funds for additional guards in the market. In addition, the perception by the vendors that the judicial system and by association the police detachment were ineffective and corrupt meant that they had little to lose by investing their own resources in developing a private police force.

The cases of solid waste management are especially interesting because the issue affected vendors differently, but the KCC was still considered to be responsible for waste management in the market. The case of the fish cleaners being approached by the Market Management Committee and the case of the flour department, which obliquely made reference to the responsibilities of the KCC in waste disposal, both touch on this issue. There is ample evidence that Owino Market had a big problem with waste disposal. There were few skips or disposal bins in the market, and the ones that were there were constantly overflowing. Not surprisingly, vendors sought other means of dealing with their waste. There were two large drainage channels running through and under the market, and many vendors used them as convenient waste depositories. The vendors further away from the channels required a waste disposal service more frequently and pushed for greater KCC involvement in waste disposal. The same sort of claims was also made in the case of facilities such as water, lighting, and toilets. Lighting existed only in the Inner Market, water was supplied at only a few standpipes in the vicinity, and the entire market had only two sets of toilets. These issues were mentioned frequently as necessary services that vendors would be more than willing to pay for.

A third level of issues relates to the operation and evolution of the market as a whole, and in the long run this issue deeply affected both vendors and the KCC. It included issues like the reconstruction project for Owino Market, the growth and apparent institutionalization of the evening market in Kampala, and the associated loss of income and revenues by the KCC from Owino Market proper. These issues were dealt with by various activity settings, including the MVA central executive, the Market

Management Committee, and the KCC administration. The account of the market administrators' meeting clearly indicates that the priority from the KCC side was the generation and monitoring of revenue from the market. Owino Market provided 25 percent of total market revenues for the KCC, and market revenues constituted about 25 percent of all KCC's income. Since the rest of the KCC's revenues came during two months of the fiscal year and were allocated immediately, the KCC would have been unable to function at all without daily income from the markets. Markets and the revenues they generated were critical to the KCC activities.

The political settings approach, then, helps to build an understanding of the scope of organization and conflict in Owino Market and of how organizations in civil society cope with, come into conflict with, and depend upon state agencies. At one moment, in one context, the MVA may be in a conflictual situation with the KCC, and on another issue it may be seeking support and assistance from the very same representative. The breadth of the issues plus the need to maintain a continuing working relationship means that relations between organizations in civil society and the state remain inextricably linked to one another.

To a large extent elections for leadership, respect for religion, adherence to agendas and protocol, and tendency to favour compromise were the order of the day for organizations in Owino Market. Inevitably, there were cases in which departments had corrupt or dictatorial leaders, and so on, but by and large the popular organizations in Owino Market were characterized by openness, in contrast to those of the state. Not surprisingly, the embodiment of the state at the local level tended to assume a more rigid and exclusionary form. The participants were generally there as poorly paid employees with little authority to implement or suggest alternatives. In general they were not well-liked by the vendors, even though they were there to assist with market issues. The vendors had chosen to create their own organizational structure to help them regulate issues that arose within the market. In Owino, market administrators had relatively little independence and were there to implement policies and regulations that emanated from the local state—the Kampala City Council.

With the lens of the political settings approach focused on Owino Market, a large, disorganized mass turns out to be a highly sophisticated and organized entity with an extremely articulate and subtle approach to politics and regulation. Indeed, while the research spotlight on local politics tends to fall on riots and political violence from below, these events may represent the culmination of much more elaborate political strategies worked out far in advance.[14] By looking for, and engaging with the politics of everyday life, local governments can deal more effectively with improving their cities.

Notes

1. World Bank, *World Development Report: Workers in an Integrating World* (Washington: IBRD, 1995), Table 31, pp.222-23.

2. See Michael Cohen and Josef Leitmann, "Will the World Bank's Real 'New Urban Policy' Please Stand Up?" *Habitat International* 18,4 (1994), pp.117-26; G. Jones and Peter Ward, "The World Bank's New Urban Management Programme: Paradigm Shift or Policy Continuity?" *Habitat International* 18,3 (1994), pp.33-51; A. Osmont, *La Banque Mondiale et les Villes* (Paris: Editions Karthala, 1995); E. Wegelin, "Everything You Always Wanted to Know about the Urban Management Programme (But Were Afraid to Ask)," *Habitat International* 18,4 (1994), pp.127-37.

3. See A. Osmont, "La Banque mondiale et les politiques urbaines nationales," *Politique Africaine* 17 (mars 1985), pp.58-73.

4. Government of Uganda, *Background to the Budget 1995/96* (Entebbe: Government Printers, 1995), p.1.

5. Compare M. Mamdani, "The Politics of Democratic Transition," in *Uganda: Landmarks in Rebuilding a Nation*, ed. P. Langseth, J. Katorobo, E. Brett, and J. Munene (Kampala: Fountain Publishers, 1995), with World Bank, *Growing out of Poverty* (Washington: IBRD, 1994).

6. World Bank, *Uganda: Report on Urban Finance and Management*, Report no. 523 (Washington: IBRD, 1985), p.i.

7. Ministry of Planning and Economic Development, *Manpower and Employment in Uganda: Report of the National Manpower Survey, 1989* (Entebbe: Government Printers, 1989), p.ix.

8. Ministry of Planning and Economic Development, *Report on the Uganda National Household Budget Survey, 1989-90* (Entebbe: Government Printers, 1991), p.46.

9. See A. Bigsten and Steve Kayizzi-Mugerwa, "Adaptation and Distress in the Urban Economy: A Study of Kampala Households," *World Development* 20 (October 1992), pp.1,423-41; and N. Musisi, "Baganda Women's Night Market Activities," in *African Market Women and Economic Power: The Role of Women in African Economic Development*, ed. B. House-Midamba and F. Ekechi (Westport, Conn.: Greenwood Press, 1995).

10. World Bank, *Staff Appraisal Report: Uganda, First Urban Project* (Washington: IBRD, 1990).

11. Kampala City Council, *Market Development Programme*, 1992, p.2.

12. Musupali (Owino) Market Vendors Association, "Constitution and Rules," drawn up by Jonathan Mattu, City Advocates Chambers, Kampala, June 1988.

13. Field Notes, "Account of a Case-Solving Meeting, Food Houses Department," Owino Market, Kampala, 1992.

14. John Walton and David Seddon, *Free Markets and Food Riots: The Politics of Global Adjustment* (Oxford: Blackwell, 1994).

Chapter 8

Claiming Space for Women:
Nicaragua during and after Revolution, 1977-94

Katherine Isbester

The women's movement in Nicaragua, because it is among the most dynamic in Latin America, has attracted the attention of academics and activists interested in popular political action, especially political action by women. Its success raises a fundamental question: how did the women's movement in Nicaragua gain such strength so quickly and then adapt itself to radically different political regimes?

Attempts to analyze the movement have been hampered by its rapidly changing content as well as by the extreme shifts in governmental regime. They have failed to notice one constant in all the flux: the consistent success of the women's movement in creating and using political settings to focus discussion and initiate action on issues. By analyzing the role of political settings in the Nicaraguan women's movement, we can understand how the movement emerged, grew powerful, and responded to the rapid and profound changes in the government and the economy. We can also make a key addition to social movement theory.

Given that political settings are the occasions and venues—the meetings, town hall gatherings, roundtables, conventions, assemblies, demonstrations, and workshops—in which people speak, converse, debate, and decide about matters of interest to a collectivity (see chapter 3), my focus here is on the political settings in which collective action confronts institutional constraint and establishes a space free of external control.[1] The freedom or subjection of a political space, however, varies in degree, and grasping how it varies is important for understanding how political space works.

The political settings at issue here reside on the boundary between civil society and the state, incorporating, in varying degrees, elements and actors of both. The sharpness of the divide between state and civil society can also vary, and its variation in Nicaragua is an important aspect of the changes in regime in the period 1977-94. At the same time, I believe that a well-formulated conception of political space has to augment existing social movement theory. Indeed, the two major social movement theories have not adequately addressed the role of public spaces.[2] By recognizing the role and broad range of locations of public spaces, we can, I hope, not just explain the Nicaraguan women's movement but also overcome the weaknesses inherent in both schools of social movement theory.

Theoretical Approaches to Social Movements and Public Spaces

Social movement theory developed in response to the rise of collective polit-ical actions that did not fit existing categories of party and interest-group and social-class activity. Movements and actions around issues relating to women, ecological damage, religious concerns, old people, young people, racial groups, and many other matters called forth new kinds of social the-ory. Two schools of analysis—commonly called resource mobilization theory and identity theory—staked out contrasting approaches. Today most social movement theorists recognize that both schools have their advantages, and they combine elements from each to explain the growth and development of a social movement.[3]

Resource mobilization theory powerfully explains what materials (or resources) are needed for a successful social movement organization. These resources are quantifiable and generally external to the group. The theory analyzes how a social movement group is able to maintain itself and grow into a social movement organization through access to resources such as means of communication (large and small), leadership skills, pre-existing support groups, and money. The theory is able to take account of the effects of changing political structures on social movements as they alter the avail-ability and utility of resources.

Two weaknesses limit the usefulness of resource mobilization the-ory. First, it fails to see the importance of political space. Access to and use of public settings could be considered a valuable resource for building a social movement, but so far the theory has not identified public space as a resource. As a result, resource mobilization theory fails to analyze how resources are mobilized through political action in public spaces. This lacuna in resource mobilization theory can be traced to the second weakness: a dichotomized conception of state and civil society relations. For the theory, civil society and the state occupy distinct arenas and pursue mutually exclusive con-cerns.[4] Because resource mobilization theory posits social movements as existing wholly in civil society, it concludes that social and political changes occur solely through confrontations between the state and civil society.[5]

It is much more realistic to postulate that civil society can have degrees of autonomy from the state. In fact, civil society and the state can be mutually embedded: for example, in a corporatist state.[6] Social movements and the political settings through which they work can also have degrees of autonomy from the state. The extent to which the state and civil society are interwoven alters the techniques of political action. In a corporatist state, a social movement's political settings can be created, funded, and directed by the state to achieve ends beneficial to both the social movement and the government. In a civil society with a high degree of autonomy from the state, political spaces can be used to lobby the state and civil society and/or strengthen the social movement's identity.

In comparison to resource mobilization theory, which emphasizes the external elements necessary for a successful social movement, identity theory emphasizes the internal dimension. Identity theory has the great merit of focusing on the internal process of constructing meanings in a social movement. It begins with the assumption that human beings are meaning-shaping; that they create identities and that each identity group develops an ethos that can organize action and give an impetus to participation. The ethos is created through individuals resisting the dominant norms of society and interacting to form a like-minded group. The group's awareness, born from resistance and reflection, activates political engagement in an attempt to enact its alternative understanding.

There is, however, a theoretical weakness here due to the absence of a concrete conception of the process of constructing political actions and meanings. Identity theory offers the possibility of understanding the unifying elements that bring actors together in political settings, but it lacks a full conception of political space and of the political work that is carried on in it. The ideas of identity theory are of particular interest for the Nicaraguan case. Theorists claim that identity-based social movements prefer to organize themselves through small collectives uniting into ad hoc networks.[7] This alignment resolves the tension over which is primary in a movement's effort to achieve specific political goals: the need for identity or the need for co-operation and compromise. In the collectives the identity remains paramount, while in the network co-operation and compromise are essential, because the goal is explicitly political. The way in which collectives and networks work together in the process of political action becomes evident in their use of political settings—spaces in which participants in the networks and the collectives meet, discuss, organize, and agitate. Political settings connect the micro-settings of the collectives with the political actions organized by the networks. In such a way, a decentralized social movement can confront a centralized state.

A fuller conception of political settings can fill the theoretical void by bringing a focus to the political work that occurs in them: choosing goals and actions; persuading the state, other groups in civil society, and a movement's own members to accept new ideas; and challenging value-laden symbols. In each of the time periods of the Nicaraguan women's movement, these three kinds of political work were found in political settings. While the resources mobilized may have been different for each political setting, and although the organization of the political space and the women's movement may have altered over the 15-year span, the actual work that the political space performed remained constant.

Political settings perform two functions for the social movement. First, they constitute the occasions for the social movement to prioritize its concerns—that is, to outline general guidelines or approaches that members or collectives may incorporate into their identity. Political settings are especially useful in this regard when the social movement is new and in the process of formation. The Nicaraguan women's movement used political settings to initiate new networks, collectives, and identities in 1977, 1983, and 1991. In closely related work, political settings also serve to organize the social movement around a specific issue and help it to strategize to achieve explicit goals. As organizing meetings or strategy sessions, political settings can, for example, involve members of the government and opposition parties, bureaucrats, and non-governmental organizations, in addition to grassroots activists. Due to their position, not all of these people would be able to demonstrate, petition, or otherwise be public about their participation in the social movement. Indeed, many of them probably would not consider themselves as participants in the social movement. Rather, they would see themselves as attempting to rectify a specific problem. In Nicaragua, political settings of this kind were most evident during the fight against AIDS, a battle spearheaded by the gay and lesbian network of the women's movement.

The second function of political space is to articulate the social movement's ethos within the political sphere. Political settings help solidify identity formation for a network, a collective, or the movement as a whole. As Alberto Melucci puts it, "No collective well-being can be assured as a final action. It has to be renewed by decisions, negotiations, and actions."[8] The Nicaraguan women's movement continually renegotiated its own identity in political settings, consolidated its understanding, and then reshaped the identity when the circumstances changed—with one notable exception. The government-controlled women's movement, AMNLAE, refused to allow a women's identity to be renegotiated in the final years of the Sandinista government. In response, women abandoned AMNLAE and began their own movement with its own political settings autonomous from the Sandinista women's movement. As Melucci states, "The formation, maintenance and alternation through time of a self-reflective identity requires social settings free from control or repression."[9] In such a way, political settings also normalize democratic procedures and expand political rights.[10]

Political settings are also sources of influence for a social movement. In the process of achieving identity, ideas are discussed, debated, and promulgated. Because members of the social movement can include state and party actors, and because the debate can occur through the media, civil society and the state may be inadvertently involved and the debate may influence civic values and state policies. Even if civil society and the state are not influenced through the debate within the women's movement, they can be influenced by the identity chosen by the women's movement. That chosen identity will necessarily influence the issues and the means of political action. Movement identities often include a sense of suffering from longstanding injustice. One of the most effective means of changing state policy in a democracy is to persuade the general public that an injustice is being committed and that policies must correct that injustice. Thus the assertion of an identity strategically enters into debates about justice and injustice in civil society.

One of the most effective methods of communicating new values and changing public norms is through changing symbols. Symbols encode values and information. These values are created by the state, civil society institutions such as the church, and social movements; they are supported by the rest of society. If the symbol is changed, societal values, norms, and common information are also changed. Political settings are arenas in which the symbols of the dominant norms and the symbols of the alternative understanding clash. Throughout the history of the Nicaraguan women's movement, women have fought to change the symbol of mothers from passive martyr to oppressed survivor, and the markers of that fight are visible in some key political settings.

Political Settings and the Nicaraguan Women's Movement, 1977-79

Before 1977 no women's movement existed in Nicaragua. Within two years the Nicaraguan women's movement went from non-existence to an influential and mobilizing force. One of the reasons it could organize itself so quickly and become so powerful was its use of political space. Still, throughout that time political settings were under threat from the dictator Anastasio Somoza, and full mobilization of a social movement was thus not feasible.

In August 1977 two women organized a mass-based women's group to protest human rights violations.[11] The women's group was called the

Association of Women Protesting the National Problem (AMPRONAC)—the national problem being Somoza. Some 60 women participated in AMPRONAC's first assembly, which, along with the meetings around it, constituted the first major usage of political space by this neophyte social movement organization. That political space was used to map out organizing principles and discuss goals. The participants adopted three objectives: to fight for women's participation in politics; to defend women's rights in all sectors of society, including social, economic, and political; and to fight against human rights violations.[12] The political space gave women the opportunity to expand their mandate beyond human rights abuses and to begin developing their common commitments, modes of discussion, and forms of action—in other words, their ethos.

AMPRONAC also made good use of its resources. Lacking experienced female leaders, the group organized itself in a decentralized and democratic way. Horizontal leadership gave the women's groups a high degree of autonomy from the capital city, Managua, and facilitated the women's development of their own identity. Although AMPRONAC based itself on existing women's human rights groups, it was able to expand thanks to financial support from bourgeois women, who also assisted AMPRONAC greatly by organizing its communication system, uniting the disparate women's groups.

AMPRONAC mobilized these resources for its first political actions. In September 1977 it organized a public demonstration against human rights abuses. In January 1978 it occupied the United Nations building in Managua for 12 days, and on the final day it organized a conference attended by 600 women demanding news of disappeared children. Somoza responded to the emergence of political settings controlled by the women's movement with increased brutality against the women, including upper-class women. As the scope of the political protest expanded, AMPRONAC became radicalized and demanded broad democratic rights and an end to economic misery. Again, this more sophisticated understanding was reached in a national conference and spread to Nicaraguan women through the use of local political settings.

AMPRONAC also used political settings to challenge commonly held symbols. It used International Women's Day, March 8, to present its demands for equality. On Mother's Day, a day of commercialized mother worship, AMPRONAC's slogan was "The Best Gift Would Be a Free Country." It was the first time in Nicaragua that either of these two days had been used for political purposes.[13] The women learned how to take popular cultural images of women and transform these images into political statements.

By 1979 AMPRONAC numbered 8,000 to 10,000 women. Its most powerful impact was its very success in presenting women's reality and needs to themselves.[14] That success could not have been attained without the canny usage of political settings to forge and then further develop AMPRONAC's understanding, and its strategies.

Political Settings and the Sandinista Women's Movement 1979-91

The Sandinista Front for National Liberation (FSLN) overthrew the dictator in July 1979. It almost immediately began implementing its ideology of social justice and liberation through subsidized food, improved education and health, and increased opportunities for political involvement. Women benefited from these policies. However, the FSLN offerings were limited in scope and became even more limited once the counterrevolutionary war began to consume 40 percent of the government's budget.[15]

True to its corporatist leanings, the Sandinista Party absorbed AMPRONAC into its party and state, renaming it the Association of Nicaraguan Women Luisa Amanda Espinoza (AMNLAE). AMNLAE performed a number of important tasks throughout the 1980s, organizing women for political work, explaining new ideas of equality and freedom, petitioning the government for changes beneficial to women, building social infrastructure such as health care, child care, and education, and persuading women of the value of the Sandinista government. To achieve its ends, AMNLAE consistently used political settings at both the micro and national levels, lobbying civil society and the state to change gender norms about women's rights and roles. It also used political settings in the form of meetings to forge a Sandinista identity within the women's movement. In the early years of the government, this campaign was not difficult, because the state was generous to women, offering them goods and services and changing the worst of the gender inequalities found in law. The organization also used political settings to choose strategies and goals for the women's movement (see Figure 8.1).

By the mid-1980s AMNLAE had been so successful at its job that rank-and-file women started criticizing the FSLN for refusing women their reproductive rights, refusing AMNLAE its autonomy from the party, and limiting women's political opportunities. The gap between the Sandinista identity and the reality of its strategies and goals created a conflict between women and their movement and both of these groups and the state. This conflict was most clearly articulated in political settings. Ultimately, political settings became the forge of a new women's movement, one that would be autonomous from the FSLN.

New political settings were created during massive national campaigns to overturn the status quo. For example, two weeks after the revolution, the FSLN initiated a campaign to teach literacy. In Nicaragua, 33.6 percent of women were illiterate, with the highest rates in the rural areas.[16] The campaign was based on the pedagogy of Paulo Freire, who encouraged literacy through the practice of groups naming their own reality. The literacy campaign empowered women by breaking the silence on women's reality.[17]

Figure 8.1
Typology of Political Spaces, 1979-90

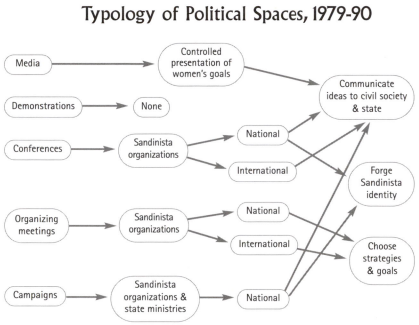

Figure 8.2
Typology of Political Spaces, 1990-94

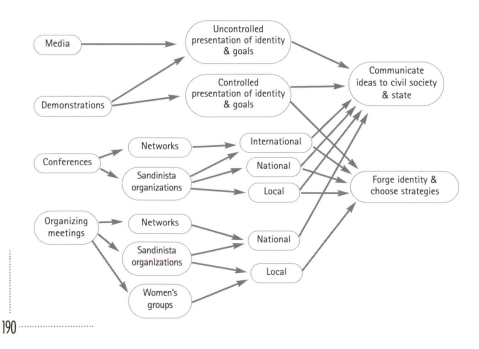

"Literacy for women is not only about learning to read and write: it is about finding a voice after centuries of invisibility, building a sense of dignity and self-confidence, and participating in the political process equally with men."[18] The Literacy Campaign was not the last time that the FSLN and AMNLAE inadvertently formed micro-political settings in which women created their own understanding and felt empowered. This would ultimately reduce the efficacy of the Sandinista control over the women's movement.

AMNLAE also created political settings to pass legal reforms benefiting women. In 1981 it proposed changes to the Patria Potesdad law, which had granted men almost unlimited rights over women and children. In sharp contrast, AMNLAE's proposed reforms created equality in the family and made a father responsible for all his children, including illegitimate ones. To overcome resistance from both the male populace and the FSLN, AMNLAE organized 285 public assemblies. Through these public forums, women developed a strong and articulate consensus in support of the legal reforms.[19] In this situation, AMNLAE used political settings to solidify women's stances and used that strength to petition the rest of civil society and the state. The reforms were passed in 1983.

In 1984, in their multiplying political settings women first formulated a women's ethos separate from the Sandinista identity. The context was one of falling agricultural productivity and dwindling rural support for the FSLN.[20] Women's labour began to replace that of the men who were away fighting the war. By 1983, women's membership in the Association on Rural Workers (ATC) reached 40 percent.[21] To increase agricultural productivity, the ATC targeted women's role in farming, but it lacked basic knowledge of women's reality. Thus the ATC created a Women's Secretariat to investigate the life of women farmers and gain that knowledge. The ATC Women's Secretariat went to small groups of women, listening to their stories. These were intimate political settings in which the women were united through their common status. From these political settings, an understanding emerged of the barriers women faced—ranging from lack of communal sinks, potable water, birth control, child-care centres, and corn mills to complaints of rape, sexual harassment, and pervasive machismo.[22]

These grassroots meetings were so successful that a National Assembly was convened in September 1986. It was attended by hundreds of women who then formally passed resolutions calling for what they had already agreed on in local meetings. The FSLN, which had sponsored the meetings, complied with the women's demands. By 1986-87, 500 new farm child-care centres were operating as well as more laundry facilities and corn mills. As for productivity, it too increased significantly, turning many men who were skeptics into cautious supporters. This, in turn, led to a greater support for women's resolutions. By 1988, women held 28 percent of union positions versus 1 percent in 1983, and 89 percent of women attended union meetings.[23] The result was an increase in the number of hours that women could work. By 1988, 90 percent of female workers surpassed the previous level of productivity.[24]

By allowing women to name their own reality, the ATC Women's Secretariat started a chain of changes of profound importance. The act of naming the system and men "machista" had implications for the possibility of consciousness.[25] Women's understanding of the sexist reality that they lived in became better accepted and their understanding became more sophisticated. Tilman Evers suggests that in the creation of political settings and new patterns of practices at the micro-level (such as the grassroots meetings), new basic values and assumptions were also created.[26] Through reconstructing fragments of autonomous identity by sharing experiences and understandings, the individual and the group change their consciousness. This new consciousness is then injected back into society through political settings sponsored by unions, political parties, and mass media. According to the ex-director of the Nicaraguan Institute for Women (INIM), the ATC Women's Secretariat public discussions of reproductive health, sexual abuse, and job constraints had repercussions throughout Nicaragua. The ATC Women's Secretariat's use of political space to forge a new women's identity and acquire new resources to help women showed the women's movement how to approach the discussion of patriarchy.

Soon after the completion of the ATC Women's Secretariat's first set of grassroots meetings, AMNLAE imitated the ATC's method of going to the grassroots to discover women's reality. In 1985 AMNLAE organized 600 public forums to ask women about what they felt were issues and needs. The forums were attended by 400,000 women. The information had two purposes: first, to create AMNLAE's own platform; and, second, to present women's needs to the new constitutional committee. Again, women came together publicly to forge an understanding of their reality. AMNLAE expected that this reality would then be enacted through FSLN public policies and/or codified in the new constitution.

These meetings were augmented by a broader public discussion about the constitution. A draft of the constitution was distributed throughout the nation and debated in 73 *cabildos abiertos*, or town hall meetings. Several town hall meetings were allotted to the topic of women. The combination of AMNLAE's meetings and the constitutional debates brought women's consciousness into full articulation, because "the constitutional process became a stage for airing women's concerns and produced heated debates among women themselves." The FSLN and AMNLAE were taken aback by the range of participants and the scope of their demands. As in the meetings organized by AMPRONAC and the ATC Women's Secretariat, women made demands that went beyond the Sandinista social justice program.[27]

Unlike its predecessors, however, AMNLAE's political spaces exposed the contradictions of a party-controlled social movement. Throughout the constitutional debate, there was an incremental increase of demands for women's rights and for improved legal language to express those rights. Questions of the legal implications of such issues as rape, abortion, battery of wives, and equality of opportunity produced further discussion. The articulation of women's rights that emerged was an organized interplay between women's everyday reality and the theoretical framework of civil rights. The process produced a clearer articulation of each. Through this convergence of theory and reality, women heard each other speak, expressing the same concerns, and became empowered through finding their own voice.[28] But the ability of women independent of AMNLAE to articulate their demands during the constitutional debates demonstrated to all AMNLAE's own failure to represent them to the government. Even more, it demonstrated that women did not need AMNLAE to express themselves. For example, AMNLAE was still not allowed to call Sandinista Nicaragua, or the FSLN, "patriarchal."[29] Women outside AMNLAE were not similarly controlled. The constitutional debates also clearly demonstrated the limits of the support that the FSLN was willing to extend to women: the two topics most discussed during the debates and long after were sex education and abortion, that is, reproductive information and control. Yet neither of those issues was included in the constitution.[30] While the opportunity to discuss ideas may have been available, the opportunity to codify these ideas was more limited.

The FSLN's control over the women's movement became untenable after AMNLAE's 1987 Second Assembly. Basing its platform on the 600 public forums and the constitutional debates, AMNLAE decided to strike a course independent of the FSLN.[31] However, at the Second Assembly, high-ranking members of the FSLN publicly resisted women's new demands for reproductive control and information. In a shocking insult, the women in the audience booed the Sandinista elite. The insult was a public protest against Sandinista control over the women's movement and over the ethos that women had created in political settings they controlled. The Second Assembly brought together women's demands that had previously been created in smaller political settings. AMNLAE incorporated this ethos into its political agenda for national socio-political change. Women had taken ownership of their own political spaces and their own movement. Effectively, that broke Sandinista control over the women's movement.

From then until 1991 the relationship between the FSLN and the women's movement became increasingly fractious. AMNLAE was put in an unsustainable position as broker between the two political groups, losing legitimacy and influence with both.[32] Women, however, had few organizational options beyond AMNLAE. Though vitiated, it nonetheless held dominance over the women's movement sheerly because it had guaranteed access to the government as a Sandinista organization. This situation changed after the FSLN lost the 1990 election to the National United Opposition (UNO), a right-of-centre coalition headed by Violeta Chamorro.

After the election the women's movement split between those who wanted to maintain a close connection with the FSLN and those who saw an opportunity for autonomy and a self-created identity. Again, political space is the best prism through which to understand the tension between the two factions and the eventual reorganization of the movement.

The leaders of the women's movement asked the grassroots to discuss what kind of movement they wanted.[33] The process of reflection was integral to the creation of identity and the choosing of strategies, and was recognized as such at the time.[34] After extensive consultation, the women's response was clear. They called for a democratic, horizontally organized structure driven by the base and autonomous from the FSLN.

The FSLN was not supportive of this suggestion. The democratic demands of the grassroots scared both the FSLN and AMNLAE's top echelon, which stopped the process of democratization. While the Sandinista ideology may have included liberation, the Sandinista reality included considerable control over mass organizations. For example, during this period AMNLAE was not allowed to raise the issue of abortion even though the majority of women polled wanted discussion on the matter. As a result, at AMNLAE's 1991 assembly the only item on the agenda was the confirmation of the appointment of the next general secretary. Most of the unions' Women's Secretariats boycotted the assembly, and so too did a number of unaffiliated women, claiming that their voices could not be heard and that the leadership of AMNLAE lacked legitimacy.[35] Women owned their political space and refused to support the Sandinista control over it. The boycott further eroded any legitimacy that the FSLN and AMNLAE had as institutional leaders of the women's movement.

The women who refused to attend the 1991 assembly organized their own conference to run simultaneously. About 200 women attended this conference, versus 600 at AMNLAE's meeting.[36] The conclusion reached at the independent conference was that women did not know what they wanted outside the structure and identity of AMNLAE and FSLN. The converging of women in a political space made the confusion and the differences among the women evident. Their only solution was to convene another political space to address this specific issue: they decided they would have to have another conference to discover it. Before women could create an alternative women's movement, they first had to convene in a political space to determine goals and understandings, that is, to determine their new ethos.

AMNLAE and the FSLN considered the competing conference a threat to their control and began a smear campaign, calling the women who attended it lesbians, prostitutes, and elitists.[37] Since many of the women who were leading the autonomous movement were Sandinistas with impeccable credentials, the charges were seen as calculated insults that demanded rebuttal. The debate over who would control the women's movement, and how, was battled in political meetings and through the media.

This fight, public and bitter, was the turning point in relations between the FSLN and the women's movement. The mass-mobilization techniques that the FSLN had used to overturn a dictatorship, fight a war, and engage in national social justice campaigns were futile against the new women's movement. The new techniques revolved around the control of micro-political settings and the media. Fistfights over ownership of office furniture erupted in AMNLAE offices.[38] Women picketed Sandinista radio stations, unilaterally declared Sandinista women's clinics autonomous, and made public statements. The FSLN could not move fast enough to block these moves, and it could hardly have used its military against the women. The FSLN's only weapon against the autonomous movement was its control over some of the media outlets.

Leaders from both sides—AMNLAE and the new autonomous movement—were sufficiently experienced to make sure that the news media were well informed about their actions. The media elevated and transformed the internal disagreement between the FSLN and members of the women's movement into a political statement about freedom versus control. The symbolic value of the battle was a huge force in a Nicaragua undergoing re-creation. As a study of Venezuela argues: "Some issues are associated with emerging value codes that, in turn, constitute a new political culture. These issues are likely to be appropriated by societies through the mass media and to be imbued with political power."[39] In Nicaragua the media focused debate by explaining ideas and validating a movement's position as valuable. The autonomous women's movement became a symbol of the new political culture of autonomy from the FSLN and of women's self-determination.

The symbolic value of the autonomous women's movement encouraged more women to participate in it.[40] Nonetheless, as María Pilar Garcia-Guadilla put it, "It is not social mobilization per se that transforms [an] issue into a new political fact but its diffusion through the mass media."[41] The autonomous women's movement learned that lesson and would later stage symbolic events solely for media diffusion.

The FSLN abdicated all responsibility for or control over the women's movement, and so the autonomous women's movement was born.[42] During the Sandinista-controlled women's movement, women had found their voices once they controlled their own political settings. They could not have taken ownership of the political spaces, however, if they had not first experienced creating an identity and achieving specific ends in a myriad of micro-political spaces. The women's movement grew slowly toward autonomy, political space by political space.

Political Settings and the Autonomous Women's Movement 1991-94

The women's movement in the 1990s made political spaces integral to its organization. Indeed, without political spaces, there would have been no women's movement to speak of. The women's movement fused identity and resources into a mutually supportive whole. It was also adept at persuading civil society and the state of the value of the ideas forged in its political spaces. As a result, the women's movement grew in numbers, increased its funding, and broadened its scope of activism.

In 1991, though, with the loss of Sandinista patronage, fundamental issues had to be resolved. The movement, newly autonomous from partisan politics, was unsure of how to lobby the government or what its focus should be. It had to reorganize itself for the post-Sandinista reality. Women's collectives sprang up. In January 1992 the women's collectives and the unions' women's secretariats organized a conference to assist the new movement in organizing itself and creating its ethos. The creation and use of the national political space had to precede the creation of the autonomous women's movement. AMNLAE did not participate and, later, the unions also withdrew, claiming that the conference did not present class as primary to understanding women's subordination.[43] The FSLN may have been weakened by its electoral loss, but it still carried clout. Despite the lack of Sandinista representation, over 800 women attended, which was 500 more than the organizers had expected.

The 1992 conference debated the value of a centralized versus a decentralized organization. Although the workings of a centralized and hierarchical organization were familiar, women's negative experience with that structure under the Sandinista government turned the majority against it.[44] Furthermore, a decentralized movement allowed for the participation of a range of organizations, from neighbourhood collectives to health and law clinics to NGOs. In that way a large segment of society could be drawn into the women's movement and its ethos. Finally, an emphasis on identity and subjectivity as the motivating principle of participation meant an increased emphasis on difference and diversity, which then suggested the need for networks as an organizing mechanism. This conference, therefore, defined the organizational structure of the movement: collectives, networks, and political settings.[45]

It seems improbable, nonetheless, that a conference with no organizational structure for the participants and no overarching ethos should be able to create both in two days. Indeed, the very emphasis on difference and the lack of an agenda allowed the conference to be successful: it allowed the participants to concentrate on their commonalities. The process of developing strategy and identity within a political space rests on the assumption that not everyone will agree with all aspects of the discussion. Unbridgeable difference is assumed. Respect for that difference, however, meant that the women could separate and accept—as a strategy—what they held in common and what they did not.

Participants in political settings create a common world of understanding, a world of commonly understood criticisms and alternatives, a world with its own common sense. In a political setting, women could focus on what they held in common in order to achieve a common goal—in this instance, the overarching organization and identity of the autonomous women's movement. The revelation of their shared world produced a consensus regarding priorities and approaches. In other words, the creation of a shared world simultaneously created both an overarching ethos and its concomitant strategies. In turn, the impact of this dual creation offered a praxis for continued growth.[46]

Despite the success of creating a shared world at the January 1992 conference, the women's movement chose decentralization without really knowing how it would work. A routine emerged for creating and operating within this shared world. Typically, a network of grassroots collectives, individuals, NGOs, and health and law clinics convened a political space, usually a conference, to acknowledge and resolve a specific problem. The conference might last as long as three days or as short as one. Before the conference the network would produce a document explaining the issue, its stance, and possible solutions, and then distribute the document through the networks so that the women could study it. Assuming that some women would not have the time to read it or that some participants might be illiterate, the organizers would have the document read aloud at the conference before it was discussed. In the end it would be revised according to the participants' recommendations, which might include criticisms of the presentation of the governing ethos or strategies to resolve the problem. The recommendations might also deepen the presentation of the issue to include new approaches. After the document was changed, all the collectives would receive a copy through the networks. The document would then become the network's blueprint for political action. The conference might attract as many as 800 women or as few as 30, depending on the strength of the network and the topic discussed. Political settings thus not only assisted in the development of a shared alternative reality but also allowed small groups to become highly political.

The growth of political settings was assisted by demography and geography. With a population of less than four million and the majority of the population under 18 years of age, Nicaragua's leaders, rank-and-file union members, NGOs, bureaucrats, and specialists could virtually meet in one room, albeit a large one. The majority of its population lived within the same geographical area, Western Nicaragua, within easy distance of the only city, Managua. Thus it was neither expensive nor time-consuming to arrange even organizational meetings in Managua. These two advantages facilitated the usage of political settings as an integral part of the women's movement.

While geography may help keep people in easy contact with one another, a social movement's long-term viability is based on its communications. In addition to internal documents, information was distributed through the media. The women's movement produced a range of publications specifically for its own purposes: *La Boletina*, which was mainstream and reported on the women's movement at large; *Afuera de la Closet*, which produced information about lesbianism and human biology; and *La Feminista,* which promulgated the radical and intellectual current of the women's movement. In addition to these magazines, the newspaper *La Barricada* had a weekly supplement, *La Gente*, which was distinctly feminist and erotic. A women's radio station and a half-hour program on the television about women's issues added to the mix. With so much access to media, the women's movement could disseminate information about its events to its own members, debate ideas, and attract new members. Through political settings and their own media, an agenda was formed to combat the government and its economic policies, and to address social problems such as violence against women.[47]

Political action was a necessity for the women's movement to combat the government because of the impact of its harsh structural adjustment policies on women. When Chamorro took power in February 1990, the economic situation was sufficiently dire that the new government decided it had little option but to engage in a stringent Structural Adjustment Program (SAP). Inflation was 13,492 percent and the debt stood at $9.7 billion, four times the gross domestic product (GDP).[48] The SAP was intended to control inflation and reduce the debt through decreased government expenditures and increased export earnings. By 1993 inflation had dropped to 12.4 percent, but the debt continued to grow at a rate of $520 million per annum and by 1994 was eight times GDP. One reason for the increasing debt was the severe economic recession. Between 1990 and 1994, per capita GDP contracted by 12.4 percent, with a cumulative growth rate over the same period of 1.9 percent.[49]

The SAP included privatization of state and parastatal companies, a reduction in the size of the army, deregulation of the economy, ceding of control of foreign trade and banking to the private sector, trade liberalization, and fiscal and monetary reform. Wages and services were reduced while previously subsidized goods, such as food staples and electricity, had their prices raised to market value.[50] The restructured economy was export-led in order to earn foreign currency, to pay the debt, and to reactivate the economy.

The government's SAP policies eroded women's standard of living. According to Richard Stahler-Sholk, "Typically of orthodox adjustment, the distributive impact fell heavily on women."[51] Of female-headed households, 72.5 percent were below the poverty line compared to 67.5 percent of male-headed households; 81.3 percent of female-headed households faced reduced food consumption compared to 75 percent of male-headed households.[52] The SAP became harsher through the 1990s, further eroding women's standard of living.

Unemployment and underemployment as a result of the SAP rose to 45 percent in 1992 and 60 percent in 1994, with formal-sector employment dropping 18 percent between 1990 and 1992 alone. It has been estimated that half of small businesses failed in the 1990s due to credit restrictions and lack of government support. Unemployment and underemployment rates for women were higher than for men, because women dominated public-sector employment. Up to 70 percent of government lay-offs involved women. In addition, the recession also forced women from private-sector employment because they were the first to be laid off.[53]

Nonetheless, women had to work to feed their families. An estimated 65 percent of urban families and 82.6 percent of rural households were headed by women. Women responded to the economic crisis by actively searching for alternative means of earning money. In comparison, men adopted a posture of resignation to or avoidance of the family crisis.[54] Thus, even having a male as the head of the household was no guarantee that the family would be supported.

Not only were women the hardest hit by the economic downturn, but their ability to find employment was also hampered by their increased domestic workload, again a product of the SAP. Florence Babb suggests a relationship between women's increased domestic labour due to the family response to the SAP and women's decreased capacity to find work outside the home.[55] Women's ability to find employment was further hindered by the cutbacks in social infrastructure spending. Social services that predominantly affected women were reduced or withdrawn. State-funded medical care was reduced, with the best hospitals privatized. State-funded hospitals providing a lower standard of care still functioned. Prescription medicine was no longer free. Funding for education was reduced at all levels of the school system, and children who attended public schools had to pay. Increased child-care concerns also reduced women's ability to work outside the home. Government-sponsored training initiatives and community programs, such as child-care services, were eliminated. This again reduced women's opportunity for leaving the home to find wage labour.

Despite facing these critical issues, the newly created autonomous women's movement found itself with no readily evident path to follow. The movement lacked an established leadership, a centralized agency to organize the movement, and experience with decentralization. Female activists were accustomed to a supportive if controlling government under the FSLN. With Chamorro's government, they faced a hostile neo-liberal regime. Even basic strategies had to be re-examined.

Fortunately, there was a continual cycle of conferences to organize and attend. Most of these were preceded by regional or urban planning meetings, followed by further meetings to communicate the discussion back to the local constituency. Some women belonged to more than one group or were sent to more than one meeting, so the same faces said the same things over and over again, persuading more people to their perspective, or not, as the case may be.

These cycles of conferences with their pre- and post-meetings meant that the women's movement was continuously redefining its identity and its strategies, continuously reshaping its shared world. Over time, its members learned that a decentralized movement can criticize government policies and even replace some services through uniting in political settings. In innumerable local political settings democratic practices became accepted as being normal, because all the women's groups were democratic and horizontally organized. The institutionalization of the women's movement into political spaces resulted in an analysis of rights, plurality, and democratic forms at all levels of the movement, enriching the politics of civil society.[56]

Sandinista women, for instance, wanted to gain a higher profile for women in the FSLN. Female superstars were well represented and respected, but at a lower level women were either invisible or had joined other political groups. The role of women at the intermediary level had progressively diminished since the revolution in 1979.[57] The leader of the FSLN, Daniel Ortega, had promised to increase the number of women on the FSLN's National Directorate (the steering committee for the party), but Sandinista women wanted more than just the appointment of another female superstar. They wanted a structural change in the system so that women would be incorporated at all levels. AMNLAE suggested that women make up 20 percent of all nominees for the 1996 election.

The realistic option of a 20 percent quota for nominees did not satisfy all Sandinista women. Some of them believed that 50 percent was more reasonable. María Dolores Ocún organized a conference for all Sandinista women, active or not, to discuss AMNLAE's proposal and what women should demand at the forthcoming May 1994 Extraordinary Congress, which would be the first to have an election for individual positions rather than for a slate. The conference called itself Las Mujeres Autoconvocadas, meaning that they belonged to neither "current." This allowed them to avoid the fissures within the party. All the women's secretariats showed up, as did AMNLAE and a number of individuals who normally did not attend conferences, both from the lowest and the highest ranks within the FSLN. The conference was one day long, with the goal of consensus that 50 percent of the party's nominees in the 1996 elections would be women. There were obviously a number of differences between the women at the conference, depending on internal party affiliation, the nature of daily work, and the range of commitment to the party. Again, however, the political space absorbed these differences because of the well-established, overarching Sandinista identity of social justice, and the immediate and focused goal of 50 percent.[58] The women thus shared and enhanced their common world.

After gaining a consensus of 50 percent representation, AMNLAE, the unions, and the rest of the Sandinista women's groups organized around that demand. The demand for 50 percent representation was included as an issue for discussion in all the regional and local meetings that would elect representatives to vote at the May 1994 Extraordinary Congress. For the structural change in the organization to occur, it would have to be approved as party policy at the Congress, which would decide who would run the party: Daniel Ortega or Sergio Ramirez. It was so difficult to predict who would win the vote that both "currents" needed to court the women's vote, although neither "current" wanted to alienate the mainstream.

The discussion of the 50 percent quota throughout the nation was spirited. The national discussion about women, politics, and rights demonstrated how a social movement organization through the use of public space could influence the debates in society and broaden its understanding of democracy. The debate brought to light questions of power and how to differentiate "good" power from "bad" power, the interplay between ethics and power, and the role of power in democracy.[59] In the end, the final decision of the Congress was for a 30 percent quota. Later other political parties, not wanting to appear sexist, also gave women a 30 percent quota for representation within their party positions and nominees.[60]

Las Mujeres Autoconvocadas had attained its explicit goal of increasing women's political participation in large part by skilfully using public space. In the process of achieving its focused goal, it broadened the discussion of the functioning of democracy within the constraints of inequality. Operating both within the women's movement and within the state, Las Mujeres Autoconvocadas is the best example of how the women's movement used public settings to influence civil society and the state through the discussion of democratic rights.

The very source and organization of Las Mujeres Autoconvocadas straddled state and civil spheres. Most of its members worked for various

NGOs, foreign government aid projects, and the UN offices in Nicaragua, or they were representatives in the National Assembly. This may have aided them in attaining their goal of increasing women's representation within political parties because it allowed them access to political leaders and sources of political power. Las Mujeres Autoconvocadas also targeted both civil society and the state with the hope of persuading both spheres about the value of women's political participation.

Those two spheres had become more distinct during the period of the Chamorro government. With neo-liberalism, most government-supplied material resources halted.[61] Neo-liberalism impoverished women, but it also allowed women increased access to international aid without Sandinista tampering. Foreign aid to the women's movement increased dramatically in the 1990s. Nonetheless, that aid did not appear to influence the women's movement overtly. It funded magazine publication, conference room rentals, day-to-day operations, and occasionally support staff. When I asked women if the funding source influenced what they said or did, they said it did not.

The perceived lack of intervention might have been because each group was usually funded by more than one agency. Thus the wishes of any one source of funds would be diluted by another. More to the point, it would be difficult for foreign aid to direct the operations of grassroots groups, because those groups are identity-based. It would be equally difficult for foreign aid to direct the happenings and decisions made in particular political settings, because there are too many variables involved in creating a shared world. A social movement made up of small groups and networks with a multiplicity of political settings may not be able to attract large sums, but by its very organizational structure it is able to avoid being subordinated to the wishes of the funding agency. However, it does seem that clinics or collectives that could write a good proposal tended to receive more money. For example, the neighbourhood women's collective, 8 marzo, had a reputation of attracting foreign aid because foreigners (that is, Western-educated women) wrote its funding proposals. This does not necessarily mean that the aid was then used in the manner proposed.

There is an important exception to this state of affairs. Ixchen, a health and law clinic, lost a large source of its funding in 1995. Ixchen was the first integrated women's health clinic (begun in 1988), and by 1995 it had become the largest and the most influential. It spawned a number of similar clinics in other cities. Its funding, which came from the United States, was cut because of persistent rumours that Ixchen performed therapeutic abortions—which it denied. Ixchen was forced to shut its doors, at least temporarily. Controlling Ixchen probably had a chilling effect on the other women's clinics. It could be that once other groups within the autonomous women's movement become more established, as Ixchen was, funding agencies will scrutinize them more closely to ensure that they are fulfilling their stated mandates. This is the weakness with funding: during the 1980s it was controlled by the FSLN, and during the 1990s it was controlled by the international community. Of the two, the international community had shown itself to be less intrusive.

In addition to a SAP and foreign aid, the insertion of Nicaragua into the global economy resulted in increased access to international conferences. Thus as the political economy went global, so too did political settings. From international conferences, Nicaraguan women gained new ideas and strategies in what Doug McAdam and Dieter Rucht call the "cross-national diffusion of ideas."[62] While the Sandinista women's movement attended the 1987 Latin American Women's Meetings, and the Sandinista professional women's group—the Women's Secretariat of the National Confederation of Professionals Heroes and Martyrs (CONAPRO H-M)—organized an international conference on women and legislation in Latin America in 1989, Nicaraguan women had not integrated themselves into the Latin American women's movement. Yet in the 1990s the autonomous women's movement attended international meetings regularly. Women's movement members attended the Central American Women's Meeting in 1992, the Latin American Women's Meeting in 1993, the Cairo Conference on Population and Development in 1994, and the Beijing Conference on Women in 1995. Each conference was preceded by extensive meetings to formulate the Nicaraguan stance—meetings steered by a network struck specifically for the purpose. International women's magazines, such as *FemPress* from Chile, became available in Nicaragua. Finally, in 1995, one of the women's networks joined La Corriente, a radical Central American feminist network, importing ideas from it into Nicaragua. International political settings had become established as part of the Nicaraguan women's movement.

Through international political settings, the Nicaraguan women's movement was exposed to new ideas and new approaches to resolving conflicts. From the Central American Women's Meeting, the Nicaraguan Women's Health Network borrowed the strategy of using Mother's Day to protest lack of funding for women's reproductive health. From the 1994 Latin American Women's Meeting, the feminist network absorbed the debate over forms of women's power. Eventually, this feminist network staged the Aquelarre Conference in March 1994 to involve the rest of the Nicaraguan women's movement in the discussion. Internationalizing political spaces thus offered the Nicaraguan women's movement new strategies and ideas for achieving their goals.

One of the most powerful strategies employed by the Nicaraguan women's movement to influence the public sphere targeted the symbols used in mainstream society. They realized that people in specific political settings could redefine common symbols and attempt to alter their meanings in the wider media. The Nicaraguan women's movement fastened on the symbol of maternity, or motherhood, and was able to change its generally perceived content. In the process the women increased political awareness of maternal mortality.

Chamorro's neo-conservative government had cut health-care spending in half, from $137 million in 1989 to $67 million (the average for years 1991-93). In per capita terms, it dropped from $45 in 1990 to $14 in 1991.[63] Despite the general decline in health care, the greatest killer of women remained in the area of reproductive health, and the statistics on maternal mortality showed that deaths were rising. The United Nations Fund on Population (FNUAP) estimated that for every 100,000 live births there were 300 maternal deaths. But even that official number was dubious. It was estimated that only 47 percent of pregnant women were registered by the health-care system, which meant that only about 50 percent of the births and deaths were known. Every 36 hours a woman died as a result of being pregnant.[64] Women had little information about birth control and less access to it. According to one study, only 26 percent of women of fertile age used birth control, including the rhythm method. Another study said that only 12 percent of fertile and sexually active women were using some form of birth control. It was very difficult to buy or acquire contraceptive products, and access to therapeutic abortions was negligible. An estimated one-third of all maternal deaths resulted from self-induced abortions.[65]

The Chamorro government celebrated the role of the housewife and mother. During the 1990 election campaign, the UNO did not refer to women as women but rather as wives and mothers.[66] Chamorro, asked if she was a feminist, replied, "I am not a feminist nor do I want to be one. I am dedicated to my home as [my husband] taught me [to be]."[67] To generate political support, Chamorro deployed her image as a loving mother who suffered from Nicaragua's political divisions. For birth control, the government advocated abstinence.[68]

The powerful and traditional symbol of motherhood became the battleground between the Nicaraguan women's movement and the Nicaraguan government. Women organized themselves into the Women's Health Network, which aimed at changing the symbol of the mother from an ever-sacrificing, passive nurturer to one of a fighter in an unfair and occasionally deadly battle against an inadequate and oppressive health-care system.

Maternal Mortality Day comes on the 28th of May, Mother's Day, a day marked by an excess of sentiment, even by Nicaraguan standards. Using the established Mother's Day to discuss maternal mortality shows the strategic canniness of the Women's Health Network. Maternal Mortality Day has increasingly dominated media coverage of Mother's Day between

1991 and 1994. The Women's Health Network was able to change the symbol of motherhood because it pointed out its inconsistencies: the paradox of worshipping motherhood in a society that denies maternal health care.

In 1991 the Mother's Day editorial in *La Barricada*, the newspaper most sympathetic toward women's rights, could only envision women's needs within a Marxist framework: "The mother as well is enslaved by invisible threads that tie her to the capitalist engine of exploitation."[69] The Women's Health Network, organized in January 1992, began to make an impact on the coverage of Mother's Day by May of that year. For the next two years the confused reporting on the role of motherhood reflected the battle over control of the symbol. In 1994 articles on maternal mortality dominated the coverage. They were on the editorial page, page 4, and in letters to the editor.[70] By 1994 Mother's Day was not merely a day to celebrate motherhood but a day of gratitude for having survived the experience. In comparison to *La Barricada*'s changing presentation of Mother's Day, *La Prensa*, the government's newspaper, continued with its saccharine presentation of the joys of motherhood.

The autonomous women's movement became adroit at using political settings to influence mass media to communicate its ideas to civil society. To change the symbol of motherhood, the Women's Health Network engaged in eye-catching demonstrations. Beginning on Mother's Day 1992, mothers whose daughters had died in childbirth carried signs with their daughters' names and their ages at death. The women paraded up and down in front of the National Assembly and marched through the street in a stunning display of pain initiating action. Many of the female deputies came out to talk to the women. The event was covered by the local media, granting the demonstration legitimacy and helping to transform Mother's Day into a political issue. The control of the women's movement over the content of the symbol of motherhood was nicely brought home in 1994, when the Catholic Church switched its annual pro-life march with its heavy emphasis on maternal suffering and passivity from Mother's Day to Father's Day.

Unfortunately, none of these political actions changed the stance of the Chamorro government. There are limitations on a social movement regardless of how well it uses political spaces: a neo-liberal government answers to the needs of international capital rather than to the needs of women. In its combative relationship with the reformed state, the women's movement may have gained strength, but Nicaraguan women as a whole ultimately remained at a disadvantage.

Conclusion

Between 1977 and 1994 there was little constancy in Nicaragua. The form of government changed, the organization of the economy changed, the goal of the women's movement changed, the leadership of the women's movement changed, the movement's relationship with the state changed, and the very structure of the movement itself changed. All of this is a challenging example of political action that social movement theories have trouble explicating. Yet the capacity of women to create political settings and to use them to develop the women's movement and to influence the public sphere was critical throughout. Examining the Nicaraguan women's movement through political spaces makes it possible to understand why the movement restructured itself, why it chose the strategies it did, and why it was successful in some areas and not others. Furthermore, analyzing the role of political settings politicizes social movement theory and explicates the relationship between the social movement and the state. Political space analysis therefore offers an important means of overcoming the weaknesses inherent in social movement theory.

Theorizing must take into account the range of political settings and of actors in them. Political settings can be small meetings, UN-sponsored conferences. and mass demonstrations. In between are organizational meetings, local demonstrations, and national campaigns. Actors in political settings can be networks, grassroots organizations, health and law clinics, individuals, NGOs, bureaucrats, and political party members. Indeed, the general public could be said to participate in political settings when it is the target of the debate. Many of the actions that accomplish the goals referred to in social movement theory—building identity, using resources, and attempting to change the public and the state—are structured in political settings. This is why political space analysis can bring a useful concreteness and specificity to the study of a social movement.

Political settings are both complex and omnipresent, yet certain processes are stable features of them. A political space functions within a social movement by directing resources and enhancing identity. Ideally, the resources and the identity mutually support each other so that the social movement has an internal logic. Thus the judicious use of political settings can strengthen a social movement by building support and membership. If the identity and the mobilized resources work against each other, a social movement tends to falter. A political space also acts as the political arm of the social movement, influencing the public sphere.[71] As the political arm, a political space will almost always engage the state. An examination of political space in Nicaragua can thus also highlight the difference in the relationship between a social movement and a supportive corporatist state versus a hostile neo-liberal state.

The consistent importance of political settings in Nicaragua's women's movement from 1977 to the present confirms the suggestion that people coming together in groups can judge a situation and respond to it, naming and sharing their own reality. As their understanding is reinforced, they are strengthened both emotionally and experientially, enabling them to become more proficient, democratic citizens. There appears to be a process of learning how to develop political spaces to build a strong social movement and to lobby civil society and the state. The ATC Women's Secretariat stumbled on an effective means of building women's identity through grassroots groups discussing their own reality. AMNLAE took this means and so successfully utilized it that women became resistant to Sandinista control over their identity. In the 1990s, grassroots groups, using the same methodology, became the backbone of the Nicaraguan women's movement.

Political settings can also be used for transmitting successful ideas and strategies from one group to another, a process evident at international conferences. The internationalization of political spaces reflects the internationalization of the state. For Nicaragua to become more integrated into the global economy, economic policies were changed and state funding for the women's movement was eliminated. In addition, the women's movement had to respond to a different set of concerns arising from the SAP. Women searched abroad for the funding necessary to develop the women's movement. This funding was limited but had fewer controls placed on it than Sandinista funding.

While the FSLN may have been generous, it controlled the women's movement. The FSLN offered services geared specifically to women, such as child care and civil liberties, and services that benefited women disproportionately, such as education and health care. The FSLN also supported a publicly active citizenry through encouraging the masses to participate in their own Sandinista political spaces. The relationship between the FSLN and the women's movement was mutually beneficial as long as the identity for both was the same. But language usage, goals, and resources were dictated from above. When goals and identities differed, the tension between the women's movement and the state weakened the women's movement. Because the Sandinista women's movement was incorporated into the state, any easy distinction between the state and civil society was eliminated. This gave AMNLAE a power base separate from the grassroots.

What really broke that power base was the creation of micro-political settings and then the connecting of them to major political settings. Women developed their language, goals, and needs through political settings. Women became empowered to move beyond the Sandinista agenda and define their own identity. Political settings assisted in delegitimizing the Sandinista identity, in resolving the power struggle within the women's movement by communicating the conflicting ideas to civil society, and in highlighting the lack of resources and strategies of the new women's movement.

Political spaces shifted the power base from AMNLAE and the FSLN to uncontrollable and autonomous micro-settings. Ironically, what made the FSLN an impressive political and military force was useless in the face of this kind of political subversion. It is difficult, though, to understand the threat of the decentralized, autonomous women's movement to Sandinista power using resource mobilization theory and identity theories. By examining political settings outside the confines of these two approaches I have tried to show why the women's movement abandoned the FSLN's patronage and sought the autonomy to continue to construct its own meanings and agendas.

In comparison, there was straightforward mutual antipathy between the women's movement and the Chamorro government. The distinction between the state and civil society became clearer. This helped to strengthen the women's movement, even though women were in a worse socio-economic position. With high unemployment, unions were weakened, and with the internationalization of the state, non-governmental organizations became major players. The women's movement had to respond to a new organizational context. With government cutbacks to education and health care, and with the government's anti-feminist ideology, the women's movement also had to respond to new concerns. The women's movement became decentralized, building on collectives and networks and unifying in political spaces to strengthen itself, change civil society, or fight the state.

The inability of the women's movement to alter the neo-liberal government's approach to women's issues points to the weakness of social movements. They are dependent on a responsive government. Yet, even under a non-responsive government, political settings can be an effective means to organize around specific goals and battle the dominant norms and symbols of society. The dispossessed can forge an alternative identity, mobilize resources around it, while engaging in the political action necessary to realize itself in the broader community. Without a responsive government, though, a social movement's influence is limited to changing civil society.

Notes

1. See Alberto Melucci, *Nomads of the Present: Social Movements and Individual Needs in Contemporary Society*, ed. John Keane and Paul Mier (Philadelphia: Temple University Press, 1989), pp.172-73.

2. See Joe Foweraker, *Theorizing Social Movements* (London: Pluto, 1995), pp.13, 92; and Mario Diani, "The Concept of Social Movement," *Sociological Review* 40,1 (February 1992), p.1.

3. For useful presentations and discussions of social movement theory, see: Jean L. Cohen, "Strategy or Identity: New Theoretical Paradigms and Contemporary Social Movements," *Social Research* 52,4 (Winter 1985), pp.663-716; A. Scott, *Ideology and the New Social Movements* (London: Unwin Hyman, 1990); Arturo Escobar and Sonia Alvarez, eds., *The Making of New Social Movements in Latin America: Identity, Strategy, and Democracy* (Boulder, Col.: Westview Press, 1992); Russell J. Dalton and Manfred Keuchler, eds., *Challenging the Political Order: New Social and Political Movements in Western Democracies* (Cambridge: Polity Press, 1990); Aldon D. Morris and Carol McClurg Mueller, eds., *Frontiers in Social Movement Theory* (New Haven, Conn.: Yale University Press, 1992); and Foweraker, *Theorizing Social Movements*.

4. Jean Cohen and Andrew Arato, *Civil Society and Political Theory* (Cambridge, Mass.: MIT Press, 1992), p.ix, offers a clear definition: civil society is "a sphere of social interaction between economy and the state, composed above all of the intimate sphere (especially the family), the sphere of associations (especially voluntary associations), social movements, and forms of public communication."

5. Ibid., pp.ix, 509.

6. See Ellen Meiksins Wood, *Democracy against Capitalism: Renewing Historical Materialism* (Cambridge: Cambridge University Press, 1995); and Kai Nielson, "Reconceptualizing Civil Society for Now: Some Somewhat Gramscian Turnings," in *Toward a Global Civil Society*, ed. Michael Walzer (Providence, R.I.: Berghahn, 1995), pp.41-67.

7. See Melucci, *Nomads of the Present*, p.60; Douglas Chalmers et al., "Associative Networks: New Structures of Representation for the Popular Sectors," in *The New Politics of Inequality in Latin America*, ed. Douglas Chalmers (Oxford: Oxford University Press, 1997), pp.564-68; and Charles Tilly, "Social Movements and National Politics," in *Statemaking and Social Movements: Essays in History and Theory*, ed. Charles Harding and Susan Bright (Ann Arbor: University of Michigan Press, 1984), p.305.

8. Alberto Melucci, "The Symbolic Challenge of Contemporary Movements," *Social Research* 52,4 (Winter 1985), p.814.

9. Melucci, *Nomads of the Present*, p.172.

10. Jean Cohen, "Between Crisis Management and Social Movements: The Place of Institutional Reform," *Telos* 52 (Summer 1982), pp.38-40.

11. See Margaret Randall, *Sandino's Daughters: Testimonies of Nicaraguan Women in Struggle*, ed. Lynda Yanz (Vancouver: New Star Books, 1981), p.2; and Clara Murguialday, *Nicaragua: revolución y feminismo, 1977-89* (Madrid: Esitorial Revolución S.A.L., 1990), p.40.

12. Latin American Working Group (LAWG), *Central American Women Speak for Themselves*, Toronto, 1983, p.10.

13. Randall, *Sandino's Daughters*, pp.14, 16.

14. Patricia M. Cuchryk, "Women in the Revolution," in *Revolution and Counterrevolution in Nicaragua*, ed. Thomas W. Walker (Boulder, Col.: Westview Press, 1991), p.144; Murguialday, *Nicaragua*, p.48; Randall, *Sandino's Daughters*, p.16.

15. Richard Stahler-Sholk, "Stabilization, Destabilization, and the Popular Classes in Nicaragua, 1979-1988," *Latin American Research Review* 25,3 (1990), p.57.

16. United Nations, *The World's Women 1970-1990: Trends and Statistics*, New York, 1991, p.52.

17. Women's International Resource Exchange (WIRE), *Nicaraguan Women: Unlearning the Alphabet of Submission*, New York, 1985.

18. Helen Collinson et al., eds., *Women and Revolution in Nicaragua* (London: Zed Press, 1990), p.123.

19. Association of Nicaraguan Women Luisa Amanda Espinoza, *Una mujer donde estee debe hacer revolución*, trans. Latin America Working Group (Toronto: LAWG, 1983), p.11; Doug Brown, "Sandinismo and the Problem of Democratic Hegemony," *Latin American Perspectives* 17,2 (Spring 1990), p.53.

20. Geske Dijkstra, *Industrialization in Sandinista Nicaragua: Policy and Practice in a Mixed Economy* (Boulder, Col.: Westview Press, 1992), p.186.

21. Collinson et al., eds., *Women and Revolution in Nicaragua*, p.44.

22. Murguialday, *Nicaragua*, pp.168-69.

23. Collinson et al., eds., *Women and Revolution in Nicaragua*, pp.47-48; Cuchryk, "Women in the Revolution," p.149.

24. Murguialday, *Nicaragua*, p.169.

25. Arturo Escobar, "Culture, Economics, and Politics in Latin American Social Movements' Theory and Practice," in *Making of New Social Movements in Latin America*, ed. Escobar and Alvarez, p.62.

26. Tilman Evers, "Identity: The Hidden Side of New Social Movements in Latin America," in *New Social Movements and the State in Latin America*, ed. David Slater (Amsterdam: CEDLA, 1985), pp.51, 59.

27. Martha I. Morgan, "Founding Mothers: Women's Voices and Stories in the 1987 Nicaraguan Constitution," *Boston University* 70,1 (1990), pp.19, 25.

28. Murguialday, *Nicaragua*, p.203.

29. The restriction was lifted with the 1987 *La Proclama*, which admitted that even with revolutionary socialism, the government and the society could be patriarchal. The women's movement considered *La Proclama* to be a major concession.

30. Association of Nicaraguan Women Luisa Amanda Espinoza, *I Was Born with the Revolution: Workshop on Women in Nicaragua, April 4, 1987* (Managua: AMNLAE and Oficina Gubernamentales de la Mujer, 1987), p.15.

31. Murguialday, *Nicaragua*, p.194.

32. Ana Criquillon, "The Nicaraguan Women's Movement: Feminist Reflections from Within," in *The Politics of Survival: Grassroots Movements in Central America*, ed. Minor Sinclair (New York: Monthly Review Press, 1995), p.221.

33. *La gente*, weekly cultural supplement to *La Barricada*, Feb. 15, 1991, p.10.

34. María Teresa Blandón, "The Impact of the Sandinista Defeat on Nicaraguan Feminism," in *Compañeras: Voices from the Latin American Women's Movement*, ed. Gary Küppers (London: Latin American Bureau, 1994), p.100; Millie Thayer, "After the Fall: The Nicaraguan Women's Movement in the 1990s," paper presented at the Latin American Studies Association Annual Conference, Atlanta, Georgia, 1994, p.12.

35. *Envío* (Universidad de Central America, Managua), June 1991, p.40.

36. Ibid.

37. *La Barricada* (Managua), March 9, 1991, p.5; Margaret Randall, *Gathering Rage: The Failure of 20th Century Revolutions to Develop a Feminist Agenda* (New York: Monthly Review Press, 1992), pp.63-64.

38. Randall, *Gathering Rage*, p.65.

39. María Pilar Garcia-Guadilla, "Gender, Environment, and Empowerment in Venezuela," in *Engendering Wealth and Well-Being: Empowerment for Global Change* (Boulder, Col.: Westview Press, 1995), p.216.

40. William A. Gamson and Gadi Wolfsfeld, "Movements and Media as Interacting Systems," *Annals, American Academy of Political and Social Science* 528 (July 1993), p.116.

41. Garcia-Guadilla, "Gender, Environment, and Empowerment in Venezuela," p.217.

42. Margaret Randall, *Sandino's Daughters Revisited: Feminism in Nicaragua* (New Brunswick, N.J.: Rutgers University Press, 1994), p.310.

43. Kaki Rusmore, "Building Women's Democratic Leadership: The Experience of the ATC's Women's Secretariat," paper presented at the Latin American Studies Association Annual Conference, Atlanta, Georgia, 1994, p.15.

44. *Barricada International* (English-language magazine, Managua), November-December 1994, p.21.

45. Thayer, "After the Fall," p.10.

46. Lisa Disch, "Please Sit Down but Don't Make Yourself at Home: Arendtian 'Visiting' and the Prefigurative Politics of Consciousness-Raising," in *Hannah Arendt and the Meaning of Politics*, ed. John MacGowan and Craig Calhoun (Minneapolis: University of Minnesota Press, 1995), p.15.

47. Blandón, "Impact of the Sandinista Defeat," p.101.

48. Bruce Jones, "Nicaragua's Economic Situation," *Congressional Record*, May 4, 1994, p.E845; José Antonio Ocampo, "Collapse and (Incomplete) Stabilization of the Nicaraguan Economy," in *The Macroeconomics of Populism in Latin America*, ed. Rodiger Dornbusch and Sebastian Edwards (Chicago: University of Chicago Press), p.331.

49. *Central American Report* (Guatemala City), Dec. 15, 1994, p.4; *Envío*, February-March 1994, p.6.

50. Rose Spalding, *Capitalists and Revolution in Nicaragua*, pp.166-69.

51. Richard Stahler-Sholk, "Breaking the Mold: Economic Orthodoxy and the Politics of Resistance in Nicaragua," paper presented at the Latin American Studies Association Annual Conference, Washington, D.C., Sept. 28-30, 1995, p.9.

52. Anna Maria Fernandez Poncela, "The Disruptions of Adjustment: Women in Nicaragua," *Latin American Perspectives* 23,1 (Winter 1996), p.56.

53. Florence Babb, "After the Revolution: Neoliberal Policy and Gender in Nicaragua," *Latin American Perspectives* 23,1 (Winter 1996), pp.32, 34; Stahler-Sholk, "Breaking the Mold," p.10; Cynthia Chavez Metoyer, "Efficiency or Burden Shifting? Gendered Outcomes of Stabilization and Adjustment Policies in Nicaragua," paper presented at the Latin American Studies Association International Conference, Washington, D.C., Sept. 28-30, 1995, p.19; Collinson et al., *Women and Revolution in Nicaragua*, p.32; Nan Wiegersma, "State Policy and the Restructuring of the Women's Industries in Nicaragua," in *Women in the Age of Economic Transformation: Gender Impact of Reforms in Post-Socialist and Developing Countries*, ed. Nahid Aslanbeigui, Steven Pressman, and

Gale Summerfield (London: Routledge, 1994), p.201; and Fernandez Poncela, "Disruptions of Adjustment," p.52.

54. Fernandez Poncela, "Disruptions of Adjustment: Women in Nicaragua," pp.55-56.

55. Babb, "After the Revolution," p.28.

56. Cohen, "Between Crisis Management and Social Movements," p.38.

57. Interview with Leticia Herrera, FSLN representative, June 16, 1994.

58. Interview with Milú Vargas, Legal Advisor for Ministry of Health (MINSA), Alternative Representative for FSLN, Co-Director of Centre for Constitutional Rights, Managua, April 27, 1994.

59. Interview with María Teresa Blandón, Co-ordinator, National Feminist Committee (CNF), Managua, June 20, 1994; Dora Zeledón, "Mujer, genero, poder: esperiencias sectoriales en defensa de un proyecto popular," paper presented to IPADE, 1993, p.2; Milú Vargas, "Por la unidad en la diversidad," paper presented at Seminario: Aspectos de Género y Cooperación en América Latina, Managua, 1994.

60. Mayra Pasos, "The Women's Movement Today," speech, York University, Toronto, March 6, 1995.

61. The only exception was the creation of the Commission of Women and Children, a program piloted in 1994. It supported women who were laying complaints about domestic abuses. Interview, Palacios, May 25, 1994.

62. Doug McAdam and Dieter Rucht, "The Cross-National Diffusion of Movement Ideas," *Annals, American Academy of Political and Social Science* 528 (July 1993), pp.56-74.

63. *NICCA Bulletin* (New York), January-March 1993, p.7.

64. Ana María Pizarro, *Encuentro nacional de mujeres sobre politicas de población y desarrollo: por un futuro digno y seguro para todas y todos* (Managua: Fondo de Población de las Naciones Unidas, 1993), p.3; *La Barricada*, May 27, 1994, p.4.

65. Pizarro, *Encuentro nacional de mujeres*, p.4; Lois Wessel, "Reproductive Rights in Nicaragua: From the Sandinistas to the Government of Violeta Chamorro," *Feminist Studies* 7,3 (Fall 1991), pp.546, 541-42; Sarah Morgan, "Toward a New Revolution in Health: The Emergence of Alternative Health Care Networks in Nicaragua since the 1990 Elections," unpublished undergraduate thesis, Hampshire College, Amherst, Mass., 1995, p.70.

66. Milú Vargas, "Las Platformas Electorales de los Partidos Políticos y la Mujer," in *Mujer y Partidos Políticos*, ed. Patricia Vargas Fernandez, Milú Vargas, and Josefina Ramos (Managua, 1989), p.25.

67. *Barricada International*, Jan. 20, 1990, p.11.

68. Michelle A. Saint-Germain, "Women in Power in Nicaragua: Myth and Reality," in *Women as National Leaders*, ed. Michael A. Genovese (Newbury Park, Cal.: Sage Publications, 1993); María Lourdes Pallais, "Violeta Barrios de Chamorro: la reina-madre de la nación," *Nueva Sociedad* 118 (March-April 1992), pp.89-98; *La Barricada*, Feb. 6, 1994, p.7.

69. *La Barricada*, May 29, 1991, p.4.

70. *La Barricada*, May 28, 29, 30, 1992; May 19, 1994, p.8; May 27, 1994, p.4; May 28, 1994, p.6.

71. Jean Cohen, "Rethinking Social Movements," *Berkeley Journal of Sociology* 28 (1983), p.111.

Chapter 9

The Mosque as a Political Space in Pakistan

Anne-Marie Cwikowski

A hallmark of the activities of new social movements is their tendency to transform social spaces into political spaces by politicizing civil society and the social relations and institutions that constitute it.[1] The mosque is a case in point. Under the influence of new actors, most notably the "new intellectuals" and leaders of the contemporary Islamic movements, and in response to changed historical circumstances, its role in Muslim society has been transformed. The mosque has become a political setting—a site of political discourse and activity, as well as a place of religious worship and sanctuary.

Perhaps the most salient feature of what is referred to variously as the "Islamic resurgence," or the "Islamic reassertion," is that Islam has become the language of politics all over the Muslim world, providing the vocabulary and idioms for the language of power and the opposition to it.[2] This is also evidenced at the micro-level, in the mosques, where the occasion of the Friday *khutba* (sermon/lecture), which precedes the noonday congregational prayer, provides a forum for the articulation of an Islamic political discourse. Depending upon the mosque, the nature of its congregation, and the leadership roles in it, Islam may be enlisted to either affirm or oppose the established political authority of a given country.

In most Muslim countries the mosques are under government control. In Pakistan, in contrast, the vast majority are private mosques—or, as they are also called, "popular mosques" or "free mosques," in that they are independent of state control.[3] It is more likely, therefore, that in assuming the proportions of political settings the mosques in Pakistan might also become venues for anti-establishment expressions of Islam, as well as staging grounds for the mobilization of political protest.

However, the definition of the mosque as a political space may be applied more generally. In Egypt, for example, a few well-known mosque preachers have become outspoken critics of government policies.

Commercially available cassette recordings of the sermons of these popular preachers have become hot items in the bazaars of Cairo and the other main towns.[4] The Egyptian authorities have also closed down a number of mosques in Cairo that were functioning as meeting places and recruiting grounds for some of the country's more notorious militant Islamic groups.[5]

Less alarming, but no less significant, is the dramatic increase in the number of mosques being built. In Egypt from 1961 to 1979 a 100 percent increase took place in the total number of mosques, which had climbed from 17,000 to 34,000. By 1984 the number had increased to about 50,000.[6] Over the last few decades a boom in mosque-building, along with an increase in mosque attendance, has occurred throughout the Muslim world, and this activity is noted generally among Western observers as being one of the major indices of the so-called "Islamic revival."

Even in Egypt, where the mosques fall under the jurisdiction of government *waqf* (religious endowment) departments and the imam (prayer leader) and other mosque functionaries such as the *khatib* (preacher/lecturer) are paid appointees of the state, most new mosques built are private mosques.[7] This is due to a variety of factors, including the inability of the state to staff, finance, and maintain so many mosques. Whatever the case, people are building their own neighbourhood and community mosques and, in many cases, deliberately circumventing state intervention in them.[8]

Most mosques being built today are also "*jamiya* mosques." That is, they are mosques that host the *khutba* and the Friday congregational prayers,[9] which represents a departure from traditional arrangements when only the main mosques of the cities and provincial towns were designated as *jamiya* mosques. Nowadays, even the most humble of mosques in the most out-of-the-way places will endeavour to acquire the services of a *khatib* to deliver the *khutba*.

Part of the revitalization of the mosque's role is also attributable to the leaders of the contemporary Islamic movements, who are returning to the mosques as part of a wider self-professed strategy of "Islamic revolution." Considered by the representatives of the older more established organizations of political Islam—religio-political parties such as the Jamaat-i-Islami in Pakistan and organizations like the Muslim Brotherhood in Egypt—as being inadequate arenas for spreading the new "Islamist" message, the mosques are being reclaimed by the new lay preachers and leaders of the Islamic movements.[10]

In the process the mosques are being turned, along with other venues in civil society such as the universities, Quran academies, recreational centres, and professional associations, not only into Islamized spaces, but also into political spaces. As political settings, the mosques have become forums in which the new leaders and lay preachers of the Islamic movements propagate their ideology, articulate their political projects, and reinforce their leadership roles in society.

Surprisingly, despite an intense Western interest in the Islamic reassertion, little attention has been paid to determining what role the mosques play in this process. After all, as Richard Antoun points out in *Muslim Preacher in the Modern World*, the mosque is the main institution in the Muslim world for the propagation of Islam. Moreover, the Friday *khutba* is the most regular occasion for the recitation of the Quran, with recitations from the Quran preceding and following the sermon, punctuating the sermon, and serving as a "proof-text" for it.[11]

Yet, outside of the historical data, and with the exception of a few important ethnological studies conducted by anthropologists, we have very little information on the role of the mosque in modern Muslim society. Discussion on the Islamic revival has taken place largely in the absence of what is for Antoun the "most vital evidence"—that is, the Islamic sermon delivered every Friday in the mosque by the "mainline carrier" of the tradition, the *khatib*.[12]

The transformation of the mosque into a political space cannot be accounted for simply by recognizing that throughout Islamic history the mosque was a place where religious and political authority met. Indeed, mosques have always been multifunctional domains: community centres, places of worship and refuge, and places where official political pronouncements were made.[13] Today, however, the mosque has become a symbolic arena of political contestation, and the *khutba* a source of countervailing symbols of political legitimacy.

As Patrick Gaffney explains in *The Prophet's Pulpit: Islamic Preaching in Contemporary Egypt*, the mosques are "ciphers" for the expression of a variety of different interests, as are the modern Islamic movements that influence them both directly and indirectly.[14] The mosques, and the activity in and around them, reflect the complex transformations going on in modern Muslim societies. Still, defining and analyzing the mosque as a political space only offers a small glimpse of the wider social processes and historical forces fuelling the modern Islamic reassertion and giving rise to the Islamic movements of political opposition associated with that reassertion. Obviously, we cannot hope to condense the big picture into such small spaces. My intention in defining the mosque as a political space is not to set it up, methodologically speaking, as a microcosm of Muslim society. Rather, by analyzing the mosque as a political setting, in its differing local contexts, I hope to illuminate one dimension of the shifting ground and changing contexts of power and politics in Muslim societies.

Spiritual and Temporal Authorities

While mosques exist in many different and varied contexts, as Gaffney explains, all of them "share elements of a common tradition." All mosques are, for example, places of devotion, which, according to Gaffney, affirm "Mecca's divine aura" as the sacred centre and sanctuary of Islam. Because most mosques contain the *mihrab* (prayer niche), which signals the direction of Mecca, which in turn is the home of the *kabah*—the centrepiece of Islamic ritual, and the central place of worship, pilgrimage, and sanctuary in the Muslim world—all mosques are in this sense "localized Meccas."[15]

The *minbar* (pulpit) and the *mihrab* are key features characteristic of most, if not all, mosques. The *minbar* is associated with the Prophet and his place of prayer at Medina.[16] It also symbolizes Muhammad's religious and political authority, because as the prophet of Islam and its first, most exemplary preacher and political leader, he customarily used the occasions when he delivered sermons to make public pronouncements concerning the affairs of the early Muslim community at Medina.[17] It is the *minbar*, usually a raised and carpeted platform, upon which the *khatib* sits or stands to deliver the *khutba*.

The intermingling of spiritual and temporal symbols inside the mosque is also linked to the practice that arose during the period of the Ummayad Caliphate (C.E. 661-750), in the tradition of the Prophet (d.632) and the first four "Rightly Guided Caliphs" (632-661), whereby the Caliph, the Prophet's successor, would deliver the *khutba* in one of the main mosques of the capital at Damascus before the commencement of the Friday prayer service. This practice continued until the advent of the Abbasid Caliphate (750-1258), when it acquired a purely religious function, which it has retained, for the most part, until the modern period.[18]

The coming to power of the Abbasids also marked the culmination of the process begun after the death of the Prophet of the progressive differentiation of the religious and political spheres of authority.[19] Along with this process and over time, the religious functions of the Caliph were divested to a *khatib*, who was a salaried official of the state and received a stipend to deliver the *khutba* in designated *jamiya* mosques on the Caliph's behalf. The Caliphs also devolved this function to governors and officials in the different provinces, regions, and towns of the empire.[20]

Thus, as the political priorities and objectives of the Caliphate overtook its religious aims, the practice also evolved that in the absence of the Caliph in the mosque, the *khatib*, as his representative, would mention the name of the Caliph at the end of the *khutba* and bestow blessings on him.[21] In this case the Caliph's authority, as the living successor of the Prophet, was summoned up in the presence of the *khatib*.

Following from this, Antoun tells us that the role of the *khatib* symbolizes both religious and political authority, because the *khatib*'s function in the mosque was closely associated with his symbolic function as a representative of the Prophet and later, the Caliph, the political leader of the Muslim community.[22] However, we should be careful not to attribute too much political significance to the symbolic features of the mosque and the *khatib*'s role in it. The practice of naming the Caliph in the mosque, for example, was less a symbol of the unity of spiritual and temporal authority than it was an expression of the primacy of the power of the de facto political ruler. The Caliphs' symbolic association with the mosque was more representative of how—as in early modern Europe, and during the heyday of the "ancien regime," when the notion of the "divine right" of Kings was proffered as a way of legitimizing dynastic succession—religion became enlisted in the service of the state.

While both Gaffney and Antoun acknowledge the secular historical basis of Muslim political practice, they privilege the place of ideal concepts and sacred symbols in it. They do not explicate the de facto separation between Islam and politics so much as they reduce politics to religious practice. Consequently, both end up by asserting the classic Orientalist assumption that in Islam there is no distinction between religion and politics.[23]

Gaffney tells us, for example, that because the symbols of spiritual and temporal authority intermingle inside the mosque, we cannot bifurcate Islam into distinct spheres of mosque and state; these symbols summarize the Islamic ideal of the unity of the Muslim *ummah* as a religious and political community.[24] However, on another more temporal plane these same symbols gave expression to the imperatives of the political Caliphate, no doubt cloaked as it was in a religious aura.

Moreover, it is misleading to argue, as Antoun does, that because the mosques in countries such as Jordan and Egypt and in other parts of the Middle East are under the control of the state, they provide us with another example of how Islam makes no distinction between religion and politics.[25] Rather, the state control of mosques merely indicates that secularism in the Islamic world has always meant state control over religion. As Fazlur Rahman argues, it is not the non-separation of religion and politics that is peculiar to Islam, but the subjugation of religion to politics.[26]

The Private Mosques of Pakistan

Gaffney's research on Islamic preaching in Egypt has led him to the conclusion that the mosque has become a potentially "volatile channel of communication."[27] Yet in Pakistan, where most mosques are institutionally autonomous from the state, the politics of Islamic reassertion has not assumed the same violent and radical proportions as in Egypt and Algeria, where the state has a tighter hold on religion and the range of religious expression in the mosques is restricted. Indeed, the Islamic movement in Pakistan has been unable to exert much influence beyond the cities and main provincial towns precisely because the mosques in Pakistani society constitute a network of relatively free spaces.[28]

In any case, a variety of other factors besides just the independent status of the mosques vis-à-vis the state determine their identity: their size, decor, location, and the events surrounding their founding, for instance. Most important of all is the question of who owns the mosque and who is responsible for its operation and financial upkeep; and it is on this question that the issue of autonomy ultimately rests, for the majority of mosques in Pakistan are private mosques independent of state control. Still, not all of those mosques are genuinely popular mosques in the sense that they are owned and operated by the community for the community, as we will see in a comparison of two mosques in particular.

As for the leadership roles inside the mosques, certain factors beyond the act of ritual preaching itself also have an impact upon the authority of the preachers and determine the extent of their influence in society. The biographies of the preachers, their personal charisma, their occupational status, and their involvement in activities outside the mosque, as well as the size and status of the congregations they serve, all combine to shape both the identity and the authority of the preachers.[29]

Dr. Israr and the Abode of Peace Mosque

Israr Ahmad is a popular preacher and self-professed radical in the Islamic movement in Pakistan. The weekly and biweekly publication of his sermons in two Lahore-based Urdu language newspapers enhances his reputation as a leader in the Islamic movement and reinforces his status as a lay preacher working on its behalf.

Israr Ahmad has also founded three organizations that operate independently of each other, but all of which are under his leadership. These include the Quran Academy, which is an Islamic educational institute; the Tanzeem-i-Islami, an organization that studies ways to implement the *shari-ah* law in society; and the Tehriq-i-Khilafah, which promotes the "rule of God" in the country.[30] His work as the amir (leader) of these organizations has earned him a measure of public respect for his commitment to the cause of Islam, if not necessarily for his views themselves.

Israr Ahmad's personal biography also contributes to his public stature. Born in 1932 in India, he migrated to Lahore after the partition of India and the declaration of Pakistan's independence in 1947. Upon his arrival in Pakistan he pursued studies at home and abroad in medicine.[31] While practising as a doctor he also acquired a masters degree in Islamic studies. His profile is similar to that of the leadership of the Islamic movements in other parts of the Muslim world—that is, of people who are secular educated professionals, primarily from engineering and science faculties, with little or no formal *madrassah* (traditional Islamic school) training.

In 1954 Dr. Israr (as he is known locally) joined the Jamaat-i-Islami party, one of the main centres of political Islam in the Muslim world outside of the offices of the Muslim Brotherhood in Egypt. In 1957 he left the party along with a few other individuals who also went on to become important leaders in the Islamic movement in Pakistan. By his telling, he quit the Jamaat-i-Islami because it had abandoned its revolutionary principles and had become just another political party, in effect reducing Islam to a political slogan and a weapon designed to increase the party's participation in the system, instead of attacking the foundations of it.

The details of Dr. Israr's breaking of ranks from the Jamaat-i-Islami are well known, but have not diminished his public stature. Nor did the break exclude him from participating in politics. Dr. Israr was recruited to work on an Islamic advisory council to the cabinet during General Muhammad Zia ul-Haq's tenure in office (1978-88), but this liaison lasted only a few months. According to Dr. Israr, General Zia was not really intent on creating an Islamic system and was interested in Islam only to the extent that it served to legitimize his rule. Dr. Israr's reputation also does not appear to have been tarnished by his brief flirtation with Zia's military dictatorship, even if it does raise doubts about his commitment to democracy. In any case, Dr. Israr's departure from the formal political realm has enhanced his singular role as an Islamic leader in society, leaving him free to devote his energy toward his self-professed goal of achieving an Islamic revolution.

Although Dr. Israr makes frequent use of the term Islamic revolution, the rhetoric should be put aside and examined in the context of the activities he engages in and the organizational structure he has built for pursuing his goals. This is an important caveat if we are to understand properly what he means by the term Islamic revolution. Indeed, a somewhat different picture then emerges. Dr. Israr's form of Islamic revolution is more akin to a strategy of building an alternative Islamic hegemony in society and of encircling the state rather than capturing or overthrowing it through violent means. The revolution involves, by his own account, practising *dawa* (propagation), that is, preaching against the current system, and disseminating an alternative Islamist ideology to convert people over to his way of thinking.

Dr. Israr also plans to transform the Tanzeem-i-Islami into a political party, but this represents the second stage in his path of Islamic revolution, which can only be attained once the work of *dawa* is done and a critical mass of Islamic consciousness has been built up in society. It is toward this end that Dr. Israr has founded his organizations with the aim of creating an educated cadre of intellectuals capable of leading the Islamic movement forward while keeping, as he puts it, the "fundamentals of Islam intact." This is also his definition of a Muslim fundamentalist, that is, one who keeps the "fundamentals of Islam intact" and strives to reunite all spheres of life under an Islamic system.

The mosque in which Dr. Israr delivers his *khutba* has connections to the Tanzeem-i-Islami, which he presides over, but is itself a privately owned mosque belonging to a military family. It is run by a mosque committee headed by one of the sons of the late Colonel who acquired the mosque, and by a staff member from the Tanzeem-i-Islami whose job it is to coordinate the affairs of the mosque with that of the Tanzeem-i-Islami and Dr. Israr's other organizations.

The mosque committee is responsible for the upkeep of the mosque and managing its finances, which include paying for the services of a full-time Imam to deliver the five daily prayers, with the exception of the Friday prayer service. The mosque is financed largely through private donations from individuals and from the Tanzeem-i-Islami.

The mosque in which Dr. Israr has regularly delivered the Friday sermons since 1978 is a small domed structure measuring about 20 feet in width and 30 feet in length. It is known locally as *masjid dar al-salaam*, which renders into English as the abode of peace mosque. It is situated in downtown Lahore, the capital of Pakistan's Punjab province, on the grounds of a major public park called Jinnah Gardens.

Dr. Israr's sermons draw crowds of over a thousand people. His topics are chosen according to the main political events going on in Pakistan and other parts of the Muslim world at the time. While many people congregate at this mosque on Fridays for the specific purpose of hearing Dr. Israr deliver the sermon, they also come for other more practical reasons. The convenience of the location of the mosque and the fixed time of its Friday prayer service also play a part. In any case, to accommodate the crowds on Fridays tents are set up on the lawns of the park surrounding the mosque, with separate areas cordoned off for men and women and loudspeakers placed around the vicinity.

The congregation of *masjid dar al-salaam* appears to follow the pattern of the Islamic movements elsewhere. It consists mainly of men drawn from the ranks of the new middle class. In attendance are doctors, businessmen, government officials (including military personnel and civil servants), university students, and other members of the largely educated urban professional class.[32] Dr. Israr's radicalism taps into the frustrations of the new middle class, as well as the downwardly mobile lower middle class. It is intended to empower a class in society whose members have benefited from modernization, and the postcolonial expansion of the state, but who are increasingly frustrated with its only partial successes, and whose lifestyles are increasingly threatened on a variety of fronts.

Pakistan in the late 1990s is in the midst of an economic and social crisis. Inflation is estimated to be running at 20 percent.[33] The decline in real wages of middle-class Pakistanis is compounded by the increasingly conspicuous consumption patterns and lifestyles of the upper classes (landlords, industrialists, and the high-ranking civil and military bureaucratic elites). Many in the middle class, a large percentage of them employed in the public sector as doctors, university professors, and lower-level civil servants, must acquire second jobs if they want to get ahead at all. The search for an authentic Islamic alternative articulated in Dr. Israr's *khutbas* is directed toward an educated audience whose expectations for upward mobility have been largely thwarted by a bureaucratic structure and political system plagued by corruption and "cronyism." The problem of corruption is particularly acute in Pakistan. One German watchdog agency reported that it had the second most corrupt political system in the world, next to Nigeria.[34] Since 1990 three successive governments have been dissolved by presidential decree on charges of corruption in high places.

Pakistanis have a real and palpable sense of frustration with the bureaucratic and political corruption, the attendant lawlessness, and the lack of equal opportunity engendered by this situation. The demands for the restoration of *shariah* law and the implementation of a system of Islamic justice are best appreciated in this context.

Dr. Israr does not speak for the vast majority of the disadvantaged rural masses, or for the urban proletariat. His discourse is representative of the Islamic right in Pakistan and elsewhere. In line with the ideology of the contemporary Islamic movements, Dr. Israr asserts that Islam is a complete way of life that offers a viable alternative to capitalism and socialism. Yet it is not so much capitalism that the Islamic movements oppose, but socialism. Rejecting the thesis of historical materialism and the communist vision of a classless society, they subscribe instead to a notion of a divinely sanctioned social division of labour.[35]

While Dr. Israr does not articulate issues of class, he does criticize the social injustices that result from the capitalist system through which wealth accumulates in the hands of a few, leading to a system of social inequality characterized by the "haves" and the "have-nots," as he terms it. Nevertheless, his basic conservatism comes to light in certain statements. In one breath he criticizes the problem of "landlordism" in Pakistan, while in the next he upholds the sanctity of private property as being an Islamic institution and rejects the idea of redistributing the landlords' estates on the grounds that it would be "un-Islamic" and unfair to do so.

In this case, Dr. Israr's political radicalism is characteristic of the class he belongs to, and of contemporary Islamic movements generally. It is explained in part by the inability of the different strata of the middle class to become part of the dominant political class on the one hand, and by the determination of the members of this class to distinguish themselves from the demands of the labour movement and the working class on the other.[36]

Dr. Israr: Two Khutbas[37]

Masjid dar al-salaam (Lahore), July 1993

Now this is 1993. Both big parties, the Pakistan People's Party and the Muslim League, have been ousted from government and, on the face of it, an impartial government has taken over. Now it is the duty of the government to make sure that all the parties accept whatever the result may be. Secondly, there should be some code of ethics—whatever it may be—acceptable to all. It is not necessary that it be a perfect code. But to start with all the parties should agree on some basic things. For example, participating parties should stop accusing each other of being traitors and spies. This custom of calling each other traitors causes a lot of damage in the country.

One more thing is this form of election is meant for the rich, only those who can spend four to five million can participate. We are not against holding free and fair elections, but this lavish spending should be curtailed. As a first step the hanging of big posters should be banned. There should be a certain size that should be allowed. Secondly, a new trend has been noticed. Posting of huge portraits of leaders by the roadsides—and this race has been joined by some religious leaders.

I want to make one thing clear. All the imams of all the religious sects agree on one thing. These hand-made portraits are strictly banned, they are *haram* in Islam. This has been strictly forbidden. There can be some controversy over camera photos, but there is no controversy whatsoever about portraits. We demand that this practice should be banned.

People ask who is better, Nawaz Sharif or Benazir. I say there is no difference between them—they are both secular—neither of them is Islamic. The only difference is that Mr. Sharif uses the name of Islam. He, like General Zia, is not sincere to the cause of Islam. Zia, for 11 years, used the slogan of Islam to prolong his regime. He could have imposed Islam but he did not. I met General Zia about the imposition of purdah for school girls and college students. General Zia expressed his inability to do so, saying that the parents of girls don't want purdah to be imposed. I remarked about the black mark on his forehead which is usually due to offering prayers. "Sir, this is a mark of shame on your forehead." I was obviously pointing out his inability to impose Islam, which he could have easily done. When he can jail thousands, hanged many because of their political differences, why couldn't he have done so?

And if you ask me, I am against the use of the slogan of Islam for elections or political purposes. No one should be allowed to use this slogan, because if one will raise the slogan others will also raise it so that there will be all sorts of different types of Islam. Each party will claim to be right. There are no two types of Islam. There is only one right path. Please don't make it a disputable point for the purposes of your own interests.

Also, the political process is equally important for the survival of the country. These are not two different things. I will try to explain it by way of example. The creation of Pakistan. It was a religious demand. We demanded a separate homeland because we were Muslims. The very foundation stone of Pakistan was on the basis of the first *kalima*— "there is no God but Allah." But it was created through a political process. So both of these things, the religious foundations and the political process, are necessary for the stability and prosperity of the country. But all this does not obviate the need for revolution. If you want to change the fate of a country you will have to go through a revolution.

Islam cannot be imposed through this political system. It can only be imposed through some kind of revolution, for which our party is working. We don't want to waste our energies participating in this useless political exercise. We want to reserve our energies for revolution. But we as a party are ready to support the religious parties in the coming general elections. I have been approached by heads of various Islamic political parties like Mawlana Fazal ur-Rahman and others, and I have made this thing clear to them—that we shall only support you if you all unite—and not as individual parties.

I am also clear in my mind about one thing. Progression in any direction is better than the status quo. Progression even if it is in a secular direction is better than keeping things as they are, because then there is always the chance of swinging things in the other direction. Keep in mind the example of Iran. They were Westernized and secular in every form, but then what happened? They completely changed. But to change the fate of the country we shall have to abolish this big landowning system if we want the political process to flourish. India's edge over Pakistan was that they were able to overcome this menace soon after independence. But unluckily we could not. That was all the more reason for the failure of the political system in Pakistan. I don't want to sound like I'm saying that these landlords don't own their land. They do, by all means, unless the government approves some law declaring the land as state and as Hazrat Umar did. Till then a different process can be thought of and landlords can be offered some privileges. Simply taking away their land is unlawful and un-Islamic.

I shall be visiting America for some time. I also want to address people there about "fundamentalism"—about why there has been this big hue and cry in the international press. Is practising the principles of Islam so condemnable a thing? What has the West to fear from Islam? And how shameful that our Prime Minister Nawaz Sharif had to make an announcement that "I am not a fundamentalist." Whom is he trying to please?

Jang, (Lahore), December 10, 1993

As a complete way of life, Islam's real and final objective is social justice, which should be reflected in the following domains: (a) equality at the social and constitutional level, (b) freedom at the political level, and (c) justice at the social level.

Consequently, Islam longs for a society where there should be no discrimination between the "superiors" and the "inferiors," and where politics should be free from coercion and alienation based on the slave-master relationship, and where the economy should be devoid of exploitation that results in the classification of the "haves" and the "have-nots."

The real basis of Islam is faith in Allah. Among the 99 names of Allah one name is "Al-adl," or sheer justice. . . . The real nature of the *shariah* is Adl, and all the individual and collective deeds of human beings should be judged according to this criterion . . . . The purpose of sending the prophets, holy books, and *wahy* [revealed knowledge] is a system based on Adl. If this objective is not attained, the claims of love for the prophets and the recitation from the holy books are of no use.

To establish this system a persuasive system of teaching can be employed. However, in some cases the obstacles in the way of achieving a just system can be removed by force. The sending of prophets, holy book, and *wahy* is to test those people who believe in the prophets and the holy books, to see whether they really devote and dedicate their lives for the establishment of a just system or not.

The climax of this subject in the Quran suggests that people should not just endure and tolerate oppression, but if necessary the aggrieved can react against the brutalities of the oppressors. In short the most important value of Islam is the establishment of social justice—and the target of Islamic revolution is to establish the God-given system of social justice.

In the end, I would like to refer to the creator of Pakistan, Quaid-i-Azam Muhammad Ali Jinnah, who explained that the objective of demanding a new country was that "We want to attain Pakistan so that we can show the rest of the world a practical example of freedom, fraternity, and equality." In 1930 Allama Iqbal wrote that if we could get an independent state for the Muslims we could show the real shining face of Islam to the world, which has been veiled by Arab kinship. But, alas, even after 46 years we are still standing at the same place. May the Muslims of Pakistan determine to work for attaining their real objective.

Imam Mahmud and a Rural Mosque

The second mosque I did research in was situated about 70 kilometres from Lahore, in a small village on the outskirts of the provincial town of Sheikhupura in Punjab province.

The mosque itself, roughly 45 by 100 feet, was the largest structure in the village. It was owned by the villagers, financed by donations from them, and staffed by an ad hoc committee of volunteers whose job it was to take care of maintenance and pay the full-time imam. It was also their responsibility to acquire the services of a *khatib* to deliver the Friday sermon.

The initial construction of the mosque was a locally funded and organized community endeavour, with some of the money being provided by a few more well-off villagers whose family members donated money from remittances earned while working abroad in the Gulf states. The land on which the mosque was built was acquired from a family living in the area who had donated it to the villagers. There had been no mosque in the village at the time.

The mosque was the most attractive building in the village, painted in pastel shades of blue and green with white trimmings. It had a walled courtyard with taps for washing and straw mats placed on the floor to accommodate the overflow of people when there was no room inside its enclosed part, which is where the *khatib* sat to deliver the *khutba* and lead the prayers. The *minbar* was a raised and carpeted platform on which stood a microphone attached to a PA system that carried the voice of the *khatib* into the courtyard of the mosque and out into the streets.

The mosque stood in marked contrast to the low-rise dwellings made of baked clay and mud-brick and inhabited by about 5,000 villagers. The housing was built around a rambling series of dirt roads leading from the suburbs of the main town toward the agricultural lands bordering the village itself.

On Fridays the number of people in attendance at the rural mosque was on average about 200 to 250. The congregation consisted primarily of middle-aged men and young boys, although usually a few older women and adolescent girls were also in attendance. During the summer harvest season the number of the congregation tended to drop off, because most of the villagers were employed as rural labourers and tenant farmers.

The women were quartered in the upstairs section of the mosque, out of sight of the men below. A hole in the floor of the upstairs section about three feet square with a wall around it allowed for the sound to pass upstairs and provided a view of the *khatib*. The generally uplifting spirit of the congregational prayers was enhanced by the communality of the activity itself. This atmosphere did not pervade the women's quarters, where the women, instead of sitting shoulder to shoulder like the main congregation of men downstairs, sat at various distances across the room. There was a distinct sense of alienation in the women's section of the mosque.

One of the *khatib*s who regularly rotated his duties in the rural mosque was Imam Altaf Mahmud. People addressed him as Imam Mahmud, although he was not really an imam in the sense of being the full-time prayer leader of the five daily prayers. The terms are interchangeable, because the *khatib* also leads the Friday prayers as well as delivering the sermon.[38] In Altaf Mahmud's case, the title of imam was used as a designation of respect for his knowledge of Islam and the responsibilities he undertook in its name. In Pakistan the term mullah is also applied to mosque preachers, but in a derogatory sense that implies religious leaders who are uneducated, parochial, and intemperate in their utterances. People speak, for example, of "mullahism" as a phenomenon.

Imam Mahmud had obtained a B.A. in history and an M.A. in educational studies from a provincial college in Punjab. He was employed as a history teacher at a Christian-run missionary school in the nearest town to the village. In contrast to Dr. Israr, Imam Mahmud had also received a *madrassah* education, in which he studied the Quran and Arabic. He did not live in the village where he preached, but in a humble dwelling with his family in an adjacent town. He also preached in other mosques in the vicinity, which he travelled to on his motorbike. Like most other preachers in the popular mosques in Pakistan, he received no stipend for his services. He performed these duties because, as he expressed it, he wanted to do service in the name of Islam.

Imam Mahmud was not associated in any direct way with the Islamic movement in Pakistan, identifying as he did with the Barelvi tradition of Islam and the religio-cultural stream of Islam associated with this network of *madrassahs* in the Indian subcontinent. The Barelvis' and the Deobandis' separate *ulama*-led organizations are both important forces in Pakistani politics.[39]

Unlike the Deobandis and the contemporary Islamic movements, which reject many Sufi practices, including saint worship, the Barelvis are noted for their populist approach to the faith. They acknowledge the tradition of the saint worship and the local role played by the *pirs/sajjada nashin* (spiritual guides who are also the hereditary custodians of the Sufi shrines) in the lives of the rural population. In this sense, Imam Mahmud and the congregation he serves are very much identified with what is referred to generally as "folk Islam."

Despite Imam Mahmud's Barelvi background, in his sermons he denounced many of the superstitious beliefs and practices associated with the shrines of the Sufis. While he acknowledged the historical role played by Sufi saints in spreading the message of Islam and uplifting the lives of the rural classes, he was particularly critical of the role of the *pirs*, whom he accused of exploiting the poor and of being charlatans. In this case, Imam Mahmud followed a distinction that successive governments in Pakistan, in assuming control of many of the Sufi shrines, had tried to impose—that is, the distinction between worshipping the Sufi saints and seeking the spiritual interventions of the living *pirs* who control their shrines.[40]

Imam Mahmud wrote out his sermons by hand and, as opposed to Dr. Israr, chose their content according to the main events of the Quranic calendar. Also, in contrast to Dr. Israr, whose sermons were delivered in what Gaffney refers to as the "metonymic" mode—that is, in a style that treats the Quran as an unambiguous collection of statements—Imam Mahmud's sermons were delivered in a metaphorical style.[41] Indeed, when Imam Mahmud gave me permission to attend his sermons and to have the written copies of them translated, he expressed most emphatically that these were to be read metaphorically, or allegorically as he expressed it. To illustrate his point, he related a story about a *khutba* he had delivered a few months earlier in a mosque in the police cantonment in a nearby town.

In that *khutba* Imam Mahmud had recounted the events of the famous battle at Karbala and the subsequent martyrdom of the Prophet's grandson Hussein at the hands of the Umayyad Caliph Yazid. The inference Imam Mahmud drew from this incident in Islamic history and Shiah hagiography, which he conveyed to the Sunni Muslim congregation in attendance, and to me later, was that people are not obliged to obey their leaders if they are not honest and do not follow the path of Allah. He explained that God does not intend the people to toil under the tyranny of dictatorial and unjust rulers.

Imam Mahmud recounted how after the *khutba* had finished he was summoned to the police commissioner's office and told that such reference to events in Islamic history were best left unspoken, and that in future he should be more careful in his pronouncements. As a result of this discussion I realized that although most of the six sermons transcribed did not raise direct political references, the political inferences were quite clear.

Imam Mahmud: Two Khutbas[42]

June 1993

All praises to God and peace be upon his prophet. In the name of Allah the all-compassionate, the all-merciful.

After all the citizens had left the city and went off to a fair where they were amusing themselves, Abraham (blessing on him) picked up an axe and went to the temple of the idols. "Quickly Abraham went to the idols and asked them, why don't you eat, why don't you speak, what is wrong with you?" From this verse it is evident that there must have been many types of fruit and food lying in front of the idols and that is why Abraham (boh) asked them, "Why don't you eat?" Now one question arises here, where did all the food and fruit come from, and who consumed it? It is clear that the common people of the city must have been delivering the food to the temple and that the priests must have been eating it.

The biggest idol of the temple was called Janar; he was the god of agriculture, industry, and commerce, and whatever the activities the people were engaged in they had to donate a share of their produce to this god, the amount of which was decided by the idol-priests. All this wealth accumulated was consumed by the priests, the politicians, and the government officials. Now we can draw parallels between those times and modern times, and examine the lives of the Hindu yogis, the priests, the popes, and the sajjada nashin, whose lives are similar to the temple priests of the old days. These good-for-nothing people are a burden on society, and are like leeches feeding off the blood of the commoners. If you look into their private lives you will see how wicked they are and what immoral customs and habits they actually have. They are like vultures in society feeding on the dead flesh of the common people.

One point I wish to make clear, however, is that Islam was spread by love and not by the sword—by the love of the Sufis and saints who lived with the common people, sharing their sorrows and joys. Islam has nothing to do with the sword of immoral conquerors, rather it was spread through the love and affection of the kind-hearted Sufis and saints, for it was they who attracted the people to the Islamic faith. However, the modern-day *sajjada nashin* and *pirs* who occupy their shrines have nothing to do with those great men, and are just selling the names of the great Sufi saints. Iqbal wrote, "Although the vulture and the eagle fly in the same sky, the universe of the eagle and the vulture are different," and "Oh God, whom shall the naive and innocent look to for guidance when the rulers and the custodians of the faith are both cunning?"

June 1993

In summing up from the previous *khutba* we see how we can draw parallels between the priests of Abraham's (boh) time and the modern-day priests and *sajjada nashin*. I was talking to you about the Quranic verse Surah Abraham and about Abraham's (boh) question to the idols of why they can't move, talk, or eat, and how this was a very philosophical way of bringing out their inherent weakness, which was their inability to do anything at all. How can you expect a thing that cannot eat or talk to help you out in times of need? "Thus he ferociously struck them with his right hand."

According to the Quran, Abraham's people said, "No doubt you are that cruel man." It is evident from this verse that it is a person's conscience that knows what's right and what's wrong even though on the face of it a person may not see the truth. While it is the conscience of a person that knows what is inherently right and wrong, in the heat of the moment people are not always inclined to weigh the pros and cons of a thing, and will act according to what is in their worldly interests. According to the Quran the people said, "You know that they don't speak." At heart the people knew their idols were impotent, that they didn't eat or speak, but it was in their worldly interests not to accept what their consciences told them.

In the verse from the Quran that I have just quoted the word *ru'us* is used. This is the plural form of *ra'is*, which means head, and everyone knows that intelligence is related to the head. The word *aql*, derived from the Arabic, means to tie. Once a friend of the Prophet (peace be upon him) came to the *masjid al-nabiy* on a camel and asked the Prophet (pbuh) about his camel, saying, "Oh Prophet of Allah, I left the camel in God's care," and the Prophet (pbuh) said, "No, first tie its legs and then leave it in God's care." The Prophet (pbuh) used the word *aql* here in the sense of meaning to tie, as the

Arabs used to tie the legs of the camels with a string and they called it *aqal*, the meaning of the word being string to tie with, and when this string was not in use they tied it around their heads. . . . Anyhow, you can seek guidance from this worldly wisdom, but it is limited and there are many things to which this worldly wisdom will be of no help to you.

According to a poet, "It is good to decide worldly matters with your logic, but you cannot decide everything with your head," and according to Iqbal, "In love of God Abraham jumped into Nimrod's fire without giving it a second thought." So we see that if the sea is very rough and a person relies solely on his worldly wisdom to decide matters it is likely that he would not jump to save a drowning man. However, if the same situation was presented to a person whose heart was filled with compassion for his fellow human beings, then there is little doubt that he would risk his life for the life of another.

In challenging Nimrod to make the sun rise in the West he challenged not only his stupid beliefs but his very power and status. Abraham (boh) made a very delicate point by challenging Nimrod in this way, for Nimrod used to call himself the son of the Sun-God. For, like all dictators, Nimrod had a very tight grip on the people. Whenever a person gains power over a people and a nation because of the grace of God, the logical thing for the ruler to do is to offer his thanks to God and to show his obedience to God by serving humanity. However, these thankless people think that the reason they have risen to power is because of their own intelligence and that it has nothing to do with God's will. Nothing gets through the thick skulls of the thankless rulers, as they grow more stubborn and proud, refusing to listen to anything that is not in their own personal interests. They act like gods on earth, and if someone questions their roles and their status these dictators display such arrogance that they wouldn't think twice about killing people.

Throughout history it has always been the case that the truth-minded people who rebuke the tyrants for their untruthful deeds, that these people are eliminated and their voices silenced. That is why our Prophet (pbuh) said, "To speak the truth against a dictator is jihad." The people of Pakistan they know that Pakistan, which was named Land of the Pure, has had many political murders and to date none of the culprits have been caught. This episode of political violence has not ended, and all the rulers who have risen to power in Pakistan behave as if they were gods, and go to every extent to prolong their tenure in public office. So too, they loot the commoners and the national treasury for their own profit and personal gain. This lust for wealth and power that our leaders display knows no limit, even if it means murder.

Conclusion

The Friday gatherings in both of these two mosques function as political settings. Insofar as the discourse in them intersects with power, it no longer serves merely to sanction it by providing doctrinal legitimation for the established political order, but it actively questions and opposes it. Nevertheless, the urban and rural mosques show important differences in discourse and leadership styles, differences brought about not just through the character and personal charisma of the preachers, but also through the differing patterns of their ownership.

In the case of the urban mosque, the connections between the Tanzeem-i-Islami and the mosque committee enable Dr. Israr to exert, if not a controlling interest, then a decisive influence over it. Indeed, *masjid dar al-salaam* is largely identified with him and the Islamic movement in Pakistan, in which he is a leading figure. It is doubtful that the urban congregation exerts much influence on the mosque except perhaps by way of providing or withholding donations, attending or not attending.

The occasion of the Friday sermon provides Dr. Israr with the opportunity to engage in a "self-authorizing" form of discourse in which Islam is articulated more as a political ideology than a theology and deployed as part of an alternative power-seeking strategy on behalf of the Islamic movement and parties he endorses.[43]

In contrast to Dr. Israr, Imam Mahmud's role is not so much that of a leader, but a voice of the people. He speaks on behalf and at the behest of his congregation. What leadership role he does exercise is more akin to that of intellectual leadership. Understanding his sermons against the background of an illiteracy rate of about 85 percent, and viewing them in the context of a highly exploitative system of agrarian relations, Imam Mahmud may be said to bring an educative function to his task.

In Imam Mahmud's sermons Islam is not formulated into a political ideology. Rather, his sermons emphasize the humanitarian spirit of Islam and articulate the meaning of faith as a guide to moral action. From this vantage point he employs Islam as a standard by which to judge the conduct of secular political rulers and traditional religious leaders alike. Islam cannot be seen in this instance to be an ideology that dupes the masses, as Imam Mahmud's sermons elaborate a conception of the world that provides an ideological framework for resistance to elite cultural domination.[44]

In any case, it is not by way of reference to ideal-type depictions of the mosque in history that we are going to be able to understand its changing role in modern Muslim societies. To posit the notion of the mosque as a political space is not a restatement of the well-worn Orientalist thesis of the non-separation of religion and politics in Islam. Rather, by defining the mosque as a political setting, we highlight the disjuncture between past and present, drawing attention to how traditional institutions such as the mosque are changed as historical contexts change, especially since the advent of modernity.

In observing the transformation of the mosque into a political space we no longer encounter religion functioning in its more customary role as simply a transmitter of tradition. As in the case of *masjid dar al-salaam*, the mosques have also become venues for the creation of new meanings and new solidarities. The tendency to view Islam as an ideology and a comprehensive system of action that encompasses all aspects of life, including the political, is itself a breaking with tradition.

Notions proffered as slogans by the leaders of the contemporary Islamic movements, such as Islam is *"din wa dawla"* (religion and state), are modern ideological constructions of Islam that the leaders of the Islamic movements deploy as a strategy for calling into question the integrity of the traditionalist *ulama* who continue to support the de facto separation of religion and politics.[45] At the same time, by raising such slogans, they challenge the legitimacy of secular rulers who subvert Islam for their own purposes.

We are not just witnessing the resurgence of primordial loyalties in the rise of the Islamic movements of opposition. They are thoroughly modern movements linked to the formation of a new middle class, and they form part of the pattern of emergence of new social movements all over the world. Tradition is no longer simply ascriptive or assimilated (if it ever was), as modern actors struggle over and contest a past that has been selectively reappropriated and reconstructed. The transformation of the mosque into a political setting does not represent the culmination of a natural evolution in the history of Islamic forms. Moreover, to define the political discourse and activity associated with the popular mosques as a "return of Islam" is to obscure the shared, yet distinct, modern historical ground on which all actors stand.

Even though not all mosques espouse the same new meanings as those occupied by a cadre of intellectuals and activists associated with the Islamic movements, many of the preachers in the popular mosques throughout the Muslim world voice the more general sentiment of political dissatisfaction that runs through it. In this sense, the popular mosques, like the Islamic movements that influence them either directly or indirectly, reflect the essentially political nature of modern Muslim societies.

Notes

1. See Alan Scott, *Ideology and the New Social Movements* (London: Unwin Hyman,1990) for a good discussion of new social movements and review of the main debates and issues in new social movement theory.

2. I am paraphrasing the observations of a few authors here. See Dale F. Eicklemand and James Piscatori, *Muslim Politics* (Princeton, N.J.: Princeton University Press, 1996), p.12; and Jean-Claude Vatin, "Popular Puritanism versus State Reformism: Islam in Algeria," in *Islam in the Political Process*, ed. James Piscatori (Melbourne: Cambridge University Press, 1983), pp.98-121.

3. Mumtaz Ahmad, "The Politics of War: Islamic Fundamentalisms in Pakistan," in *Islamic Fundamentalisms and the Gulf Crisis*, ed. James Piscatori (Chicago: University of Chicago Press, 1991), p.172.

4. The blind preacher—Shaykh Abdul-Hamid Kishk—for instance, is one such popular dissident preacher in Egypt: he has been barred from preaching since the 1980s. Another preacher and activist is Shaykh Hafiz Salaama, whose mosque was eventually closed down by the Egyptian authorities. See John L. Esposito, *The Islamic Threat: Myth or Reality* (New York: Oxford University Press, 1992), p.98. Case studies of certain other mosques in Egypt and biographies of their preachers are provided in two articles by Patrick D. Gaffney: "The Local Preacher and Islamic Resurgence in Upper Egypt," in *Religious Resurgence: Contemporary Cases in Islam, Christianity, and Judaism*, ed. Richard Antoun and Mary Elaine Hegland (Syracuse, N.Y.: Syracuse University Press, 1987), pp.40-41; and "Authority and the Mosque in Upper Egypt: The Islamic Preacher as Image and Actor," in *Islam and the Political Economy of Meaning*, ed. William R. Roff (London: Croom Helm, 1987), pp.199-225. For an interesting analysis of the role of the mosque and the preacher in modern Muslim society based on extensive field research of a Jordanian mosque, its preacher, and congregation, see Richard Antoun, *Muslim Preacher in the Modern World: A Jordanian Case Study in Comparative Perspective* (Princeton, N.J.: Princeton University Press, 1989).

5. See Hamied N. Ansari, "The Islamic Militants in Egyptian Politics," *International Journal of Middle East Studies* 16 (1984), pp.123-44. Much of Ansari's information was acquired from official government transcripts of the prison interrogations of a number of Islamic militants charged with involvement in a series of violent incidents in 1981, including the assassination of President Anwar Sadat.

6. See Patrick Gaffney, *The Prophet's Pulpit: Islamic Preaching in Contemporary Egypt* (London: University of California Press, 1994), p.14.

7. Ansari, "Islamic Militants in Egyptian Politics," p.129, reports that in 1981, out of a total of 46,000 registered mosques, only 6,000 were under the control of the Ministry of Religious Endowments. The government admitted to being unable to supervise the activity of so many new mosques.

8. Gaffney points out that we should be careful not to assume that all private mosques are antigovernment establishments. In many cases people build private mosques and then actively solicit official sponsorship from the Ministry of Religious Endowments, because this will ensure steady sources of funding and provide them with the services of a preacher paid for by the government. Gaffney, *Prophet's Pulpit*, p.49.

9. Gaffney, *Prophet's Pulpit*, p.47. See also "Khatib," *The Encyclopedia of Islam* (Leiden, Neth.: E.J. Brill, 1994), p.1110.

10. Gaffney explains, "It was not an expansion of the arena for public speaking that was sought so much as an altogether new and urgent mode of communicating: action, not talk, was needed." See "Local Preacher and Islamic Resurgence," p.41.

11. Antoun, *Muslim Preacher in the Modern World*, pp.4, 8.

12. Ibid., p.3. See also "Khutba," *The Shorter Encyclopaedia of Islam* (Leiden, Neth.: E.J. Brill, 1965), pp.258-59.

13. Antoun, *Muslim Preacher in the Modern World*, p.68. See also "Masjid," *Shorter Encyclopaedia of Islam*, pp.335-50.

14. Gaffney, *Prophet's Pulpit*, p.17.

15. Ibid., pp.13-14, 23-25.

16. Ibid., p.18.

17. Antoun, *Muslim Preacher in the Modern World*, p.186.

18. Ibid., p.68.

19. Albert Hourani, *A History of the Arab Peoples* (Cambridge Mass.: The Belknap Press of Harvard University, 1991), p.33. For a discussion of the issue of the relationship between religion and politics in theory and practice, see Erwin I.J. Rosenthal, "Some Reflections on the Separation of Religion and Politics in Modern Islam," *International Studies* 3 (1964), pp.249-83; Ira M. Lapidus, "The Separation of State and Religion in the Development of Early Islamic Society," *International Journal of Middle East Studies* 6,4 (1975), pp.242-385; and Nazih Ayubi, *Political Islam: Religion and Politics in the Arab World* (London: Routledge, 1991), pp.1-34.

20. Ayubi, *Political Islam*, p.68. See also "Khatib," *Encyclopedia*, p.1110.

21. "Khutba," *Shorter Ecyclopaedia*, p.259.

22. Antoun, *Muslim Preacher in the Modern World*, pp.68-69.

23. The argument that Muslim societies are "organic societies" in which religion permeates every sphere of life and all institutions, including the political, is a classic Orientalist assertion. Following this line of reasoning, Antoun concludes, "The separation of religion and politics or religion and government has no traditional place in Muslim society, and still has no place, as recent events at the end of the twentieth century are making all too clear." See Antoun, *Muslim Preacher in the Modern World*, pp.68, 187.

24. Gaffney, *Prophet's Pulpit*, pp.16-17.

25. Antoun, *Muslim Preacher in the Modern World*, p.189.

26. Fazlur Rahman, *Islam and Modernity* (London: University of Chicago Press, 1982), pp.139-40, 43.

27. Gaffney, "Local Preacher and Islamic Resurgence," p.40.

28. The mosques in Pakistan are highly denominationalized. The majority of the mosques are controlled by the traditionalist *Sunni ulama* (religious scholars) organization known as the Society of Muslim Ulama, who are identified with the Deobandi religio-cultural stream of Islam in the subcontinent. The Deobandis also control the largest network of *madrassahs* (religious schools) in Pakistan. For a description of the main religious organizations in Pakistan, including the Deobandis, see Ahmad, "Politics of War," pp.158-59.

29. See also Gaffney, "Local Preacher and Islamic Resurgence," p.44; and Gaffney, "Authority and the Mosque in Upper Egypt," pp.204-5.

30. The information on Israr Ahmad, and *masjid dar al-salaam*, was acquired during a personal interview with him in Lahore, July 20, 1993, and during a follow-up interview with a staff member of the Tanzeem-i-Islami organization.

31. Barbara D. Metcalf, "Islamic Arguments in Contemporary Pakistan," in *Islam and the Political Economy of Meaning*, ed. William R. Roff (London: Croom Helm, 1987), p.146.

32. The details of Dr. Israr's congregation are compiled from a variety of sources. A local researcher and I gathered some of the information at the mosque during a number of Friday visits. The staff at the Tanzeem-i-Islami also provided information based on their records of donations to the mosque.

33. *The Economist*, Feb. 8-14, 1997, p.22.

34. Ibid., Feb. 8-14, 1997, p.22.

35. S. Abul Ala Maududi, *Islamic Law and Constitution* (Lahore: Islamic Publications, 1992), pp.194-95.

36. See Klaus Eder, *The New Politics of Class: Social Movements and Cultural Dynamics in Advanced Societies* (London: Sage Publications,1993). Eder makes this observation regarding the class bias of the new social movements emerging in the West, but it is also applicable to the contemporary Islamic movements.

37. The first *khutba* here was transcribed and translated from notes and a rather poor tape-recording. The second *khutba* is taken from the daily Urdu-language newspaper, the *Jang*. All translations were done with the aid of a local translator and research assistant.

38. Gaffney, *Prophet's Pulpit*, p.31.

39. The Barelvi *ulama* organization, known as the Society of Pakistan Ulama, has its strongest support in Punjab province. The Deobandis, who control the largest number of *madrassahs* and mosques in Pakistan, find most of their support in Baluchistan and the North-West Frontier Province, where they were able to form provincial governments during the years 1973-74. See Ahmad, "Politics of War," pp.157-59. For more information on the relationship between the *ulama* and the state in Pakistan, see Mumtaz Ahmad, "Islam and the State: The Case of

Pakistan," in *The Religious Challenge to the State*, ed. Matthew C. Moen and Lowell
S. Gustafson (Philadelphia: Temple University Press), pp.230-67.

40. For a discussion of the policies pursued by different Pakistani governments toward the shrines, see Katherine Ewing, "The Politics of Sufism: Redefining the Saints of Pakistan," *Journal of Asian Studies* 42,2 (February 1983).

41. The metonymic mode of discursive reasoning is characteristic of Muslim fundamentalists such as Dr. Israr. Gaffney explains that the main feature of the metonymic mode is its literal quality and the refusal to acknowledge any distinction between the Quran as a text and social reality. See Gaffney, *Prophet's Pulpit*, pp.53-55, 165, 238-39.

42. These excerpts from two *khutbas* were delivered in the rural mosque by Imam Mahmud in June 1993. The *khutbas* were transcribed and translated from his written copies in Urdu. The quotes in the text of the sermon represent Imam Mahmud's own loose translations from the Quran, which he recited in Urdu. According to the custom in many mosques, he integrated the Quranic quotes into the text and did not provide references to the surah (chapter) numbers. The bracketed letterings are my own shortened references to the ritual blessings, which are liberally scattered throughout the sermon text.

43. Olivier Roy refers to this style of preaching as being "self-authorizing," in the sense that the new breed of lay preachers such as Dr. Israr assumes the traditional role of a *khatib* and acquires the social status accompanying that role, without actually having a proper *madrassah* education, as, for example, Imam Mahmud had. See Olivier Roy, *The Failure of Political Islam* (Cambridge, Mass.: Harvard University Press, 1994), p.86.

44. I am paraphrasing David Arnold's terminology, which is derived, in the context of his analysis of the peasantry in India, from Antonio Gramsci's theorizations on the role of religion in relation to the southern Italian peasantry. See David Arnold, "Gramsci and the Peasant Subalternity in India," *Journal of Peasant Studies* 11,4 (1984), pp.156, 160.

45. Ayubi explains that the notion that Islam is religion and politics, or religion and state—the main battle cry of contemporary Islamic activists—represents a reversal of the traditional historical pattern of the state appropriating religion and Islamizing politics in order to impart legitimacy to itself. See Ayubi, *Political Islam*, pp.123, 156-57.

PART IV

Lessons and Conclusions

Chapter 10

Local Action and Global Power:
Shifting the Balance

Jonathan Barker

The case studies in this book—despite the geographical and cultural distances that separate them—have one important similarity: they are far from the centres of global power. Moreover, the political settings described carry little weight in the national politics of the countries in question. We are talking here about collective political action at the margins of global and national power. The cases chosen share two characteristics that are frequently found at the margins of global power, but that are far from universal.

One characteristic is the compactness of dwellings and public spaces. Neighbouring vendors in Owino Market could organize a meeting in seconds and complete it in minutes. It was easy to move around in both Oskaloosa and Leyburn, although Oskaloosans were reluctant to go further than across the street without driving a car, and sometimes they even drove across the street. Kanyakumari, Machina, and Dagona were all pedestrian communities in which people could readily walk from anywhere to a central place for a meeting. They even had town criers to announce meetings. Nicaragua is a small and densely populated country in which many populous areas can readily send representatives to central meetings. The mosques in Pakistan drew upon a local population for the bulk of their membership.

The second characteristic is the large proportion of the population represented by small-scale producers and merchants who own some property and operate in the market but employ few workers and by lower-middle-class government employees who in some cases may earn much less than a living wage. Class division in these localities is neither sharp nor extreme, with old and new petty bourgeoisies predominating.

We have taken an empirical approach to the topic of street-level democracy on the grounds that the evolving new realities of local politics within the context of globalization call for careful descriptive understanding if the raw material is going to be useful for theoretically informed interpretations. Our accounts of political settings have left open many important practical questions raised by politics at the margins, and these practical questions in turn raise important issues about the theories and concepts that we can use to consider those matters. Among the practical questions are:

The energy question:
- What drives collective political action at the margins of global power?

The linkage question:
- How does local political action at the margins relate to the larger national and international worlds of political action?

The leadership question:
- What is the role of leaders in political action at the margins of global power?

The democracy question:
- How can people at the margins of global power exercise control over the conditions of their own lives?

The approach question:
- What does the political settings approach contribute to efforts to answer the above questions?

Each of these questions carries with it a cluster of related questions, all of which bear upon how we think about politics at the margins. Given that the image of nation-states as unified and sovereign political spaces is far from the current reality (chapter 2), for the study of local political action we need to abandon that image in favour of an empirical approach that tries to ascertain how local political action relates to the claims and influences of states and other centres of power, some of them global. The case studies in this book support an image of a fluid and complex boundary between the state and civil society. The range and kinds of activities under direct government control vary from time to time and place to place. It is less a boundary than a zone of interaction and contestation.

The activity settings I call "political settings" or "political space" form a crucial part of the boundary zone. Because they do not fall under government control they count as part of civil society, but unlike the rest of civil society their activity is oriented toward government or other matters of broad public concern. The power exercised in the boundary zone emanates from several sources; local associations and institutions, certain local individual citizens, transnational NGOs, foreign governments, and international agencies all vie for power and recognition. Centres of local power may aspire to control of activity settings that in name come under state authority. States may privatize activities by handing them over to private businesses or to voluntary associations. States may also attempt to assert control over activity settings that until then belonged to political space or to the non-political part of civil society. They may assert their influence in the boundary zone via background rules (to criticize government officials is made a crime) or indirect influence (informers, government funding, sham voluntary associations), and when government leaders perceive a crisis they may declare a state of emergency to establish direct state control over what was part of the boundary zone. In this contested boundary zone, then, state and civil society interact and global forces enter both directly and indirectly.

The Energy Question: Where Does the Energy for Local Political Action Come From?

Humans may be "political animals," as Aristotle says, but then humans in different places and times are also not equally active in public life. What energizes political action? The cases in this book were selected because of the political actions they demonstrated and because they provide a basis for grounded reflection. Livelihood issues are in the foreground of the political action in most of the cases, and those issues are of two kinds. One set unites the locality against outside forces and the other set divides the locality into groups that compete for resources and power. The locally divisive actions can sometimes inhibit unified action against external forces, but it is striking that the local conflicts seem also to increase the ability and readiness to act and thereby to enhance the capacity for unified local action in crucial instances. The fishing villages in south India in Aparna Sundar's vivid account are bitterly divided between those who use small craft and those who operate trawlers. Political authorities both local and higher up have failed in repeated efforts to mediate a durable compromise. Physical and verbal conflict breaks out again and again. Yet both groups were able to support the one-day strike directed against the licensing of factory fishing vessels. The local conflict seems both to increase political skills and to feed a willingness to act.

Local energies stimulate wider political action in other ways, too. In Owino Market in Kampala, as Christie Gombay shows, the everyday work of political settings—to resolve conflicts, handle issues of market hygiene, and communicate information—sustained an organizational infrastructure that was also used to represent the interests of market vendors to outside forces, including government and the World Bank. In northern Nigeria Kole Shettima tells about how settings established from above to promote specific development activities became venues in which more general issues of change and of the responsibility of government authorities were raised, if only in a guarded manner. Katherine Isbester portrays how women in Nicaragua established networks and national meetings specifically designed to link the local meetings, in which women explored the difficulties they faced in their homes and neighbourhoods, to larger agendas of action. Although they can compete and interfere with one another, local actions, issues, and conflicts can bring new energies to political actions that focus on external forces.

With respect to women's participation more generally, the data from Oskaloosa and Leyburn suggest another aspect of the energy question. The study of small towns in England and the United States shows that the time and energy committed to political space were substantially greater in the U.S. town. A large part of the difference is accounted for by the much greater participation by women in Oskaloosa than in Leyburn. How women's political energies are tapped or suppressed is an important topic for future research. We know that in northern Nigeria and Pakistan the culture associated with Islam specifically excluded women from most political settings to which men had access, but in Kanyakumari, India, and in Owino Market, Uganda, where women were not excluded, they were substantially underrepresented in political settings. Still, in Kanyakumari women did have their own organizations, and in certain demonstrations and protests in which men had a role, women predominated and took the lead. Localities clearly differ greatly in the extent to which they tap the energies of women in political action, but with the exception of Oskaloosa, the localities studied here failed to draw women into political activity to nearly the extent that they attracted men. The success of the women's movement in Nicaragua shows that, in that country at least, women had considerable energy to commit to political action once the opportunity was created for them to experience political action and address issues of their choosing.

Kinds of exclusion or suppression other than gender also operated, but we have only incomplete evidence about them. For example, people associated with opposition political tendencies in Machina, Nigeria, were almost completely absent from the activity settings set up by the theoretically politically neutral Northeast Arid Zone Development Project (NEAZDP), while in Dagona the immigrant Sakkwatawa people were excluded from most political activity. We have less data on class barriers to participation in meetings, but the information from the towns in England and the United States indicates that upper classes were disproportionately active in all public settings while middle and lower classes had similar participation rates. Clearly, such exclusions and biases will curtail the proportion of available political energy that can be mobilized.

Based on our evidence the energy for political action comes from three main sources: the drive felt by individuals, families, and groups to defend a threatened source of livelihood; from local conflicts over economic resources, political influence, and social autonomy; and from the assertion of political and social identities. Each of these sources of political energy corresponds to a prominent theory of social action. Action in defence of livelihood fits well with Marx's view that social and political activity grows out of relations of production. Action deriving from conflicts over resources, influence, and autonomy corresponds to theories of relative deprivation and changing relative status. Action to assert social and political identities matches theories of the construction of collective identities.

People in every locality perceived that major livelihood issues were at stake and that government policies had an effect upon the availability of work and the adequacy of income and basic living conditions. The pressures on livelihood could often be traced to forces of globalization. In the case of Owino, there was expanding commercial activity in Uganda due to the aid and loans flowing in to support economic adjustment programs and due to the peace dividend that followed upon the seizure of power by the National Resistance Movement. Vendors benefited from the expansion, but the working conditions in the market deteriorated and the growth of the evening market outside the formal bounds of Owino posed a grave challenge to Owino's vendors. In Kanyakumari small-scale fishers faced new competition from mechanized trawlers and giant factory ships. At the same time they were gaining access to markets for kinds of fish they had not been able to sell at all in earlier years. To meet the competition, many small-scale fishers bought outboard motors, fished longer hours, and covered a wider area. Some women tried to replace the net-making they lost to manufactured nets with selling fresh fish to local markets. The dwindling availability of some species and the continuing precariousness of earnings pushed both men and women to form a fishers union, a fish-marketing co-operative, and fishing village neighbourhood associations.

In Nigeria and Pakistan the political settings we looked at were linked to globalization indirectly through the effects of economic adjustment on government spending. In Yobe state, Nigeria, farming was troubled by low rainfall, limited possibilities for irrigation, and poor transportation. At the same time financing and ideas for new kinds of production were limited while the feeling was acute and widespread that new water sources and new health services were needed. In Pakistan economic adjustment hit middle-class professionals and their plight fed into the growth of Islamic movements. A similar retrenchment of government spending under the neo-liberal program of the Chamorro government removed government support for programs and services of vital interest to the work and the health of women in Nicaragua.

The idea expressed by Katherine Isbester that both resource and identity theories of social movements have validity is upheld by cases other than hers. If both resource conflict and identity expression can energize political action, both also appear to be closely bound up with concerns about protecting livelihood. Indeed, the defence of livelihood, in our cases, appears to be the most general and fundamental energizer of political action, although it usually works with more or less clearly identifiable conflicts over resources and expressions of social identities.

These three related sources of energy do not exhaust the evidence. Other forces also seem capable of attracting action; at the very least they shape action that may be driven by other motives. One is strong attractive leadership of the kind exemplified by Dr. Israr in the Lahore mosque. The other is the availability of the venue, of the setting, of political action. Leadership can stir, awaken, and perhaps in some contexts create the motive of action in others. That is the message of Max Weber's category of charismatic authority. More original to the perspective I am asserting is the idea that the sheer availability of political settings will attract action. ("Build it and they will come!") Once the setting is established people are drawn to it by peer pressure, habit, friendship, vanity, and the whole range of human social motives, in addition to those connected to livelihood, relative deprivation, and identity. This attraction means that the act of creating a setting has a kind of multiplier effect on the motives that prompted the creation of the setting. It gives added value to the energy expended by originators of political settings. It does not, of course, guarantee that the energy drawn forth by the setting results in the kind of action intended by the originators. After all, the actions that political settings will take have an inherent unpredictability. Especially when there is scope for participant control, participants may choose to adopt agendas and directions not anticipated by the founders.

The Linkage Question: How Are Local Actions Related to National and International Forces?

Good physical communication assists the wider networking that successful local action needs. The good roads and bus service in India and Nicaragua were crucial to the wider organizing successfully pursued in those countries. The participation in Dagona and Machina and the surrounding villages was limited in scope by the difficulty of wider popular organization, although NEAZDP itself had excellent networks throughout its zones of activity in the state.

Another way that local action is linked to national forces is as important as it is obvious. Local action is more common, more varied, and easier where the right to engage in political action, which is the right to create political settings, is protected by law and by law enforcers. The countries of our case studies had fairly broadly protected civil rights, with England, the United States, and India having the broadest rights. Uganda, Nigeria, Nicaragua, and Pakistan had greater political restrictions at the time of the research. A survey of political settings would look very different in a country ruled by a highly repressive regime; research of the kind we accomplished would be extremely difficult to carry out.

The organizational structure in which many of the impressive local meetings were nested stretched upward to middle and upper levels of state power. In Yobe state NEAZDP had formal contracts with the state and the national government, giving it strong links to top office-holders. The Catholic Church of Tamil Nadu had a strong regional presence in India as a whole, as well as international connections. The Market Vendors Association in Kampala cultivated support from prominent city officials. The key to the success of the women's movement in Nicaragua was, first, its connections within the Sandinista leadership and, later, its strong and recognized national leadership. The leading speaker at the mosque in Lahore was a national figure with personal connections to leading politicians. It may be ironical that effective local political action against the rules and actions of government requires support from within the power structure itself, but irony is a common form of humorous banter in and around local political settings.

Although governments, at their best, can defend the right to create political settings, they are not especially good at establishing political settings under citizen control; governments tend to create settings that fall under their own hierarchical control. In Machina and Dagona, Nigeria, the two government development agencies that employed the ideology of participatory development in describing their work established few participatory political settings, while the European agency with a similar ideology was a major generator of political settings with significant participation—again, taking "political settings" as referring to settings whose activity is oriented to issues of common or broad concern and not necessarily referring to party politics. In Nicaragua the women's movement took on a stronger control from below when it lost its official connection with government. In Oskaloosa and Leyburn government-controlled settings rated consistently lower in participation than did activity settings controlled by voluntary associations.

Local government itself rarely organized local political settings with any significant participation. They did run local offices of varying effectiveness and held information meetings in which officials explained a policy or gave advice to a gathering of citizens. Offices in Kanyakumari were sometimes lightning rods for popular demonstrations. In Machina the presence of resident government employees contributed to the defeat of the Emir's favoured candidate for local council president, but the offices the government employees ran were in no way participatory. The quasi-governmental status of the priest in Kanyakumari made it easier for him to inaugurate new forms of popular organization, but it seemed to have made it harder for him to fade into the background and allow citizens to take control of the new popular political settings. In Owino the offices of the local-level resistance councils, the base-level government organizations, were remarkable for their nearly complete vacancy. They contained hardly a table, chair, or file shelf, not to mention a live office-holder. All staff members were busy at other, more remunerative, activities, though these same officials did manage to collect formal and informal payments from vendors who put up stalls in the growing evening market that competed on a semi-legal footing with Owino Market. It was because the mosques in Pakistan were not under government control that they were able to operate as autonomous political spaces. In some countries governments have seized control of mosques, no doubt in part to extinguish an unwanted political independence. The importance of local government structures raises the question of whether forms of local government can be instituted that favour productive local political settings.

To make effective decisions on matters relating to the actions of governments and international business and governmental organizations, people in local political settings not only need to recognize the role of the large-scale organizations and forces that influence them, but also need to gain necessary information. Successful local leaders take on the key role of information broker or agent for other information brokers. In Nigeria the Northeast Arid Zone Development Project trained and appointed village agents whose explicit task was to act as a trusted link between villagers and the project, with its strong research and information capacity. In Tamil Nadu the priests and the fishworkers' organizations both had links to national and international organizations that gathered research and intelligence about changes in the fishery. In Uganda's Owino Market one weakness of the Market Vendors Association was its lack of a direct channel to the World Bank department that was planning to support market upgrading. Indeed, MVA leaders tried to get information about the Bank's plans from our researchers, who were there to study local political space. In Pakistan local mosques can and do have links with active transnational Islamic organizations. And the women's movement in Nicaragua made up for some of the resources it lost when it separated from government by knitting new ties of support and information with international women's organizations. Good international information can even give local political activists a modicum of leverage over government officials, who may be less well connected internationally.

Several of the case studies also reveal a broad connection of currents of opinions, ideological outlooks, and organizational models. The model of participatory development embodied by NEAZDP in Yobe state is part of a wider current that finds application in many parts of the world and may eventually be applied by other agencies in Nigeria. The women's movement and the reform movements in Islam and Christianity move through specific linkages, but the general ideas put forward by these movements sometimes find a broader currency in the mass media. The case studies here in India, Nicaragua, and Pakistan show movements trying, with some success, to get their messages into national publications and broadcasts and to engage a general public in their causes. Themes of resource conservation, women's health, and religious integrity had resonance beyond their immediate constituencies. The relevant space of communication based upon trust and confidence is clearly much larger than the locality and spreads beyond national borders. The role of religious and social movements in creating translocal and transnational zones of trusted communication is very significant for local action.

The Leadership Question: What Is the Importance of Leadership and What Role do Leaders Play?

In all the case studies the actions of leaders were essential in the creation of venues and the eliciting of action. In the mosques in Pakistan religious leadership gave direction to the use made of the mosques' public space. The urban mosque was an example of a movement-driven leadership in which the mosque took its place alongside other vehicles of ideological action such as speeches, campaigns, publications, and an educational institution. The rural mosque was a more representative venue in which the *khatib* reflected a version of local beliefs on public issues. In Kanyakumari religious leadership was also crucial, but it self-consciously pursued questions of social welfare. Position in an organization, both religious and secular, gave scope for leadership in Yobe state. NEAZDP's status and administrative power provided resources, legitimacy, and consistency for the actions of its local development officers, who in turn had to work with or around the influence of the Emir, who sought to keep NEAZDP from detracting from his own power. In Owino Market leadership came from within the vendors themselves. They solidified their role with a formal administrative structure that included an office building, regular meetings, elected committees, procedures for adjudicating conflicts, and many other elements of good organization.

The case studies suggest, further, that individuals with local roots— but with the education, experience, and connections to communicate with confidence with national and international centres of ideas, research, and information—play a crucial role in shaping local political action. Localities without such individuals would look very different. The parish priests who brought liberation theology and base communities to Kanyakumari; the Development Area Promoter (DAP), Bashir Bukar Albishir, who initiated NEAZDP projects in Machina; Dr. Israr, with his sermons and newspaper columns in Pakistan; the "horizontal organization" pioneered by AMPRONAC in Nicaragua that brought bourgeois and village women together; and the MVA leaders in Owino: all of them brought home to their localities ideas and sensibilities discovered or sharpened through national and international networks.

Leaders who can make use of existing local traditions and practices to establish new public settings to promote their projects can make a significant impact on local society. The religious traditions of Christianity and Islam appear repeatedly in our case studies. The role of priests and *khatibs* was noted, and the mosque itself, as Anne-Marie Cwikowski details, had in many circumstances become a political space in its own right. The same can be said of the churches in Kanyakumari. The church that rises large and majestic near the centre of each village serves as meeting hall and committee room for a variety of gatherings and forums. The frequent use of prayer to open and close meetings of all kinds reveals a felt affinity between the core religious values and the interpersonal respect required by open speaking.

Religious ideas, of course, also implicitly uphold the institutional leadership embodied in existing churches and mosques. In the cases we studied, the institutional frame was able to contain considerable innovation, including relatively democratic practices through which some aspects of local leadership could be challenged. Although our cases cannot be regarded as representative, and the kind of openness we found is unlikely to be typical of more deeply class-divided or tyrannically governed localities, they do give grounds for some thoughts about local democracy at the margins of global power.

The comparison of Oskaloosa and Leyburn adds another angle of vision to the leadership question. It shows that in the whole range of settings, a much larger proportion of the citizens of Oskaloosa than of Leyburn exercised leadership functions—although leadership positions were less stable in Oskaloosa and more subject to passing pressures. More participation stood in the way of concerted and directed change.

The Democracy Question: What Kind of Democracy and What Kind of Participation Can Grow in the Soil at the Margins of Global Power?

Local political settings themselves often combined key elements of democratic practice. The local leaders we interviewed were almost always quick to defend the civil freedoms of gathering and expressing opinions. Organizers of meetings and actions depended on support from local government organs and local popular culture to protect those freedoms, or at least not to suppress them. In several of the cases local leaders and organizers tried to keep their meetings clear of identification with political parties. In Owino some market activists recalled the days when party commitments created conflict among vendors, and they wanted to avoid repeating the problem. NEAZDP in Yobe state tried to present itself as neutral in partisan politics, but with only partial success given its ties with the government. The women's movement in Nicaragua had to fight alongside the FSLN for freedom to organize, but once the FSLN was in power the movement chaffed under Sandinista domination. It used the hard-won freedom to advance its case for more autonomy.

In most of our case studies the ethic of open discussion was grounded in religious thought. It was widely accepted that the chair of a meeting should allow everyone to speak. The idea of open discussion was reinforced during nationalist movements a generation or two ago and supported in some places by trade union and other associational activism. In practice, though, women and people holding minority views may well have felt inhibited and faced sanctions outside the meeting for voicing their ideas.

At the margins of global power, power itself is elusive and unstable. The sources of the forces that change or protect local livelihoods and social practices are not easy to discern. What does it mean to say that a village, a development project, or a mosque is self-governing, when the livelihoods of the participants are at the mercy of environmental change, the actions of distant resource companies, and changes in world market prices that in no way respond to local views or actions? The mismatch between the forces that change the locality and the control exercised by holders of local authority ensures that local power often cannot address some of the most vital issues that people face.

In the cases we are considering democratic forces might control a host of local political spaces and still muster negligible political impact. The effort and drama of local political action are often out of all proportion with the results, and it does not take very many experiences of futile effort to breed a culture of cynical resignation. With a few repetitions of action without outcome, even the engine of anger eventually sputters to a halt. In most of the cases we studied, local political action chose to address issues that could be resolved locally, and they were issues of material and social importance. In Tamil Nadu the tension between local trawler owners and local small-boat fishers could not be resolved, but it could be repeatedly addressed and brought to temporary truces. Women could organize to take a share of local fish marketing and gain significant income. Continual efforts were made, particularly by women, to keep alcohol consumption in the villages within bounds.

In Yobe state NEAZDP worked hard to find local solutions to material problems, establishing locally replenished village development funds to promote projects such as training oxen for animal traction, establishing tailoring businesses, digging wells, building small irrigation schemes, and training women to build wood-saving cook stoves out of local clay to use and to sell. The MVA in Owino spent most of its effort resolving conflicts in the market and coping with immediate issues of cleanliness and day-to-day market administration. In Nicaragua local women's groups could address immediate issues of domestic abuse, reproductive control, and gaining a voice in local affairs. Mosques retain prayer and worship as core activities that draw support and commitment.

The fishers of Kanyakumari won a victory in their fight to exclude factory ships from waters near their fishing grounds, but they could do so only in an unusual alliance that included other localities along India's long coast, coastal trawler owners, nationalist politicians, and middle-class contributors to the environmental movement. Local fishers were in a position to combine their local knowledge about changing fish stocks with the broader information gathered by fishery researchers; and they were sufficiently organized to accept the leadership and strike plans of a national fishworkers' union. More typical of local participation in Kanyakumari is the periodic eruption of conflict between small-boat fishers and trawler owners, a conflict that reflects social and economic tensions but does nothing to protect the local economy from overfishing and instability in international fish markets.

The mismatch in scale and the limited grasp of democratic action is visible in other cases as well. In Owino the Market Vendors Association was by all accounts a model of active and representative organization reflecting the needs and interests of vendors. Yet it had a difficult time gaining the information and the voice it sought in the plans being formulated by the World Bank and the Uganda government to upgrade the market. Moreover, the vast growth of the evening market activity around Owino appeared likely to render the planned upgrading obsolete in short order. In Machina and Dagona the relative success of participatory meetings around local development projects was achieved through the work of a professionally managed hierarchical development bureaucracy that was answerable not to the people it served but to the military governments of Yobe state and Nigeria as a whole. In addition even a well-managed development organization was finding it extremely difficult to address the fundamental difficulties posed by inadequate and irregular rainfall and poor market outlets for local crops in Machina and the absorption of large numbers of recent settlers in Dagona.

The Oskaloosa-Leyburn comparison and the Nicaragua experience under different political regimes supply an additional piece of the local democracy puzzle. In Oskaloosa the greater citizen control and stronger local autonomy corresponded with a much greater turnover in local leadership, which made it difficult for participants to sustain innovative initiatives. Yet the local energy available to invest in change was much greater in Oskaloosa. In Nicaragua the women achieved their most rapid and extensive gains when their movement was closely connected with, but subordinated to, the Sandinista government. When the government changed and drew apart from the women's movement, the women's organization gained in autonomy and in self-definition; but it ceased to deliver as many benefits and changes as it had done when the FSLN was in power.

Street-level democracy on its own, then, is no match for the difficulties of power and livelihood at the margins of globalization. It needs to be linked to wider organizations of interest and information and to enter into dialogue with centres of power in government and elsewhere that have an impact on the locality. It needs to balance the opening of intralocal conflicts against the advantages of coherent action vis-à-vis external threats. Making the linkages and balances is likely to be easier when civil rights are protected and information moves freely. Local voices with real power behind them contribute two essential ingredients: (1) local knowledge about environment and skills; and (2) local understanding about the commitments and tendencies of local people: what they like, what they can accept, and what they cannot tolerate. The knowledge and the understanding are not simply there to be mined like a vein of ore in a geological layer; they are the outgrowth of the process of discussion and consultation with extralocal centres of power and information in which local voices speak and local listening hears.

The Approach Question: What Does the Political Settings Approach Contribute to Efforts to Answer All of These Questions?

The descriptive approach taken in our research has proved itself to be open to and useful for theoretical innovation. It can inform both ideas and policies, both theory and practice. One of its particular strengths is that it divides and names the world of social action in ways familiar to the people who inhabit that world. The idea of political settings not only has a rigour and consistency that makes it appropriate for systematic research and theoretical reflection, but also possesses a common-sense realism that opens the door to fruitful discussion about the shape and structure of the political spaces in which people build their politics.

The settings approach builds on a diverse tradition of qualitative and quantitative empirical research into the local contexts of action and the symbols through which people invest action with meaning and translate meanings into actions. Recognition of the generality of social settings and of the political content of the idea of settings and of political settings in particular can aid researchers (both academic and action-oriented) to delimit and engage their theoretical assertions and their policy imperatives with more precision and effectiveness.

The focus on political settings provides insight into the importance of meetings in local political life. It is impressive that in all the localities studied, people understood how to organize and hold meetings in which there were relatively open discussions of some set of issues. Except in the mosques in Pakistan, the meetings were not religious in purpose, but it was striking how often prayer and religion played a part in the meetings. An opening prayer would invoke spiritual protection and guidance for a harmonious and productive discussion. In Kanyakumari parish priests instigated many meetings, and in Yobe state Muslim dignitaries sponsored meetings, giving general approval to the work of the most active development organization, the Northeast Arid Zone Development Program. In all cases participants and chairs, when asked, said that all opinions were welcome and all points of view could be expressed and considered. We witnessed several vigorous debates and a few highly emotional ones. Yet, as the case studies show most markedly about the participation of women, the openness of the discussions was relative; regulations and customs limited access and activity.

Despite the restrictions, most meetings in all the localities were attended by people of sufficiently different backgrounds, statuses, and viewpoints that the makings of a good discussion were present and Hannah Arendt's criterion of a variety of speakers and listeners was met. The settings had, then, a firm potential for argument, drama, and misunderstanding. Most decisions were by consensus. Outside of the United States and England we did not find examples of public or recorded votes. In the other places, when decisions were wanted, after discussion participants assented to the predominant view as announced by the chair.

The democratic impulse and democratic practice are alive and well in the streets and gathering places at the margins of global power. But the reach of the impulse and the impact of the practice will be overwhelmed and undermined all too often unless those acting nationally and internationally learn how to construct their own institutions and shape their own actions in ways that engage productively with street-level democrats and the political settings they create. Pursuing better understandings of the workings of local political settings on the part of activists and researchers is a good place to start.

Appendix

Mapping Local Politics: Methods, Measures, and Morals

Jonathan Barker

Good research on social change usually builds its analysis on the foundation of several sets of data, wherever possible including time series. Some of the more common kinds of data sets used by researchers are:

1. open-ended interviews with selected individuals
2. structured interviews with a random sample of some population
3. information on a series of cases of a type of social interaction
4. government reports
5. census data on population, perhaps over a period of time
6. statistics on health, education, elections, or the economy
7. quantitative and qualitative information about production units
8. quantitative and qualitative information about organizations.

It is always useful for researchers to consider what kinds of data sets would work best for their particular projects. Good research usually requires data sets that are complete or representative of some kind of entity, whether it is an individual person, production units, households, novels, a government policy, or something else. A bit of this and a bit of that can stimulate preliminary thinking about social change, but it can rarely adequately ground research that aspires to be definitive for its time and place.

The importance of good sets of data is quite independent of whether the interpretation takes a naturalistic or an interpretive turn.[1] Accounts of the way in which a social regime or situation is constructed must be based on some kind of information. Court documents may show official constructions of social conflicts, while interviews with litigants can show the popular construction of the same conflicts.[2] But a researcher needs a set of documents and a set of interviews as the foundation of an interpretation. Another example: a researcher may want to gather the set of all the interpretations people have of some social event; from that set of data the researcher may seek to deduce what "really" happened, or seek to show how different persons interpret that event; in either case she or he needs the set of interpretations.

For some purposes the number of entities may be very small: perhaps a single novel will exemplify a change of social perception in a society, or a single government policy deserves its own story.[3] Usually there is an implicit set of all novels of a certain kind that the one exemplifies, but a set with a single item in it is a logical and a practical, if infrequent, possibility.

The purpose of this appendix is to describe a kind of entity about which it is possible to gather information, to argue that for many kinds of issues of social change and for several kinds of analytical strategies a set of data about these entities can be extremely useful, and to put forward practical ways of going about gathering information on them. The name of the entity in question is "activity setting," which has a logical compatibility with research on political action and local social participation.

Activity Settings

An activity setting refers to an episode of human activity, often collective activity, but it consists of more than that; it includes the physical environment that surrounds the activity and the material objects that connect with the activity. Each activity setting is bounded in time and space and has a unique spatial-temporal address.[4] All human activity can be assigned to one or another activity setting. In the course of a day a person moves from one activity setting to another. One setting is usually in the person's home, another might be at a workplace, and others still in shops and streets and other places. Political activity settings are those in which the main part of the activity consists of discussing and deciding about matters of joint concern for some set of people. In ordinary language, the entities are meetings of various kinds.

Activity settings and meetings in particular lend themselves to descriptive and interpretive research.[5] A researcher can readily identify a set of relevant activity settings and systematically seek information and interpretations of them. Much research does just that without knowing or noticing that it has selected a kind of activity setting from among many. Research on social relations in workplaces selects for study settings in which people produce goods and services.[6] Research on "interfaces" selects for study activity settings in which local people encounter representatives of outside authorities.[7] Research on hidden politics chooses encounters or meetings that are designed to be hidden from public view, but that treat of matters of power and community relations. Within such activity settings it also looks for a set of stories or "scripts" that openly or disguisedly represent and comment upon relations of power.[8] Some research on government-society relations recommends special study of "street-level" offices in which citizens and officials transact business.[9]

There are real advantages to making use of activity settings to get information about many specific kinds of activity. The reason is the simple one that particular kinds of activity tend to concentrate in particular kinds of activity settings. If you are interested in the activity of economic production, you will do well to learn about what people do in production units. If you are interested in public discourse on community matters, you will do well to study public meetings. It is quite feasible to get a list of *all* the activity settings in a community or neighbourhood that are dedicated mainly to economic production or mainly to public discussion of community matters. By getting information about the appropriate list of activity settings it is possible to canvass almost all of the relevant activity or to sample it in a systematic way.[10]

The other way to learn about public discourse is to start with a sample or a set of individuals and to ask them about their participation in such discourse. But starting with individuals has three disadvantages compared to starting with activity settings. First, it takes more work to find in a sample of individuals those with knowledge of an activity than it does to go to the activity where the relevant individuals are already gathered. The easiest way to find the participants in meetings is to go to the meetings, to their records, or to their organizers. Second, the activity in question is by its nature collective activity, and it is appropriate to describe and understand it as such. Third, the activity settings in question are objects of knowledge and feeling for many different people. By taking meetings as the objects of research the study can ask about the different constructions placed on them. Therefore, it may be important to talk with individuals and to discover if there are different ideas about what happened and what it meant. The perceptions and attitudes of different individuals can easily be investigated once the activity settings themselves are known.

Compiling a List of Activity Settings

To compile a list of relevant activity settings you need to know the spatial and temporal boundaries of the society, community, neighbourhood, or population that interests you, and you need to know what kinds of activity settings are relevant to your project. The community might be a certain urban neighbourhood over the past year or a particular village over the last five years. For questions of political action and participation, all public meetings relating to community affairs might be relevant. Newspapers, telephone books, and community directories are all good sources of information. Elders and activists in the locality are always a primary resource. Since many meetings are organized by official bodies and voluntary associations, it will be useful to approach the offices and leaders of such organizations for information about what meetings were held when and where and under what sponsorship.

In research I did with Aparna Sundar in a fishing village in southern India we knew that we wanted information on all the public meetings that had taken place over the preceding year. We asked a group of young men in the village to make a map of the community on which could be indicated all the places where meetings were regularly or occasionally held.[11] As they drew the map the men discussed among themselves the different associations and meetings. Their collective knowledge added several significant meetings to the list we had begun with the help of village leaders. The map itself proved to be an extremely helpful aid when we talked with other groups about kinds of political action in the village. It showed us a great deal about how the village was divided into neighbourhoods with social as well as geographical organization. Also, by representing the separate existence of the activities in question, it gave the people we were talking to the role of experts with special knowledge rather than objects of research.

Why Study Meetings?

Information about meetings is relevant to many kinds of local research.[12] Global, national, and local pressures of social change impose difficulties on people in all localities. There are, of course, all kinds of personal and family responses to the pressures. People lose their jobs, start new businesses, move to new places, rent out a room in their house, seek assistance from relatives, drop out of school, enrol in school. People also seek collective solutions either to block some change from outside or to accomplish some collective goal. The action to respond to change may or may not be democratic. It may be organized from above or below. In the meetings that take place people may speak from the heart or for the ears of power-holders they fear. Whatever the case, the meetings and the collective action are an important part of the local response to change and social pressure.[13]

The meetings are the venues for public dialogue about social pressures and difficulties and what to do about them. They also dramatize in a public way those voices and interests that are willing and able to make themselves heard. The existence of relatively open meetings does not mean that all politics is open. Prudent citizens and researchers will suppose that there may well be a hidden politics of power as well as a hidden politics of resistance. Methods of research to discover those guarded zones may be appropriate. Nonetheless, the form and the content of open politics are also vital features of the social reality of a place, especially when democratic participation is an issue. For broad popular participation in politics, nothing can substitute for open political meetings.

Meetings do not exist in isolation. Information on changing social and class relations, government policies and actions, popular attitudes and perceptions, and social networks and organizations can readily be integrated with study of meetings as a kind of activity setting. Meetings have formal and informal rules that attract or even oblige participation by certain people and that repel or even forbid participation by others. They also have rules or customs about who speaks and about the forms of speech and the kinds of issues raised. All these rules and customs can be seen in operation, and they can be related to class hierarchies and cultural differences. Some interests or viewpoints may be amplified and others silenced in the public arenas. They may be raised in certain venues but not in others.

A set of data about how meetings work, for whom, and on what issues can add significantly to many kinds and topics of local research.

Attributes of Meetings

Our research has focused on popular participation in communities and localities in Nigeria, India, Uganda, Nicaragua, and Pakistan. The communities include rural towns, large urban centres, and coastal villages. The type of activity settings include meetings related to market vendors, mosques, development projects, local self-government, fishing-ground conflicts, fish marketing, and many other matters. We found that meetings and government offices carry many different attributes connected to our interest in social change and political participation. Some of the most salient are:

- the size and richness of the public space
  - How many meetings?   How many people participate?
  - Under what different auspices?   Addressing how many different topics?

- power in public space
  - Who comes?   Who speaks?
  - Who controls directly?   What indirect controls?

- content and style of public action
  - What topics?   How addressed?
  - Who speaks and who does not?   What emotional tone?
  - What decision method?   What decisions or actions?

Given this kind of information, we can ask a series of further questions. How does public political action relate to class and the political structure of the community? How does it relate to differences in gender, age, and culture in the community? How does it relate to the issues that we think and residents think face the community? What does it show about the role of external powers and authorities within the locality? How are meetings changing over time?

The sample question guides used in some of the research reported in this book, and reproduced in this appendix, indicate the kinds of information that can be gathered on meetings, offices, and organizations. Study them to see how we worked our interests into the research instruments and to get your own ideas about good questions to ask about activity settings. We collected and used both qualitative and quantitative information. Chapter 5 on the U.S. and English towns makes the most extensive use of quantitative measures. The note on ways of measuring the size and richness of social or political space discusses the basis for the urb, a measure used in that study, but the discussion also demonstrates how research on activity settings can reveal the power of social context.

What Are Government Settings? What Are Political Settings? A Note for Research Assistants

An activity setting is specific and concrete organized activity. Each instance or occasion of an activity setting happens in a definite place at a definite time with particular people and objects as its components. Some activity settings happen only once, like the governor's visit to Machina to promote education. Other activity settings occur again and again, like the Friday evening gathering at the Abode of Peace Mosque in Lahore.

Most settings belong to clusters or organizations. The governor's visit was one of a set of visits he made to local government towns in Yobe state. It is also an example of a type of setting: a governor's official visit, which has a pattern to it. The police station in Kanyakumari is part of Tamil Nadu's police system and falls under the authority of the state government. It is a type of setting that is found all over India and the world, including Owino Market in Kampala.

Government settings are activity settings that are part of government, and political settings are activity settings in which people try to influence government or inform themselves about government. Practically, government settings include all the offices of government and political settings include all public meetings about government. Offices and meetings, as activity settings, are of particular interest for our research. Together they constitute the tangible political space of the locality.

Background on Settings or Clusters of Settings

The following form or list of "Basic Information on Organizations," which can be used to help describe an activity setting, does not have a place for essential background information. Often it makes sense to write down the background information for a cluster of related settings, perhaps all those connected to a single organization.

You can write out background information in the form of a short essay. The following questions and suggestions provide a guide to the kind of information necessary for the research project; but be sure to include other points that you find important, striking, interesting, or amusing.

Basic Information on Organizations

1. What is the name of the organization?
2. Why did you decide to write about it?
3. When was the organization founded?
4. What were the circumstances of its founding?
5. Who played an important role in the founding?
6. What people currently play key parts in the cluster of settings?
7. In what ways are they central?
8. What are the significant changes in the organization?
9. What are the important events in the organization's history?
10. What connections outside the locality does the organization have?
11. What control does the external body have over rules and resources?
12. What is the official governing body of the organization?
13. How is it made up?
14. How often does it meet?
15. What other bodies are part of the organization?
16. What kinds of meetings do they hold?
17. What offices are staffed by the organization?
18. What other kinds of meetings take place in the organization?
19. What are the powers and responsibilities of these meetings?
20. How often does each one take place?
21. Who could tell us about each kind of meeting?
22. Make a diagram of the organization and its parts, indicating where the different kinds of meetings and offices fall. If possible, include the hierarchy of settings or offices related to the activity settings in question. Discuss the kinds of power and influence exercised between and among settings. Note any power, formal or informal, held by subordinate settings to resist directions imposed from above. Use as many diagrams as necessary.
23. Write down any other large or small ideas you have about the setting or cluster: how it works, what its function is, how it is misunderstood, etc.

Activity Setting Forms

The following forms are not questionnaires; they are records of information about settings that you get from several kinds of sources. How complete your information is will depend upon the sources you find and the effort you devote to interviewing people. You will have to decide which settings and which particular meetings or offices are worth devoting special energy to.

There are three sources of information: written records, other people, your own attendance. Use them all.

Be sure to inform the people you seek to interview about the aims of the research and tell them that they are free to decline to take part. Assure them that you will not reveal their identities without their permission.

A good way to get information from experts is to ask them about the last meeting they attended, then ask them about the one before that, and so on. This is a much better method than asking, in general, "What do you do in your meetings?"

You may want to fill out forms for particular meetings and for the regular meetings as a group.

Write the number of each question and then the answer to it in an exercise book.

1. IDENTIFIERS

These entries give basic information about the name and location of the setting along with the name of the researcher and the time of the research.

1.1 What name do people call this setting in their language?

Comment on any interesting significance the local name for the setting may have.

1.2 What is the English equivalent?
1.3 What are the mailing address and telephone number, if any, for this setting?

The address could be useful if we need to write for further information or if we wish to send some of the research results or a note of thanks. Having a mailing address or a telephone is a resource of significance in itself.

1.4 What city, town, or village is it in?
1.5 What country is it in?
1.6 What are the names of the researchers who got the information recorded here?
1.7 What is the name of person filling out this form?
1.8 On what date is the form being filled out?

There may be more than one date if you include information gathered at different times from various sources.

2. TIME (FOR MEETING)

If you are recording information about a meeting you attended or know about, the date will be no problem. If you are interviewing a local expert, ask first about the most recent meeting the expert knows about. Then ask about earlier meetings. If the meetings are supposed to be monthly or at some other regular interval, ask if any regular meetings were missed. Note whether or not the length of the current meeting is more or less typical. If not indicate what a typical length is. We want to be able to estimate the total time this setting was open or available during the course of a year.

2.1 What time did the meeting begin?
2.2 What time did it end?
2.3 How long did it last?
2.4 On what date did the meeting take place?
2.5 How many other meetings of the same kind with the same name took place over the past 12 months?

This is a convenient place to ask whether any of the previous meetings had special importance. If so, fill out a separate form for each of the interesting meetings (you make the final judgment about this). You may have to conduct interviews with other people.

2.6 On what dates did these other meetings, if any, take place?

2.7 Are there separate setting records for these meetings?

2.8 What other information do you have about the time of the meeting? (For example, did many people wait a long time for it to begin? Was the time changed? Was it convenient or inconvenient for people who wanted to attend?)

> *This is a good place to note any special qualities of the year for this setting. For example, political party meetings may be much more numerous and intensive during election years, or an environmental crisis may spark extraordinary activity by an environmental organization.*

3. TIME (FOR OFFICE)

> *Again the point here is to learn how "available" the setting was over the past year. The questions are designed to take account of formal and informal realities.*

3.1 What time does the office usually open?

3.2 What time does it close?

3.3 For what hours does it regularly close between these hours, for lunch or prayer, etc.?

3.4 How many hours is the office open and working in a normal week?

3.5 For how many normally open days or weeks was it closed in the past 12 months? (For example, because the key person travelled or was ill, or because of a religious or other holiday?)

3.6 How many hours in total was the office open and working in the past 12 months?

3.7 Other information and explanations about the time the office is open.

> *Here is the place to take note of facts that alter the degree to which the setting is fully operative when it is open. For example, if the key officer who has most of the information and the power to sign and make decisions is often absent, requiring people to return for service, this is the place to note that information.*

4. PLACE

> *The information sought in this section is meant to give a clear picture of who the setting looks. It would be useful in addition to give a narrative account of how the setting looks with your own reactions and interpretations. That could be part of item 4.11. If the setting is identified with a particular person, class, or group, indicate how that identification is made apparent.*

4.1 What is the official name, if any, for the place of this setting?

4.2 What is the usual name that people give to the place in their language?

> *Note any special significance of the name.*

4.3 What is the English equivalent of the usual name?

4.4 Is the place outdoors or indoors?

4.5 If outdoors, describe any fence or wall that forms a boundary.

4.6 If outdoors, describe any roof or shelter.

4.7 If outdoors, what is the approximate length and width of the setting in metres?

4.8 If indoors, what is the approximate length and width of the room (or each of the rooms) the setting occupies?

4.9 How is the setting furnished?

4.10 How are the people in it arranged?

4.11 Provide other information or ideas about the importance of the place or its symbolic value.

5. PEOPLE (FOR MEETINGS)

> *The aim here is to get information about how the setting selects its members and leaders. Does it reflect social forces such as class and culture? Does it reflect differences in power and participation by gender? Does its internal hierarchy reproduce the wider social hierarchy, or does it reflect an internal dynamic? Note that one way new organizations change society is by themselves reflecting new values. Moreover, the broad stratification of a society may not always be reflected in particular meetings and organizations.*

5.1 Who is in charge of the meeting?

5.2 What is the title of that person for the meeting?

> *Note any special significance the title may have.*

5.3 What other jobs or titles does that person have?

> *The answer to this question relates to the issue of the concentration of leadership positions in an organization or a community in the hands of a few people. From another standpoint it may reveal the concentration or dispersion of creative input into the social life of the community.*

5.4 What are all the other official positions for the meeting (for example, secretary, guest speaker, prayer-giver)? Write the names in the local language with their English equivalents.

> *It may turn out that there is a conventional list of offices that many different settings have. Or*

there may be two or three conventional models. The existence of such models and the differences in the conventional models from country to country are themselves of great interest. In section 5.18 you might want to comment about how this setting reflects or departs from a particular model.

5.5 What minor jobs, such as arranging chairs or serving drinks, are assigned to particular persons for the meeting?

Note here or in 5.18 if these jobs have more significance than meets the eye, as reflectors of social stratification or as carrying more influence than at first appearance, for example.

5.6 Give the following information for the holders of all the positions noted above, including the person in charge:

Generally, the point here is to see what kinds of people are found in positions of influence and action. You may have particular hypotheses to test that require other questions. By all means add them in and give any new questions new numbers, starting with 5.19 if they go into this section.

Sex (M, F)
Age (child, young adult, adult, old adult, very old)
Cultural groups (ethnic, caste, religious—locally relevant ones)
Can speak English (yes, no)
Years of schooling
Person dwells (in community, other community)
Economic level (high, medium, low)
Political party or faction

5.7 How many other people, not leaders or helpers, are members of the meeting?

Note whether numbers at this particular meeting are unusual compared to other meetings of the same kind. If it is a regular meeting, try to do an estimate of the total number of participants and participant-hours over the period of one year.

5.8 How many onlookers are present?

Onlookers can have a very important role. Often young people learn how the meeting works and what the current issues are. Onlookers carry the news to sections of the population that may not be present or even allowed to be present as participants. Make note of the importance of the onlookers in this case.

5.9 Estimate what percentage of ordinary members fall into each of these categories:

Sex (M, F)
Age (child, young adult, adult, old adult, very old)
Cultural groups (ethnic, caste, religious—locally relevant ones)
Person dwells (in community, other community)
Economic level (high, medium, low)
Political party or faction

5.10 Estimate what percentage of onlookers fall in each of these categories:

Sex (M, F)
Age (child, young adult, adult, old adult, very old)
Cultural groups (ethnic, caste, religious—locally relevant ones)
Person dwells (in community, other community)
Economic level (high, medium, low)
Political party or faction

5.11 Why do you think the people who came decided to attend?

Is it social pressure, interest in an issue at hand, strong social habit, pressure from powers that be, or something else? This and the next entry are intended to reveal something of the social forces that regulate participation.

5.12 Why do you think the people who did not attend decided not to?

5.13 How are people informed about the meeting? (For example, town crier, newspaper, radio, word of mouth, some other means? How systematic is the call for a meeting?)

5.14 Is there any special pressure to attend? If so, describe the pressure.

5.15 Are people paid for attending, with an allowance, for example? If so, how much are they paid?

5.16 Are there penalties for those who fail to attend?

5.17 Do women face any special obstacles if they want to attend?

Include here matters such as difficulty of arranging child care, opposition of men to allowing women to go out alone or at night, religious restrictions on women's activities.

5.18 Write down any other ideas or comments you have about people at this meeting.

This is a place to enter comparisons, if any, with other settings. For instance, is this setting different or remarkable in the kind of people it includes and the activities they undertake and the relations they establish?

6. PEOPLE (FOR OFFICES)

Many of the basic relations between government and people are enacted in government offices. The staffing of the office reveals a great deal about the local face of government. Is it local people or outsiders? Does it represent all groups or only a few? How fast or slowly does it deliver its services? You could note at the end of the form, under item 13.1, your assessment of the popular evaluation of this office, especially if it is particularly loved or reviled.

6.1 Who is in charge of this office?

6.2 What is the official title of the person in charge, in the local language and in English?

6.3 What do most people call the person in charge in the local language?

6.4 What are the other paid positions in the office?

6.5 For the person in charge and the other paid positions, give this information:

Sex (M, F)
Age (child, young adult, adult, old adult, very old)
Cultural groups (ethnic, caste, religious—locally relevant ones)
Person dwells (in community, other community)
Economic level (high, medium, low)
Political party or faction

6.6 How many other people are usually in the office?

Some offices are meeting places or communications hubs for a social group that may or may not have much connection with the function of the office. Under 13.1 or here you could note if the other people around the office reflect some secondary or unofficial function.

6.7 How many people are waiting to get into the office?

6.8 How many people received services from the office the day before the interview or the day of observation?

6.9 How many people receive services over a typical week?

The point here is to get an idea of the offices that serve a large number of people and the ones that serve few people, but perhaps a special group of some interest.

6.10 What are the important seasonal variations (rains, dry season, times of religious observance, etc?)

6.11 How many visits for services were made in the past 12 months?

This means person-visits. One person returning on a second day would count as two visits. A group of five visiting together would count as five visits.

6.12 Estimate the percentage of the visits to the office made over the past 12 months by people who fall into each of the following categories:

Sex (M, F)
Age (child, young adult, adult, old adult, very old)
Cultural groups (ethnic, caste, religious—locally relevant ones)
Person dwells (in community, other community)
Economic level (high, medium, low)
Political party or faction

6.13 What brings people to this office?

6.14 Do any groups (by sex, age, ethnic group, etc.) face special obstacles in coming to this office?

6.15 Are there special incentives for coming to this office?

6.16 Are there special penalties for not coming to it?

7. ACTIVITY (FOR MEETINGS)

Although the content of the discussion may be important for the research, the form and quality of the interactions are also crucial. The assumption is that how groups do politics influences the success of the participation they mediate. Moreover, the ability to raise issues and solve conflicts depends upon political practice, some of it in meetings. You may want to reflect directly on these matters under items 7.17 and 7.18 or 13.1. It can also be helpful to make comparisons with other settings under those items.

7.1 How was the meeting opened?

7.2 What were the main items on the agenda?

7.3 Describe what was said under each agenda item.

7.4 What questions were asked, and by whom?

7.5 Who answered the questions and what did they say?

7.6 What decisions were made?

7.7 How were the decisions arrived at?

7.8 Was there voting?

7.9 What was the tone of the discussion?

7.10 If there was conflict or disagreement, how was it expressed?

7.11 What was the role of women in the discussion?

7.12 What was the role of young adults?

7.13 Did the very old have any particular role?

7.14 What further meetings or further work was announced?

7.15 Was there a prayer? Where in the meeting? Who gave the prayer or prayers?

7.16 How was the meeting closed?

7.17 In your opinion, was the meeting a success? Explain why or why not.

7.18 What did the meeting reveal about conflict, co-operation, and influence in the community?

7.19 What are the striking or important symbols used in the setting, or symbolic qualities of the setting itself?

7.20 Does the kind of language and words used in the setting focus attention on certain topics and exclude others? Explain.

7.21 Does the kind of language used attract certain kinds of people to speak and exclude or discourage others? Explain.

8. ACTIVITY (FOR OFFICES)

The kind of services, the tone of interaction, and the existence of special projects are all important features of offices that provide services directly to citizens. You might want to get special detail on services that pertain to your research.

8.1 What is the normal work of people in the office?

8.2 How does the work change with dry season, rainy season, etc.?

8.3 Have there been any special campaigns or projects for this office in the past 12 months? Describe each special project.

8.4 What services do people get from this office?

8.5 What is the tone of the relations between the officials and the people in this setting?

9. THINGS

Occasionally objects have central importance. For example, the office with the only telephone in town has capabilities unmatched in other offices. Or possessing a symbol of authority may set an office or meeting apart from others that claim to have similar importance. People may feel that they cannot hold a certain kind of meeting unless they have essential equipment, such as a podium or loudspeakers or chairs for dignitaries. Without the equipment the community or group will simply forgo the setting. In other cases the objects might have very little importance at all.

9.1 Describe any furniture that seems important for the activity of this setting.

9.2 Describe any other objects that are important for the work of this setting.

9.3 Do any objects have important symbolic value? Explain.

10. POWER AND AUTONOMY

The aim here is to gather information that reveals the extent to which the setting is controlled within the community or from higher levels of authority in government or in the private sector. Decisions about the meeting, its leaders, its activity, its participants, its rules, and its funding all relate to the location of control. Develop your own conventions about what constitutes local, state, federal, and international locations of power. You might add information on other aspects of the location of control. Which agency of government? What political party? Additional information can go under 10.13 or 13.1, or you can add questions by including numbers 10.16, 10.17, etc.

10.1 Who made the decision to have this setting?

10.2 Was the decision to have the setting made mainly in the community or mainly outside the community but in the state, mainly outside the state but in the federation, or mainly outside the federation? Explain.

10.3 At what level are the leaders of the setting chosen? Local, state, federal, international.

10.4 How were the leaders chosen? Self-selection, election, appointed (by whom?), etc.

10.5 At what level is the program of activity (or the agenda of the meeting) for this setting decided—local, state, federal, or international?

10.6 Describe how the program of activity is decided.

10.7 At what level are the rules about who can enter this setting made—local, state, federal, or international?

10.8 Describe how the rules are made about who can enter.

10.9 Does this setting get any funding? If so, where does its funding come from?

10.10 What percentage of funding comes from the local level? The state level? The federal level? The international level? Make the best estimate you can.

10.11 What other resources does the setting use (building, food, water, P.A. system, vehicle)? From what level are these resources provided—local, state, federal, international?

10.12 Comment on what agency at what level you think has the main power over this setting. Comment especially on what power local people have over the existence and the activity of the setting.

10.13 Is the setting directly a part of government at any level?

10.14 If not directly a part of government, how dependent is it on government? Give your interpretation.

10.15 If not a part of government, how important a part in the setting do government employees play?

11. HISTORY

The questions here, and your elaborations around them, can provide valuable information about political change and political creativity. Many important political changes are reflected in the founding of new settings, new organizations. And new practices within continuing settings also mark important changes. Changes such as the first admission of women, the first use of internal elections, the appointment of a leader for life (eliminating elections), the first meeting of a new organization, and the final meeting of an organization that is closing down can all inform our understanding of basic changes.

11.1 When was the setting founded? Give at least the year or the approximate year.

11.2 What were the broad circumstances of its founding? Was it part of a larger campaign or a larger institutional change?

11.3 What have been the circumstances of any important changes in the setting over the years?

11.4 Describe any striking, revealing, or historically important instances of the setting, or a related one. An example is a historic meeting in which a leader was chosen or deposed. In some cases oral traditions or myths will be pertinent.

11.5 Describe any aspects of the setting that you think are connected to the quality of communications between government and citizens.

11.6 What have been the major conflicts or controversies in this setting or about this setting in the past 12 months? In the past ten years?

11.7 What role has the setting played in political or social alignments or conflicts?

11.8 Have particular people or particular social or political groups been important in sustaining this setting? Or in limiting or opposing it? Explain.

12. SOURCES

It is useful to comment on the quality of the different sources. Plans for follow-up can include getting more information to revise this report or getting information on another related setting or learning more about a particular person, etc.

12.1 What people were sources of the information recorded on this form?

12.2 What documents or records provided information on this setting?

12.3 Note here any information that you think is weak or missing.

12.4 What are the plans, if any, for follow-up work on this setting?

13. FINAL COMMENTS AND IDEAS

This section is completely open to all kinds of comments—perhaps general points about the setting or specific ideas that did not seem to fit under the questions above. Be sure to include thoughts that might help with interpretation later on. Ideas that seem totally obvious and unnecessary to record now may be forgotten, and lost, a few months later.

13.1 Please write down here any other comments or ideas or information you have about this setting and about the quality of this record.

Measuring Size and Richness of Political Space: A Technical Note

A fundamental measure of social space focuses precisely on use. It is occupancy time. For a given activity setting or group of activity settings, you can calculate occupancy time by multiplying mean hours per occurrence *times* number of occurrences per year *times* mean number of people present per occurrence. This gives the number of person-hours that people commit to the setting over the course of a year. A very populous setting that lasts only a few hours, such as a major soccer match, may have the same occupancy time as a much-repeated or continuous setting with many fewer people. The measure makes no distinction among different temporal patterns and counts all person-hours equally.

Total occupancy time is not easily expandable. The non-domestic activity settings of a town can pull person-hours away from domestic activity and they can pull in outsiders as temporary inhabitants, but short of a permanent gain in population the number of person-hours available is a fixed and finite number. This basic fact opens the way for use of economic modes of analysis. The distribution of person-hours among settings can be seen as a process of allocation of a scarce resource. How do people decide how much time to reserve for domestic pursuits? How do they choose where to "spend" their non-domestic hours? Person-time offers a clear-cut way to measure and compare how people in a locality allocate their time. The research in Yorkshire and Kansas (see chapter 6) made extensive use of measures of the person-time committed to different activity settings and types of activity setting.

The researchers in Yorkshire and Kansas also sought a summary measure of amount or extent of activity the locality makes available to its inhabitants. In a sense all localities are equal, because everyone "spends" 100 per cent of their time in one or another activity. Yet we know that some localities offer a greater wealth of possible activities than others, and some activities may be much more readily available than others. How can we measure the activity-resources a locality makes available? How can we measure the richness and extent—the *amplitude*—of activity?

The starting point is to recognize three qualities of social space and one characteristic of people related to their use of social space.

1. Every social space is structured into a finite number of activity settings, each of which channels activity into a pattern characteristic for that setting.
2. Activity settings exist only when they function; they have a temporal dimension defined by the frequency with which they occur and the duration of each occurrence.
3. Each activity setting has its own program of activity, its own set of inhabitants, and its own responsible positions through which its activity is accomplished. (The particular inhabitants and position-holders may change from occurrence to occurrence of a setting; the program may change as well, but a radical change would signal the demise of an old setting and the advent of a new one.)
4. People have the capacity to be flexible in choosing the means to achieve relatively stable purposes, and they exercise this capacity as they allocate their participation among the activity settings available to them and take part in the programs of particular settings.

The way in which the structure of social space interacts with the purposes and experiences of people suggests a way to measure the amplitude of social space. Each activity setting has its own program of activity and requires its own positions of competence and responsibility. The variety of experience and the opportunity (and pressure) to engage in competent and responsible action will almost certainly be greater when political space is organized into more numerous, less populous, and more various settings than when it is organized into fewer, more populous, and less various settings. Furthermore, people can arrange their time commitments to political activity in ways that accomplish more diverse purposes if political space is more variegated.

This line of reasoning can be applied without pretence of great rigour for impressionistic comparisons of different social and political spaces. What we are comparing is the *richness* as well as the sheer temporal *quantity* of social space; hence my preference for the term "amplitude" to designate this general quality of social space. The meaning of non-rigorous applications of the idea of amplitude is clarified by consideration of a rigorous, quantitative application. The extensive and thorough research data from Oskaloosa and Leyburn invite such an application, and Roger Barker spent much time and thought developing one. He called his measure of the amplitude of social space the urb.

The temporal dimension of activity settings is central to measuring the amplitude of social space. When the gavel closes the meeting of the city council, that activity setting ceases to exist until the next meeting is opened. When the grocery store closes for the night at 9 p.m. it no longer exists as a setting, at least until it opens the next morning at 8 a.m. A few settings are open and operating every hour of every day: most trafficways and certain 24-hour copyshops, grocery stores, and restaurants, for example. But most activity settings exist intermittently according to a schedule that is often, but not always, regular. Clearly, the 24-hour grocery store is more available for shopping than is the annual church bakesale that holds forth for five hours on a Sunday afternoon once a year. A club that meets weekly is more available for participation than a club that meets monthly. Still, these comparisons of availability of activity say nothing about either the geographic size of the setting or the number of its participants. Availability or amplitude is a measure of the degree to which activity is convenient, reachable, handy, at hand. Being available does not mean any particular person will want to enter it, nor does it guarantee entry to anyone who wishes to enter. Many settings have few or no restrictions on entry, but some are selective about their participants. Barriers to entry and patterns of selectivity are important topics to be considered, but they are separate from the measure of amplitude. Amplitude is one basic measure of the amount and variety of activity and experience that is on offer in the social environment. Since each activity setting includes a distinctive program of activity, and most require the exercise of skill and responsibility, an overall measure of the number, frequency, and duration of activity settings (singly or in groups) promises to be useful.

The researchers in Kansas and Yorkshire argued that the availability of settings is not a simple function of the number of hours they operate. A new setting that operates for only one hour per year adds a whole new activity, while increasing the opening time of an existing setting by one hour only makes already available activity slightly more available. Similarly, adding an hour in a new day to the operation of a setting increases availability more than adding an hour in a day already served. This point is clear in the case of elections, for example, because they take up little social time but have a large influence on the quality of political life.

Think, for example, of three shopping malls, each making 2,600 setting-hours of shopping activity available to the locality. The first mall has one shop open ten hours a day and five days a week for two weeks a year. The second has five shops open ten hours a day for only one day a week for fifty-two weeks a year. The third has ten shops open only one hour a day for five days a week and fifty-two weeks a year. Which affords the greatest amplitude of shopping activity?

malls	no. of shops	hours/day	days/week	weeks/year	amplitude/ year	setting-hours
1.	1	10	5	52	0.501 cu.	2,600
2.	5	10	1	52	0.697 cu.	2,600
3.	10	1	5	52	2.361 cu.	2,600

According to the urb measure the third mall has about 4.7 times the amplitude of the first mall and about 3.4 times the amplitude of the second mall. The measure makes intuitive sense. Since each shop offers opportunity for significantly different activities and must include its own set of responsible positions, the mall with the most shops open on the most different days is more ample in the opportunities it provides for shopping activity. But more shops with many fewer days of opening does not mean much greater availability of shopping activity. The shops are there, but it is difficult to schedule visits to them.

Now compare the following changes to the *second mall*: (1) adding five new shops; (2) adding a second day per week of operation for the five existing shops; and (3) adding ten hours of operation per day for the five existing shops.

Mall	shops	hours/day	days/week	weeks/year	amplitude
2.	5	10	1	52	0.697cu.
2a.	10	10	1	52	1.389cu.
2b.	5	10	2	52	1.144cu.
2c.	5	20	1	52	0.987cu.

Although the added number of store operating hours is 2,600, doubling the number of open shop hours, in the three kinds of expansion the amplitude of activity is not increased equally. The new shops add opportunity for new kinds of shopping and create new responsible roles requiring new skills. In comparison, the new opening day for existing shops offers no new kinds of activity and demands no new skills, but people will find it easier to schedule participation in the five shops now open two days each week instead of one. Finally, the lengthened hours of operation add the least availability of activity, although they do make participation a little easier for people who work long hours during the day.

The qualitative differences in the two comparisons of shops in a shopping mall derive from the tendency of people to use flexible means to overcome obstacles in the environment in order to accomplish relatively stable goals. In the case at hand, they adapt their schedules to make use of the activities on offer. A new activity setting creates opportunity for new activity goals, while extending days and hours only reduces obstacles to reaching already available goals.

The urb is a measure of activity-availability that gives independent weight to the threefold time dimensions of activity settings: their existence in the research year, the number of days on which they operate in the research year, and the number of hours during which they occur in the research year. All settings that occur in a given year gain the same year score, whether they occur on one day or on every day of that year. The day score reflects the number of days out of the year's supply of 365 (or 366 in leap years) days during which the activity setting operated. The hour score reflects the number of hours on which the setting functioned out of the year's 8,760 (or 8,784) hours. These scores are then weighted according to the findings of the research about the mean number of settings available in Oskaloosa and Leyburn each year, each day, and each hour. The index is scaled to a standard town in which there are 680.5 settings per year, 151 per day, and 34.1 per hour. The figures are the mean for these variables in four sets of data: Oskaloosa and Leyburn in 1954-55 and 1963-66. By this convention, adding one new activity setting that occurs for one hour in the year contributes about 81 times the amplitude of activity that adding one day to an already existing activity setting contributes. The new hour-long setting adds about 440 times the activity-availability that one extra hour of an existing setting would contribute. The same logic can be applied to a single setting, groups of settings, or all the non-domestic settings in a town.

The amplitude of activity settings in the standard town is set at 100 centiurbs. The research employs this measure a great deal for comparisons of the relative availability of different sets of activities. Keep in mind that all the non-domestic activity in the standard town totalled 100 centiurbs and that the actual measure in the four data sets remains close to that figure; they range from 90 to 113. In some of the tables the extent of zones of activity or clusters of activity settings is given as the percentage of the town's total centiurbs accounted for by the activity settings in question, rather than by their absolute size in centiurbs.

Turning now from technical details to questions of approach and imagination, we need to emphasize the differing perspectives of the two measures. Two localities with the same population have the same number of person-hours to allocate among activities, but the amplitude of the activities they generate can be very different. The locality that divides its activity into a larger number of distinct activity settings at the expense of the number of participants per setting and of number of hours per day of operation will generate activity of greater amplitude than the locality that arranges its activity in fewer settings with larger numbers of participants and longer hours per day of operation.

Occupancy-time can be thought of as a measure of the allocation of a scarce resource. It is like an accounting of the choice of desserts made by the customers in a restaurant. How many chose apple pie as compared to chocolate cake and creme caramel? The centiurb measure can be thought of as a measure of activity-richness. It is like a measure of the abundance of the offerings on a dessert tray that takes account of the size of each dessert, the number of different desserts, and their arrangement on the tray for ease of serving.

The two measures reflect two different perspectives on social space; they have very different contributions to make to a theory of political space. People do choose among activities. That power of choice has a big impact on activity settings. If people stop choosing to enter a certain shop, it will go out of business; if people stop attending a certain church, it will close its doors. But activity settings exert power over people as well. Within the setting, custom and authority enforce the expected program of activity, and deviation is actively countered and persistent deviants are often ejected from the setting. The quality of life offered by a locality is in large part a function of the depth, character, and variety of experience its activity settings generate. The power of a setting extends beyond its boundaries. Shops advertise and entice customers; meetings announce themselves and designate people to remind waverers that they are expected to show up. Simply by being there, settings induce people to decide whether or not to enter and take part. Creating activity settings can have a powerful effect on the action and experience of people.

We have here the two sides of social analysis. The economistic side stresses individual choice in a context of scarcity and sees the control that choices exercise over social arrangements. The contextual one stresses the structuring and motivating side of social arrangements and sees their power to create goals, values, and energy fields that attract and induce participation and shape how people conceive of normal social relations. The political space approach seeks to bring into equal focus both kinds of analysis. It recognizes, with much political science analysis, that political activity is often about the efforts to influence and control directly the choices people make. But it also notices that political action often shapes social space and thereby influences the actions and the experiences of people. The political space approach tries to understand the kinds of influence that the structuring of social space can exert. Unlike more familiar kinds of structural analysis, the political space approach adopts a scale of analysis that is appropriate to the understanding of local-level actions by individuals and small groups of people.

The data from Oskaloosa and Leyburn suggest that the size and activity-richness of a cluster of settings may bear centrally on issues of social and economic change. The connection lies in the energizing or motivating capacity of activity settings. They are not just the place-times at and in which people choose to go to do something, they are organized fields of social energy that activate and direct people. They do not completely determine what people do, but their forces do interact with the motives and directions that people bring to the setting. Different patterns in the structure of activity settings may account for differences in the energy people commit to public activity. More numerous settings, with greater collective variety, and involving fewer people on average, may well be socially more energizing than a smaller number of settings, exhibiting less variety, and involving more people on average. Certainly differences in setting richness are reflected in the quality of experience of the people who participate in them.

Whose Knowledge, What Power, Which Values?

In designing the research and applying for funding I observed the rules about research with human subjects and committed the project to informing interviewees of the subject of the research and giving them every opportunity to decline to be interviewed and to decline to answer any particular questions. I also agreed not to expose research subjects to danger and to get research permission for the project from the governments and authorities in question. Although these rules are basic, some of them assume an ability to communicate that may not always be present, and they do not cover all the ethical issues our research faced and in some sense resolved.

For example, in one place people we wanted to interview often asked to be paid for the interview. In another there were simmering tensions that periodically erupted into open violence. In all the research sites the university researchers living on very modest student grants appeared to the local people as being very wealthy and potentially influential, and with reason. And as head researcher and professor from Canada, I was seen as being far more wealthy and powerful than the student researchers.

My account may be of interest to others who have faced or who will face similar questions and to ethicists looking for real-life situations that they can use to try out their precepts and tools of reasoning. I have not looked into the philosophical literature to place an elaborate sheen to my homespun solutions, but an account of ethics from below may be of interest for its own sake. And I will risk a few reflections of a more general kind.

The research in question is a project to study local political action in different contexts, but using similar methods of research. We were working in locales on the distant periphery of world power in which the majority of people would be classified as poor and vulnerable. The locales were Owino Market, the largest open wholesale and retail market in Kampala, Uganda; Machina, a town of several thousand people in the semi-arid farming zone of Yobe state in northern Nigeria; and several coastal fishing villages in Kanyakumari District at the southern tip of India in Tamil Nadu state. For the research on political settings I worked alongside each of the researchers: Christie Gombay in Owino; Kole Shettima in Machina; and Aparna Sundar in Kanyakumari.

Our aim was to gather detailed and systematic descriptions of many local meetings and offices having some public or political character. If there were demonstrations or confrontations they also counted as political settings. We believed that factual accounts would increase our understanding of how local power was wielded, how issues were raised and squelched, who spoke and who did not, how central power limited local action, and what political capacities local people had.

The research did not include the familiar kind of questionnaires in which people are asked about their opinions on a series of topics. It did make use of interviews in which people were taken as experts who could give us information about the meetings and offices and demonstrations that have occurred in the locality and about the organizations that have created and supported them. We also observed meetings and wrote down information about them and what took place in them. We did some of this work ourselves, and we hired local research assistants to act as interpreters and do interviews and make observations on their own. The interviews were often with local leaders, officials, dignitaries, or activists, but we also talked with many ordinary citizens.

In Owino Market in Kampala the project was to collect information about a sample of the hundreds of meetings that take place there each week, especially those among market vendors. Most officials in the market and office-holders in the very active Market Vendors Association were quite willing to co-operate. Ordinary vendors usually requested compensation for the time they spent on interviews with us, about 50 cents per interview. We acceded to these requests and set a standard rate for interviews. Once the word got around the transactions went smoothly. The reason for our decision was that many official transactions had a price attached to them—called "eating money"—in a society in which the monthly salary of officials would cover living expenses for less than a week. Furthermore, many relationships in the market were based on the exchange of money, and there was a definite opportunity cost for vendors who might have been using their time usefully instead of doing an interview with us.

The World Bank project was important for the market vendors, and it turned out that we knew more about that project than the Market Vendors Association did. Should we convey some of this knowledge to the MVA leaders? Whose knowledge was it? There was an implicit contest over who would control the World Bank's redevelopment money and what bodies would have standing in the decisions about the project. We decided that the MVA, as affected citizens with a well-run and representative organization, had a strong claim to be part of the discussions. We did give its leaders information we thought might be useful to them. That strengthened our rapport with the MVA leaders and facilitated our research.

We also got hints of other kinds of information that we chose not to pursue very far, although it was germane to our research. The overcrowded market had spilled over into a technically illegal evening market in the streets around Owino after 6 p.m. when Owino itself closed. We learned that there was a complex system of legal and illegal payments from vendors to political figures to protect the stalls in the evening market. Relations between Owino and the evening market were an important subject in the meetings of vendors that we were learning about. The amount of money changing hands informally was substantial. Nonetheless we decided it was too dangerous to pursue the money trail very far—dangerous for the research and for the researchers. We thought it sufficient to have uncovered a pattern of some importance for the politics of the market. There was more than a façade of rule of law in Uganda, but there was also a complex double or triple standard about legality. Imposing our values about legality of market payments seemed imprudent.

In all the research locales my visit as a professor from Canada lent credibility and *gravitas* to the research project. In one case the student researcher was asked by influential local people to take a position in a local educational institution. It was an honour for the researcher to be recruited; it was an offer difficult to refuse. The researcher wanted above all to complete a Ph.D. My professorial presence was instrumental in convincing the local elite that for the researcher to finish the research and get the degree were in the best interests of all concerned. Here was another way in which the institutional power of the professoriate protected the integrity of a research project, but it had to use its own local power to do so.

All the research sites were home to significant splits and conflicts. To understand political settings we needed information from all sides. The research would suffer if we became so identified with one side that other sides cut us off. In Machina a powerful Emir held sway through his own long-standing power and the skilful placement of his children in key positions. Yet a large part of the population identified with an opposition tendency that was pretty well shut out of power. It took all the considerable skills of the student researcher to keep the confidence of the Emir's party and still gain the trust of the opposition groups. Again the claims we could make on behalf of science and research were instrumental, and my presence to symbolize them was of great help. The researcher provided the key argument: out of all the small towns in the world, Machina was one of six that researchers in Toronto had chosen for this research on the quality of social and political life. The researcher also got some key school teachers on side by hiring them as research assistants.

The point here can be stated more generally. Although professorial and academic power has an important role to play in protecting the research function, do not underestimate the power of local society and its social relations. In the Muslim society of Machina we had to accept the exclusion of women from almost all public meetings and the impossibility of women research assistants interviewing men or men interviewing women. But beneath the outer forms we needed to look for how women informed themselves and conveyed opinions. If research was an instrument of change in gender relations, the change would take place over a long period of time.

In Kanyakumari in India the research identified sources of local tension, and the researcher had to take personal account of the dangers the tensions held. Small-craft fisherman with centuries of tradition behind them found themselves competing with merchant-owned small trawlers that fished much the same waters as the smaller craft. Periodically the two groups came to blows. The fishers burned trawlers and the trawler operators cut the nets of the fishers. There were times when they even attacked one another's houses. Since the conflict had more or less standard forms of confrontation, it was interesting from the point of view of political settings. But I fully supported the decision of the researcher to stay away from a village if violent conflict seemed a distinct possibility. Our research was not worth risking personal injury, and we could get much of the needed information through interviews after the fact.

In assessing danger, trying to grasp local power relations, and searching for expressions of local value commitments there is no substitute for wide-ranging conversations with thoughtful local people. Through our hiring of local researchers, our seeking out of local leaders and activists, and our contacts with local research institutions we were well placed to have such conversations and to seek the information we needed to decide about paying for interviews or assessing local dangers or understanding patterns of local power.

In all of this I could discern several ethical principles at work.

• Make sure the people in the research locale understand as well as possible the nature of the research and give them a clear choice to participate or not.

• Regard the activities and people being researched as meaningful in their own terms. Look for ways to create venues of relative equality and free exchange. But do not underestimate insurmountable differences and inequalities. Seeing them in their material and cultural context is crucial.

• Think about what you mean to the people you are relating to as researcher. What is your value to them? What do they think your value might be? A meal ticket, a way to get abroad, a bit of prestige, a source of danger, a petty annoyance, an interesting interlocutor? Notice the power they have over you.

• Allow research *information to flow freely* among co-operating researcher and people in the research locale, but recognize that researchers in training need an individual research record for career advancement.

- Do no harm in conducting research. In particular arrange research so that it does not reinforce social injustices and so that it does, when possible, work against social injustice. In other words, acknowledge that existing social arrangements may contain injustices, and recognize that they cannot be taken as the standard for judging the ethics of the research.
- At the same time, recognize that your ability as a researcher to understand the real content of social relations and meanings is limited, especially when you are doing research in an unfamiliar social situation and your ability to communicate with people is limited.
- Remember that after you have left the place of research, people have to go on living pretty much the same way as before. Don't raise expectations or hopes. This means not overpaying researcher helpers of various kinds and not responding too strenuously to requests for personal help. There are two kinds of ethical danger here. One is that you will fail to understand the true nature of the relationships and will mistakenly identify a relationship as oppressive or free when it is the opposite. The other danger is that you will correctly identify an element of injustice in a situation, but in shaping your research you will inadvertently bring about even worse injustices.
- Do not expose yourself or other researchers to known dangers and caution them about taking unwarranted risks.
- Be alert to *ethical dilemmas and trade-offs*. Free flow of information in the research locality may work to the benefit of local powerful groups that seem to support social injustice. Emphasizing the opportunity to refuse participation in research may make it difficult to get crucial information.
- Find a way to describe the research so that people will understand it sympathetically and accurately.

A way to deal with many ethical dilemmas is to open them for discussion in a venue of relative equality. Generally the discussion with research students and research employees in the research zones was successful at dealing openly with conflicting interests and perceptions. Being able to identify and discuss such issues quickly and openly was valuable. The great familiarity of the student researchers with the research locales and their good local social relations provided a basis for good conversations about the research with selected capable local people. But such conversations were not easy to organize.

Whose Knowledge? In the research process we respected and used the expert knowledge of local people. We recognized a claim to knowledge on the part of the people researched and gave them some relevant information. Only with the publication of this book can we send them an account of the research, but it is difficult to claim that it is in a form they can grasp. The very finding of such a form would be a major project.

What Power? In the research situation we outsiders had the power of wealth and institutional prestige and education (and sometimes it could be used to shield the research and the researchers), but the local people had the power to give or withhold co-operation, to be honest or to manipulate. It is not so unequal and there is instrumentalism on both sides. And both often did gain. There is something to be said for the power of witnessing; it may discourage some outrages. In the long run the research may contribute to a process that does empower local people, but the connections are distant and tenuous.

Which values? We hew to a belief in the long-term virtue of better knowledge. I add a commitment not to increase injustice and where possible to strengthen the oppressed in their efforts for more justice. The first is easier than the second, but the impact of these commitments is mitigated by the power of the existing social forces. It is always possible that locally powerful groups can turn the research to their own advantage.

Some researchers see an insurmountable issue of values: that of transgressing some boundary of moral meaning that prevents ideas of injustice from being valid in another cultural-social context. I resist this claim on the grounds that humans and their situations give people enough in common to discern common principles of justice when they are stated in a general way. However, the problem of uncertain meanings does make me skeptical of my ability to state and apply general values correctly in situations in which cultural, social, and linguistic differences are great.

I take comfort in the idea that as a researcher I am also a kind of temporary citizen or participant with other people and we owe one another the consideration of co-participants. Working out our value relations is part of our relationship. Researchers do not stand apart and obey ethical rules different from others. We can take counsel with certain people in the research locale as well as among researchers and with colleagues on the issues the research raises. In this project, due to the good connections of the students and the local assistants we hired such conversations were frequent.

Conclusion

People doing research on social change and social action in local neighbourhoods, villages, groups, and communities will do well to consider collecting, in a systematic way, information about those kinds of activity settings that are relevant to the research issues. Our research on political participation and social action in a range of different local contexts found that getting information on all kinds of public meetings is feasible and fruitful. The work raises interesting and sometimes difficult ethical issues, but they could often be resolved through discussion. The information and the process of getting it proved to be extremely revealing about the scope and limits of local political participation and action. It added a dimension to the analysis that could not have been supplied by other sets of information.

Notes

1. Alexander Rosenberg, *Philosophy of Social Science* (Boulder, Col.: Westview Press, 1988).
2. S.F. Moore, *Social Facts and Fabrications* (Cambridge: Cambridge University Press, 1986).
3. Benedict Anderson, *Imagined Communities: Reflections on the Origins and Spread of Nationalism* (London: Verso, 1983), chapter 2.
4. Phil Schoggen, *Behavior Settings: A Revision and Extension of Roger G. Barker's Ecological Psychology* (Stanford, Cal.: Stanford University Press, 1989), chapter 3.
5. Helen B. Schwartzman, *The Meeting: Gatherings in Organizations and Communities* (New York: Plenum Publishing, 1989).
6. Edward S. Greenberg, *Workplace Democracy: The Political Effects of Participation* (Ithaca, N.Y.: Cornell University Press, 1986).
7. Norman Long and Magdelena Villareal, "Exploring Development Interfaces: From the Transfer of Knowledge to the Transformation of Meaning," in *Beyond the Impasse: New Directions in Development Theory*, ed. Frans J. Schuurman (London: Zed Books, 1993).
8. James C. Scott, *Domination and the Arts of Resistance: Hidden Transcripts* (New Haven, Conn.: Yale University Press, 1990).
9. Michael Lipsky, *Street-Level Bureaucracy: Dilemmas of the Individual in Public Services* (New York: Russell Sage Foundation, 1980).
10. Allan W. Wicker, *An Introduction to Ecological Psychology* (New York: Cambridge University Press, 1983), chapter 2.
11. James Mascarenhas, "Participatory Rural Appraisal and Participatory Learning Methods: Recent Experiences from MYRADA and South India," *Forests, Trees and People Newsletter*, no.15-16 (February 1992), pp.10-17.
12. John Gastil, *Democracy in Small Groups: Participation, Decision Making, and Communication* (Philadelphia: New Society Publishers, 1993).
13. Sara M. Evans and Harry C. Boyte, *Free Spaces: The Sources of Democratic Change in America*, 2nd ed. (Chicago: University of Chicago Press, 1992).

Selected Bibliography

Arendt, Hannah. *The Human Condition*. Garden City, N.Y.: Doubleday/Anchor, 1959.

Barker, Jonathan. "Political Space and the Quality of Participation in Rural Africa: A Case from Senegal." *Canadian Journal of African Studies* 21,1 (1987).

Barker, Roger G. *Ecological Psychology: Concepts and Methods for Studying the Environment of Human Behavior*. Stanford, Cal.: Stanford University Press, 1968.

Barker, Roger G. and Phil Schoggen. *Qualities of Community Life*. San Francisco: Jossey-Bass Publishers, 1973.

Brecher, Jeremy and Tim Costello. *Global Village or Global Pillage: Economic Reconstruction from the Bottom Up*. Boston: South End Press, 1994.

Burawoy, Michael. *The Politics of Production: Factory Regimes under Capitalism and Socialism*. London: New Left Books/Verso, 1985.

Cohen, Jean L. "Rethinking Social Movements." *Berkeley Journal of Sociology* 28 (1983).

Cohen, Jean and Andrew Arato. *Civil Society and Political Theory*. Cambridge, Mass.: MIT Press, 1992.

Evans, Sara M. and Harry C. Boyte. *Free Spaces: The Sources of Democratic Change in America*. 2nd ed. Chicago: The University of Chicago Press, 1992.

Foley, Michael W. "Organizing, Ideology, and Moral Suasion: Political Discourse and Action in a Mexican Town." *Comparative Studies in Society and History* 32,3 (1990).

Fox, Karl A. "Behavior Settings and Social System Accounting." In Phil Schoggen, *Behavior Settings: A Revision and Extension of Roger G. Barker's Ecological Psychology*. Stanford, Cal.: Stanford University Press, 1989.

Fox, Karl A. *The Eco-Behavioral Approach to Surveys and Social Accounts for Rural Communities: Exploratory Analyses and Interpretations of Roger G. Barker's Microdata from the Behavior Setting Survey of Midwest Kansas in 1963-64*. Ames, Ia.: Iowa State University, North Central Center for Rural Development, 1990.

Fuhrer, Urs. "Bridging the Ecological-Psychological Gap: Behavior Settings as Interfaces." *Environment and Behavior* 22,4 (July 1990).

Gadgil, Madhav and Ramachandra Guha. "Ecological Conflicts and the Environmental Movement in India." *Development and Change* 25,1 (1994).

Ghai, Dharam. *Participatory Development: Some Perspectives from Grassroots Experiences*. Geneva: UNRISD, 1988.

Gupta, Akhil. "Blurred Boundaries: The Discourse of Corruption, the Culture of Politics, and the Imagined State." *American Ethnologist* 22,2 (1995).

Kaminski, G. "Cognitive Bases of Situation Processing and Behavior Setting Participation." In *Issues in Contemporary German Social Psychology*, ed. Gun R. Semin and Barbara Krahé. Beverly Hills, Cal.: Sage, 1987.

Long, Norman and Magdelena Villareal. "Exploring Development Interfaces: From the Transfer of Knowledge to the Transformation of Meaning." In *Beyond the Impasse: New Directions in Development Theory*, ed. Frans J. Schuurman. London: Zed Books, 1993.

Magnusson, Warren. *The Search for Political Space: Globalization, Social Movements and the Urban Political Experience*. Toronto: University of Toronto Press, 1996.

Manor, James, ed. *Rethinking Third World Politics*. New York: Longman, 1991.

Melbin, Murray. "The Colonization of Time." In *Human Activity and Time Geography*, vol.2, *Timing Space and Spacing Time*, ed. Tommy Carlstein, Don Parkes, and Nigel Thrift. London: Edward Arnold, 1978.

Melucci, Alberto. *Challenging Codes: Collective Action in the Information Age*. Cambridge: Cambridge University Press, 1996.

Mitra, Subrata K. *Power, Protest and Participation: Local Elites and the Politics of Development in India*. London: Routledge, 1992.

Nayak, Nalini. "The Kerala Fishworkers' Struggle." In *A Space within the Struggle*, ed. Ilina Sen. New Delhi: Kali, 1990.

Oldenberg, Ray. *The Great Good Place: Cafes, Coffee Shops, Community Centers, Beauty Parlors, General Stores, Bars, Hangouts and How They Get You through the Day*. New York: Paragon House, 1989.

Parkes, Don and Nigel Thrift. "Putting Time in Its Place." In *Making Sense of Time*, vol.1, *Timing Space and Spacing Time*, ed. Tommy Carlstein, Don Parkes, and Nigel Thrift. London: Edward Arnold, 1978.

Putnam, Robert. "Bowling Alone: America's Declining Social Capital." *Journal of Democracy* 6,1 (January 1995).

Putnam, Robert. *Making Democracy Work: Civic Traditions in Modern Italy*. Princeton, N.J.: Princeton University Press, 1993.

Routledge, Paul. *Terrains of Resistance: Nonviolent Social Movements and the Contestation of Place in India*. Westport, Conn.: Praeger, 1993.

Schoggen, Phil. *Behavior Settings: A Revision and Extension of Roger G. Barker's Ecological Psychology*. Stanford, Cal.: Stanford University Press, 1989.

Scott, James C. *Domination and the Arts of Resistance: Hidden Transcripts*. New Haven, Conn.: Yale University Press, 1990.

Touraine, Alain. "Beyond Social Movements." In *Social Movements: Critiques, Concepts, Case-Studies*, ed. Stanford M. Lyman. Houndmills, Basingstoke, Eng.: Macmillan, 1995.

Walton, John and David Seddon. *Free Markets and Food Riots: The Politics of Global Adjustment*. Oxford: Blackwell, 1994.

Whitehead, Lawrence. "Bowling in the Bronx: The Uncivil Interstices between Civil and Political Society." In *Civil Society: Democratic Perspectives*, ed. Robert Fine and Shirin Rai. London: Frank Cass, 1997.

Wicker, Allan W. *An Introduction to Ecological Psychology*. New York: Cambridge University Press, 1983.

Wicker, Allan W. "Behavior Settings Reconsidered: Temporal Stages, Resources, Internal Dynamics, Context." In *Handbook of Environmental Psychology*, ed. Daniel Stokols and Irwin Altman. New York: John Wiley and Sons, 1987.

Index

Achari, T.R. Thankappan 110
activity setting research 252-72
  clusters 256
  data and analysis 252-67
  ethical aspects 4, 268-72
  in government settings 255-56
  in meetings 253-55
  in offices 255
  measurements 263-66
  political settings 256
activity settings 28, 29, 30-38, 53-56. *See also*
  political settings
  amplitude/range 24, 34, 120, 122-26, 129,
    263-67
  autonomy 42-43, 121, 123, 126, 141, 143-44
  classification 38-40, 117-20
  data and analysis 38-40, 252-67
  defined 31-32, 252-53
  government agencies 40-42, 45, 47, 122-35
  identification 33, 61-64, 253
  individual goals/growth 34, 54, 55-56, 121,
    126-27, 129, 141-44, 146
  participant analysis 39-40, 121, 126, 127-29
  program patterns 37, 39-40, 120
  social/political controls 34, 37-38, 42-43, 48,
    50-52, 55, 156-79
  space-time units 33, 53
  stability and change 46, 55, 144-47
  time analysis 39, 118-19, 120, 122-23
Ahmad, Mumtaz 233, 234, 235
Ahmed, Zanna Abubakar 74
aid. *See* development agencies, international
Alvarez, Sonia 209
AMNLAE 186, 189-96, 200, 207-8
amplitude 120, 263-66. *See also* activity
  settings, amplitude/range
AMPRONAC 21, 188-89
Anderson, Benedict 272
Ansari, Hamied N. 233
Antoun, Richard 215, 233, 234
Arato, Andrew 209
Arendt, Hannah 10-11, 25, 251
Aristotle 9, 25, 240
Arnold, David 236
associational politics 47, 141, 169-70. *See*
  also micro-politics; non-governmental
  authority systems
associations 47-48, 61, 63-4, 66-67, 209. *See*
  also civil society; voluntary associations
ATC 191-92, 207
Athen's effect 9, 11-12
Athenian democracy 9-10. *See also* Greek
  political thought
authority systems 43, 48, 49, 120-21. *See also*
  non-governmental authority systems;

government authority systems
Ayubi, Nazih 234, 236

Babb, Florence 211, 212
Bailey, Connor 109
Barker, Jonathan 5, 6, 25
Barker, Roger 5, 53, 56, 115-48, 264, 272
Basic Christian Communities 92, 99-100, 102,
  107
Basu, Amrita 80, 108, 109, 114
Bavinck, Maarten 109
Baviskar, Amrita 109
behaviour settings 53, 54, 56
Benjamin, Craig S. 114
Better Life Program for Rural Women 59, 60,
  61, 63-64, 73
Bigsten, A. 182
Blandón, Maria Teresa 210, 211, 212
Boyte, Harry C. 20, 26, 272
Brandell, Inga 26
Brown, Doug 210
Burawoy, Michael 55

Casanova, J-C. 74
centiurbs 120, 266
central/local relations 18-20, 21, 42, 69, 109,
  244. *See also* political action, local/central
  scale mismatch; state/local interactions
Chalmers, Douglas 209
Chamorro government 194, 198-99, 200, 204,
  208, 242
church role 87, 98, 99, 106-7, 113-14, 244-47,
  251. *See also* Basic Christian Communities
  and women 92, 107
church social action 85, 97, 91-92, 99
churches 24, 61, 64, 90, 91-92, 96
civil rights 13, 187-88, 193, 207, 244, 248
  and women 59, 60, 73, 93, 167, 174, 193, 202
civil society 3, 15, 16, 19-20, 58, 114-15,
  156-58, 171-72, 181, 200, 209, 213-14, 233,
  239-40. *See also* associations; state/civil
  society interactions
class analysis 3, 13, 16-18, 138-40, 221-22,
  224, 232, 238, 241
Cohen, Jean L. 209, 212
Cohen, Michael 182
collective action 4, 19, 23, 28, 252-53. *See also*
  political settings approach
collectives 185-86, 196-97, 208. *See also*
  networks
Collinson, Helen 210, 211
corporatist state 185, 189, 206
corruption in Pakistan 221
  Islamic movement critique 219-25
  popular Islam critique 228-33

Criquillon, Ana 210
Cuchryk, Patricia M. 210
Cycon, Dean 109

Dagona 59, 61-67, 72-73, 238, 241, 243-49, 251
Dagona/Machina comparison 63-65, 72-73, 244
Dalton, Russell J. 209
deep-sea fishing campaign 79, 85, 88-89,
    103-4, 107-8, 240
democracy. See Athenian democracy; Greek
    political thought; political participation
development agencies 58-61, 66, 75, 249-50
    autonomy 60, 64, 73-74
    empowerment 58, 62-66, 72-74
    funding 59, 60, 73
    government 59, 60, 62
    international 58, 59, 92, 202-3, 207
development projects 58, 59, 249-50
Diani, Mario 209
Dickey, Sara 113
Dietrich, Gabriele 112
Dijkstra, Geske 210
Directorate of Food, Road, and Rural
    Infrastructure (DFRRI) 59-61, 63-64, 73
Disch, Lisa 211
domestic space. See private space
Draper, Hal 25

Easton, David 25, 36
ecological psychology 35, 53-56
Eels, K. 139
Eicklemand, Dale F. 233
employment/wages 152-53. See also
    government workers
empowerment 4, 58, 61-66, 72-74, 94, 106-7,
    189, 191-93, 207. See also leadership
    development
    women 87, 107, 189, 191-93, 207
England 116-48, 241, 244, 251
environmental movement 9, 13
Escobar, Arturo 209, 210
Esposito, John L. 233
Evans, Sara M. 20, 26, 272
Evers, Tilman 192, 210
Ewing, Katherine 235
export promotion policies 17, 85, 199

Fernandez Poncela, Anna Maria 211, 212
fish marketing co-operatives 84, 87-88, 91-92
fisheries depletion 79, 81-83, 106, 110-11
fisheries development 81-83, 109
    deep-sea policy 79, 82-83, 88, 103-4, 111
    see also deep-sea fishing campaign
    export 85
    Kanyakumari 83-85
    sustainability 89
fishers, artisanal 96, 104, 105, 110-11
fishers, trawlers 84-85, 96, 104

fishing industry 83
fishing mechanization 81-83, 84, 104, 105, 110.
    See also trawling
fishworker castes 86-87, 105, 112
fishworkers' movement 79-80, 85-89, 109. See
    also National Fishworkers' Forum (NFF)
    women 87, 112
fishworkers, women 85, 86, 92, 93
Foley, Michael W. 114
food security 86, 89
Forgas, Joseph P. 53
Foweraker, Joe 209
Fox, Karl A. 56, 147
Fuhrer, Urs 54

Gadgil, Madhav 87, 109, 112
Gaffney, Patrick D. 215, 216, 217, 227, 233,
    234, 235
Gamson, William A. 211
Garcia-Guadilla, Maria Pilar 211
Gastil, John 272
Geetha, V. 113
Ghai, Dharam 58, 74
Ghosh, Amitav 114
Gillet, Pierre 111, 113
Giudicelli, M. 111
global forces 2, 6, 9, 16, 49, 245
globalization 2, 8, 17-18, 25, 26, 49-50, 79-80,
    103, 203, 207, 242, 248. See also
    neo-liberalism
government agencies 40-42, 45, 47, 63, 65-66,
    77, 122-35
    participatory structures 63, 65-67, 126-29, 246
government authority systems 40-45, 47, 56,
    59, 63, 76, 77, 97-98, 105-6, 122-29, 170,
    172-78, 189-96, 207-8. See also activity
    settings, government agencies
    political participation 65-66, 127-29, 132,
    244-45. See also government agencies,
    participatory structures
government space 40-42, 61-62, 63, 66, 90-91,
    122-35, 158, 172-78, 213, 216, 217
government workers 153
    corruption 153, 172, 173-74, 178
Gramsci, Antonio 16, 23, 26, 113, 236
Gran, Guy 26
Greek political thought 10-11, 41. See also
    Aristotle; Athenian democracy
Greenberg, Edward S. 272
Guha, Ramachandra 87, 109, 112
Gupta, Akhil 19-20, 26, 108, 109, 110, 114

Hansen, Mogens Herman 11, 25
Herrera, Leticia 212
Hourani, Albert 234
human rights. See civil rights

identity politics 13, 14, 15, 18, 185-88, 196-97,
    200, 208, 242, 243
India 81-114, 240-49
informal sector 153. *See also* civil society
    conflict adjudication 162-64
    politics 151
Islam 5, 6, 59, 60, 68, 70-71, 74, 213-36.
    See also mosques
Islam, state/religion relationship 213, 216-17,
    232, 234, 236
Islamic militants 214, 218-19, 233
Islamic movements 213-15
    Egypt 213-14, 233
    Pakistan 213, 217-25, 234
    middle class 218, 220-22, 231-33
Israr, Ahmad (Dr. Israr) 218-25, 231, 235, 243,
    247
    Tanzeem-i-Islami 218, 219, 220, 235

Jamaat-i-Islami party 214, 219
Jones, Bruce 211
Jones, G. 182
Kalavathy, M.H. 111
Kaleekal, Jose 112
Kaminski, G. 53
Kampala 152-55, 178, 238, 240-41, 242, 245-49
Kampala City Council (KCC) 154-55, 157-58,
    172, 176-78, 180-81, 182
Kanyakumari 21, 79, 83, 89-99, 105-8, 111,
    238, 240-43, 245-49, 251
    fishing economy 83-85
Kayizzi-Mugerwa, Steve 182
Keuchler, Manfred 209
khatib 214-18, 226-27, 233
khutba 213, 214, 215, 216, 227
    anti-government 222-25, 228-31
Kiondo, Andrew 74
Kocherry, Thomas 88, 103, 113
Kohli, Atul 26, 108
Koran. *See* Quran
Korten, David C. 26
Kumar, K.G. 112, 113
Kurien, John 109, 110, 111, 112, 113, 114
Kuruvinakunnel, Patricia 109

Laing, R.D. 34, 53
Lapidus, Ira M. 234
Latin American Working Group 209
leadership development 87, 107, 121, 134, 136,
    141-43, 146, 207, 239, 243, 246-47. *See also*
    activity settings, individual goals/growth;
    empowerment
Leitmann, Josef 182
Leyburn 116-48, 238, 241, 244, 247. *See also*
    Oskaloosa/Leyburn comparison
Leys, Colin 25
liberation theology 9, 87, 247
Lipsky, Michael 272

livelihood issues 11, 22, 69, 85-88, 94-103,
    221, 238, 240-41, 242, 243, 249. *See also*
    Owino market, evening market; Owino
    Market Vendors Association
Long, Norman 19, 26, 272

Machina 59-60, 63, 67-73, 238, 241-49, 251.
    See also Dagona/Machina comparison
Magnusson, Warren 26, 108, 109
Mahmud, Altaf (Imam Mahmud) 226-31, 235
Mamdani, M. 182
Manor, James 109
Market Vendors Association. *See* MVA/KCC
    relationship; Owino Market Vendors
    Association (MVA)
Marxism 13, 16, 242
Mascarenhas, James 272
Mathew, George 113
Mathew, P.M. 109, 112
Maududi, S. Abul Ala 235
Mayer, Margit 25
McAdam, Doug 203, 212
McGuire, John 110
McPhee, John 53
media 20, 195, 198, 205, 209
Meeker, M. 139
meeting venues
    closed 164, 166
    open 161, 163, 164
meetings 4, 5, 29, 31, 238, 248, 251. *See also*
    collectives
    Dagona/Machina 62, 64, 66-67, 75
    Kanyakumari 95, 99, 109
    Nicaragua 183, 191-93, 194-95, 198
    Oskaloosa/Leyburn 128-29, 132, 136-38
    Owino Market 156, 161-79
Melbin, Murray 53
Melucci, Alberto 26, 186-87, 209
Metcalf, Barbara D. 235
Metoyer, Cynthia Chavez 211
Meynen, Wicky 110
micro-politics 18-19, 35-38, 47-48, 141, 146,
    151, 158, 179, 181, 207-8
Migdal, Joel 108
Mill, John Stuart 47
Mitra, Subrata K. 108, 112, 114
Moore, Barrington 16, 26
Moore, S.F. 272
Morgan, Martha I. 210
Morgan, Sarah 212
Morris, Aldon D. 209
Morris, Michael 109
mosques 6, 22, 61, 62-63, 64, 213-16, 225-26,
    238, 241, 243-47, 251. *See also* Islam
    Egypt 213-14, 217, 219, 233
    popular 226-33
    private/autonomous 213, 214, 218, 225, 245
    women's section 226

mosques, Islamic fundamentalist 220, 222-25
   political ideology 218-19, 221-22, 231-33
mosques, political role 213-15, 231-33
   political parties 21, 219-20, 223
   rural 225-31, 246
   urban 218-25, 246
Mueller, Carol McClurg 209
Mukul 111
Murguialday, Clara 209, 210
Murickan, Jose 112
Musisi, N. 182
Muslim Brotherhood (Egypt) 214, 219
Muslim society 213-15, 221, 222, 233
MVA/KCC relationship 156, 166-67, 176-77
   See also Owino Market, management
   committee

Nash, June 114
nation-state 3, 8, 35, 103, 239
National Fishworkers' Forum (NFF) 86-88, 93,
   111, 112, 113
National Resistance Movement 151-52, 158.
   See also resistance councils (RCs)
Nayak, Nalini 109, 110, 112
neo-liberalism 2, 8, 9, 151, 154, 202, 208, 243.
   See also structural adjustment
networks 185, 190, 196-97, 208. See also
   collectives
Newman, Robert S. 110
Nicaragua 187-212, 238, 241, 243-50
Nie, Norman H. 56
Nielson, Kai 209
Nigeria 58-78, 238, 240-49, 251
non-governmental authority systems 43, 47,
   60, 91, 95-96, 159-61, 162-64, 167-68. See
   also associational politics
non-participatory culture 64, 139, 143-44, 175,
   178, 181. See also participatory culture
Northeast Arid Zone Development Project
   (NEAZDP) 59, 61, 62, 63-64, 67-74, 241,
   244-51

Ocampo, José Antonio 211
Oldenberg, Ray 56
Omvedt, Gail 109
Oskaloosa 115-148, 238, 241, 244, 247
Oskaloosa/Leyburn comparison 116-18, 119,
   122-29, 132, 144, 250
Osmont, A. 182
overfishing. See fisheries depletion
Owino Market 151, 154-81, 238, 240-41, 242,
   245-48
   administrators meeting 172-74, 181
   decline 155, 180, 242, 249
   evening market 155, 165, 176, 180, 242,
   249
   government agencies 172-81

   management committee 155, 157-58,
   176-78, 181
   police 172, 174-75
   security services 155, 157
   Umoja Securicor 170-171, 180
   upgrading 154-55, 167, 180-81, 249
Owino Market Vendors Association (MVA)
   156, 157, 159-69, 178-81, 240-41, 246-47,
   249

Pakistan 213, 217-33, 238, 241-47, 251
Pallais, Maria Lourdes 212
Pandian, M.S.S. 113
Parkes, Don 53
participation. See political participation
participatory culture 47, 63, 66-67, 72, 115,
   138, 141, 158, 163-64, 171-72, 178, 181,
   200. See also non-participatory culture
participatory research 55, 255, 268-71
Pasos, Mayra 212
Pelzer, Knut 109, 110
Piscatori, James 233
Pizarro, Ana Maria 212
Platteau, Jean-Philippe 110
pluralism 42, 63, 64, 72
pluralism, religious 165, 168
Pokrant, Bob 110
Polanyi, Karl 13, 25
police 96-97, 101-2, 106, 172, 174-75
political action 2, 18, 19, 28, 30, 62, 101-3, 106,
   132, 239-44, 248-49
   defined 40, 43-44
   local/central scale mismatch 17-20, 26, 240,
   248-50
   local/international links 21, 203, 207, 239,
   245, 249, 250
   symbols 186, 187, 188, 204-5, 250
   women 87, 97, 98, 107, 109, 183, 186-212
political actions/settings
   blockades 88, 97-98
   boycotts 194
   communications 101, 188, 190, 192, 195,
   197-98, 200, 245
   conferences 194-96, 197, 200, 201
   demonstrations 23, 29, 87, 101-3, 205
   fasts 87, 88, 91, 101-3
   government offices 4, 45, 46, 56, 62, 172-73
   meetings 4, 5, 29, 31, 62, 64, 66-67, 75, 95,
   99, 109, 128-29, 132, 136-38, 156, 161-79,
   183, 191-93, 194-95, 198, 238, 248, 251
   occupation of buildings 188
   pickets 11, 195
   polling stations 30, 45
political discourse 9, 11, 35, 44, 146-47, 191-93,
   213, 222-25, 248, 251
   hidden 19, 58, 64, 70-73, 228-31. See also
   Quran interpretation, metaphorical

political participation 5, 27, 46-47, 67-70, 94,
126, 132, 136-38, 158, 179, 244-45, 247, 248
language access 86, 166, 168, 170, 177
women. *See* women and participation
political parties 46, 62, 64, 67, 68, 70, 72, 92,
113, 214, 219, 241, 248, 269
political setting studies
Dagona/Machina 61-74, 238, 241-49, 251
Kanyakumari 90-99, 100-103, 238, 240-43,
245-49, 251, 254, 269-70
mosques 217-36, 238, 241-47, 251
Nicaragua 187-212, 238, 241, 243-50
Oskaloosa/Leyburn 117-46, 238, 241, 244,
247, 249-50
Owino market 159-69, 171-72, 238, 240-41,
242, 245-49, 268-69
political settings 4, 11, 30, 100-103, 106-7,
129-32, 159-69, 171-72, 239-40, 243. *See
also* activity settings; political space
amplitude/range 130-34, 243
autonomy 185-86, 189, 191, 192-96, 202,
207-8
classification 38-40
data and analysis 21-24, 75-78
defined 21, 40, 44, 129, 132, 255
geographic factors 198, 238, 243
growth of individual 134, 136
identification 21, 44-46, 61-64, 120, 130-32
interrelations 20, 169
international 89, 203, 207
methodology 21-22, 61-62, 252-68
participant analysis 68, 70, 139-40
social/political controls 20, 23-25, 29-30,
134, 158, 181, 183, 188, 193-96, 202, 227,
240, 244, 251
time analysis 134, 179
political settings approach 3, 4, 20-23, 28,
49-50, 58, 80-81, 89, 157-58, 183-87, 206,
250-51, 266-67, 272
ethical issues 4, 267-71
political space 28, 44-46, 65, 74, 96, 106,
129-39, 184-86, 190, 246, 247, 248, 266-67.
See also political settings approach; public
space
expansion 20, 22, 27, 52, 58, 66, 73, 118,
146-47, 157-58, 171-72, 183, 187-88,
191-96, 206-8, 215
politicization 38, 80, 108, 182, 191-96, 197, 213
politics, defined 35
Pope, Andrew 110
popular action. *See* political action
popular participation. *See* political participation
private space 74, 90, 118, 147
public space 58, 64, 74, 118-19, 147, 184, 255.
See also political space
Putnam, Robert 16, 18, 26, 58, 61, 75, 148

Quran 215, 225, 227, 229
Quran interpretation
metaphorical 70-71, 227-31
metonymic 220, 235

Rahman, Fazlur 217, 234
Rajadurai, S.V. 113
Rajagopal, A. 113
Ram, Kalpana 90, 113
Randall, Margaret 209, 210, 211
Rao, N. Subba 110
Reeves, Peter 110
resistance councils (RCs) 151-52, 160, 178, 245
resource mobilization theory 13-14, 18, 184-85,
208
revolutionary action 16, 29, 52. *See also*
Marxism
Rosenberg, Alexander 53, 272
Rosenthal, Erwin I.J. 234
Roy, Olivier 235
Rucht, Dieter 212
Rusmore, Kaki 211

Saint-Germain, Michelle A. 212
Sakkwatawa 59, 72, 75, 241
Sandinista government, women's movement
relations 186, 189-96, 207-8
Sandinista movement, women's participation
200-201
Sato, Seizaburo 74
Schattschneider, Elmer Eric 26
Schoggen, Phil 53-56, 115-48, 272
Schwartzman, Helen B. 272
Scott, A. 209
Scott, James C. 19, 26, 272
Seddon, David 182
Sethi, Harsh 109
Shah, Ghanshyam 109
Shiva, Vandana 109
Shue, Vivienne 108
Sivakumar, S.S. 104, 106, 114
Sivathamby, Karthigesu 113
social action research 3-4, 242, 250, 254-72
ethical issues 4, 267-71
social capital 61, 67, 73, 75
social forces 28, 29, 30, 34, 51. *See also*
activity settings, social/political controls;
political settings, social/political controls
social movement analysis 3, 5, 13-14, 15, 21-22,
58, 184-86, 206, 208, 242-43. *See also* identity politics; resource mobilization theory
social movements 185-87, 206, 209, 213, 232,
246. *See also* women's movement
decentralized structure 185-87, 188, 194,
196, 197, 202, 208
social/political environment 48, 51, 64, 136,
138, 244, 247, 248

social science research
     interpretivist perspective 53, 252
     naturalistic perspective 53, 55, 115, 252
space-time units. *See* activity settings, space-
     time units
Spalding, Rose 211
sports 117, 122, 169-70
Srinivasan, Bhaskar 111
Stahler-Sholk, Richard 199, 210, 211
state/civil society interaction 239-40, 250.
     See also Islam, state/religion relationship
     Kanyakumari 81, 91, 93, 104, 106
     Nicaragua 183-87, 192-96, 200, 201-2, 206,
        207-8
     Owino market 151, 157-58, 163, 170, 171,
        172, 176-78, 180-81
state/local interactions 19-20, 70, 95-96, 105,
     240, 244. *See also* central/local relations
structural adjustment 151, 152, 198-99, 207,
     242-43
     urban 151-53
     women 198-99, 207
Subramaniam, Ajantha 111
Sundar, Nandini 113
Swift, Jamie 26

Tamil Nadu Fishworkers' Union (TFU) 93, 99,
     100, 101, 102, 107
Tanzania 74
Tarrow, Sidney 25, 26
Thayer, Millie 210, 211
Thomson, K.T. 111, 113
Thrift, Nigel 53
Tilly, Charles 209
time-space units. *See* activity settings, space-
     time units
Tocqueville, Alexis de 15, 16, 47, 138
Tombeur, James 113
Touraine, Alain 25
Trawler Wars 94-99, 104-8, 112, 240, 248
trawling 82, 84, 86, 110. *See also* fishers,
     trawlers
Turner, Terisa E. 114

Uganda 150-82, 241, 242, 244-49
Umoja Securicor 170-71, 180
unions 65, 67, 89. *See also* National
     Fishworkers' Forum
     social movement unionism 87
United States of America 115-48, 241, 250, 251
urb 255, 264-65. *See also* amplitude; centiurbs
urban infrastructure/services 152, 154
     costs 179-80
     economics 152, 154, 179-81
     informal sector 156, 179-80
urbanization, Africa 150, 152

Vargas, Milú 212
Vatin, Jean-Claude 233
Verba, Sidney 56
village development plan 67-70
Villareal, Magdalena 19, 26, 272
Visvanathan, Susan 109
voluntary associations 13, 15, 62-65, 78, 132,
     137-38, 157, 169-70, 209

Walton, John 182
Ward, Peter 182
Warner, W.L. 139
Washbrook, David A. 113
Waterman, Peter 87, 112, 114
Weber, Max 16, 26, 41, 243
Wegelin, E. 182
Wessel, Lois 212
Whitehead, Lawrence 26
Wicker, Allan W. 54, 55, 272
Wiegersma, Nan 211
Wignaraja, Poona 106, 114
Wolfsfeld, Gadi 211
Wolin, Sheldon 54
women and participation 22, 241, 244, 248-51
     Dagona/Machina 68, 72-73
     Kanyakumari 87, 92, 93, 97, 107, 112
     Oskaloosa/Leyburn 139
     Owino Market 160, 161, 175
     Nicaragua 190, 192-93, 200-202
     Pakistan mosques 220, 226
Women's International Resource Exchange
     (WIRE) 210
women's movement 3, 13, 15, 246
     international 203, 207, 245
     Nicaragua 183-212, 238, 241, 243, 244, 245,
        246, 247, 248, 249, 250
Wood, Ellen Meiksins 209
World Bank 150-51, 182
     First Urban Project (Uganda) 152, 154-55,
        167, 180, 245, 249, 269
     *Uganda Report on Urban Finance and
     Management* 152, 182. *See also* structural
     adjustment

Zeledón, Dora 212